RPG AND RPG II PROGRAMMING:
Applied Fundamentals
A Job Approach to Learning

WILLIAM E. BUX
EDWARD C. CUNNINGHAM

Prentice-Hall, Inc., Englewood Cliffs, New Jersey 07632

Library of Congress Cataloging in Publication Data

Bux, William E
    RPG II programming, applied fundamentals.

    Includes index.
      1. RPG (Computer program language)   2. Business—
Data processing.   I. Cunningham, Edward C.
II. Title
HF5548.5.R2B87   001.6′425   78-25733
ISBN   0-13-783423-3

Editorial/Production Supervision by Lynn Frankel
Interior Design by Cathy Van Yperen
Cover Design by Jorge Hernandez
Manufacturing Buyer: Gordon Osbourne

10   9   8   7   6   5   4   3   2

Printed in the United States of America

Prentice-Hall International, Inc., *London*
Prentice-Hall of Australia Pty. Limited, *Sydney*
Prentice-Hall of Canada, Ltd., *Toronto*
Prentice-Hall of India Private Limited, *New Delhi*
Prentice-Hall of Japan, Inc., *Tokyo*
Prentice-Hall of Southeast Asia Pte. Ltd., *Singapore*
Whitehall Books Limited, *Wellington, New Zealand*

CONTENTS

PREFACE

RPG and RPG II Programming, Applied Fundamentals, is a textbook-workbook designed as a hands-on, how-to-do-it approach to teaching and learning the most popular business-oriented computer programming language — RPG. It also enables the student programmer to self evaluate the degree of mastery attained upon the completion of each segment or project.

The textbook-workbook has been developed in response to a need for educational materials that are more than purely expository, with problems having to be developed by the instructor or only alluded to within the textbook that must be heavily used in conjunction with the computer manufacturer's manual. There is a need for teaching and learning materials that are developed pedagogically, with stress placed upon proceeding from the known to the unknown, from the simple to the complex, and with challenging learning experiences gained by applying the knowledge and skill mastered in earlier problem-solving situations to each program's solution. Instructional materials should be conceived so that they are adaptable, flexible, and thus usable in conjunction with any computer installation that uses a RPG compiler.

New concepts necessary for developing the project are presented at the beginning of each project. As the need for additional concepts arises, then and only then, are they illustrated. This method of presentation allows the student programmer to immediately apply the given theories.

The fundamentals of RPG programming are applied to the planning, compiling, and executing of programs that student programmers will be exposed to when initially employed. Students gain additional meaningful experience by modifying the programs within the textbook to provide more information in the print-out, especially in the area of sales accounting.

All source data, forms, and working papers needed to plan, compile, and execute each program are contained within the textbook-workbook.

THE MARKET FOR RPG PROGRAMMING

The market for RPG programming, exists in high schools, community colleges, junior colleges, private business schools, and four-year universities that have a computer on the premises or access to a computer via a time-sharing system or service center. Like the teaching and learning materials prepared for any skill development (typewriting, shorthand, key punching, etc.), the same basic instructions and philosophy of teaching may be used regardless of the level at which the skills are offered.

DESIGN AND LAYOUT OF THE TEXTBOOK-WORKBOOK

1. The instructional materials with the many illustrations take the student programmer step by step through the development of each project. Each project is designed to utilize the source data supplied within the body of the textbook.

2. The expository material is based on realistic business applications and the student is placed in the role of completing projects that would normally be developed on the job. Background information is provided to show students the *why* of each project.

3. Twenty programming projects have been developed for completion by student programmers.

4. Text exercises are provided periodically throughout the textual materials with three objectives:

    a. to evaluate the student programmer's understanding of the textual theory

    b. to test the student programmer's knowledge and skill in solving short application problems prior to planning and executing the projects

    c. to enable the student programmer to self-evaluate his work by comparison with textual illustrations.

5. All coding sheets, Print Chart forms, and other special forms needed for completion of the course are perforated and bound within the projects of the textbook-workbook.

6. In completing the work in *RPG and RPG II Programming, Applied Fundamentals* the student programmer will need approximately 2,000 punched cards.

STUDENT PROGRAMMER ATTAINMENTS

At the completion of the course the student programmer will have a basic understanding of:

the material as it is presented, chapter by chapter — project by project.

one of the most widely used computer programming languages in the world.

coding RPG.

applying a computer language such as RPG to business applications.

application development.

coding techniques in an increasingly complex manner.

Those projects completed will be used by the student programmer as a reference manual. Project Twenty will reinforce the knowledge gained in the first nineteen projects. Project Twenty requires independent study, thought, and development of a complete application system.

DESIGN AND LAYOUT OF THE INSTRUCTOR'S MANUAL

The contents of the instructor's manual are:

1. Suggestions for adapting the textbook-workbook materials to offerings of various lengths such as one semester, one quarter, and a full year.

2. Print-outs for each of 19 projects, with solutions based upon source data contained in the textbook-workbook.

3. Answers to exercises.

William E. Bux

Edward C. Cunningham

INTRODUCTION

One of the major objectives of business today is to handle economically, efficiently, and accurately the volume of data that must be processed. The handling of facts or the processing of data can be accomplished by one or more of the following data processing systems.

1. *Manual.* In a manual system information and data are recorded in handwritten form (with pencil or ink), and usually one or a very few copies are made at a time.

2. *Electromechanical.* An electromechanical system, which involves the use of simple machines and other equipment, is generally more economical and efficient than a manual system. As a rule, the information and data are typewritten, and arithmetic processes are performed on desk calculators. The *write-it-once principle* lies at the core of the electromechanical system. This principle stresses the initial recording of all repetitive or constant data in such a form that it can be later electromechanically reproduced — that is, reproduced by machines.

3. *Punched Card.* In a punched card system the numeric and alphabetic data and special symbols are converted into a code language that can be interpreted by all the machines and equipment used in the system. The data on source documents, such as invoices, purchase orders, and time cards, is recorded on punched cards. Because a punched card is usually prepared to record information about each item or unit appearing on the source document, the term *unit record system* is used synonymously with the term punched card system. Other names commonly applied to this type of system are *tabulating* and *electric accounting machine* (EAM). When the punched card system is properly planned and installed, it can prove extremely valuable to small businesses and can supply accurate and more detailed records than the manual and electromechanical systems.

4. *Electronic Data Processing.* In an electronic data processing (EDP) system a computer is used to process the facts and information that have been converted into a code consisting of electrical impulses. This code may be based on binary language, a number system that uses 2 as its base instead of 10 as in the decimal system. Or the code may be based on the octal system, using a base of 8, or the hexadecimal system, which uses a base of 16. The data (input) is read into a central processing unit by means of direct keyboard, magnetic tape, paper tape, optical scanners, or punched cards and is then treated

mathematically, classified, sorted, and stored. Output is called forth from the central processing unit as needed and recorded on magnetic tape, paper tape, or punched cards; or automatically printed on business forms and reports; or displayed on cathode-ray-tube (CRT) output terminals; or transferred from magnetic tape to microfilm for storage; or transmitted orally to the user via telephone (voice response).

WHAT IS RPG?

With the introduction of computers the unit record user needed a programming language that was easy to understand, code, and use. The RPG (Report Program Generator) programming language provided all the programming features and techniques with which the unit record user was familiar. Thus RPG helped make the move to the use of computers smoother and easier.

RPG is unlike any other programming language, for it runs on a computer in a fixed cycle, which will be discussed later. What it lacks in flexibility is compensated for by its ease of use. Other computer languages have functions that RPG does not possess, but since its introduction, improvements have made it flexible enough for programming the vast majority of commercial applications.

It is capable of being used on most small computers. In addition, RPG will support many computer configurations, such as on-line, real-time systems, telecommunication with terminals, and telecommunication with other computers.

The past 10 to 15 years have seen a rapid development of computers. Technological advances in the computer industry have produced computers that not only process data of high volume in seconds but also process that data with less cost to the world's businesses. At present every large business has a computer. It could not operate in today's business environment without one. Most medium-sized businesses have computers for the same reason. Until recently small businesses, defined as having a gross sales volume of 1 to 10 million dollars of sales per year, could not afford a computer installation. Today over 50,000 small businesses have computers, and almost 500,000 more businesses possess the potential of having a computer installation. Because of RPG's relative ease of coding and its applicability to all areas of the business world, it has been widely adopted.

The Programmer

"Feeding" the data into the computer system for processing requires the services of a trained technician, known as a *programmer*, who plans the conversion of original data into a medium that is acceptable to the computer, such as punched cards, punched paper tape, or magnetic tape. The programmer plans the logical arrangement, sequence, and correlation of data taken from several sources. The sequence of instructions to the computer is called the *program*.

The Program

A group of instructions — the program — is written to direct or instruct the computer to perform functions on the data to be processed. In order to develop a logical program, the programmer must fully understand the nature of the problem to be solved by the computer. The problem must first be defined by the person or office wanting assistance. In general, much explanation is necessary in order for the programmer to understand fully exactly what is wanted or desired. The problem must undergo in-depth analysis so that the most logical approaches to its solution will be undertaken. Methods for checking the accuracy of the data must be developed. The form of the output (printed reports, punched cards, or tape) must be known in advance because special routines may be necessary to carry the problem to its final solution.

The programmer writes a *source program* on specially designed sheets of paper called *coding sheets* or *specifications sheets*. In the source program the name of the program is written, the data is described, and the procedures for acting on the data are indicated. The specific parts of the computer configuration are also designated. The source program is usually punched into cards by means of a keypunch machine or data recorder. The source program deck of cards, together with the necessary control cards, is then fed into the computer.

In the computer the RPG compiler (a special program supplied by the computer manufacturer) analyzes the source program. The compiler checks the source program for such violations as misuse of programming rules, syntactic errors, and incorrect sequence of program statements. Any violations found are printed out in the form of diagnostic messages. These messages identify the degree of error and pinpoint the individual card containing the error. Once the source program is completely free of syntactic errors, the compiler uses it to generate a new program, called the *object program*, in a machine language acceptable to the computer.

Finally, the programmer must test the program. The programmer designs test data to simulate the actual or "live" data that will be processed later by the computer. Running the program with test data shows either (a) that the program works and will execute the desired results when it is run later with live data or (b) that the program does not work yet. Most programs do not work when they are first written. A number of test runs are often necessary before all errors are found and corrected. Making a test run is commonly referred to as *debugging*.

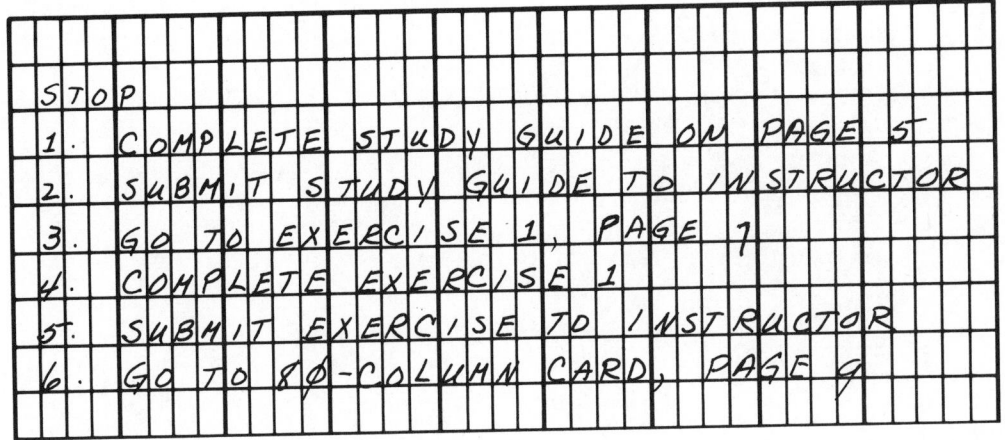

```
STOP
1. COMPLETE STUDY GUIDE ON PAGE 5
2. SUBMIT STUDY GUIDE TO INSTRUCTOR
3. GO TO EXERCISE 1, PAGE 7
4. COMPLETE EXERCISE 1
5. SUBMIT EXERCISE TO INSTRUCTOR
6. GO TO 80-COLUMN CARD, PAGE 9
```

STUDY GUIDE

Date _____   Name _____

DIRECTIONS: *Answer the following questions in the spaces provided. Your answer should indicate the depth of understanding that you have toward the concepts and definitions presented. If insufficient space is provided, complete your answer on the reverse side of this Study Guide Sheet.*

1. Name the four types of data processing systems and give a brief definition of each.

2. What is RPG? How does it differ from other programming languages?

3. Why has RPG become a popular language in the business world during the past few years?

4. Explain the job of the programmer.

5. What is a program?

6. What is meant by the term debugging?

7. Explain the terms source program and object program. How do these terms relate to each other?

5

EXERCISE 1

Date _____   Name _____

TRUE–FALSE: *Each of the following statements is either true or false. Indicate your choice in the Answers column by encircling "T" for a true answer or "F" for a false answer.*

		Answers
1. A compiler produces the Object Program		T F
2. Diagnostic messages are printed out by the computer		T F
3. A Source Program is written on coding sheets		T F
4. A machine language program is the same as a Source Program		T F
5. A deck of keypunched cards may contain the Source Program		T F
6. Data description is found in the Object Program		T F
7. Most newly written programs do not execute the desired results		T F
8. The problem must be fully explained to the programmer before the program is written		T F
9. A program may take the form of a Source Program or an Object Program		T F
10. Test data is specifically designed to simulate the actual or "live" data that will be processed by the computer		T F

Matching: *In the Answers column, write the letter that represents the word or expression in Column 1 that matches each item in Column 2.*

COLUMN 1

A. Compiler
B. Computer
C. Diagnostic messages
D. Printed reports
E. Program
F. Programmer
G. Punched card system
H. Reproducing
I. Storage
J. Sorting
K. Merging
L. All cycles

COLUMN 2   *Answers*

1. A computer program supplied by the manufacturer   _____

2. Output   _____

3. Handles volumes of data in seconds   _____

4. Duplicating   _____

5. A group of instructions   _____

6. Writes programs   _____

7. Files, card, tape, or disk   _____

8. Unit record system   _____

9. Printout of code violations   _____

7

COMPLETION: *Complete each of the following statements by writing the appropriate word or words in the Answers column.*

Answers

1. A program written on coding sheets is known as   _____

2. The special program that converts the Source Program to machine language is called the   _____

3. The principle lying at the heart of the electromechanical system is the   _____

4. Another name for unit record system is   _____

5. Making a test run is commonly referred to as   _____

6. The Source Program is translated into the machine language program and is understandable to the computer when the Source Program is completely free of   _____

80-COLUMN CARD

The 80-column card, commonly known as the IBM card, is 3¼ inches high and 7½ inches long. The thickness is 0.007 inch. Because cards are fed rapidly through various data processing machines, their manufacturing tolerance must be strictly adhered to.

Cards can have one of the four corners cut off (called a corner cut), be color coded, and have printing on them. These characteristics are aids to the humans who use them.

On the card shown in Fig. 1,

1. The upper left corner is cut; therefore it is known as a left corner cut card.

2. There are ten rows of printing on the card.

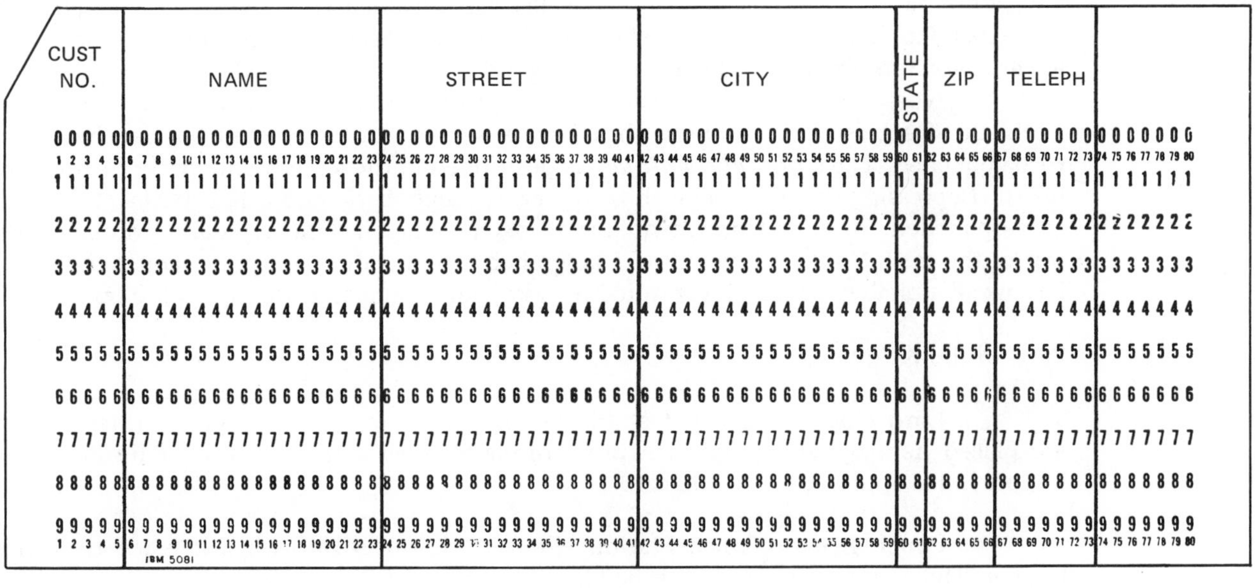

Figure 1

3. Rows zero and nine have digits (left to right) going from 1 through 80. These 80 numbers refer to columns. Each column can be punched to represent one character. Columns are vertical, whereas rows are horizontal.

4. There is a rather large blank space above the zero row. This area is known as the zone portion of the card. The uppermost zone is known as the 12 zone or row. The row immediately below the 12 zone is the 11 zone or row. The zero row is often considered the 10 zone or row when it is used for any characters except pure digits.

5. The 12 row (12 zone) is known as the 12 edge of the card and the 9 row is known as the 9 edge. Cards are fed into various data processing machines with either the 12 or 9 edge leading.

6. The card in Fig. 1 is fielded. A fielded card is one on which consecutive columns are set aside for specific purposes. It was determined that the following fields are required to punch the input data.

Card Columns		
	1–5	Customer Number
	6–23	Name
	24–41	Street
	42–59	City
	60–61	State
	62–66	Zip Code
	67–73	Telephone Number

KEYPUNCH (029)

The keypunch is the machine used to transcribe original data from a source document into the form of punches, or rectangular holes, in the proper fields of 80-column cards. Fig. 2 is an illustration of the IBM 029 keypunch machine.

The keypunch machine's keyboard is very much like a typewriter. Unlike a typewriter, however, a keypunch machine has a *combination keyboard*. This means that each key except two (the A and Z keys) has two different characters printed on it. A key with a double character printed on it is called an *expanded key*. The upper characters of the expanded keys are punched when the keyboard machine is in numeric mode. The lower characters are punched when the keyboard is in alphabetic mode.

Note that the *numeric shift key* is positioned in the lower left corner of the keyboard. Depressing the numeric shift key causes numeric and certain special characters to be punched. The *alphabetic shift key* is positioned in the lower right corner of the keyboard. Depressing the alphabetic shift key causes alphabetic and other special characters to be punched. When the print switch is on, each character punched is also printed at the top of the card. Unlike a typewriter, a keypunch machine does not print capital and small letters; all alphabetic characters printed by a keypunch machine are capital letters.

Parts of the Keypunch

Card Hopper: Located at the upper right side of the keypunch. Blank cards are placed here by the operator. A pressure plate forces cards forward for feeding. The hopper holds approximately 500 cards.

Punch Bed or Punch Station: First station of a card when it is fed from the hopper. The card positioned in this bed has two positions.

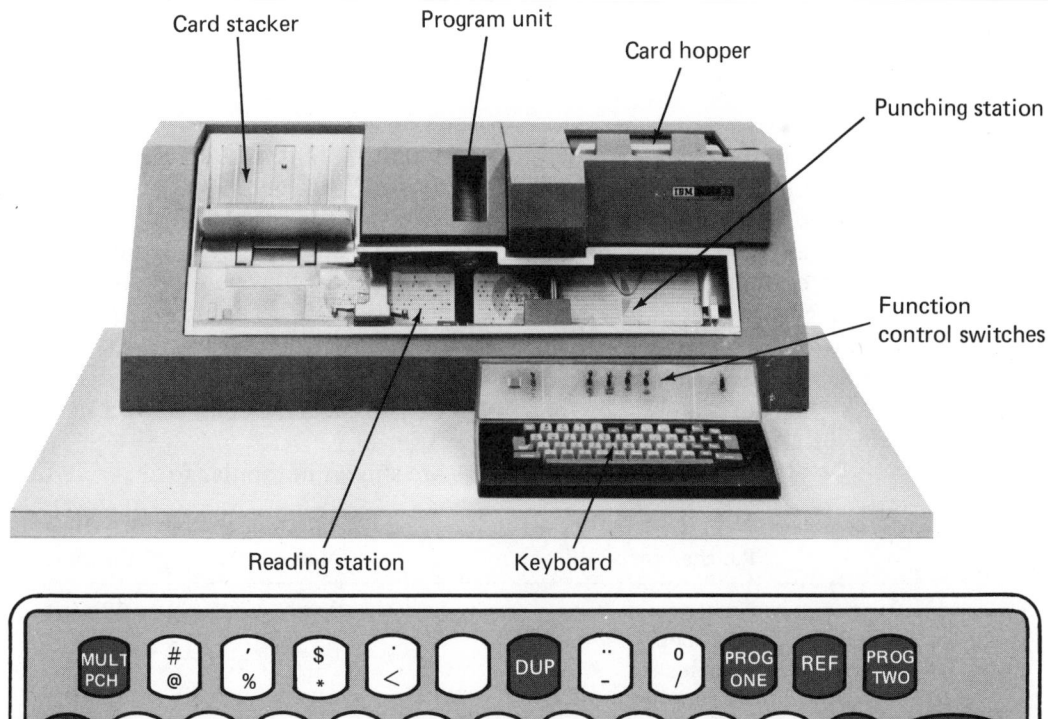

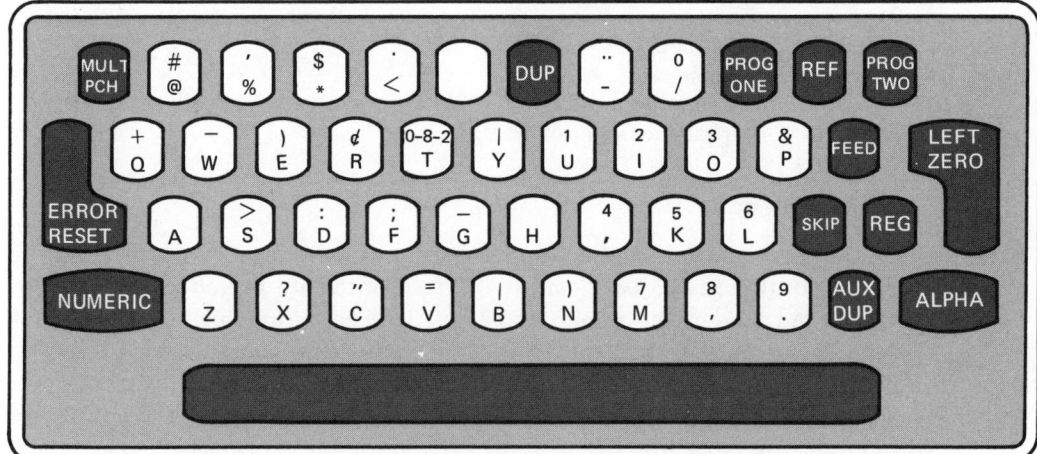

Figure 2

a. Preregistered —holes cannot be punched into the card while in this position.
b. Registered —holes can be punched into the card while in this position.

Read Bed or Read Station: Card has two positions in this bed, or station.
a. Preregistered —holes cannot be read by the machine while the card is in this position.
b. Registered —holes can be read by the machine while the card is in this position.

Eject Bed or Eject Station: Cards are moved into this station or bed after moving from the read station.

Stacker: Located at the upper left side of the keypunch. Punched cards are stacked here on the 12 edge on a slant. The face of the card is stacked away from the operator. The stacker holds approximately 500 cards. The cards are in the same order as the source document data from which they were punched.

Program Card

In order to give the operator more automatic ability when punching data, codes have been established that will change the mode of the keypunch automatically. Such codes are known as *program card codes*. The five most common codes of a program card will now be discussed. A *program card* must have a punch in every column of the entire card. The first column of each field is the most important because it contains the coded punch that directs the keypunch to use the desired mode for that entire field. The remaining columns of the field are usually punched with codes called *field definition punches* that serve to continue the mode — that is, until the first column of the next field is reached. The mechanism that senses that the code for the first column of a new field is reached is called the *star wheels*.

The five most common codes are shown in tabular form.

Field to be Punched for	First Column	All Other Columns
Numeric	Space	12's (&)
Alphabetic	1	A's
Skipping	—	12's (&)
Numeric Duplication	0	12's (&)
Alphabetic Duplication	/	A's

Card Movement

The cards are placed in the hopper 9 edge down, face forward. If the *feed key* is depressed continuously, two cards will feed into the *punch station*. Only when a card is registered under the *punch head* will it accept punches, or holes. The punches are placed in the card from beneath the punch bar one column at a time. The proper combination of punches is controlled automatically by the internal workings of the keypunch machine. Punching a character in each column until the card is completed is known as *serial punching;* a typewriter uses the same principle.

When the 80th columns of the cards have passed the *punch head* and the *read head* respectively, the card passing the *read head* moves automatically into the *eject station* and the card passing the *punch head* moves automatically into the *read station*. When the 80th column of the second card passes the *read head*, the first card moves automatically into the *stacker*. In the *stacker*, cards lie on a slant with the 12 edge down, facing away from the operator.

The card movements through the machine are

1. *Hopper* to *Punch Station.*

2. Registered under *Punch Head.*

3. After the 80th column passes under *Punch Head*, card is in the *Read Station.*

4. Card is registered under the *Read Head.*

5. After the 80th column passes under the *Read Head*, it is in the *Eject Station.*

6. The card is *Stacked.*

An example of a fielded data card is shown in Fig. 1. The punching of a *program card* for this fielded data card is as follows.

Customer Number   A space is punched into column 1
                   12's are punched in columns 2 through 5

Name Field   A 1 is punched in column 6
                   A's are punched in card columns 7 through 23

Street Field   A 1 is punched into column 24
                   A's are punched into card columns 25 through 41

City Field   A 1 is punched into column 42
                   A's are punched into card columns 43 through 59

State Field   A 1 is punched into column 60
                   An A is punched into column 61

Zip Code Field   A space is punched into column 62
                   12's are punched into card columns 63 through 66

Telephone Field   A space is punched into column 67
                   12's are punched into card columns 68 through 73

Unused Field   A – is punched into column 74
                   12's are punched into columns 75 through 80

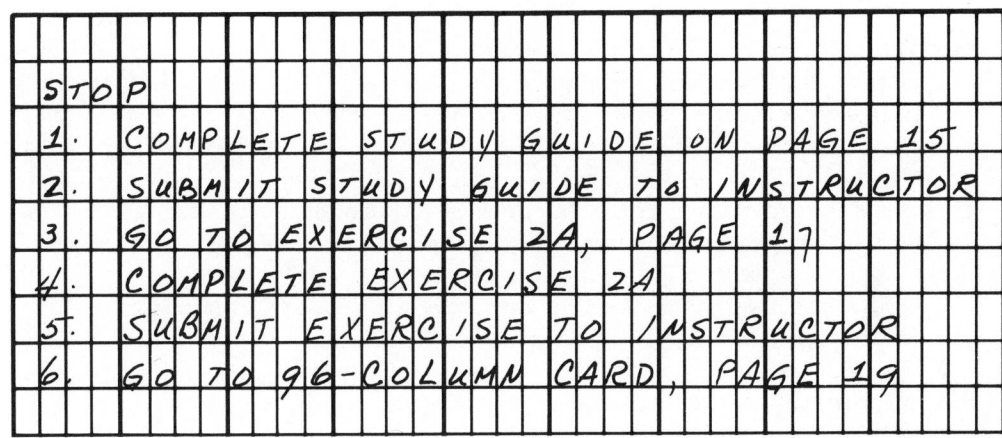

	STOP
1.	COMPLETE STUDY GUIDE ON PAGE 15
2.	SUBMIT STUDY GUIDE TO INSTRUCTOR
3.	GO TO EXERCISE 2A, PAGE 17
4.	COMPLETE EXERCISE 2A
5.	SUBMIT EXERCISE TO INSTRUCTOR
6.	GO TO 96-COLUMN CARD, PAGE 19

STUDY GUIDE

Date _____   Name _____

DIRECTIONS: *Answer the following questions in the spaces provided. Your answer should indicate the depth of understanding that you have toward the concepts and definitions presented. If insufficient space is provided, complete your answer on the reverse side of the Study Guide Sheet.*

1. Explain some of the features of the 80-column card.

2. Explain the keyboard of the 029 keypunch machine.

3. List the five parts of the keypunch machine. Give a short explanation of each part.

4. What is a program card and why is it used?

5. List and illustrate the five most common program card codes.

6. Explain the card movement through the keypunch machine.

EXERCISE 2A

Date ———————————————— Name ————————————————

TRUE–FALSE: *Each of the following statements is either true or false. Indicate your choice in the Answers column by encircling "T" for a true answer or "F" for a false answer.*

Answers

1. Because cards are fed rapidly through data processing machines, there is no need for manufacturing tolerances .... T F

2. Cards can have only one corner cut off of them .... T F

3. There are 12 rows for punching on an 80-column card .... T F

4. Columns of a card are vertical .... T F

5. The 12 zone is the uppermost zone on a card .... T F

6. The 12 zone is not known as the 12 edge .... T F

7. Consecutive columns set aside for a specific purpose are known as a field .... T F

8. The keys that do not have expanded characters are the A and W keys .... T F

9. The keypunch machine has two modes — alphabetic and numeric .... T F

10. The upper character of an expanded key is obtainable when the machine is in numeric mode .... T F

11. The numeric shift key and the alphabetic shift key are located on the lower left and right sides of the keyboard .... T F

12. The mode change is constant as long as the shift key is held depressed .... T F

13. The card hopper of an IBM 029 holds approximately 600 cards .... T F

14. Cards are forced forward in the hopper by the pressure plate mechanism .... T F

15. Cards are placed in the hopper 12 edge down, face forward .... T F

16. The registered position is the first position of the punch bed .... T F

17. Holes are punched in the card from beneath the punch head bar .... T F

18. There are three positions for the card when it is in the read bed .... T F

19. Cards move to the eject bed from the stacker .... T F

20. The card stacker is located in the upper left corner of the keypunch .... T F

21. The stacker holds approximately 500 cards .... T F

22. The punched cards are in the same order in the stacker as the data of the source document .... T F

23. The program card causes the keypunch to change mode according to the codes punched into it .... T F

24. The first column of a field of a program card contains the code to shift the machine to the desired mode .... T F

25. The program card does not need to have a punch in each and every column T F

17

26. There are four basic or common codes for a program card   T   F

27. The program card does not contain punches that serve to follow the field   T   F

28. Depression of the feed key causes cards to feed into the punch station from the hopper   T   F

29. The keypunch machine places the punches in the card in the proper combination   T   F

30. Punching one character at a time into the card is known as serial punching   T   F

31. Cards move in syncronization through the card beds   T   F

32. A keypunch programmed for automatic duplication will lock up if a card containing the data to be duplicated is not registered at the read head   T   F

33. Cards are placed in the hopper 9 edge down, face forward   T   F

Completion: *Fill in the blank with the appropriate word or words.*

1–3. The three zones of an 80-column card are _____ , _____ _____ , and _____ .

4–5. The two keys that are not expanded on the key punch are the _____ _____ and _____ keys.

6–10. The five parts of the keypunch are the _____ , _____ _____ , _____ , _____ , and _____ _____ .

Matching: *Match Column 1 to Column 2.*

COLUMN 1	COLUMN 2	*Answers*
A. 0.007	1. Shift key in the lower left corner of keyboard	_____
B. 80		
C. 12	2. Shift key in the lower right corner of keyboard	_____
D. Fielded Card		
E. Numeric	3. The number of rows on a card	_____
F. Alphabetic		
G. Star Wheels	4. A punched card thickness	_____
H. Card Hopper		
I. Feed Key	5. Mechanism that senses different codes on a program card	_____
	6. Consecutive columns set aside for specific purpose	_____
	7. The number of columns on a card	_____

96-COLUMN CARD

The 96-column card differs from the 80-column card in several ways. See Fig. 3.

1. The card is punched on a machine called a Data Recorder.

2. The 96-column card is one-third the size of the 80-column card, and yet it has 20% more storage capacity.

3. The card is divided into two segments, the Print Area Segment and the Punch Area Segment.

4. When data is punched into the card by the Recorder, the holes are round instead of rectangular.

5. Each of the corners is beveled for ease of transport through the Recorder and other equipment.

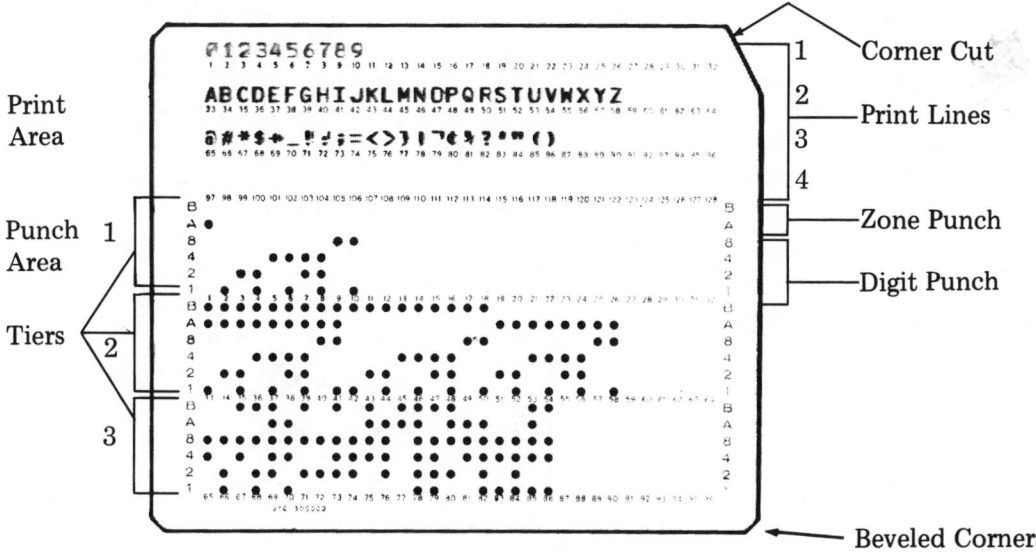

Figure 3   96-column Card

6. Each of the upper corners (left or right) can be cut for identification purposes.

7. Data is recorded in the Binary Coded Decimal (BCD) Format instead of the Hollerith Code Format.

8. Each tier has the card column number represented.

PRINT AREA SEGMENT

1. There are four print lines, each having 32 positions for a total of 128 print positions.

2. Of the 128 possible printing positions, only the first 96 are directly associated with the Punch Area Segment.

3. Print positions 97 through 128 are allocated to some printing device other than the Recorder.

PUNCH AREA SEGMENT

1. There are three horizontal punching areas known as tiers.

2. Each tier is subdivided into two groups of punch positions — zone punches and digit punches.

3. The zone punches are A and B.

4. The digit punches are 1, 2, 4, and 8.

5. Each tier has 32 sets of punch positions called card columns, making a total of 96 columns. Each column has six punch positions. Each column is punched to represent one character.

NUMERIC CHARACTERS

The numeric characters 1 through 9 are represented by various combinations of the digit punches 1, 2, 4, and 8. The numbers 1, 2, 4, and 8 are represented by a punch in their respective punch positions. However, the numbers 3, 5, 6, 7, and 9 are represented by two or more punches. For example, the number 5 is represented by a combination of digit punch 1 and digit punch 4 in the same column.

The numeric character zero is represented by a punch in zone A. Numeric punching on the 96-column card is illustrated in Fig. 4.

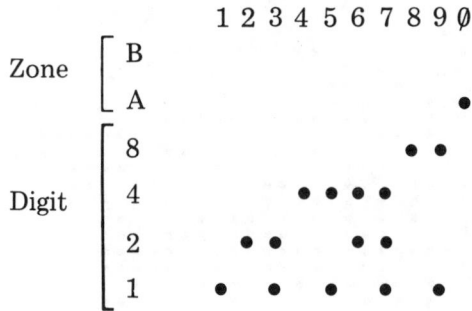

Figure 4   Numeric Punching — BCD Code Format

ALPHABETIC CHARACTERS

Alphabetic characters include the 26 letters of the alphabet. RPG II also considers the characters $, #, and @ to be alphabetic. Alphabetic characters are represented by a combination of one or more digit punches and one or two zone punches in the same column. The zone punches are A and B. The alphabet is broken down into three segments. The letters A through I are represented by punches in zones A and B; the letters J through R are represented by a punch in zone B; the letters S through Z are represented by a punch in zone A. Digit punches are combined with the zone punches to represent each letter. Notice the following examples in Fig. 5.

1. Letter A is represented by zone punches A and B plus digit punch 1. Letter G is represented by zone punches A and B plus digit punches 4, 2, and 1.

2. Letter J is represented by zone punch B plus digit punch 1. Letter O is represented by zone punch B plus digit punches 4 and 2.

3. Letter S is represented by zone punch A plus digit punch 2. Letter X is represented by zone punch A plus digit punches 4, 2, and 1.

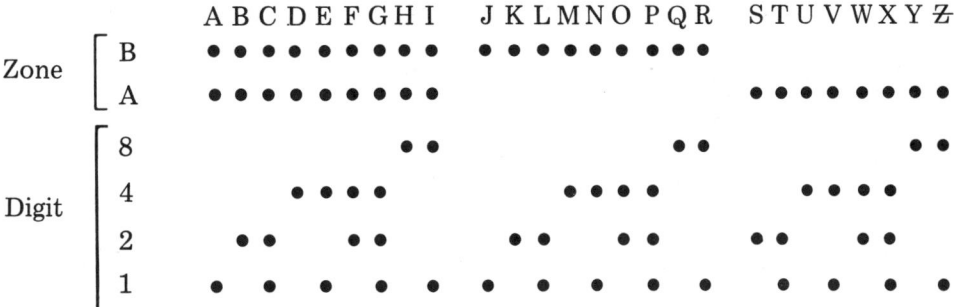

Figure 5   Alphabetic Characters — BCD Code Format

SYMBOLIC CHARACTERS

Symbolic characters are represented by special combinations of zone punches and/or digit punches in one column. Not all the special characters illustrated in Fig. 6 can be used on all computers' configurations. However, the symbols shown are relatively standard.

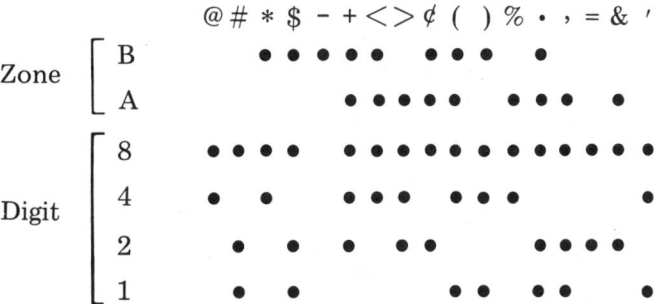

Figure 6   Symbolic Characters — BCD Code Format

21

```
STOP
1.  COMPLETE STUDY GUIDE ON PAGE 23
2.  SUBMIT STUDY GUIDE TO INSTRUCTOR
3.  GO TO EXERCISE 2B, PAGE 25
4.  COMPLETE EXERCISE 2B
5.  SUBMIT EXERCISE TO INSTRUCTOR
6.  GO TO PROJECT ONE, PAGE 27
```

STUDY GUIDE

Date_____   Name_____

DIRECTIONS: *Answer the following questions in the spaces provided. Your answers should indicate the depth of understanding that you have toward the concepts and definitions presented. If there is insufficient space provided for your answer, complete your answer on the reverse side of the Study Guide.*

1. Explain the relationship of the printing lines to the punch tiers.

2. Explain how the zone punches of a 96-column card are positioned.

3. Explain the makeup of a punching tier.

EXERCISE 2B

Date_____   Name_____

TRUE–FALSE: *Each of the following statements is either true or false. Indicate your choice in the Answers column by encircling "T" for a true answer or "F" for a false answer.*

Answers

1. The 96-column card is one-third the size of the 80-column card   T   F

2. The 96-column card has 20% more storage capacity than the 80-column card   T   F

3. The machine used to punch the holes into the 96-column card is called the Data Recorder   T   F

4. There are four printing lines on the 96-column card   T   F

5. Each printing line on the card is tied in with a punching tier   T   F

6. Each printing tier has 33 possible printing positions   T   F

7. The corners of the 96-column card are beveled for ease of transport through the computer equipment   T   F

8. The letters BCD stand for Before Coding Decisions   T   F

9. Punching positions representing any character are in a vertical arrangement in each tier   T   F

10. Six-position punching allows for the possible combination of numeric, alphabetic, and symbolic characters   T   F

11. Each punching tier is subdivided into zone punches and digit punches   T   F

12. There are only two hole–punch combinations for an alphabetic character—that is, one zone punch and one digit punch   T   F

13. The digit punches on a 96-column card are 8, 4, 2, and 1   T   F

14. B and A punches on the 96-column card correspond to a 12 punch on the 80-column card.   T   F

15. Digits 1, 2, 4, and 8 are not represented by holes being punched in their relative positions   T   F

16. The number zero (0) is represented by a punch in zone 11   T   F

17. The punching for the letter C is zone A, zone B, digit 1, and digit 2   T   F

18. The fourth printing line does not have any corresponding punching tier   T   F

19. A zone punch is made up of either zone punch A, zone punch B, or a combination of the two   T   F

20. The number 9 is represented by zone A plus digit 8 and digit 1   T   F

Completion: *Fill in the blank with the appropriate word or words.*

1, 2. The zone punches on a 96-column card are _____ and _____
_____ .

3, 4. The segments of a 96-column card are the _____ area and the
_____ area.

5. Data is recorded in _____ format instead of Hollerith Code format on the 96-column card.

6. There are _____ possible printing positions on a 96-column card.

7, 8. The 96-column card is _____ the size of an 80-column card and yet has _____ % more storage capacity.

Matching: *Match Column 1 to Column 2.*

COLUMN 1   COLUMN 2   *Answers*

A. Recorder   1. The digit represented by a punch in Zone A   _____
B. 3
C. 32   2. Number of punching positions in each tier   _____
D. Ø
E. 6   3. Number of punching tiers   _____
F. 20
G. Keypunch   4. Number of positions on each column of the card   _____
H. Card Format
                     5. Machine used to punch 96 column cards   _____

PROJECT ONE

PROJECT SPECIFICATIONS

For the purpose of each of the remaining projects in this book, you are to assume that each of your classmates is the owner of a business.

As a student programmer, you have been exposed to

1. Card Formats

2. Keypunch Machine

Using a card format, do the following:

1. Punch a program card.

2. Mount program card on drum.

3. Punch a card containing the required data of each member of the class while the machine is under programmed control.

4. Submit these data cards to your instructor.

Your instructor will insert the cards into an already existing source program deck that will produce the output report illustrated on the Print Chart on pages 28 and 29.

PRINT CHART

The Print Chart serves as a tool in planning the printed computer output. Although the forms vary somewhat, most charts are similar to the standard form shown in Figs. 7a and 7b. The Print Chart is 150 spaces (columns) wide and has 50 vertical lines. Each line represents one line of print; and each column is the size of one printed character. Because the types of printers vary, not all columns on the form will be used. If the printer in question has a capacity of 120 print positions, only 120 of the 150 print positions on the Print Chart will be used.

If a computer does not specifically instruct the printer, through the Source Program, as to exactly which print positions should be used, the printer automatically justifies the printing at the left on the output form. That is, the leftmost print position of the printout will be the first print position of the printer. Notice the following characteristics of the Print Chart in Figs. 7a and 7b.

1. There are print position indicators across the top and the bottom of the form.

2. There are 150 possible horizontal print positions.

3. There are 15 sections (columns), each of which is indicated by a darker line. In each of these sections there are 10 print positions.

4. Each horizontal section (10 printing positions) represents 1 inch.

5. There are 50 numbered vertical lines. Lines were removed to save space.

6. There are 8 sections (horizontal rows), each of which is indicated by a dark line. In each of these sections there are 6 print lines.

7. There are 2 print lines (49 and 50) in a section by themselves at the bottom of the Print Chart.

8. Each vertical section (6 print lines) represents 1 inch.

Computer printers normally accommodate 120, 132, or 144 print positions. The Print Chart is, of necessity, governed by the printer capacity. If the printer has a 120-character capacity, the centering point is print position 60; for a 132-character capacity, it is 66; for a 144-character capacity, it is 72.

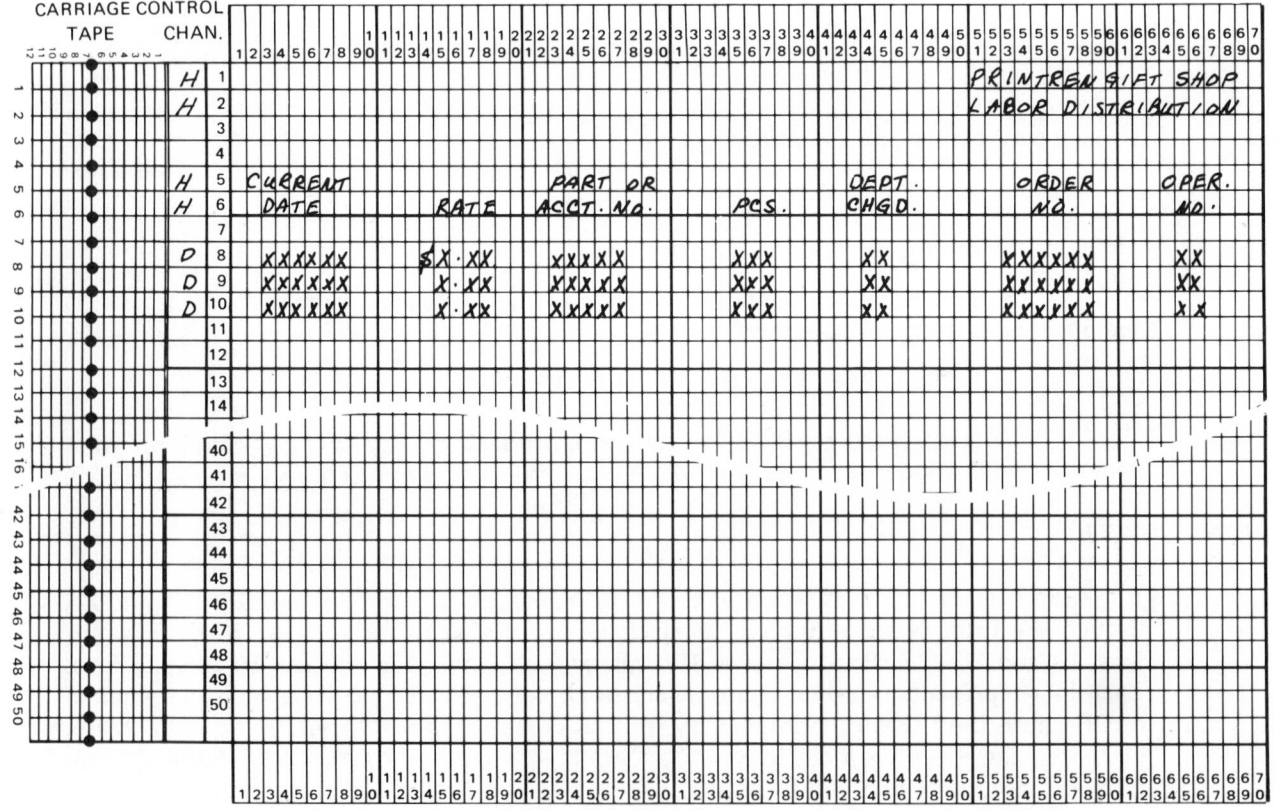

Figure 7(a)   Print Chart Sheet Development (Left Portion)

In general, the stock paper used on the printer measures 14⅞ inches wide by 11 inches long. However, special paper or forms are obtainable for printing special jobs or projects. If other than standardized stock paper or forms are to be used for the printout, the programmer must plan the print positions accordingly.

A carriage control tape is to be punched by the computer operator to correspond to the Print Chart. The one illustrated on the Print Chart is not used. The punching of the hole alignment for form spacing and skipping takes place prior to running the Source Program and test data. This operation is included in the debugging process, which occurs when the program is submitted to the computer to see if it contains programming errors. Any errors must be corrected and the program submitted again to the computer. The process could be repeated several times until the computer indicates that the program is completely free of any programming errors.

The placement, or positioning, of each of the several levels of headings — main, sub, and columnar — is illustrated on the Print Chart. The actual titles of the headings are written on the coding sheets. Since the headings appear first, they are placed in the program before the data that will be listed under them.

The placement of the data to be taken from the input record must also be planned and illustrated on the Print Chart. The columns are often illustrated by using A's or X's for the data. The A's and X's used in Fig. 7 are to be considered only as print positions. Actual editing symbols, such as the dollar sign and decimal point, which are used to make reading the output easier, are also sometimes used on the Print Chart to make it more meaningful.

To further develop your understanding of how a print chart acts as a tool in planning the output layout, note the following characteristics of the Print Chart shown in Fig. 7(a) and (b).

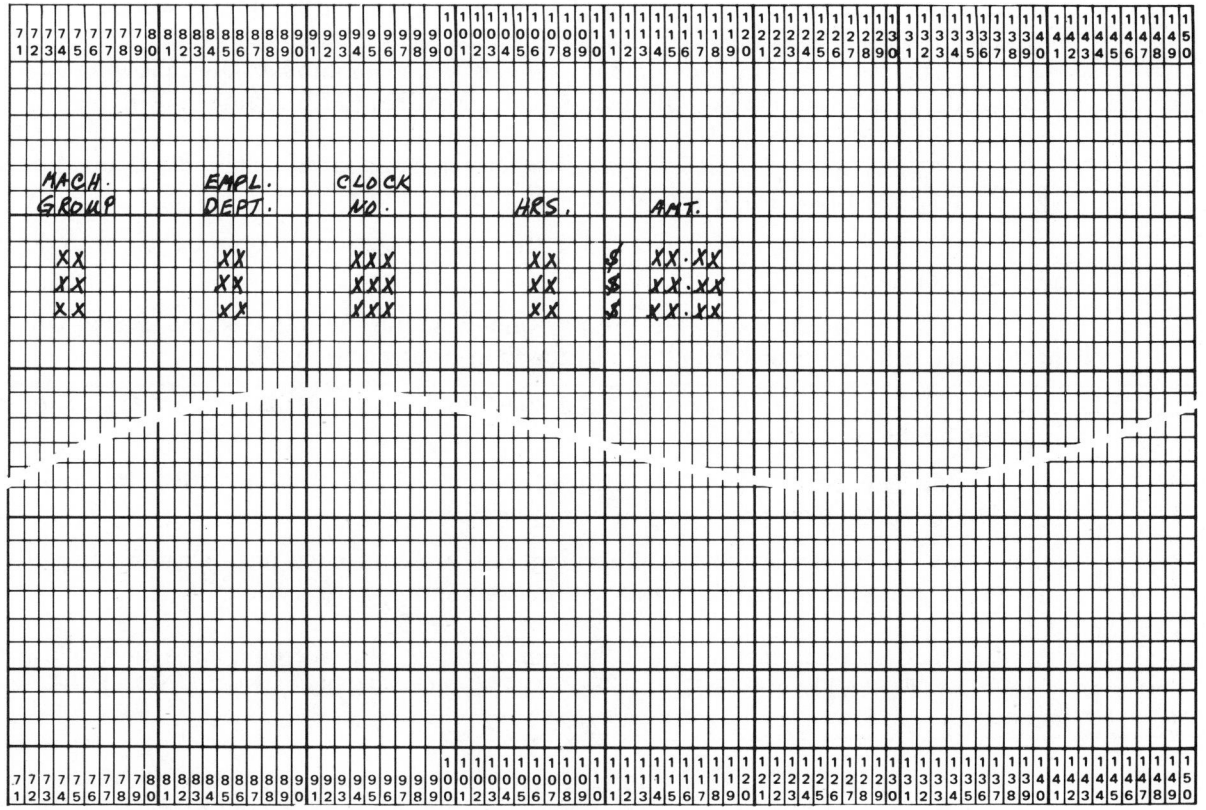

Figure 7(b)   Print Chart Development (Right Portion)

1. The main heading requires two lines of print.

2. The columnar headings require two lines of print.

3. There are two blank spaces between the main heading lines and the columnar heading lines.

4. The detail lines are illustrated by X's and have editing symbols contained within some of them.

5. The print line is 120 positions in length.

6. The H and D coded to the left of column 1 illustrate the type of line that is to be printed.

Main Heading

The main heading PRINTREN GIFT SHOP must be centered, commencing at the centering point, the 60th print position. To determine the starting print position backspace one print position (toward print position one) for each two characters of the heading. All spaces and symbols are included in the character count. If a single character remains, the programmer has the option of moving or not moving back one print position.

Using the backspacing method, the P of PRINTREN is placed in print position 51 of the Print Chart. The heading is then coded once the starting point has been determined. The LABOR DISTRIBUTION line is centered in a similar manner.

Columnar Headings

The columnar headings require two print lines. Each of the 12 columns will be centered within the ten print positions of each section of the Print Chart.

The first line of the columnar headings will accommodate the following words: CURRENT, PART OR, DEPT., ORDER, OPER., MACH., EMPL., and CLOCK.

1. The word CURRENT, which requires seven print positions, is positioned within the first section. The C is positioned in print position 2.

2. Since there are no words for the second section, it is unnecessary to determine any centering.

3. The words PART OR are positioned within the third section. PART OR requires seven print positions. The P is positioned in print position 23.

4. Since there are no words for the fourth section, it is unnecessary to determine any centering.

5. The word DEPT. is positioned within the fifth section. DEPT. requires five print positions. The D is positioned in print position 43.

6. Steps similar to the preceding ones are continued until all remaining first-line columnar headings are positioned within their appropriate sections.

The second line of the columnar headings will accommodate the following words: DATE, RATE, ACCT.NO., PCS., CHGD., NO., GROUP, DEPT., NO., HRS., and AMT.

1. The word DATE requiring four print positions is positioned within the first section. The D is positioned in print position 3. DATE is now centered below CURRENT.

2. The word RATE is positioned within the second section. RATE requires four print positions. The R is positioned in print position 15.

3. The words ACCT.NO. are positioned within the third section. ACCT.NO. requires eight print positions. The A is positioned in print position 22. ACCT.NO. is now centered below PART OR.

4. The word PCS. is positioned within the fourth section. PCS. requires four print positions. The P is positioned in print position 35.

5. The word CHGD. is positioned within the fifth section. The C is positioned in print position 43. CHGD. is now centered below DEPT.

6. Steps similar to those above are continued until all remaining second-line columnar headings are positioned within the appropriate sections.

Detail Lines

The data composing the detail line of print must also be centered within its appropriate section.

1. The actual digital date, which requires six print positions, is positioned within the first section. The first digit that represents the date is positioned in print position 3. The five remaining X's (columns 4 through 8) finish the coding for this section.

2. The RATE amount is illustrated by X's, along with the editing symbols ($ and .). Since the rate amount requires five print positions, the $ is positioned in print position 14.

3. The PART OR ACCT.NO. figure is illustrated by X's. It requires five print positions. The first X is positioned in print position 23.

4. Steps similar to those above are continued for the remaining sections.

5. However, observe the AMT. field. The editing symbols ($ and .) are also illustrated in this field. There are blank spaces between the $ and the first X. This type of coding illustrates the possibility of figures being printed in the blank spaces.

The main objective of a Print Chart is to illustrate the appearance of the data on the OUTPUT report.

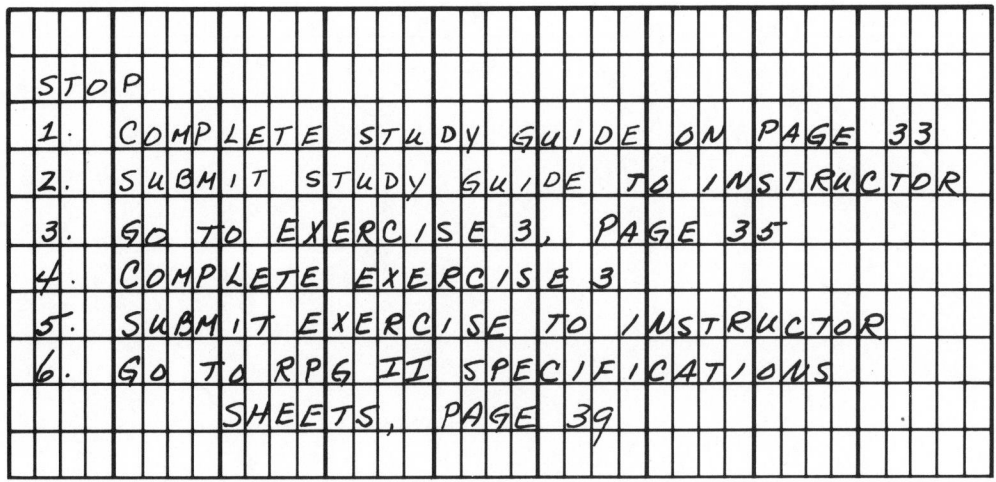

Date_____   Name_____

　　　　DIRECTIONS: *Answer the following questions in the spaces provided. Your answer should indicate the depth of understanding that you have toward the concepts and definitions presented. If there is insufficient space provided for your answer, complete your answer on the reverse side of the Study Guide Sheet.*

1. Explain the characteristics of a Print Chart form.

2. Explain the relationship between the diagramming on the Print Chart and the Output Report produced by the printer of the computer.

3. Explain how the carriage control tape (if used) relates to the Output Report and printer of the computer being used.

4. Why and who makes up the carriage control tape?

5. Explain why the symbols H, D, X, $, and period are used on a Print Chart form.

EXERCISE 3

Date_____   Name_____

TEST YOUR KNOWLEDGE: *Develop a print chart layout, using the following data, on the print chart form provided on pages 36–37.*

1. A two-line main heading of your own choice.

2. The print line is 120 print positions in length.

3. The following columnar headings are to be used.

        (a) Employee number   6 positions

        (b) Employee name   20 positions

        (c) Department number   4 positions

        (d) Position number   6 positions

        (e) Grade of pay   2 positions

        (f) Date of hire   6 positions

4. Allow ten spaces for the intercolumnar columns.

Upon completion, submit your print chart layout to your instructor.

150/10/6 PRINT CHART PROG. ID ________ PAGE ________

(SPACING: 150 POSITION SPAN, AT 10 CHARACTERS PER INCH, 6 LINES PER VERTICAL INCH) DATE ________

PROGRAM TITLE ________

PROGRAMMER OR DOCUMENTALIST: ________

CHART TITLE ________

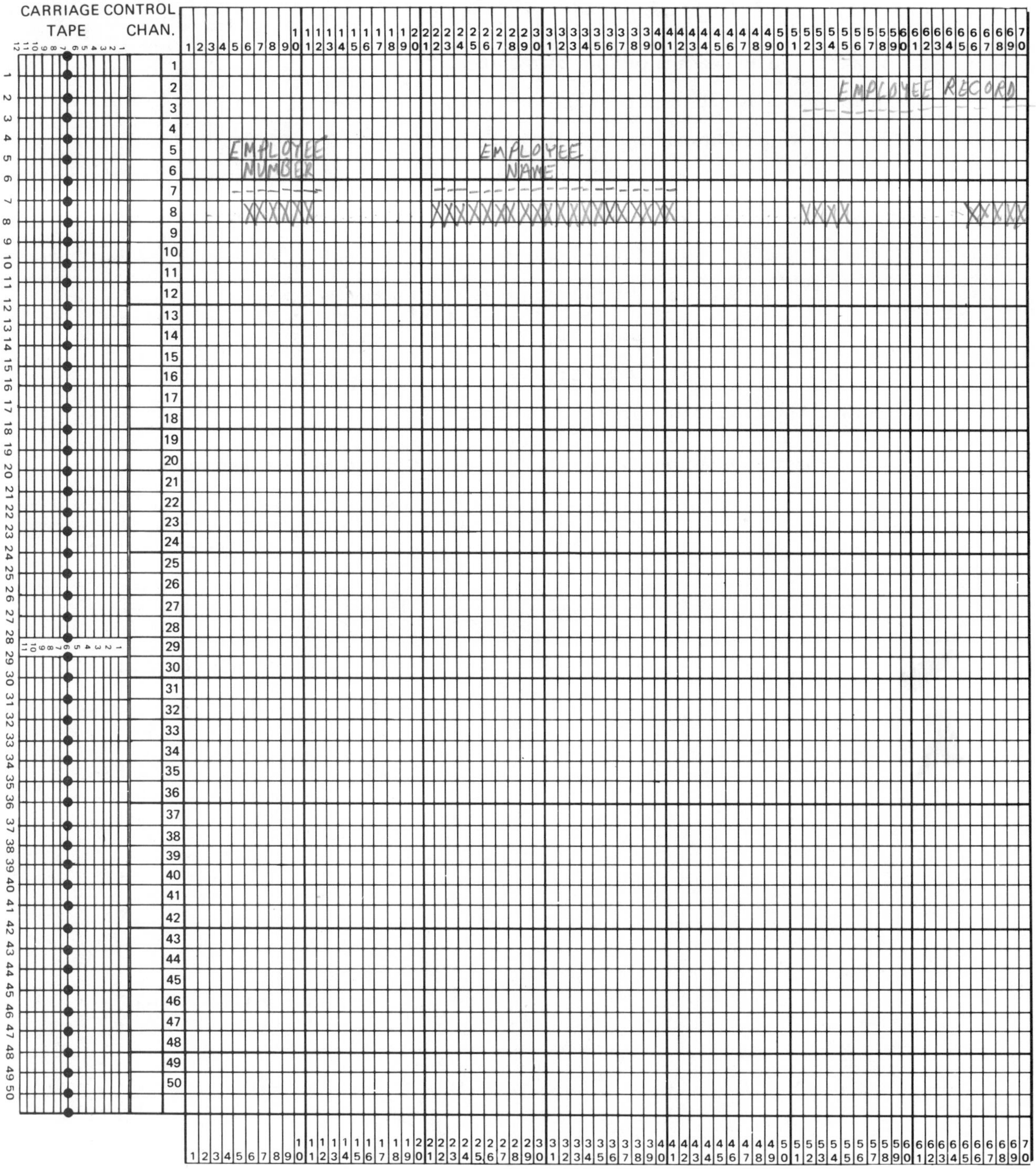
CARRIAGE CONTROL
TAPE
CHAN.
EMPLOYEE RECORD
EMPLOYEE NUMBER
EMPLOYEE NAME

IBM GX20–1816–0 U/MO25*
Printed in U.S.A.

NOTE: Dimensions on this sheet vary with humidity.
Exact measurements should be calculated or scaled
with a ruler rather than with the lines on this chart.

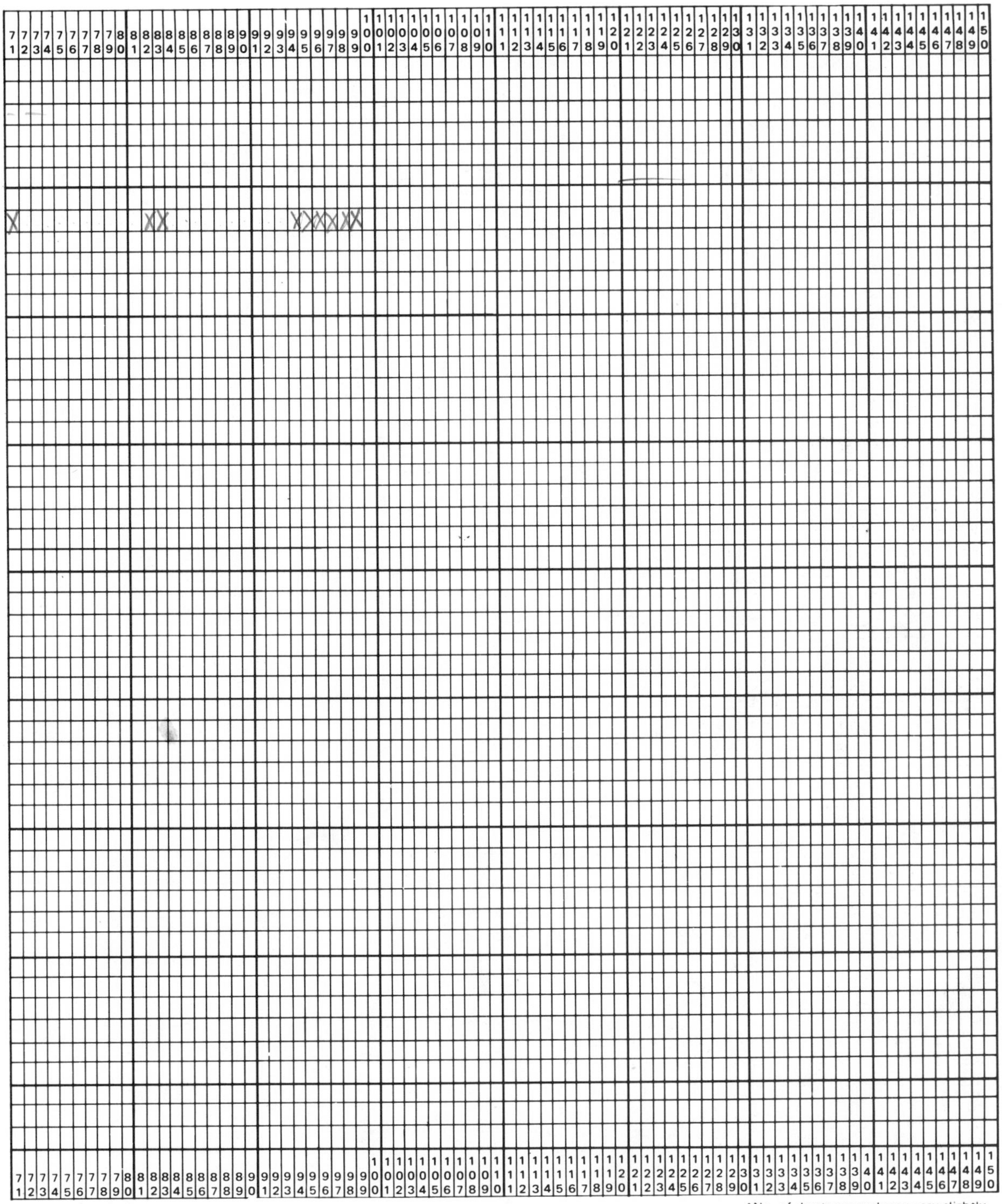

*No. of sheets per pad may vary slightly.

RPG II SPECIFICATIONS SHEETS

ELEMENTS OF RPG STRUCTURE

RPG (Report Program Generator) is a problem-oriented computer language. Coding is quickly accomplished and easily understood. To make any instruction machine sensible, it must be first converted to a machine language. This conversion takes place in a translator program, called the *compiler*, which is furnished by the manufacturer. The compiler is an internally stored program. The compiler accomplishes two objectives.

1. It checks for coding errors in the program being compiled.

2. If no major errors are found, the compiler translates the Source Program into an Object Program.

Since the compiler is expected to operate on each of the elements described by the programmer, the elements discussed on the following pages must be thoroughly understood. RPG instructions are written, or coded, on Specifications Sheets (also known as coding sheets). Statements coded on the sheets are later punched into cards that make up the Source Program (sometimes known as the Source Deck). Each line on a coding sheet is punched into a separate card. The various portions of the sheets will be explained as they are needed to complete the coding of the source program pertaining to each project. RPG coding sheets are designed to meet the following needs.

1. They are a convenient aid for the programmer to use in organizing the program and are extremely vital to the person who punches the cards.

2. They enable the programmer to specify those items that are used by the compiler to create the Object Program.

3. The printed listing of the Source Program can be checked against the coding sheets.

A programmer's first job is to describe the data that makes up a file. A *file* is any number of cards having a similar format. Each card of a file is known as a *record*. A file may contain several different types of records, but all the records of a file have the same length. Records are divided into *fields* — that is, groups of columns set aside for specific purposes.

39

FIELDS

Like other records, RPG Specifications sheets are also divided into fields. These fields are of predetermined length and are printed on the Specifications sheets. There are many different fields on the various types of Specifications sheets. However, the common fields listed below appear on all RPG Specifications sheets. See Figs. 8 and 9.

Page Number Field   (Columns 1 through 2)

This field is used to identify each page of the program. The pages are numbered sequentially. Many pages (or Specifications sheets) may be needed to complete a program. They should be kept in order. The page number is punched into columns 1 and 2 of each card in the Source Deck.

Line   (Columns 3 through 5)

This field is used to sequence the lines on each page of the program. Each line will be punched into one card of the Source Program. The lines on each Specifications sheet are preprinted in ascending order in multiples of ten.

Form Type   (Columns 6 through 6)

There are seven different types of RPG Specifications sheets. Each type is identified by a preprinted alphabetic character in the Form Type Field.

H	Control Card Specifications (Header Card)
F	File Description Specifications
E	Extension Specifications
L	Line Counter Specifications
I	Input Specifications
C	Calculations Specifications
O	Output Specifications

Every card of an RPG Source Program must have one of these characters punched into column 6. The header, or control, card (H) must always be the first card of the Source Program. The other types of Specifications sheet cards must follow in the order of F, E, L, I, C, and O. Some programs do not use every type of specifications card. The H and F specifications appear on the same Specifications sheet. The E and L specifications are also found together.

Comments   (Columns 7 through 7)

A programmer often wishes to write comments pertinent to the program and its operation and logic. The compiler recognizes a comment card by the asterisk (*) in column 7. Comment lines have no effect on the program or its compilation. They serve merely as documentation. Comments CANNOT be written on a control card, however.

Program Identification (Columns 75 through 80)

Programmers identify each program that they write by coding in an abbreviated name or code by which the program will be later known. If a card is misplaced or dropped, it can easily be collated into the proper sequence of the Source Program by the coding in the Program Identification Field, in the Page Number Field, and in the Line Field. The programmer can use any alphabetic or numeric characters in the chosen name. The following points, however, should be observed.

1. The name must be unique.

2. The first character of the name must be alphabetic.

3. There can be NO embedded blanks within the name.

See Figs. 8 and 9 for the common fields.

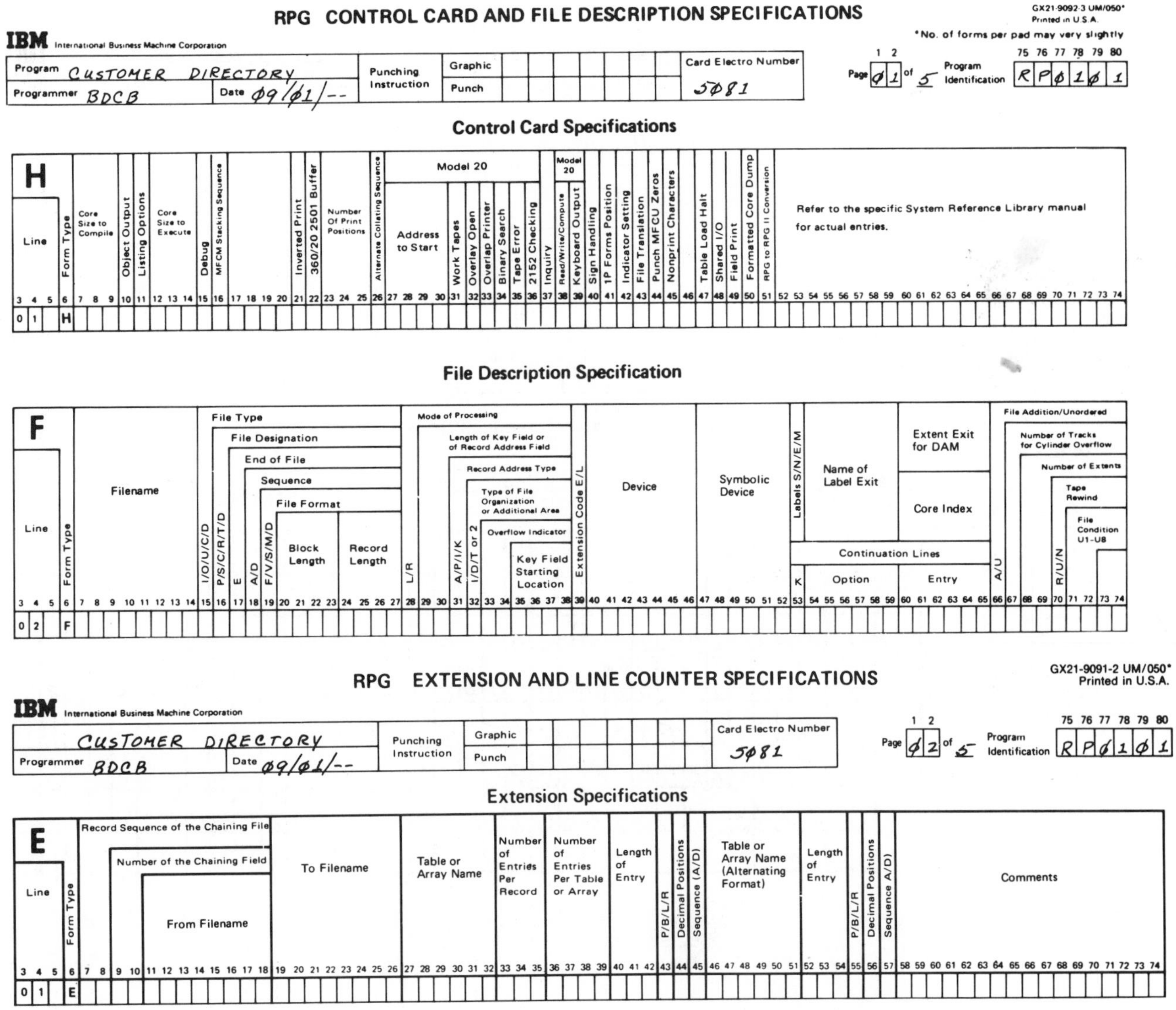

RPG CONTROL CARD AND FILE DESCRIPTION SPECIFICATIONS

GX21-9092-3 UM/050*
Printed in U.S.A.

*No. of forms per pad may very slightly

IBM International Business Machine Corporation

Program CUSTOMER DIRECTORY
Programmer BDCB   Date 09/01/--

Punching Instruction — Graphic / Punch
Card Electro Number 5081
Page 01 of 5   Program Identification RP0101

Control Card Specifications

Refer to the specific System Reference Library manual for actual entries.

(H — Control Card Specification form)

File Description Specification

(F — File Description Specification form)

RPG EXTENSION AND LINE COUNTER SPECIFICATIONS

GX21-9091-2 UM/050*
Printed in U.S.A.

IBM International Business Machine Corporation

CUSTOMER DIRECTORY
Programmer BDCB   Date 09/01/--

Punching Instruction — Graphic / Punch
Card Electro Number 5081
Page 02 of 5   Program Identification RP0101

Extension Specifications

(E — Extension Specification form)

Figure 8

41

Line Counter Specifications

L			1		2		3		4		5		6		7		8		9		10		11		12	
Line	Form Type	Filename	Line Number	FL or Channel Number	Line Number	OL or Channel Number	Line Number	Channel Number	Line Number	Channel Number	Line Number	Channel Number	Line Number	Channel Number	Line Number	Channel Number	Line Number	Channel Number	Line Number	Channel Number	Line Number	Channel Number	Line Number	Channel Number	Line Number	Channel Number
1 1	L																								

GX21-9094-2 U/M 050*
Printed in U.S.A.

RPG INPUT SPECIFICATIONS

IBM International Business Machine Corporation

Program: CUSTOMER DIRECTORY
Programmer: BDCB Date 09/01/--

Punching Instruction — Graphic / Punch

Card Electro Number: 5081

Page 03 of 5   Program Identification: RP0101

I						Record Identification Codes			Field Location					Field Indicators		
Line	Form Type	Filename	Sequence	Number (1-N)	Option (O)	Record Identifying Indicator or **	1 Position / Not (N) / C/Z/D / Character	2 Position / Not (N) / C/Z/D / Character	3 Position / Not (N) / C/Z/D / Character — Stacker Select P/B/L/R	From / To / Decimal Positions	Field Name	Control Level (L1-L9)	Matching Fields or Changing Fields / Field Record Relation	Plus	Minus	Zero or Blank
0 1	I															

GX21-9093-2 UM/050* Printed in U.S.A.
*No. of forms per pad may vary slightly

RPG CALCULATION SPECIFICATIONS

IBM International Business Machine Corporation

Program: CUSTOMER DIRECTORY
Programmer: BDCB Date 09/01/--

Punching Instruction — Graphic / Punch

Card Electro Number: 5081

Page 04 of 5   Program Identification: RP0101

C			Indicators			Factor 1	Operation	Factor 2	Result Field				Resulting Indicators			Comments
Line	Form Type	Control Level (L0-L9, LR, SR, AN/OR)	And / Not	And / Not	Not	Factor 1	Operation	Factor 2	Name	Length	Decimal Positions	Half Adjust (H)	Arithmetic: Plus / Minus / Zero — Compare 1>2 / 1<2 / 1=2 — Lookup (Factor 2) is High / Low / Equal			Comments
0 1	C															

GX21-9090-2 U/M 050*
Printed in U.S.A.

RPG OUTPUT SPECIFICATIONS

IBM International Business Machine Corporation

Program: CUSTOMER DIRECTORY
Programmer: BDCB Date 09/01/--

Punching Instruction — Graphic / Punch

Card Electro Number: 5081

Page 05 of 5   Program Identification: RP0101

O				
Line	Form Type	Filename		
			STOP	
			1. COMPLETE STUDY GUIDE ON PAGE 43	
0 1	O		2. SUBMIT STUDY GUIDE TO INSTRUCTOR	
			3. GO TO EXERCISE 4, PAGE 45	
			4. COMPLETE EXERCISE 4	
			5. SUBMIT EXERCISE TO INSTRUCTOR	

Figure 9

STUDY GUIDE

Date _____   Name _____

DIRECTIONS: *Answer the following questions in the spaces provided. Your answers should indicate the depth of understanding that you have toward the concepts and definitions presented. If there is insufficient space provided for your answer, complete your answer on the reverse side of the Study Guide.*

1. List and explain the fields that are common to all coding sheets.

2. Explain how human language is translated into machine language.

3. List and explain how the coding sheets are designed to meet prescribed needs.

4. List the order in which the different types of coding sheets must be assembled.

5. List the rules of Program Identification.

43

EXERCISE 4

Date _____   Name _____

TEST YOUR KNOWLEDGE

DIRECTIONS: *Assume that you would be coding the common fields on the coding sheets of Exercise 3. Use only the specifications sheets illustrated below.*

RPG OUTPUT SPECIFICATIONS

GX21-9090-2 U/M 050*
Printed in U.S.A.

IBM International Business Machine Corporation

| Program | | Punching Instruction | Graphic | | | | | | Card Electro Number | | Page | 1 2 | of | Program Identification | 75 76 77 78 79 80 |
| Programmer | Date | | Punch | | | | | | | | | | | |

| O | | T/E Fetch(F) | Space | Skip | Output Indicators | | | | Commas | Zero Balances to Print | No Sign | CR | – | X = Remove Plus Sign |

RPG INPUT SPECIFICATIONS

GX21-9094-2 U/M 050*
Printed in U.S.A.

IBM International Business Machine Corporation

| Program | | Punching Instruction | Graphic | | | | | | Card Electro Number | | Page | 1 2 | of | Program Identification | 75 76 77 78 79 80 |
| Programmer | Date | | Punch | | | | | | | | | | | |

| I | | | | Record Identification Codes | | | Field Location | | L9) | | Field Indicators |
| | | | 1 | 2 | 3 | | | | | |

RPG CONTROL CARD AND FILE DESCRIPTION SPECIFICATIONS

GX21-9092-3 UM/050*
Printed in U.S.A.
*No. of forms per pad may vary very slightly

IBM International Business Machine Corporation

| Program | | Punching Instruction | Graphic | | | | | | Card Electro Number | | Page | 1 2 | of | Program Identification | 75 76 77 78 79 80 |
| Programmer | Date | | Punch | | | | | | | | | | | |

Control Card Specifications

H		Form Type	Core Size to Compile	Object Output Listing Options	Core Size to Execute	Debug											
Line																
3 4 5 6	7 8 9 10 11 12 13 14 15															
0 1 H																

```
STOP
1. COMPLETE EXERCISE 5, PAGE 47
2. SUBMIT EXERCISE TO INSTRUCTOR
3. GO TO CONTROL CARD AND FILE
   DESCRIPTION SPECIFICATIONS,
   PAGE 49
```

File Description Specification

| F | | File Type | Mode of Processing | | | | M | Extent Exit | File Addition/Unordered |
| | | File Designation | Length of Key Field or | | | | | | Number of Tracks |

Figure 10

45

EXERCISE 5

Date_____   Name_____

TRUE–FALSE: *Each of the following statements is either true or false. Indicate your choice in the Answers column by encircling "T" for a true answer or "F" for a false answer.*

1. The Print Chart serves as a tool in planning the output format   T   F

2. The Print Chart does not have any indication of print positions   T   F

3. The print positions on the Print Chart are divided equally into sections   T   F

4. On the Print Chart eight vertical lines of print equal 1 inch   T   F

5. The center point for a 120-print position printer is 60   T   F

6. Normal stock paper for the printer is 14⅞ inches by 11 inches   T   F

7. The carriage control tape illustrated on a Print Chart is cut off and used by the operator of the computer   T   F

8. The same spacing is used regardless of the size of output form being utilized for the job   T   F

9. The debugging process requires that the program be submitted to the computer many times if necessary until all errors are eliminated   T   F

10. A computer program may require several levels of headings, which must be illustrated on the Print Chart   T   F

11. The characters that the programmer uses to illustrate print positions on the Print Chart are the same characters that will appear on the printout   T   F

12. Those symbols that make reading the output report more meaningful are known as editing symbols   T   F

13. RPG is a problem-oriented language used by the computer   T   F

14. The language conversion from source language to machine language takes place in the translator   T   F

15. Any number of like records can be classified as a file   T   F

16. RPG instructions are coded on Specifications sheets   T   F

17. Not all the Specifications sheets have common fields   T   F

18. Characters identifying the different types of Specifications sheets are punched into column 7   T   F

19. Comment statements have an effect on the program when it is being compiled   T   F

20. Programmers identify each program by assigning it a unique name   T   F

21. There can be embedded blanks within the assigned unique name of a program   T   F

22. The compiler recognizes a comment card by an asterisk (*) in column 7   T   F

23. Application programmers must make up the rules that govern the working of the compiler   T   F

24. Each card in the Source Program is known as a specification   T   F

25. The Source Program is translated into an Object Program by the compiler   T   F

Completion: *Fill in the blank with the appropriate word or words.*

1. RPG (Report Program Generator) is a _____ -oriented computer language.

2, 3. A _____ is any number of cards having a like format, each of which is known as a _____ .

4. Specification Sheets have _____ fields.

5. The Source Program cards of each type are numbered in ascending order in multiples of _____ .

6. Comment lines have _____ effect on the program or its compilation.

7. In assigning a name to a program, the programmer must begin with a/an _____ _____ character.

Matching: *Match Column 1 to Column 2.*

COLUMN 1	COLUMN 2	*Answers*
A. Compiler	1. Checks for coding errors	_____
B. File		
C. Source Deck	2. Another name for Source Program	_____
D. *		
E. Embedded	3. Always the first card of Source Program deck	_____
F. Object Program		
G. Header Card	4. Converts to machine language	_____
H. Identification Characters	5. Spaces within an assigned name	_____
	6. Source Program is translated into	_____
	7. Like-formatted cards	_____
	8. Denotes a comment card	_____

CONTROL CARD AND FILE DESCRIPTION SPECIFICATIONS

Only those Specifications sheets fields necessary for the completion of a program will be described. Additional fields will be described as they are needed to complete other programs.

CONTROL CARD

A control card (illustrated in Fig. 15) is required for each program. This card describes the program to the compiler, thus enabling the Source Program to be translated into an Object Program.

The control card must have an H punched into column 6. Any other column not needed is left blank.

FILE DESCRIPTION

Every computer program must have one or more input and output files. Each file is made up of records. Also, each file used must be described and defined so that it can be translated into the Object Program. Only one file can be defined on a single line of the coding sheet. All common fields have been previously described. Each field of the File Description Specifications sheet (shown in Fig. 15) necessary for the completion of the program will now be explained.

FIELDS

Filename (Columns 7 through 14)

The rules that must be considered when coding in this field are as follows:

1. Filenames must be left-justified. In this case, the Filename must begin in column 7.

2. Filenames must begin with an alphabetic character. (The characters $, #, and @ are considered to be alphabetic in RPG.)

3. Filenames must be made up of alphabetic, or numeric characters. No special, or symbolic characters can be used in a Filename. In order to be more meaningful, Filenames are usually composed of characters that describe the file's use.

4. Filenames cannot be more than eight characters long.

5. Filenames cannot contain embedded blanks.

6. Each Filename on the File Description Specifications sheet must be unique.

7. Each filename coded on the File Description Specifications sheet must be identical to the corresponding Filename to be coded later on the Input Specifications, Output Specifications, and Extension Specifications sheets.

Each file must be described and defined so that the input and output file processing routines can be included in the Object Program. Fig. 11 shows examples of correct and incorrect coding in the Filename field.

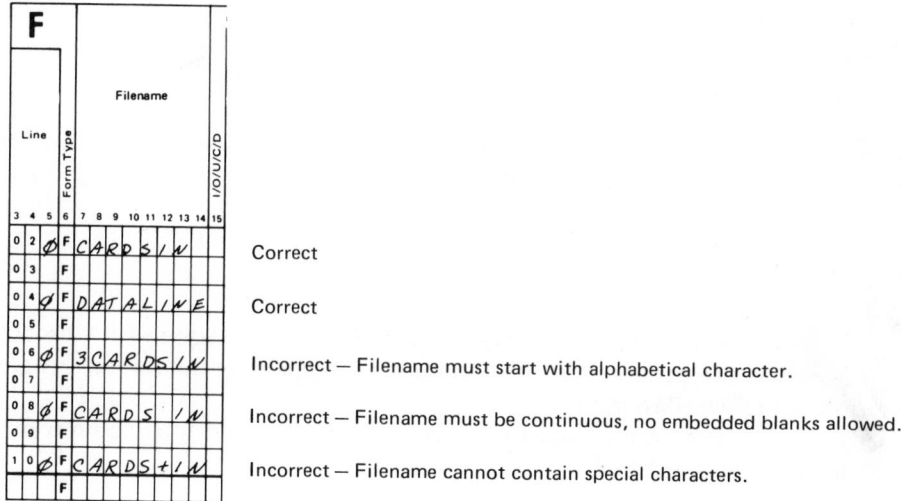

Figure 11

File Type (I/O/U/C/D) (Columns 15 through 15)

The alphabetic character coded in this field describes the file type. If the character I is coded, it signifies that the file is an INPUT file. If the character O is coded, it means that the file is an OUTPUT file. Characters U, C, and D will be discussed later in the book.

File Designation (P/S/C/R/T/D) (Columns 16 through 16)

This field is used only in relation to INPUT files. The alphabetic character coded here refers to the type of file that makes up the INPUT file. If the character is a P, then the file is a PRIMARY INPUT file. If there is more than one INPUT file, then PRIMARY designates which file will be processed or read first. Primary can also be understood to mean that the file is the master or main input file from which records are read. Only one primary file can be defined for a program. Characters S, C, R, T, and D will be discussed later in the book.

Some examples of coding files for the *File Type* and *File Designation* fields are shown in Fig. 12.

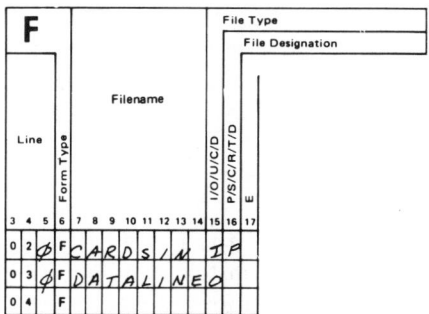

Figure 12

End of File (E) (Columns 17 through 17)

An E in this column is optional. If the column is left blank, all INPUT files (one or more) must be completely processed before the program will go to END-OF-JOB. Its use will be explained later when more than one INPUT file is discussed.

File Format (F/V) (Columns 19 through 19)

An F should always be coded in this column for INPUT and OUTPUT files. The F designates that all records are of a fixed length. The V designates that the record length will vary or that such lengths are variable. Most small computers do not support V length records. Variable-length records will not be discussed in this book.

Record Length (Columns 24 through 27)

This field is right-justified. If an 80-column card is being used as the input record, the length is determined at 80 columns or positions. However, if a 96-column card is being used as the input record, the length is determined at 96 columns or positions. The maximum number of printing positions for the output record is governed by the number of printing positions on the printing device that is part of the computer configuration being used. Most printers have either 120 or 132 printing positions. Some input/output devices, such as tape, allow 9999 positions.

In Fig. 13 examples are given of the coding of the *End of File*, *File Format*, and *Record Length* fields.

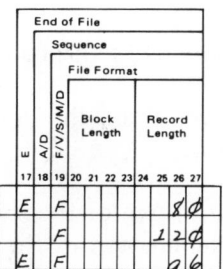

Figure 13

Overflow Indicator (Columns 33 through 34)

The overflow indicator is used only on OUTPUT printer files. There is a direct relationship to the OUTPUT INDICATOR field on the OUTPUT Specifications. Whenever an OA through OG or OV condition is specified on the output specifications coding sheet, it must also be specified in this field. If no indicator is coded here, most printers will automatically skip to the top of a new page when the printer detects an overflow condition.

Device (Columns 40 through 46)

This field is left-justified. It is the name of the INPUT or OUTPUT device. The device name is designated by the computer manufacturer, and your instructor will give you the device names for your specifications sheet coding. The names appearing in this book are valid device names and will be used for purposes of illustration.

Figure 14 depicts coding of the Overflow Indicator and Device fields.

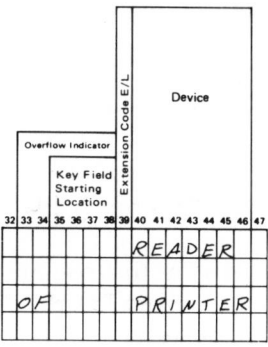

Figure 14

Symbolic Device (Columns 47 through 52)

Most systems require a name here. It is used to link the file defined in the program with the physical device on the computer. Consult your systems reference manual for further definition of this field.

Tape Rewind R/U/N (Columns 70 through 70)

This column is used to indicate to the system where to leave the tape reel when using tape devices. Tapes can be automatically rewound or left where they have currently stopped. Consult your systems manual for a further description of this field if you are using tape.

File Condition U1-U8 (Columns 71 through 72)

This field can be used to condition the use of this file by the systems job or operation control. Not used in this text.

The amount and degree of theory to be mastered on each specifications sheet require that a thorough examination of the material be given. If the student programmer does not do well in each examination, he/she should go over the material again and again until he/she has good mastery before progressing to the next specifications sheet.

```
STOP
1.  COMPLETE STUDY GUIDE, PAGE 55
2.  SUBMIT STUDY GUIDE TO INSTRUCTOR
3.  GO TO EXERCISE 6, PAGE 57
4.  COMPLETE EXERCISE 6
5.  SUBMIT EXERCISE TO INSTRUCTOR
```

Date _____   Name _____

DIRECTIONS: *Answer the following questions in the spaces provided. Your answers should indicate the depth of understanding that you have toward the concepts and definitions presented. If there is insufficient space provided for your answers, complete your answer on the reverse side of the Study Guide.*

1. What is the purpose of the control card?

2. Explain the rules that govern the use of the Filename field.

3. Explain the purpose of the File Designation field.

4. Explain the purpose of the Overflow Indicator field.

5. Explain the purpose of the Record Length field.

6. What is the purpose of the Symbolic Name field?

7. Explain the purpose of the File Format field.

EXERCISE 6

Date _____   Name _____

DIRECTIONS: *The CONTROL CARD AND FILE DESCRIPTION SPECI-*
FICATIONS sheet on page 58 is to be used to complete the necessary coding for the
following.

1. Control card required for the program.
2. READIN is the input file as well as the primary file.
3. End of file is to be coded.
4. The Input File Format is fixed in length.
5. The Record Length is 80 positions.
6. The Device name of the input file is (your instructor's specifications).
7. READOUT is the output file.
8. The Output File Format is fixed in length.
9. The Output File record length is 120 positions.
10. There should be coding for Overflow Indicator.
11. The Device name of the output file is (your instructor's specifications).
12. Code the data in the common fields.

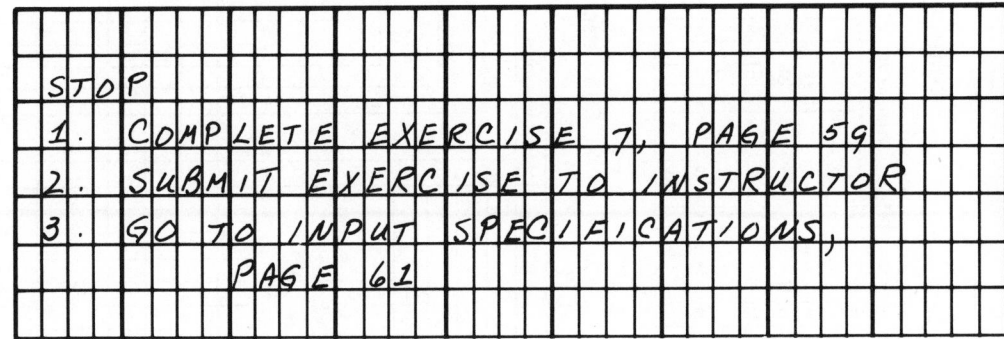

STOP
1. COMPLETE EXERCISE 7, PAGE 59
2. SUBMIT EXERCISE TO INSTRUCTOR
3. GO TO INPUT SPECIFICATIONS,
   PAGE 61

RPG CONTROL CARD AND FILE DESCRIPTION SPECIFICATIONS

IBM International Business Machine Corporation

GX21-9092-3 UM/050*
Printed in U.S.A.

*No. of forms per pad may very slightly_

Program		Punching Instruction	Graphic		Card Electro Number		75 76 77 78 79 80
Programmer	Date		Punch				E M P P R O

Page 01 of 5

Program Identification

Refer to the specific System Reference Library manual for actual entries.

Control Card Specifications

H

File Description Specification

F

Line	Form Type	Filename				File Type	File Designation	End of File	Sequence	File Format	Block Length	Record Length		Mode of Processing	Length of Key Field or of Record Address Field	Record Address Type	Type of File Organization or Additional Area	Overflow Indicator	Key Field Starting Location	Extension Code E/L	Device			Symbolic Device		Name of Label Exit		Extent Exit for DAM				File Addition/Unordered	Number of Tracks for Cylinder Overflow	Number of Extents	
0 2	F	READIN										80									READER												
0 3	F	READ OUT O										132				OF					PRINTER												
0 4	F																																
0 5	F																																
0 6	F																																
0 7	F																																
0 8	F																																
0 9	F																																
1 0	F																																

Figure 15

EXERCISE 7

Date _____   Name _____

TRUE–FALSE: *Each of the following statements is either true or false. Indicate your choice in the Answers column by encircling "T" for a true answer or "F" for a false answer.*

		Answers	
1.	A control card is not required for each program	T	F
2.	Every computer program must have two input files	T	F
3.	More than one file can be described on a single coding line	T	F
4.	All specifications sheets have common fields	T	F
5.	Filenames are left-justified and can contain no more than eight characters	T	F
6.	The Filename field begins in column 7 of the coding sheet	T	F
7.	The first character of a Filename need not be alphabetical	T	F
8.	Embedded blanks are allowed within Filenames	T	F
9.	Numeric characters can be included within the Filename	T	F
10.	The Filename assigned on the File Description Specifications coding sheet must also be identically coded on the Input, Output, and Extension Specifications sheets	T	F
11.	The alphabetic character coded in column 15 of the File Specifications sheet indicates the type of file that is being coded	T	F
12.	The code I in column 15 indicates that the file is incomplete	T	F
13.	More than one primary file is allowed in a program	T	F
14.	The E coded in column 17 of the File Description Specifications sheet designates which input file will cause an end-of-job condition	T	F
15.	The F coded in the File Format field signifies that all the records are of the same length	T	F
16.	Only 80-column records are allowed in RPG programs	T	F
17.	Most computer printers have the print capacity of 120 or 132 print positions	T	F
18.	The Overflow Indicator is used only for output print files	T	F
19.	Device names need not be left-justified	T	F
20.	Symbolic device names are usually mandatory	T	F

59

COMPLETION: *Fill in the blank with the appropriate word or words.*

1. Every computer program must have _____ or more input and output files.

2. The name of the file is coded so that it is _____ in the Filename field.

3. Filenames may not begin with a _____ character or contain embedded blanks.

4. Only _____ primary file(s) can be defined in a RPG program.

5, 6. The letter codes _____ and _____ designate the file format.

MATCHING: *Match Column 1 to Column 2.*

COLUMN 1	COLUMN 2	Answers
A. Input File	1. Designates which file will be read first	_____
B. Record Length	2. Used only on Output Print Files	_____
C. Filename		
D. Overflow Indicator	3. Another designation for the Primary File	_____
E. Symbolic Device	4. Defined on a single coding line	_____
F. File	5. Field that is right-justified	_____
G. Primary	6. The coding of an I in the File Type field indicates	_____
H. Master		
	7. Most systems require that a name be coded in this field	_____

INPUT SPECIFICATIONS

The format of the records that are to be entered into the computer as input is described on the Input Specifications sheet (see Fig. 21). Furthermore, the fields within each record must be individually defined or described so that the RPG Compiler can create the necessary instructions to process the data. Even though the source documents may contain such symbols as the dollar sign ($), commas (,), and decimal points (.), they will not be included when describing the input data. These editing symbols will be taken into consideration later when the Output Specifications Sheet is described.

On the Input Specifications sheet, columns 7 through 42 define file(s) and describe the record(s) within each file. Columns 43 through 70 define fields within the record. Columns 75 through 80 are reserved for program identification (see Fig. 21, lines 11–12).

FIELDS

Filename (Columns 7 through 14)

1. The filename must be identical to the one used to describe the INPUT files on the File Description Specifications sheet.

2. The Filename must appear on the first line that contains information that will be used to further explain the file.

Sequence (Columns 15 through 16)

Since the file is made up of individual records, it must be determined if the sequence (the order in which the records follow each other within the file) is essential. If the sequence is paramount, records are given numbers, usually starting with 01. In a situation where the name record must precede the street record, where the street record must precede the city-state record, the proper sequenceing of these three records would be critical. The name record would be assigned sequence number 01, the street record would be assigned sequence number 02, and the city-state record would be assigned record number 03. A record out of sequence would cause the program to halt.

If other records are part of the file, they must be numbered in ascending order.

61

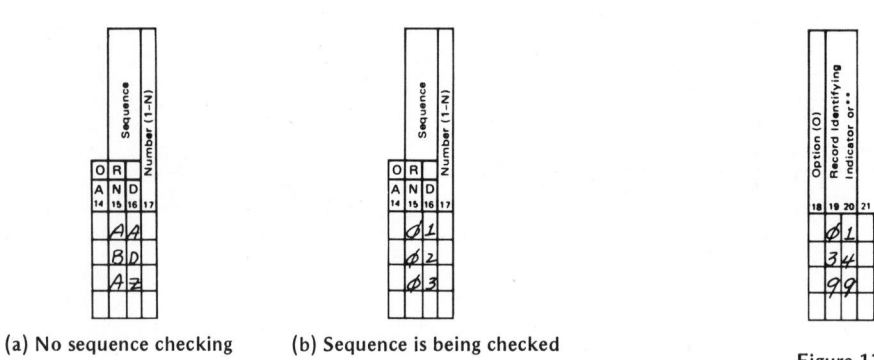

(a) No sequence checking   (b) Sequence is being checked

Figure 16

Figure 17

However, the numbering need not be in consecutive order. That is, 5 followed by 7, followed by 12, followed by 98, is correct. If the sequence of records within a file is unimportant, then columns 15 and 16 should contain two alphabetic characters. Figure 16 illustrates the correct coding.

Record Identifying Indicator (Columns 19 through 20)

If the record number assigned by the programmer is going to be one of the digits 1 through 9, a leading zero must be included in column 19. This assigned record number is coded on the line above the line of the coding for the fields of the record. On succeeding lines of the coding sheet, each field of the record is coded. The numbers punched into these columns identify a specific type of record that must be described to the computer. Any two-digit number from 01 through 99 can be assigned to identify the record. However, if it is the first or only record being read from the file, programmers normally assign the number 01. This number, or indicator, allows for record referencing on subsequent RPG Specifications sheets.

If the value placed in columns (19 and 20) becomes associated with one type of record (card) of the input file, then when this type of record is read, the indicator (01) comes ON. When Record Identifying Indicator 01 is ON, the information from this record can be processed by using indicator 01. Immediately before the next record is read, the indicator goes OFF.

An example of Record Identifying Indicator numbers appears in Fig. 17.

Record Identification Codes
(Columns 21 through 41)

This field is subdivided into three equal and identical seven-column subfields.

Position: Columns 21 through 24 indicate the record column containing the character that identifies the specific code.

Not (N): Columns 25 through 25. If this column is coded with an N, the code indicated in column 27 should NOT be present. If column 25 is left blank, the code in column 27 should be present.

C/Z/D: Columns 26 through 26 will indicate that portion of the control code that is to be used for identification. There are three possibilities.

Z The zone portion only.

D The digit portion only.

C Both portions (zone and digit).

If the code is an alphabetical character and the complete character is to be used, a C is coded in this column; if the code is to be only the zone portion of the character, a Z is coded in this column; if the code is to be only the digit portion of the character (0–9), a D is coded in this column.

For example, if a D is coded in column 26 and a 6 is coded in column 27, then characters F, O, W, and 6 will satisfy this condition because the digit portions of each of these characters is 6.

Character: Columns 27 through 27 will contain the control code assigned by the programmer. If the control code is 1, it is coded in this column. If the control code is –, it is coded in this column. If the control code is F, it is coded in this column. Whatever the specific code is, it is coded in column 27.

The second subfield is contained in columns 28 through 34. The third subfield is contained from columns 35 through 41. The same rules govern these two subfields as govern the first subfield. The only difference is that the column numbers will be changed, depending on the subfield being used. The purpose of this field is to indicate to the computer which conditions or codes must be present in the input record to turn on the Record Identifying Indicator described in columns 19 and 20 of this Input Specifications sheet. To illustrate, if you have input records with a possible combination of characters A, B, and C in column 15 and you want to process only those records having an A in them, your coding would be as shown in Fig. 18, line 010.

I

Line (3–5)	Form Type (6)	Filename (7–14)	Sequence (15–16)	Number (1–N) (17)	Option (O) (18)	Record Identifying Indicator or ** (19–20)	Record 1 Position (21–24)	Not (N) (25)	C/Z/D (26)	Character (27)	
01Ø	I	CARDSIN	AA			Ø1	15		C	A	
02Ø	I	CARDSIN	AA			Ø1	15	N	C	B	
03Ø	I	CARDSIN	AA			Ø1	8Ø		C	F	Both portions of the character are the code.
04Ø	I	CARDSIN	AA			Ø1	8Ø		D	F	The digit portion only is the code.
05Ø	I	CARDSIN	AA			Ø1	8Ø		Z	F	The zone portion only is the code.
06Ø	I	CARDSIN	AA			Ø1	8Ø	N	D	6	The code (6) should not be present.
07	I										

Figure 18

Here the Record Indentifying Indicator 01 would turn on only when an A in column 15 was read from the input file. However, if you wanted records with both A and C in column 15 of the input record to turn the Record Indentifying Indicator 01 ON, your coding would be as shown in Fig. 18, line 020. In this figure the coding is such that it indicates that the Record Identifying Indicator is not to come ON if the character in column 15 is the character B.

Several examples of correctly coded Record Identification codes are shown in Fig. 18, lines 030, 040, 050, and 060.

Field Location (Columns 44 through 51)

This field is further subdivided into two subfields.

From (Columns 44 through 47)
To (Columns 48 through 51)

The FROM field indicates the record column number(s) in which the field begins. It is right-justified. The TO field indicates the record column(s) in which the field ends. It is also right-justified. Whenever a field location is specified or defined, the same factors should be considered — that is, (a) the column of the record in which the field begins and (b) the column of the record in which the field ends. The field being described, record columnwise (FROM–TO), will be named in columns 53 through 58. If the field is one column in length, the record column number is coded in FROM and is again coded in TO. Leading zeros need NOT be coded.

Figure 19 shows examples of correctly coded entries of the Field Location field.

Decimal Positions (Columns 52 through 52)

In order to specify that an input field is alphabetic or numeric, the programmer signifies this fact by the presence or the absence of a digit in column 52. Numeric data that is to be used in calculations, to be zero suppressed, or to be edited on the output report is implied in this field. That is, if a numeric field does not contain a decimal point, a 0 (zero) must be placed in this field. Doing so indicates that the field is a whole number and that there are no values to the right of the assumed (implied) decimal point.

If the numeric field is not a whole number and does contain a decimal point, the number of positions to the right of the assumed decimal point must be indicated. Dealing with dollars and cents, the entry in column 52 would be a 2. The decimal point is not punched into the field of the input record because it would take up a valuable column.

Some examples of entries showing the use of column 52 are illustrated in Fig. 19 shown below.

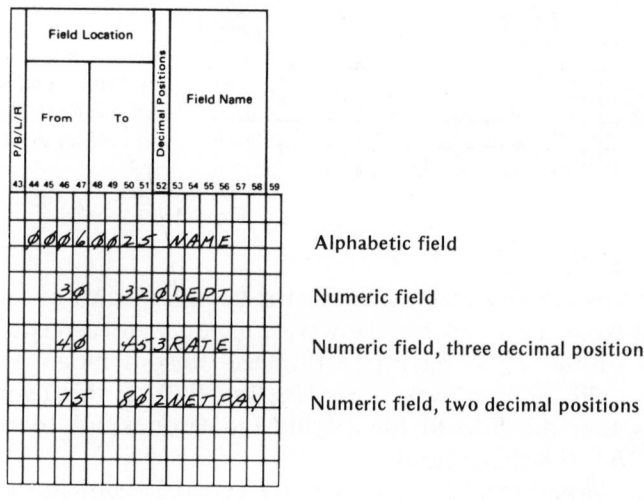

Figure 19

64

Field Name (Columns 53 through 58)

When fields of a record are being defined, they must NOT be on the same coding line that specifies the FILENAME. Each field is defined on a separate coding line. The fields need not be described in the same order that they appear on the input record. The name of the field should be meaningful. The name is left-justified and restricted to six continuous positions in length. The name must begin with an alphabetical character. However, numeric characters can be used as part of the name. Each field name must be unique — once it has been assigned, it CANNOT be assigned again.

Figure 20 illustrates correct and incorrectly coded field names.

The Input Specifications Sheet shown in Fig. 21 is an example of correct coding.

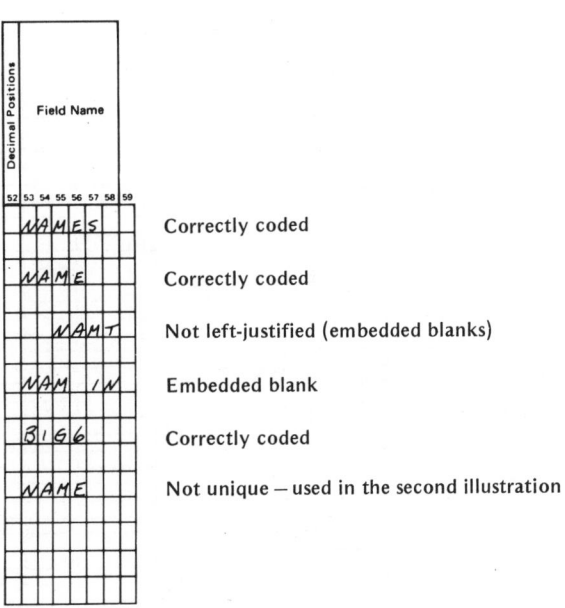

Figure 20

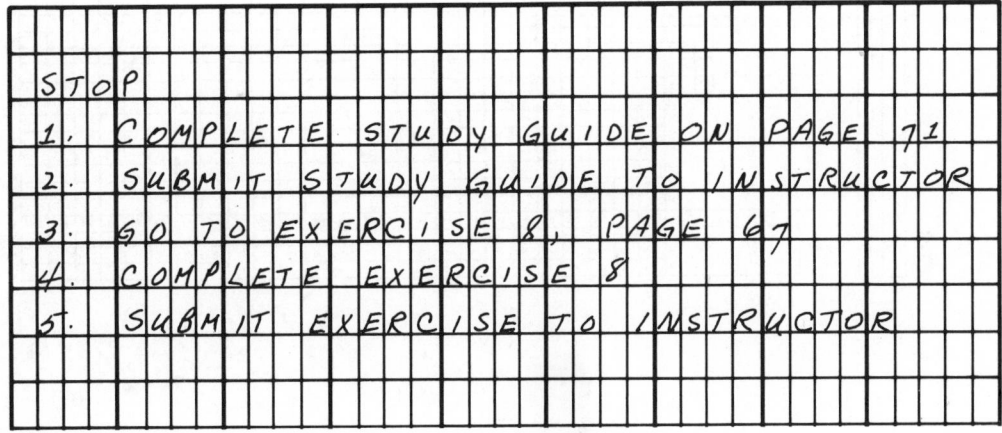

IBM International Business Machine Corporation

RPG INPUT SPECIFICATIONS

Program	Punching Instruction	Graphic
Programmer Date		Punch

Card Electro Number

GX21-9094-2 U/M 050*
Printed in U.S.A.

Page 1 2 of ___

Program Identification

Line	Form Type	Filename	Sequence	Number (1-N)	Option (O)	Record Identifying Indicator or *	Position	Not (N)	C/Z/D	Character	Position	Not (N)	C/Z/D	Character	Position	Not (N)	C/Z/D	Character	Stacker Select	P/B/L/R	From	To	Decimal Positions	Field Name	Control Level (L1-L9)	Matching Fields or Changing Fields	Field Record Relation	Plus	Minus	Zero or Blank
0 1	I	CARDSIN AA				01																								
0 2	I																			1	5		NUMBER						
0 3	I																			6	30		NAME						
0 4	I																			31	50		STREET						
0 5	I																			51	70		CITY						
0 6	I																			71	72		STATE						
0 7	I																			76	80		ZIP						
0 8	I																												
0 9	I																												
1 0	I																												
1 1	I																												
1 2	I																												
1 3	I																												
1 4	I																												
1 5	I																												
1 6	I																												
1 7	I																												
1 8	I																												
1 9	I																												
2 0	I																												

Figure 21

EXERCISE 8

Date _____   Name _____

DIRECTIONS: *Code the Input Specifications Sheet (Fig. 22) to describe the following conditions. The file is a Salesman file.*

1. Use your own filenames.

2. Supply your own field names.

3. Use your own Indicator number.

4. Differentiate the numeric data of the input record.

5. Each card contains an S in column 80.

6. Your fielded input card is as follows:

    a. Salesman Number   CC 1–4

    b. Salesman Name   CC 5–24

    c. Territory Number   CC 25–28

    d. Region Number   CC 29–30

    e. Commission percentage   CC 31–33 (two decimal places)

    f. Sales dollar plan for year   CC 34–42 (two decimal places)

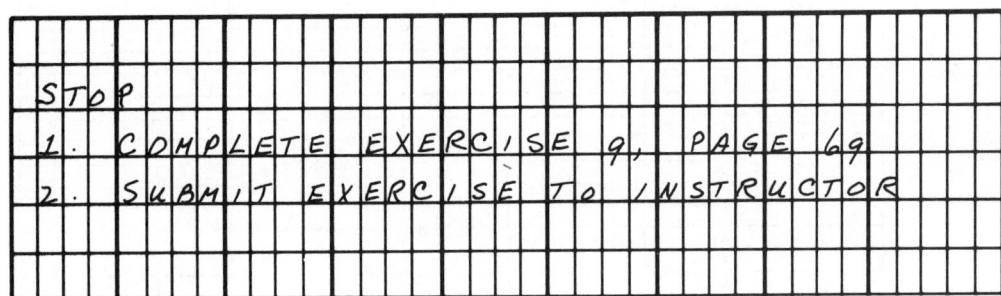

STOP
1. COMPLETE EXERCISE 9, PAGE 69
2. SUBMIT EXERCISE TO INSTRUCTOR

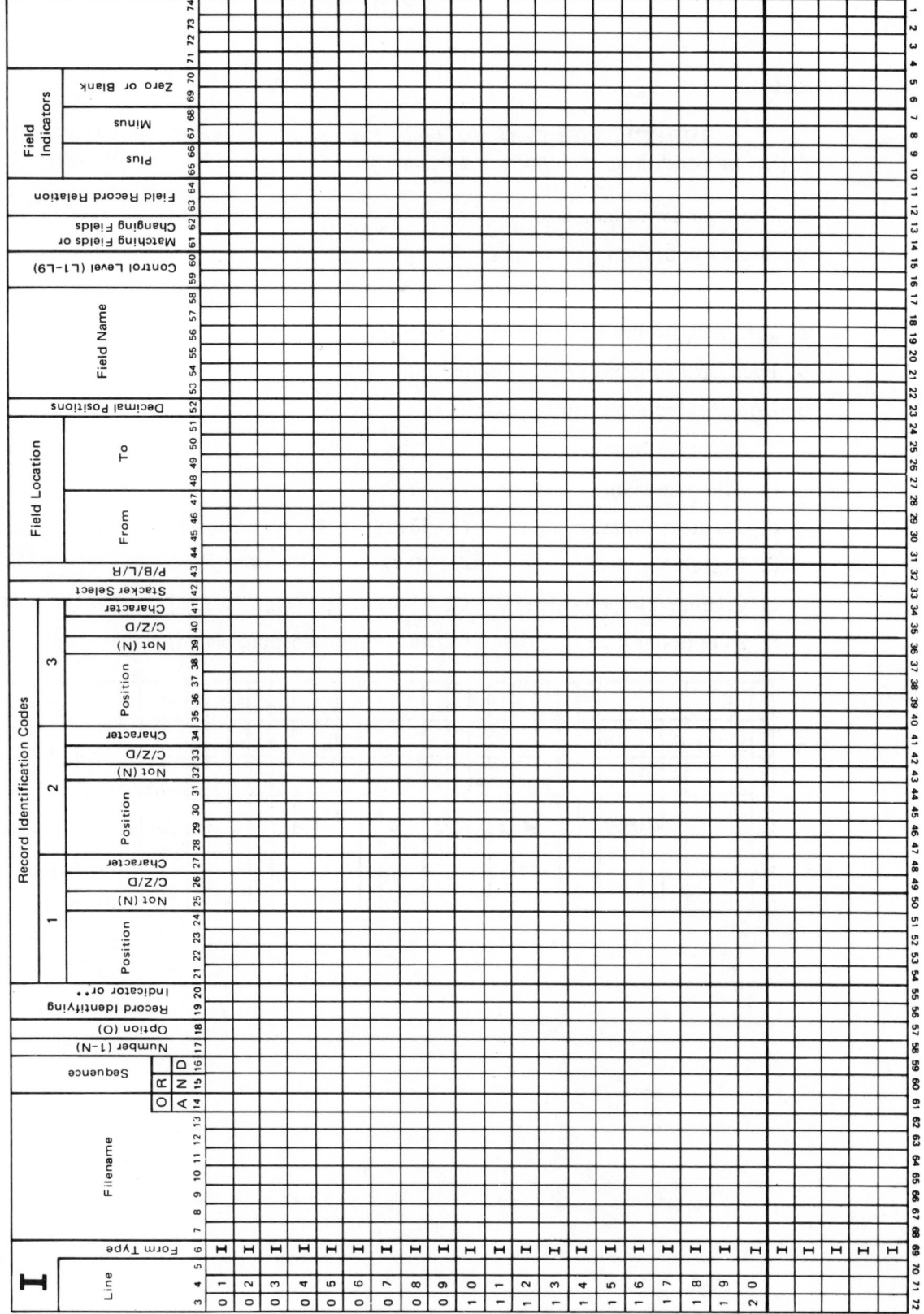

Figure 22

68

Date _____   Name _____

TEST YOUR KNOWLEDGE: *Each set of coding lines A, B, C, etc., of Fig. 23 should be treated as a separate entity. On page 70 you are to give the necessary explanation(s) of any incorrect coding.*

RPG   INPUT SPECIFICATIONS

GX21-9094-2 U/M 050*
Printed in U.S.A.

IBM International Business Machine Corporation

	Program				Punching Instruction	Graphic					Card Electro Number			Page	1 2	of ___	Program Identification	75 76 77 78 79 80
	Programmer		Date			Punch												

Record Identification Codes / Field Location / Field Indicators form.

	Line	Form Type	Filename	Sequence	Number (1-N)	Option (O)	Record Identifying Indicator or **	Position 1	Not (N)	C/Z/D	Character	Position 2	Not (N)	C/Z/D	Character	Position 3	Not (N)	C/Z/D	Character	Stacker Select	P/B/L/R	From	To	Decimal Positions	Field Name	Control Level (L1-L9)	Matching Fields	Field Record Relation	Plus	Minus	Zero or Blank
A.	01	I	CARDS/W AA	Ø1				1		C	F											1			506 CUSNO						
	02	I																													
B.	03	I	CARDS/W A1	Ø3																		1	1		STATUS						
	04	I																													
C.	05	I	CARDS/WAA	ØL						C	F		2		C	M						1	5		CUSTNO						
	06	I																				6	30		CUSNAM						
	07	I																				31	350		CUSTNO						
	08	I																													
	09	I																													
D.	10	I	6BIGBOYSAZ	AZ																		1	556		CUSTNO						
	11	I																				6	30		CU NA						
	12	I																													
	13	I																													
E.	14	I	BIG%%BOYS AA	Ø1																											
	15	I																				1	50		CUSTNO						
	16	I																				6-30			CUSNAM						
	17	I																				75	802		AMOUNT						
	18	I																				45	500		AMTZ						
	19	I																													
	20	I																													

*No. of forms per pad may vary slightly

Figure 23

Underscore the area on page 69 that is incorrect in each illustration. List the reasons for its incorrectness.

A. _____

B. _____

C. _____

D. _____

E. _____

```
    STOP
  1.    GO  TO  EXERCISE  1Ø,  PAGE  73
  2.    COMPLETE  EXERCISE  1Ø
  3.    SUBMIT  EXERCISE  TO  INSTRUCTOR
```

STUDY GUIDE

Date _____   Name _____

DIRECTIONS: *Answer the following questions in the spaces provided. Your answers should indictate the depth of understanding that you have toward the concepts and definitions presented. If there is insufficient space provided for your answers, complete your answer on the reverse side of the Study Guide.*

1. Explain the purpose of the Sequence field (columns 15–16).

2. Explain the association of the number assigned, in the Record Identifying Indicator field (columns 19–20), with the file.

3. Explain the hierarchy of the Sequence Field.

4. Explain the importance of the Field Location field on the Input Specifications sheet to the Input Record.

5. Explain the importance of coding a digit in the Decimal Position field.

6. Explain why fields must be defined in the Field Name field.

EXERCISE 10

Date _____   Name _____

TRUE–FALSE: *Each of the following statements is either true or false. Indicate your choice in the Answers column by encircling "T" for a true answer or "F" for a false answer.*

		Answers	
1.	The fields of a record need not be described	T	F
2.	Symbols found on the source document usually are not included when describing the input data	T	F
3.	Columns 1 through 42 of the Input Specifications sheet pertain to record identification	T	F
4.	Columns 43 through 70 of the Input Specifications sheet define fields within the record	T	F
5.	A maximum of nine characters is allowed for the Filename	T	F
6.	Filenames must be left-justified	T	F
7.	Filenames can begin with numeric characters	T	F
8.	Each Filename on the Input Specifications sheet must be identical to one coded on the File Description Specifications sheet	T	F
9.	If there is to be no sequence checking in the program, any two alphabetic characters can be coded in the Sequence field	T	F
10.	Record Identification Indicators can be any two digits from 01 through 99	T	F
11.	When a record is printed, the Record Identifying Indicator is On or Off	T	F
12.	The Record Identification Codes field is subdivided into three equal seven-column subfields	T	F
13.	A Record Identification Code cannot be both the zone and the digit portion of a character	T	F
14.	If the control code is the digit portion of a character, the programmer codes a D in column 26	T	F
15.	Field Location numbers must be right-justified	T	F
16.	The two subfields of the Field Location field are FROM and TO	T	F
17.	If the field being described in the Field Location field contains only one column, only the FROM portion is coded	T	F
18.	All fields must have a code placed in the Decimal Positions field	T	F
19.	If leading zeros are to be suppressed, the programmer codes a Z in the Decimal Positions field	T	F
20.	Field Names are left-justified	T	F
21.	Field Names cannot contain embedded blanks	T	F
22.	Numeric characters can be part of the Field Name but cannot be the first character	T	F

73

23. Any numeric field that is to have an arithmetical computation applied to it must have a code in the Decimal Positions field · · · · · · · · · · · · · · · · · · · T   F

24. If a zero (0) is coded in the Decimal Positions field, the field must be considered a whole number field · T   F

25. When sequence checking is important, the programmer codes numbers in the Sequence field · T   F

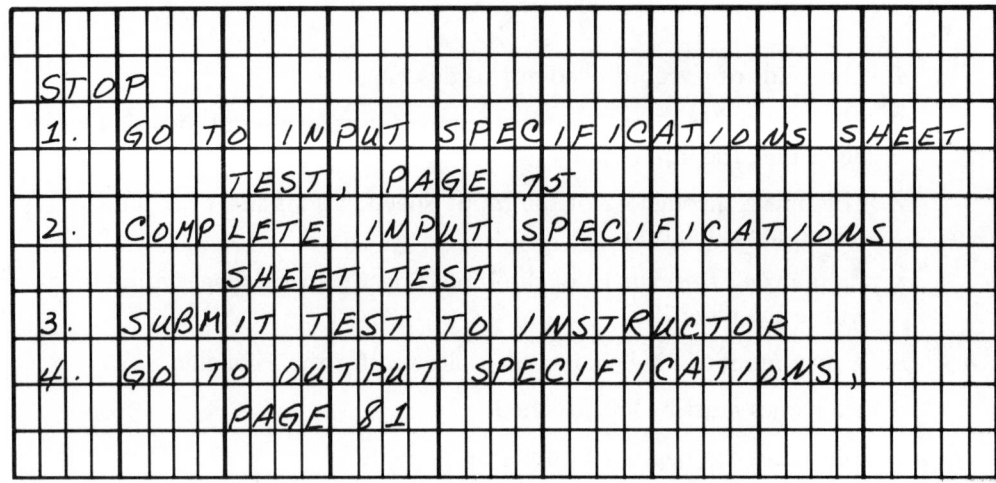

```
STOP
1.  GO TO INPUT SPECIFICATIONS SHEET
        TEST, PAGE 75
2.  COMPLETE INPUT SPECIFICATIONS
        SHEET TEST
3.  SUBMIT TEST TO INSTRUCTOR
4.  GO TO OUTPUT SPECIFICATIONS,
        PAGE 81
```

INPUT SPECIFICATIONS SHEET TEST

Date ______________________________ Name ______________________________

PART I: *Fill in the blank with the appropriate word or words (3 points each).*

1. A ____________________ coded in the Decimal Position field indicates that the field must be considered a numeric whole number field.
2. An example of a Device Name is ____________________ .
3. Columns 43 through 70 of the Input Specifications sheet are used to describe ______ ______________ .
4. A collection of related data items treated as a unit is called a ____________________ .
5. Columns 44 through 51 on the Input Specifications sheet that are used to identify the position of a field in a record are called ____________________ .

PART II: *Multiple Choice (3 points each)*

1. In Fig. 24 the Record Identifying Indicator 03 is considered turned ON only when
   a. A in column 1 was read from the Input file.
   b. A in column 1 and B in column 2 was read from the Input file.
   c. B in column 2 was read from the Input file.
   d. Any card is read from the Input file.

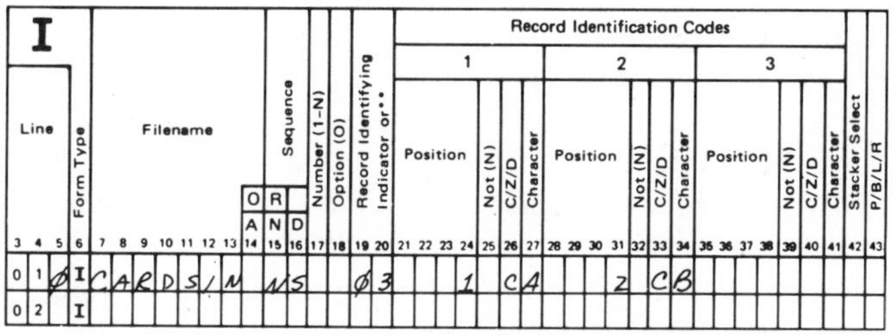

Figure 24

2. Observe the following field names. Which field name/s is/are CORRECT? Explain why the field may be INCORRECT.
   a. DEPTNO ______________________________
   b. DESCRIP ______________________________
   c. LFIELD ______________________________
   d. 1FLD ______________________________
   e. FLD$1 ______________________________
   f. AMT. ______________________________
   g. A-FLD ______________________________
   h. B111 ______________________________

3. Refer to Fig. 25. Which specification line/s is/are INCORRECT?

Line	Form Type	Filename	O R A N D	Sequence	Number (1-N)	Option (O)	Record Identifying Indicator or **	Position (1)	Not (N)	C/Z/D	Character	Position (2)	Not (N)	C/Z/D	Character	Position (3)	Not (N)	C/Z/D	Character	Stacker Select
0 1	I	CARDIN	NS				Ø1	1		C	A									
0 2	I																			
0 3	Ø I	CARDSIN	NS				Ø1	1		D	9	2		4	D8					
0 4	I																			
0 5	Ø I	CARDSIN	NS				Ø1	1		C	B	2		C	C					
0 6	I																			
0 7	Ø I	CARDS	NS				Ø1	1		7	3									
0 8	I																			
0 9	Ø I	/NCARDS	NS				Ø1	1		7	4									
1 0	I																			
1 1	I																			
1 2	I																			

Figure 25

4. The purpose of the Decimal Positions field on the Input Specifications sheet is _____

   a. To specify that an input field is alphabetic.

   b. To specify that an input field is numeric.

   c. To specify that an input field is numeric and contains decimals.

   d. All the above.

   e. None of the above.

PART III: *True or False (2 points each). Write the letter "T" for true and the letter "F" for false, in the space provided.*

1. Columns 1 through 42 of the Input Specifications sheet pertain to record identification _____

2. Field Location numbers must be right-justified _____

3. A Ø coded in the Decimal Positions field indicates that the field is alphabetic _____

4. When sequence checking is required, the programmer codes any two letters in the Sequence field _____

5. The Overflow Indicator on the File Specifications sheet is used with all output files _____

6. Editing symbols are included in the coding of fields on the Input Specifications sheet _____

7. A Filename must begin in column 7 of the Input Specifications sheet _____

8. A maximum of eight characters is allowed for the Field Name _____

9. Overflow Indicators can be any two characters from OA to OI or OV   _____

10. The Record Identification Codes field is subdivided into three equal seven-column subfields   _____

PART IV: *Application problem (25 points). Using the following data and the File Description Specifications sheet (Fig. 26) and Input Specifications sheet, (Fig. 27) complete the problem.*

1. Date — Columns 3 through 8

   Name — Columns 9 through 28

   Hours — Columns 29 through 31

   Rate — Columns 32 through 35 (2 decimal positions)

   Gross Pay — Columns 36 through 41 (2 decimal positions)

   Federal Withholding Tax — Columns 42 through 46 (2 decimal positions)

   Social Security Tax — Columns 47 through 51 (2 decimal positions)

   Other Deduction — Columns 52 through 56 (2 decimal positions)

   Net Pay — Columns 65 through 70 (2 decimal positions)

2. The Input File is to be called *PAYROLL* and is 80 positions in length. The device is card input.

3. The Input File is not in any sequential order.

4. The Output file is 120 positions in length and is called *YOURNAME*. Assign an Overflow Indicator to the Output File.

PART V: *Short Answer Essays (28 points). Complete all the following essays. Use the back of the test paper for your answers.*

1. What do the entries C, Z, and D indicate when they are used with the Record Identification Codes in columns 21–41 of the Input Specifications sheet?

2. List and explain fully the purposes of the File Description Specifications sheet and the Input Specifications sheet.

3. Explain the rules for the construction of a Field Name.

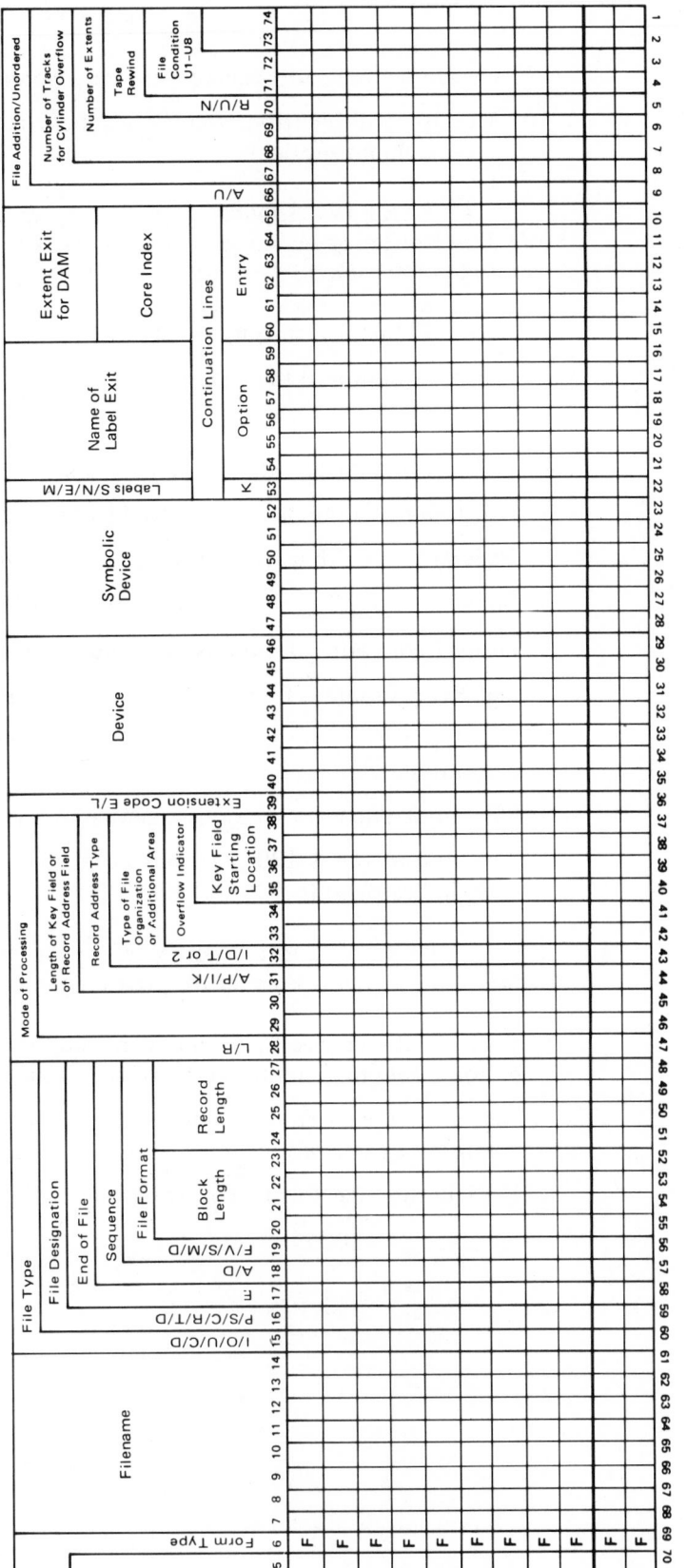

Figure 26

78

IBM International Business Machine Corporation

RPG INPUT SPECIFICATIONS

GX21-9094-2 U/M 050*
Printed in U.S.A.

Program		Punching Instruction	Graphic	Card Electro Number
Programmer	Date		Punch	

Page (1 2) of ___ Program Identification (75 76 77 78 79 80)

Line	Form Type	Filename	Sequence (OR / AND)	Number (1-N)	Option (O)	Record Identifying Indicator or**	Record Identification Codes 1: Position	1: Not (N)	1: C/Z/D	1: Character	2: Position	2: Not (N)	2: C/Z/D	2: Character	3: Position	3: Not (N)	3: C/Z/D	3: Character	Stacker Select	P/B/L/R	Field Location: From	Field Location: To	Decimal Positions	Field Name	Control Level (L1-L9)	Matching Fields or Changing Fields	Field Record Relation	Field Indicators: Plus	Field Indicators: Minus	Field Indicators: Zero or Blank	
3 4 5	6	7 8 9 10 11 12 13	14 15 16	17	18	19 20	21 22 23 24	25	26	27	28 29 30 31	32	33	34	35 36 37 38	39	40	41	42	43	44 45 46 47	48 49 50 51	52	53 54 55 56 57 58	59 60	61 62	63 64	65 66	67 68	69 70	71 72 73 74
0 1	I																														
0 2	I																														
0 3	I																														
0 4	I																														
0 5	I																														
0 6	I																														
0 7	I																														
0 8	I																														
0 9	I																														
1 0	I																														
1 1	I																														
1 2	I																														
1 3	I																														
1 4	I																														
1 5	I																														
1 6	I																														
1 7	I																														
1 8	I																														
1 9	I																														
2 0	I																														
	I																														
	I																														
	I																														
	I																														
	I																														

Figure 27

RECORD LAYOUT FORM

Company _____

Application _____

by _____

Date _____

Job No. _____

Sheet No. _____

Figure 28

OUTPUT SPECIFICATIONS

The output of RPG can take a variety of different forms: punched cards, magnetic disk, magnetic tape, and printed reports. The data coded on the Output Specifications sheet describes the format of the output report. (See page 92) When the output is to be a printed report, the Output Specifications sheet follows the format of a Print Chart. When the output is designed for some other device, a record layout sheet similar to the one in Fig. 28 is used.

On the Output Specifications sheet, columns 7 through 31 are used to describe the output file. Columns 23 through 70 are used to describe the various fields on the output record. The overlap in columns 23 through 31 will be explained later in this section.

FIELDS

Filename (Columns 7 through 14)

The Filename on the Output Specifications sheet must be identical to an output Filename coded on the File Description Specifications sheet. The RPG compiler uses this name to keep track of the records belonging to each file. Those rules that apply to Filenames on the File Description Specifications sheet also apply to Filenames coded on the Output Specifications sheet. Observe the rules pertaining to Filenames beginning on page 49.

OR (Columns 14 through 15)
AND (Columns 14 through 16)

Coding OR in columns 14 and 15 or AND in columns 14 through 16 refers to the Output Indicators in columns 23 through 31. The codes in columns 14 through 16 are not indicators themselves; they represent the words "or" and "and". If the output record can be conditioned by more than one set of indicators, OR is coded on the line of each set of indicators following the first set. However, if more than three indicators are needed to complete a set that will condition the output record, AND is coded on the line of additional indicators. Fig. 29 illustrates coding in the OR/AND fields.

81

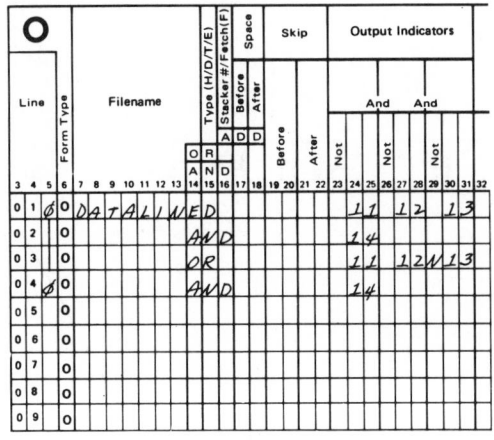

Figure 29

Type (H/D/T/E) (Columns 15 through 15)

When the character H is coded in this column, it indicates that report headings or columnar headings are to be printed. The data contained in a heading record is constant—that is, it identifies and thus does not change. These headings can be printed on the first page only of the output report or at the top of each page of the output report.

If the heading is to appear ONLY on the first page of the output report, the necessary coding is a 1P in the Output Indicator Field. The 1P indicator (first page) is turned ON for the first cycle of the Object Program. This type of coding is depicted in Fig. 30, line 010.

If the heading is to appear on ALL pages of the output report, the necessary coding is an OR coded in columns 14 and 15, plus an OF coded in columns 24 and 25. (See Fig. 30, line 020.) The OF means OVERFLOW.

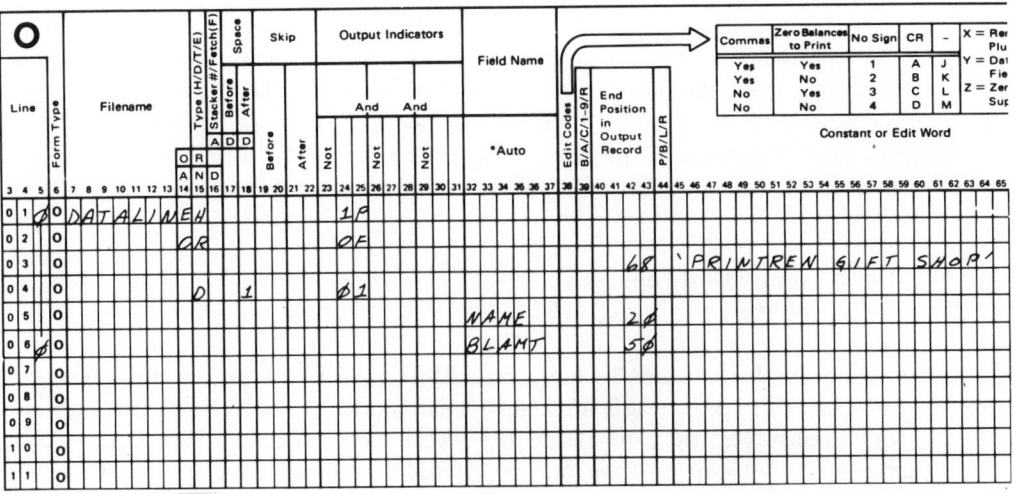

Figure 30

82

When the character D is coded in column 15, it indicates that the record line of print is a detail line. Most printed lines of an output report are classified as detail lines of print. The data constituting this type of print line represents either the input record data or the results of calculations performed on the input record data.

If the character T is coded in column 15, then total records are to be printed. Total records are the accumulated results of calculations done on portions of detail records. Total output records will be covered in a later section. When the character E is coded in column 15, it indicates exception output. Any line properly conditioned with indicators when the EXCPT operation is performed in the Calculation Specifications will output.

Figure 30 points out that

1. There are two types of print lines:

      H   Heading

      D   Detail

2. The heading PRINTREN GIFT SHOP will be printed on every page of the output report.

3. One detail line will be printed for every input record that turns on indicator 01. The data printed will be determined by the data in the input record fields NAME and BLAMT.

Note the coding of the Input Specifications sheet in Fig. 31.

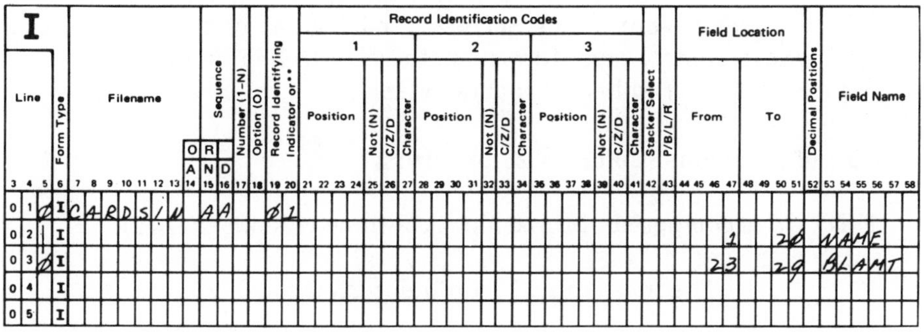

Figure 31

Space (Columns 17 through 18)

This field is subdivided. The coding in column 17 (the Space Before subfield) indicates the number of spaces (1, 2, or 3) that the printer is to advance before an output line is printed. The coding in column 18 (the Space After subfield) indicates the number of spaces (1, 2, or 3) that the printer is to advance after an output line is printed.

Skip (Columns 19 through 22)

The Skip field is used either when the printer is to advance more than three lines before or after printing an output line or when the printer is to advance to a certain position on the page. Like the Space field, the Skip field is subdivided.

For printers that use line number control, the number coded in columns 19 and

20 (the Skip Before subfield) instructs the printer to skip to that line before printing an output line. A line number coded in columns 21 and 22 (the Skip After subfield) instructs the printer to skip to that line after printing an output line.

Forms may be from 6 to 120 lines in length. To skip from any print line on the form to another print line that is greater than three print lines, code

01–99 for lines 1 through 99

A0–A9 for lines 100 through 109

B0–B9 for lines 110 through 120

for skip before printing in columns 19 and 20. For skip after printing, use columns 21 and 22.

For printers that use a carriage control tape, the number coded in 19 and 20 instructs the printer to skip to that channel number in the control tape before printing an output line. A channel number coded in columns 21 and 22 instructs the printer to skip to that channel number after printing an output line.

The skipping operation should not be greater than the length of the form except when skipping to a new page. Skipping to a new page always occurs if the channel or the line number has been passed on the current page.

Skipping to lines within a page is usually done only on special printed forms, such as invoices and report cards. Skipping to a new page is done on any type of form; and for good appearance, skipping to line $\emptyset 3$ or $\emptyset 6$ is standard operating procedure, although any line can be used.

Printed forms can be of any length. To specify this fact to the computer, the Line Counter Specifications Sheet is used for line controlled printers. For printers with the carriage control tape, forms length is controlled by the carriage control tape. All output (for this text) will be 11 inches in length.

Output Indicators (Columns 23 through 31)

This field is composed of three identical three-column subfields.

1. The first subfield — Columns 23 through 25

2. The second subfield — Columns 26 through 28

3. The third subfield — Columns 29 through 31

The main function of an output indicator is to control when an output record is to be written. All RPG II indicators can be used in the output indicator columns. An N can be used in columns 23, 26, and 29 for the negative conditions.

Two special-purpose indicators, lP and OA–OG, OV, are used in these columns to control "top of forms" or "headings." lP is the first-page indicator. lP is ON only during the first cycle. It can be used to print headings at the top of the first page of the report. OA through OG or OV are used to condition the printing of lines when the overflow condition occurs. The overflow condition occurs on line 60 or on the overflow line indicated on the Line Counter Specification Sheet if it is used.

For printers that use the carriage control tape, overflow is conditioned when channel 12 is detected. The overflow indicators must be defined on the File Specifications sheet in columns 33–34 for the printer file. If an overflow indicator is not assigned, the printer will skip automatically to the top of the form (page) when the overflow condition is detected. This skipping will be to line 6 or in the case of carriage control tapes to channel 01.

Field Name (Columns 32 through 37)

The output Field Name must be left-justified. The field names used on the Input Specifications sheet or defined in calculations can be used when describing the field. If a field name is coded, columns 7 through 22 must be blank. Columns 7 through 31 are reserved for Record Descriptive data, whereas columns 23 through 70 are reserved for individual Field Descriptive data. The overlapping columns (23–31) are to allow indicators to control both the printing of the line and each field within that line. The fields need not be coded in the same sequence that they appear on the output record. The determining factor is the ending print position coded in columns 40 through 43. Generally, however, they are listed sequentially for better readability and understanding. The maximum length of the output record is determined by the number of positions defined on the File Description sheet for the file.

Edit Codes (Columns 38 through 38)

Insertion of special symbols or editing characters, such as the period, comma, dollar sign, and leading zero suppression, occurs within amount fields to make the output report more meaningful to the reader. These special editing symbols are coded on the Output Specifications sheet, using column 38. Editing codes are used to accomplish any one or all of the following on numeric fields: Suppression of leading zeros; Omission or insertion of a sign or CR symbol to the right of the rightmost position of the field; Insertion of decimal points and/or commas.

If any of the editing codes are to be used, printing space allowance must be given when diagramming the Print Chart.

The programmer analyzes the necessary requirements of the output report and selects from the Edit Code Block the symbol that is required for the particular result necessary on the output report. See Fig. 32. Notice, in Fig. 32 that

1. The arrow, column 38, points to the EDIT CODE BLOCK.

2. The Edit Code Block is composed of

   a. a COMMAS column.

   b. a ZERO BALANCES TO PRINT column.

   c. a NO SIGN column.

   d. a CR column.

   e. a MINUS SIGN (–) column.

   f. the X, Y, Z column.

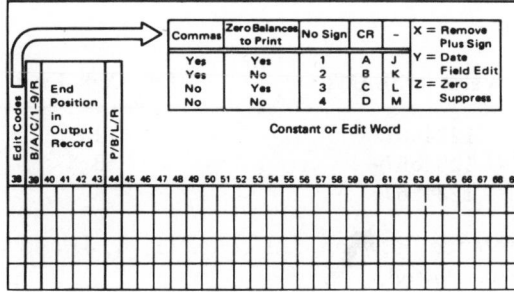

Figure 32

85

The (X, Y, Z) column is treated as a separate entity. The NO SIGN, CR, and MINUS SIGN (-) columns list the options of the editing codes open to the programmer.

The codes in the NO SIGN column dictate whether comma(s) or a zero balance is to be printed on the output field. The BLAMT field on the Input Specifications sheet (Fig. 31) shows that it is a seven-position field with a decimal position of two places from the right. The sign does not take a position of the input field (observe the value in BLAMT in the following table). BLAMT is a seven-position field and it takes just seven positions of memory. However, in the table note the effect that codes 1, 2, 3, and/or 4 will have on the data in BLAMT.

Value in BLAMT	Edit Code Used	Printed Result
$01234567^{\pm}$	1	1,2345.67
0	1	.00
$01234567^{\pm}$	2	1,2345.67
0	2	
$01234567^{\pm}$	3	12345.67
0	3	.00
$01234567^{\pm}$	4	12345.67
0	4	

The codes in the CR and MINUS SIGN (-) columns are used only if a negative amount figure is a possibility when printing a numeric field. If a negative figure is to be represented by the CREDIT SYMBOL (CR), then that column must be given consideration and the appropriate code (A, B, C, or D) is used to indicate if COMMAS and ZERO BALANCES TO PRINT are to apply. If a negative figure is to be represented by the MINUS SIGN (-), then the appropriate code (J, K, L, or M) is used to indicate if the COMMAS and ZERO BALANCES TO PRINT are to apply. In other words, the difference between these edit codes depends on whether the credit indication is represented by the symbols (CR) or (-).

To show the effect of the editing codes, assume the following:

Value in BLAMT	Edit Code Used	Edited Result
1234567±	1	12,345.67
1234567-	A	12,345.67CR
1234567-	J	12,345.67-
1234567+	A or J	12,345.67

Note that the comma(s) was automatically inserted. The decimal point was printed with two positions to its right. However, if the amount in BLAMT was either 0000009 or 0000000 and any of the above codes were used, the edited result would be .09 and/or .00. Of specific interest is the fact that the leading zeros are automatically suppressed. If an amount in BLAMT were not large enough to require the insertion of a comma(s), they would not print.

Value in BLAMT	Edit Code Used	Edited Result
1234567±	2	12,345.67
1234567-	B	12,345.67CR
1234567+	K	12,345.67

The only difference between edit codes (1, A, J) and (2, B, K) is that the zero balance indication is not printed.

Value in BLAMT	Edit Code Used	Edited Result
1234567±	3	12345.67
1234567-	C	12345.67CR
1234567-	L	12345.67-

The difference between edit codes (1, A, J) and (3, C, L) is that the comma(s) is not inserted in the Edited Result. However, if the balance is a zero balance, it would be printed as .00 — that is, the decimal is printed along with the zeros to its right.

Value in BLAMT	Edit Code Used	Edited Result
1234567±	4	12345.67
1234567-	D	12345.67CR
1234567-	M	12345.67-

The difference between edit codes (2, B, K) and (4, D, M) is that the comma(s) is not inserted. However, zero balances are not printed.

Each character symbol will take a print position on the Print Chart. Therefore the number of field positions is of extreme importance and must be considered when developing the Print Chart. Remember that editing codes can be applied only to fields that are described as numeric.

The X, Y, Z column of the Edit Code Block, as noted, serves a different purpose. These codes DO NOT provide an automatic punctuation (commas, decimal points) to a field.

Edit Code X: The code causes the input field to print with no comma(s) or decimal(s). The field is printed with all zeros shown. No sign is printed even if the input field is negative. Observe the following.

Value of BLAMT	Edit Code Used	Edited Result
001234	X	001234
000123-	X	000123

Edit Code Y: Dates are often required on a report. Date fields are punctuated by using the Edit Code Y. This code is known as the Date Edit Code. In order for the code to be effective, the date field must contain at least three digits. The code is only effective on numeric fields. The Y code suppresses leading zeros of a date field. This would apply to the months of January through September. The date is broken down as to month, day and year, or day, month, year with two digits for each. The Y edit code also inserts slashes in the date.

UDATE	Edit Code	Edited Result
01127-	Y	1/12/7-

Your Own Date Field	Edit Code	Edited Result
0112	Y	1/12
11237-	Y	11/23/7-

There are two common ways of programming for the date to appear on the output report. The first method is by using UDATE, and the second method is a six-position numeric field defined by the programmer.

Note that UDATE is a field that can be used by the programmer to date his reports or output records. UDATE is known as a reserved field supplied by a function of RPG II. Check your system for reserve field availability. Other reserved fields available for use are UMONTH, UDAY, UYEAR, and PAGE. UMONTH, UDAY, and UYEAR are two-position fields, whereas PAGE is a four-position field that starts at 0001 and is automatically advanced by 1 each time a skip is performed to the top of a new page on the printer. Figure 33 shows the use of UDATE, PAGE, and the use of the Constant or Edit Word.

Edit Code Z̶: The Z̶ code places no punctuation [insertion of comma(s) or decimal(s)] within the field. However, all leading or nonsignificant zeros (zeros to the left of the first significant digit) will be suppressed. The suppression is effected by the leading zeros being changed to blanks so that no printing will appear on the output report. Significant zeros (zeros within an amount) will print. If the amount to be printed represents a zero balance, a 0 (zero) is printed. In order for this code to be effective, the field must be defined as being numeric. Note that the letter Z has a line through it (Z̶). This type of coding is done to prevent the character from being mistaken for the digit 2.

Figure 33, line 060 is an Output Specifications sheet coding using Edit Code Z̶.

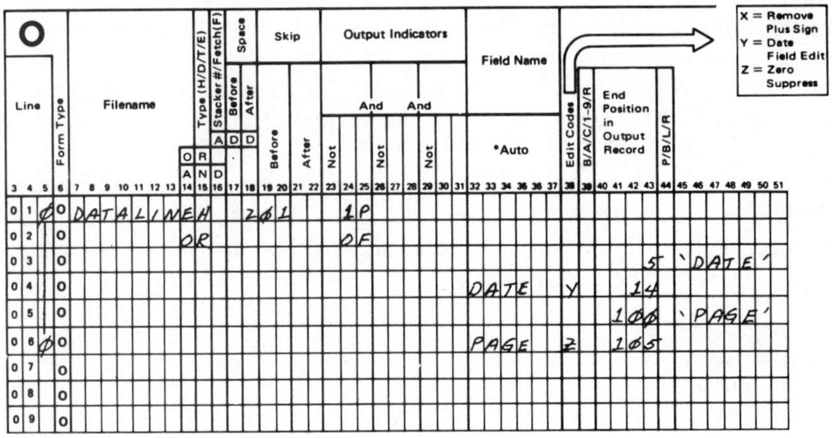

Figure 33

End Position In Output Record (Columns 40 through 45)

This field is right-justified. The rightmost or end position in the output record of the output field is indicated in these columns. This position is obtained from the Print Chart or Record Layout, which has been previously developed by the programmer.

Constant or Edit Word (Columns 45 through 70)

This field is left-justified. The constant (word or phrase not changed within the program execution) is placed between literal signs. Whatever is coded between the literal signs will be printed exactly as coded. The literal signs are not printed. The programmer represents literal signs by the use of a single quotation mark. In general, constants are used to represent report or columnar headings. Quotation marks are printed by coding an additional quotation mark. Line 060 of Fig. 34 shows how a quotation mark is obtained.

If the programmer uses an Edit Word, he has greater control over the type of editing (punctuation) of a numeric field in comparison to the Edit Code Block editing codes. Edit Word symbols can be coded always to print in specific print positions or they can be floated before the left-most significant digit based on suppression of leading zeros.

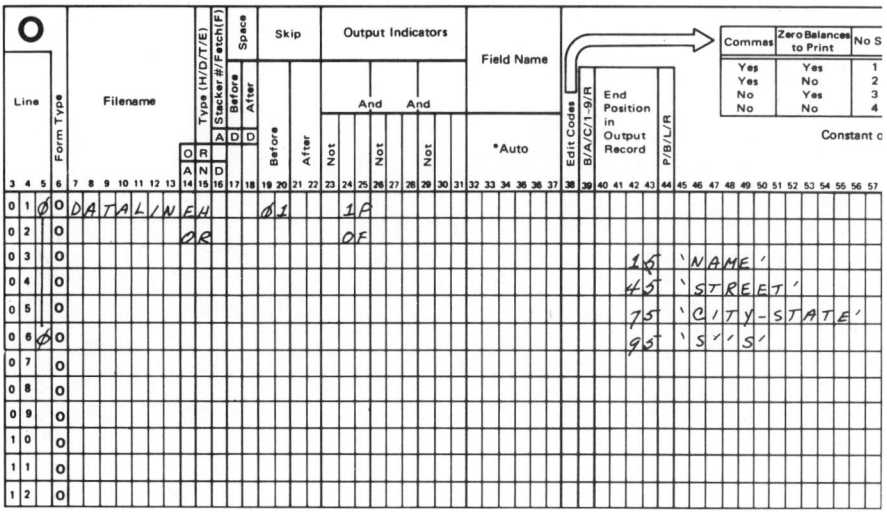

Figure 34

If the Edit Word is used, it is coded on the same line as the field being described. Note the following.

1. Illustration A in Fig. 35 has the dollar sign in a fixed position. The zero (∅) to the left of the decimal point will automatically suppress all leading zeros.

2. Illustration B in Fig. 35 has the dollar sign floating. The zero (∅) to the immediate left of the decimal point will automatically suppress all leading zeros. However, the dollar sign will be placed to the immediate left of the first significant digit.

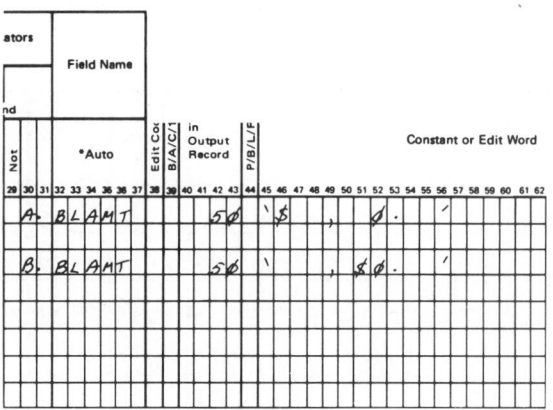

Figure 35

BLAMT	Example	Result
0012345	A	$ḅḅḅ123.45*
0012345	B	$123.45
0	A	$ḅḅḅḅḅḅ.00*
0	B	$.00

*The leading (ḅ) are merely to show that the area would be completely blank. In this illustration, they are placetakers. They would not show in an actual situation.

TIP TO PROGRAMMER

RPG moves the fields coded on the Output Specifications sheets to the output area one at a time. The fields are moved in the same sequence that they are coded. Normally this fact would not cause a problem because the programmer would be careful to use the Print Chart or Record Layout to code the correct ending positions for each field. But this fact can be used to advantage.

If the programmer wanted to suppress printing of the NAME (line 020) on some detail lines of the report, he would code a constant of 20 blanks on the very next line of the specifications sheet and condition the output of the blank constant with an indicator. The indicator could be turned on when the name was the same as in the last record. To see how to accomplish this type of coding, refer to Fig. 36.

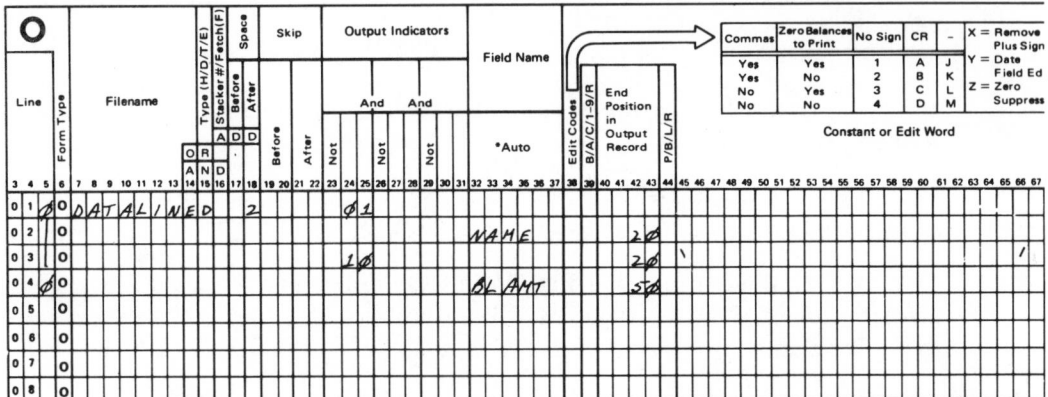

Figure 36

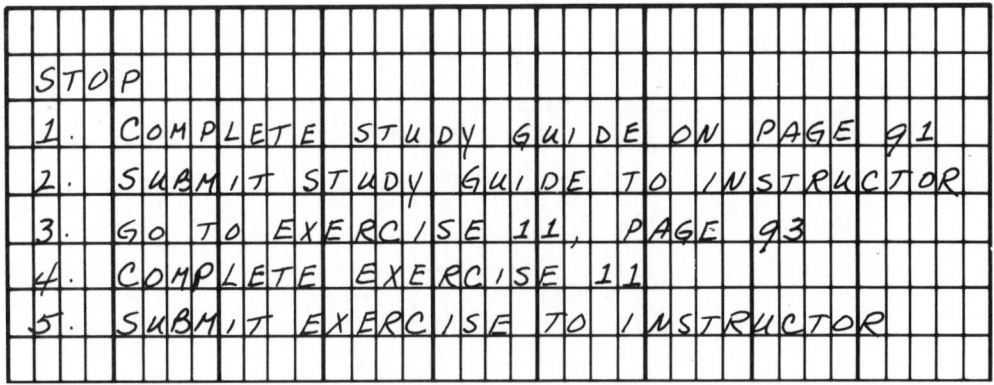

STOP
1. COMPLETE STUDY GUIDE ON PAGE 91
2. SUBMIT STUDY GUIDE TO INSTRUCTOR
3. GO TO EXERCISE 11, PAGE 93
4. COMPLETE EXERCISE 11
5. SUBMIT EXERCISE TO INSTRUCTOR

STUDY GUIDE

Date _____ Name_____

DIRECTIONS: *Answer the following questions in the spaces provided. Your answers should indicate the depth of understanding that you have toward the concepts and definitions presented. If there is insufficient space provided for your answers, complete your answer on the reverse side of the Study Guide.*

1. Explain the heading line and how positions of print are determined by the programmer.

2. Explain the coding needed to turn ON an indicator that causes printing to occur from an input record.

3. Explain the fields that will need to be coded for the spacing of the Output Report.

4. Explain the reasons for the use of Edit Codes.

5. There are six columns to the Edit Code Block. Describe the function of each of the columns.

6. Explain the coding for constants in the Constant or Edit Word field.

IBM   International Business Machine Corporation

GX21-9090-2 U/M 050*
Printed in U.S.A.

Program _____
Programmer _____

Punching Instruction

Graphic | | Punch | |

Card Electro Number

Page [1] [2] of ___

75 76 77 78 79 80
Program Identification

Date _____

Commas	Zero Balances to Print	No Sign	CR	-
Yes	Yes	1	A	J
Yes	No	2	B	K
No	Yes	3	C	L
No	No	4	D	M

X = Remove Plus Sign
Y = Date Field Edit
Z = Zero Suppress

Constant or Edit Word

Field Name

*Auto

Edit Codes
B/A/C/1-9/R
End Position in Output Record
P/B/L/R

Output Indicators
And   And
Not   Not   Not

Skip
After   Before

Space
After   Before

Stacker #/Fetch(F)
Type (H/D/T/E)
D A D
R N D
O A

Filename

Form Type
Line

O

EXERCISE 11

Date _____   Name_____

DIRECTIONS: *Page 94 contains an Output Specifications sheet that is coded with 12 errors that you are to circle. In the spaces below, explain what should be done to correct the error(s). Letter your answer with the corresponding letter on the line of code in error on page 94.*

____ _____
____ _____
____ _____
____ _____
____ _____
____ _____
____ _____
____ _____
____ _____
____ _____
____ _____
____ _____

```
STOP
1.  GO TO EXERCISE 12, PAGE 95
2.  COMPLETE EXERCISE 12
3.  SUBMIT EXERCISE TO INSTRUCTOR
4.  GO TO OUTPUT SPECIFICATIONS
        SHEET TEST, PAGE 97
5.  COMPLETE OUTPUT SPECIFICATIONS
        SHEET TEST
6.  SUBMIT TEST TO INSTRUCTOR
7.  GO TO PROJECT TWO, PAGE 103
```

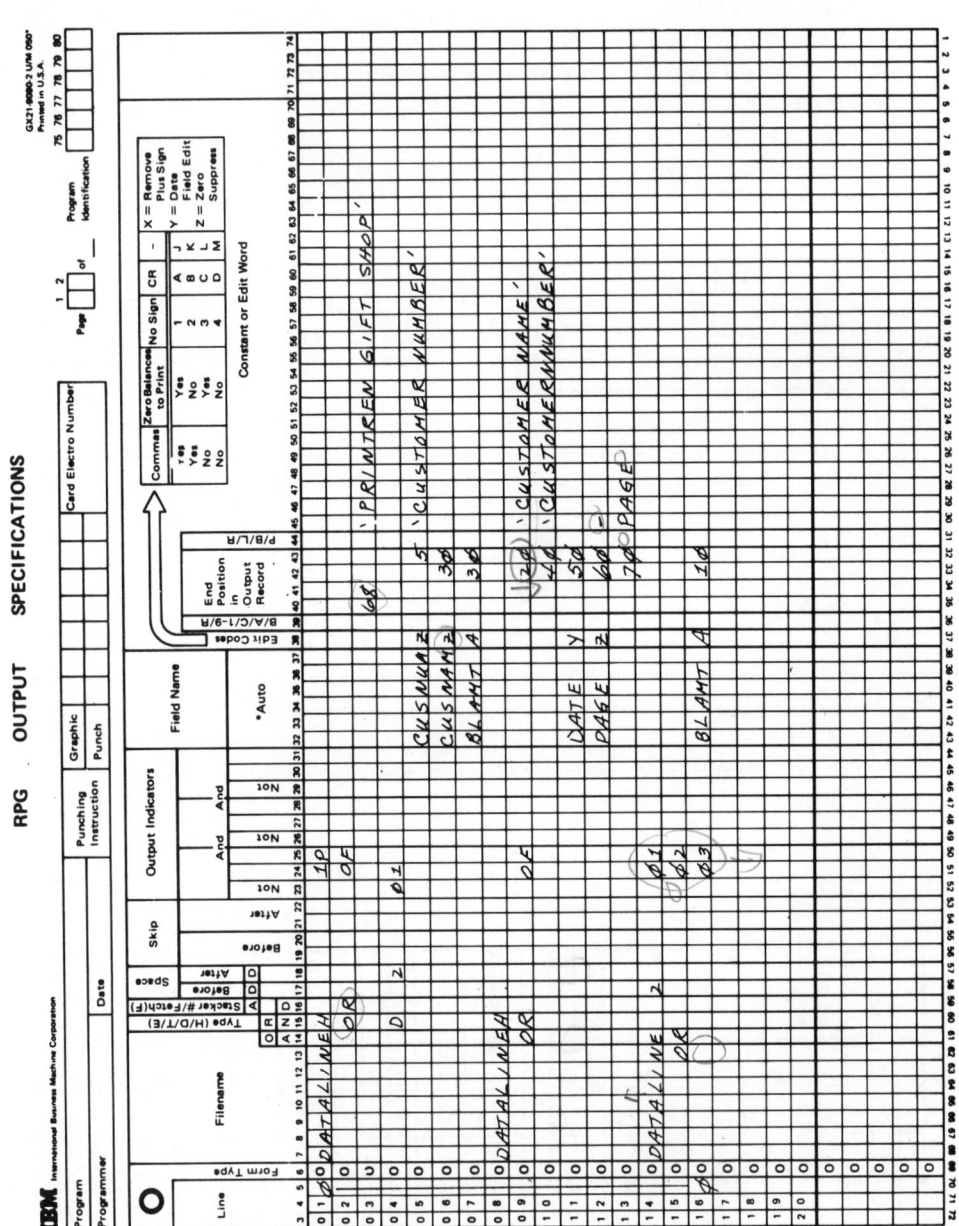

Figure 37

94

EXERCISE 12

Date_____   Name_____

TRUE–FALSE: *Each of the following statements is either true or false. Indicate your choice in the Answers column by encircling "T" for a true answer or "F" for a false answer.*

		Answers	
1.	Every part of the input record must be coded on the Output Specifications sheets	T	F
2.	The Output Specifications sheet has no direct bearing on any other form in data processing	T	F
3.	Each Filename of the Output Specifications sheet must be identical to an output filename coded on the File Description Specifications sheet	T	F
4.	As on the Input Specifications sheet, the record description entry on the Output Specifications sheet is coded on a line by itself	T	F
5.	The Filename need not be left-justified	T	F
6.	The Filename can contain embedded blanks	T	F
7.	The letter H coded in column 15 indicates that a header record is being described	T	F
8.	Header record data are usually constant	T	F
9.	Header records must be printed on every page of the output report	T	F
10.	The Print Chart is the basic tool used to determine End Position in Output Record fields	T	F
11.	The letter D coded in column 15 indicates that a dump record is being described	T	F
12.	The coding lP in columns 24 and 25 of the Output Indicators field signifies that the heading will print on the first page	T	F
13.	Literal marks are actually apostrophes	T	F
14.	The code OF means overflow	T	F
15.	Channel 12 of the carriage control tape is known as the OFF channel	T	F
16.	The detail print line closely approximates the data of the input record	T	F
17.	Coding the Skip After field always causes the printer to skip to a new page	T	F
18.	Spacing can be effective only after the printing of a record line	T	F
19.	The codes in the Skip field are effective only when a new form is positioned	T	F
20.	The function of the Output Indicator is to control when an output record is printed	T	F
21.	There is a direct connection between the Record Identifying Indicator and the Output Indicator	T	F

22. Data is moved from the input area to the output area before it can be printed   T   F

23. Before an Overflow Indicator can be effective, it must have been previously assigned on the File Description Specifications sheet   T   F

24. The Field Names used in the Output Specifications sheet can be the same as those used on the Input Specifications sheet   T   F

25. Field Names on the Output Specifications sheet must be listed in the same order as the Input Specifications sheet   T   F

26. Another name for editing could be punctuating   T   F

27. Edit Codes of the Edit Code Block can be used interchangably   T   F

28. Print Chart spacing need not be considered when Edit Codes are used   T   F

29. The Edit Code Block is composed of six columns   T   F

30. Negative figures can be represented by the CR or – symbol   T   F

31. Some Edit Codes allow zero balances to be printed as .00   T   F

32. The X, Y, Z codes provide for comma punctuation   T   F

33. The Y code automatically suppresses leading zeros   T   F

34. The primary function of the Z code is to suppress leading zeros   T   F

35. The Z code will suppress significant zeros   T   F

36. Zero suppression is effective on numeric fields only   T   F

37. The reason Z is coded with a slash through it is to prevent mistaking it for the digit 2   T   F

38. End Position in Output Record numbers must be sequential   T   F

39. Constants are most often used for the printing of heading data   T   F

40. The Constant or Edit Word field gives the programmer greater control over the punctuation or editing of a field   T   F

41. Editing symbols cannot be floated   T   F

42. Columns 7 through 31 are used to describe the output that is to be written   T   F

43. The word OR indicates that an alternate condition exists   T   F

44. Headings can be either printed or omitted on the top of each output page of a report   T   F

45. Most printed lines of a report are classified as detail lines   T   F

46. For printing to occur, the control indicator can be either ON or OFF   T   F

47. There can be coding in both the Field Name field and the Filename field on the same specification line.   T   F

48. The literal marks are printed on the output report   T   F

49. Edit Word coding is used in conjunction with Edit Code Block codes   T   F

50. Any symbol can be coded so that it is both fixed and floated on the same output field   T   F

OUTPUT SPECIFICATIONS SHEET TEST

Date _____   Name _____

PART I: *Fill in the blank with the appropriate word or words (3 points each).*

1. The _____ is the basic tool used to determine End Position in Output Record fields.

2. Coding the indicator _____ in columns 24 and 25 of the Output Indicators field signifies that the heading will print on the first page.

3. _____ are symbols used to enclose constants.

4. Insertion of special symbols, such as the period, comma, and dollar sign, that add more meaning to the output report is called _____ .

5. Three types of print lines include _____ , _____ _____ , and _____ .

6. Observe the coding on the Output Specifications sheet (Fig. 38). This coding is incorrect because _____ _____ .

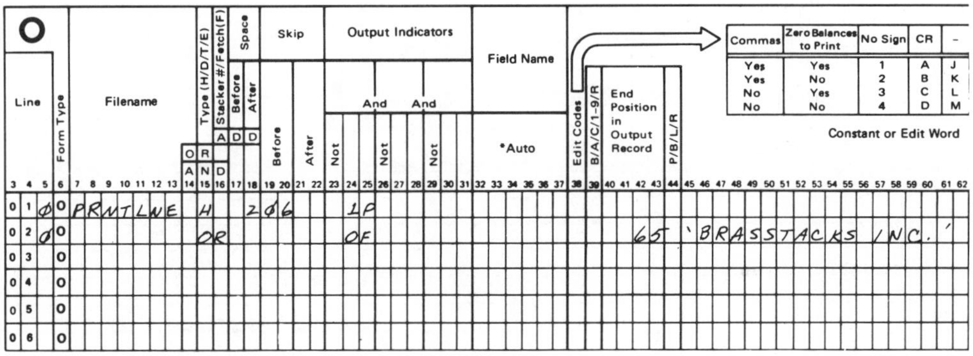

Figure 38

7. The character T coded in column 15 indicates _____ _____ .

8. The purpose of the SKIP field in columns 19 through 22 is _____ _____ .

9. _____ means the dropping off of character(s) of a field of print.

10. Observe the following coding (Fig. 39). Which specification lines is/are correct?

_____

PART II. *True or False (2 points each). Write the letter "T" for a true answer and the letter "F" for a false answer in the spaces provided.*

1. Comment cards are identified by an asterisk in column 7   _____

2. If the file does not require any particular sequencing of records, the Sequence Field can be coded with any two alphabetical characters   _____

3. The numbers coded in the End Position in the Output Record field are obtained from the formatted card used as input   _____

4. Comment statements have an effect on the program or its compilation   _____

5. Every part of the input record must be coded on the Output Specifications sheet   _____

6. The word OR in columns 14–15 on the Output Specifications sheet is classified as an indicator   _____

7. When the character D is coded in Column 15, it indicates that the record line of print is a detail line   _____

8. Printer forms can be of any length from 6 to 120 lines   _____

9. In order for the data to be printed, it must be moved from the input area of the computer to the output area of the computer   _____

10. The X symbol in the edit block is used when editing the date field   _____

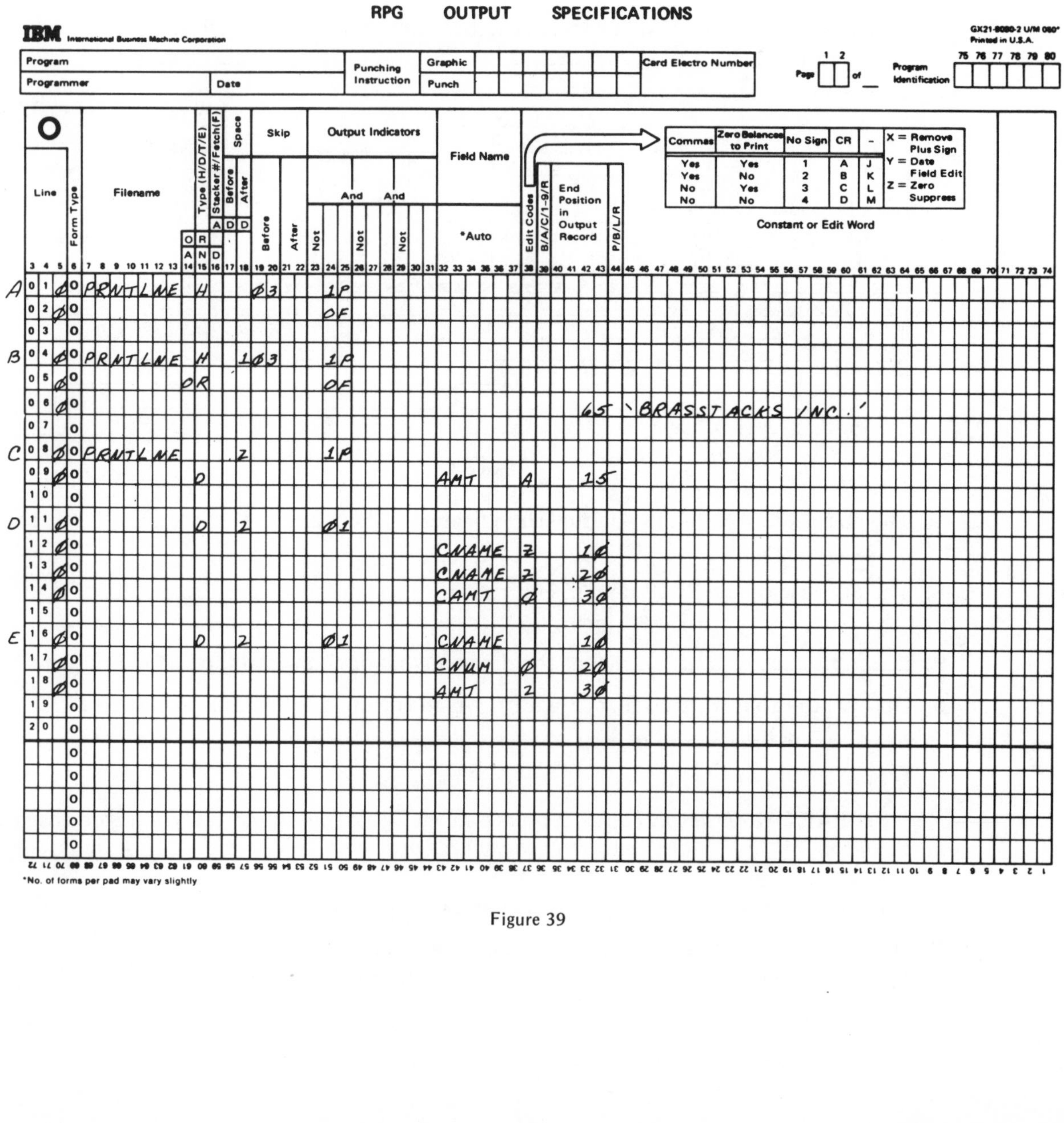

Figure 39

PART III. *Application problem (40 points). Using the following data, complete the problem on the specifications sheets provided. Use Print Chart on page 454.*

1. A report is to be printed with the information from the following formatted data.

Date	CC 1–6
Salesman Number	CC 7–11
Salesman Name	CC 12–31
Customer Number	CC 32–36
Item Number	CC 37–41
Quantity	CC 42–44
Cost Price	CC 45–49 (two decimal places)
Selling Price	CC 50–54 (two decimal places)

2. The input file is to be called 'SALESUM' and is 80 positions in length.

3. The output file is 120 positions in length and is called 'SLSRPT.'

4. Headings are to be printed on the first page only.

5. Design a Printer Spacing Chart, using the necessary information from the card format shown above.

6. The major heading should be indicated as 'SALES SUMMARY REPORT.'

7. Provide your own appropriate columnar headings.

8. Insert proper editing symbols in the Cost Price and Selling Price fields.

9. Double space detail data.

IBM

International Business Machine Corporation

RPG CONTROL CARD AND FILE DESCRIPTION SPECIFICATIONS

GX21-9092-3 UM/050*
Printed in U.S.A.

Program _____

Programmer _____ Date _____

Punching Instruction	Graphic		Punch	

Card Electro Number _____

Page [1] [2] of ___

*No. of forms per pad may very slightly

Program Identification 75 76 77 78 79 80

Control Card Specifications

H

Refer to the specific System Reference Library manual for actual entries.

File Description Specification

F

Line	Form Type	Filename	File Type	File Designation	Record Length	Device
0 2	F	SALESUM	I	P	80	READER
0 3	F	SLSRPT	O		120	PRINTER
0 4	F					
0 5	F					
0 6	F					
0 7	F					
0 8	F					
0 9	F					
1 0	F					

100

Program		
Programmer		Date

Punching Instruction — Graphic / Punch

Page 1 2 of __ — Program Identification (75 76 77 78 79 80)

Card Electro Number

I — INPUT SPECIFICATIONS

Line	Form Type	Filename	Sequence			Number (1-N)	Option (O)	Record Identifying Indicator or **	From	To	Decimal Positions
01	I	SALESUM	AA					01			
02	I								1	6	0
03	I								7	11	0
04	I								12	31	
05	I								32	36	0
06	I								37	41	0
07	I								42	44	0
08	I								45	49	2
09	I								50	54	2
10	I										
11	I										
12	I										
13	I										
14	I										
15	I										
16	I										
17	I										
18	I										
19	I										
20	I										

RPG OUTPUT SPECIFICATIONS

IBM International Business Machine Corporation

GX21-9090-2 U/M 050*
Printed in U.S.A.

Program		Punching Instruction	Graphic		Punch		Card Electro Number		Page 1 of __ 2
Programmer	Date								Program Identification 75 76 77 78 79 80

Commas / Zero Balances to Print / No Sign / CR / - (Edit Codes)

Commas	Zero Balances to Print	No Sign	CR	-
Yes	Yes	1	A	J
Yes	No	2	B	K
No	Yes	3	C	L
No	No	4	D	M

X = Remove Plus Sign
Y = Date Field Edit
Z = Zero Suppress

Constant or Edit Word

Output lines

Line	Form Type	Filename	Type (H/D/T/E)	Stacker#/Fetch(F)	Space Before/After	Skip Before/After	Output Indicators	Field Name	Edit Codes	End Position in Output Record	Constant or Edit Word
01	O	SLSRPT	H			0303		1P			
02	O										
03	O		D		2			01			
04	O							UDATE Y			
05	O							SLNUM			
06	O							SLNAME			
07	O							CUSNUM			
08	O							ITMNUM			
09	O							QUANT			
10	O							COST			
11	O							PRICE			

Constant: 00 'SALES SUMMARY REPORT'

102

PROJECT TWO

SPECIFICATIONS: LISTING

In order to provide a better understanding of how a Source Program in RPG is collated or assembled, an analysis of Project Two coding sheets on pages 110 through 112 will be undertaken. It is suggested that you remove these precoded specification sheets from the book so that you can follow the following text material.

A Source Program consists of all or some of the following Specifications sheets. The statements on these sheets are then punched into cards. Once the cards have been punched, they are then assembled in the following order:

1. Control Card Specifications

2. File Description Specifications

3. Extension Specifications

4. Line Counter Specifications

5. Input Specifications

6. Calculation Specifications

7. Output Specifications

SPECIFICATIONS SHEETS

Each Specifications sheet has common fields. These common fields will be reviewed.

Page Number Field (Columns 1 through 2)

This field is used to identify each page of the program. The pages are numbered sequentially.

Line (Columns 3 through 5)

This field is used to sequence the punching of the deck of cards that eventually becomes

103

known as the Source Program. The sequencing is in ascending order in multiples of ten for each type of specification.

The programmer may wish to add statements to the program after it has been punched into cards. Column 5 of the Line field on the Specifications sheets is blank for this purpose. By coding a number (1 through 9) in column 5, the source deck of cards can be kept in proper sequence.

Maintaining the Line field is important so that the source deck can be reassembled in case it should get out of order. It also makes documentation and maintenance of the program easier by providing a Source Program statement number to which the programmer can refer.

Form Type (Columns 6 through 6)

This preprinted alphabetical character indicates whether the data being read into the RPG compiler is

H	Control Card Specifications (Header)
F	File Description Specifications
E	Extension Specifications
L	Line Counter Specifications
I	Input Specifications
C	Calculation Specifications
O	Output Specifications

Every card of an RPG Source Program must contain one of the preceding identification characters punched into column 6.

Comments (Columns 7 through 7)

The compiler recognizes a comment card by the asterisk (*) in column 7. Comment lines have no effect on the program or its compilation. They serve merely as documentation. Comment indication CANNOT be written in a control card. See Fig. 41, line 020 and 030 of the File Description Specifications sheet.

Program Identification (Columns 75 through 80)

Programmers identify each program that they write by coding in an abbreviated name or code by which the program will be known later. The programmer can use any alphabetic or numeric character in the chosen name. The following points, however, should be observed.

1. The name must be unique.

2. The first character of the name must be alphabetic.

3. There can be NO embedded blanks within the name.

At the conclusion of the analysis of the Project One coding sheets, you should be able to write an RPG program that will list data from input cards.

Figure 41 illustrates the Control Card Specifications sheet.

CONTROL CARD SPECIFICATIONS

The coding of the Control Card is unique to the system that you are using. Check your system reference manuals for the necessary coding required.

FILE DESCRIPTION SPECIFICATIONS

Lines 020 and 030

These two statements (each punched on a separate card) are known as comment statements. The symbol or sign that makes them comment statements is the asterisk in column 7. Comment statements can involve as many columns as necessary as long as they do not go beyond column 70. If the comment requires two or more cards to complete, the programmer codes an additional asterisk in column 7 and continues the comment on each succeeding card. Comment statements serve as aids to persons reading the program and help as flow chart checkpoints. To further aid your instructor, always have your name printed after the number of the project. See Fig. 41.

Lines 040 and 050

The purpose of these two lines of coding is to describe the INPUT and OUTPUT files to the computer. See Fig. 41.

Line 040

Filename (Columns 7 through 14): The name assigned to the file (a group of like cards) by the programmer is CARDSIN. It is left-justified.

File Type (Columns 15 through 15): The I coded in this column indicates that the file is an INPUT file.

File Description (Columns 16 through 16): The file is the Primary or main file, which is indicated by the P coded in this column.

End of File (Column 17 through 17): Since this is a single INPUT file, the E coded in this column will designate the end-of-file condition when all the cards have been read.

File Format (Columns 19 through 19): The file is of a fixed length, thereby necessitating that an F be coded in this column.

Record Length (Columns 24 through 27): The length of the record is indicated as 80. If a 96-column card is being used, the number coded would be 96. The field is right-justified.

Device (Columns 40 through 46): This field is left-justified. The device named here "READ42" is required by the configuration or manufacturer. Figure 41 is for an IBM 1442 Card-Read-Punch device. If the illustration was for a DEC DATA SYSTEM Card Reader on a PDPll, the coding would be "READER." If the configuration being used is of another type or manufacturer, then that device must be appropriately named. You may also need to code the symbolic device in columns 47–52. Your instructor will furnish you with the appropriate data or refer to the manufacturer's reference manual.

Line 050

In Fig. 41 observe that

Filename (Columns 7 through 14): The name assigned to the file by the programmer is DATALINE. It is left-justified.

File Type (Columns 15 through 15): The O in this column indicates that the file is an OUTPUT file.

File Format (Columns 19 through 19): The file is of a fixed length, thereby necessitating that an F be coded in this column.

Record Length (Columns 24 through 27): The length of the record is indicated as 120. This will not hold true if the printing device has a 132 or 144 printing capacity. The field is right-justified.

Device (Columns 40 through 46): The field is left-justified. The device named here is "PRINTER." This name is required by the configuration or manufacturer. Figure 41 is for DEC SYSTEM, IBM 1130, or SYSTEM 3 configurations. However, if the configuration being used is different from either of the above, then that device must be appropriately named and coded in this field. Also check to see whether coding is required in the Symbolic Device Field.

The File Description Specifications sheet has now been completely explained. The next Specifications sheet to be discussed will be the Input Specifications sheet.

INPUT SPECIFICATIONS

Refer to the INPUT card shown in Fig. 1 on page 9. The formatted card, the one that you punched for Project One, is the same card that will be discussed as the Input record. The entries coded on this specifications sheet describe the data that is to be read into the input area of the computer. See Fig. 42.

Line 010

Filename (Columns 7 through 14): The name of the Input file CARDSIN is spelled exactly as it was on the File Description Specifications sheet. The columns for this field are identical to those used on the File Description Specifications sheet. The field is left-justified.

Sequence (Columns 15 through 16): Whenever one input file and one record format are to be defined as Input, any two alphabetical characters can be used in this field. The programmer decided to use the letters "AA."

Record Identifying Indicator (Columns 19 through 20): The numeric code "01" will turn ON when a card is read. Indicator "01" will be used for the printing of the data as described on the Output Specifications sheet. It is a referencing indicator in that when the type "01" record is read, the Record Indicator is turned ON. The File Description's statement is coded on a line by itself. See Fig. 42.

Lines 020 through 070

Of special note is the method used in coding the zeros to be punched in column 5.

106

Field Location (Columns 44 through 51): The FROM field, columns 44 through 47, is right-justified. The numbers coded in this field represent the beginning column of the field being described.

The TO field, columns 48 through 51, is right-justified. The numbers coded in this field represent the ending column of the field being described.

The fields need not be described in the exact order that they appear on the INPUT record (left to right), but any field containing data that must be used in the program must be described.

Field Name (Columns 53 through 58): The names in this field are programmer supplied. The programmer codes names that best illustrate the type of data found in the record (card) columns. The names assigned here are unique to this program. If the field is referenced again in the program, the same name is used. The field is left-justified.

Field Definition Statement Lines are coded on lines by themselves. They are never coded on File Definition Statement Lines.

The next Specifications sheets are the Extension Specifications sheet, Line Counter Specifications sheet, and the Calculation Specifications sheet. Since no coding is necessary on these sheets, this section of the program need not be considered at this time. However, the programmer must now turn his attention to what the user of the report wishes the appearance of the Output report to take. The Print Chart layout must now be taken into consideration.

PRINT CHART

Before the programmer codes the Output Specifications sheets, he must give a great deal of thought to the appearance of the Output Report. The tool used to generate the appearance is, of course, the Print Chart. The Print Chart illustrated in Fig. 40 is explained below.

1. The coding on line 3, indicated by the letter H, shows that the programmer coded in the six heading fields NAME, STREET, CITY, STATE, ZIP, and TELEPHONE. This line will be discussed in Project Four.

2. On line 6 the programmer coded the six detailed line fields.

   a. The D coded to the left of the vertical numbered lines indicates which type of print line is to be used. The D, in this case, represents a detail line.

   b. The NAME field starts with print position 1 and ends with print position 18. Notice that print positions 1 and 18 have A's coded in them. Print positions 2 through 17 have a straight line drawn through them. The programmer decided that this would be the method used to indicate these alphabetic print positions. A's could have been coded in columns 2 through 17, but doing so would be tedious as well as giving a cluttered appearance.

   c. The STREET, CITY, and STATE fields were also coded with A's because the data in these fields is primarily alphabetic. However, the STREET field could contain digits for the number of the address. The programmer, however, realized that alphabetic characters were the dominant factor and so indicated this fact.

   d. The ZIP field, starting in print position 76 and ending in print position

80, is coded differently from the other fields of the Print Chart. This field is coded with X's because it is primarily a numeric field. However, X's could have been coded in all the fields of the Print Chart. The programmer decided that his method would allow for greater clarification.

e. The TELEPHONE number field is also coded using X's because it is a numeric field.

Once the Print Chart has been completely coded by the programmer, he turns his attention to the Output Specifications sheet. He must use the Print Chart as his source document for specific areas of the Output Specifications sheet.

OUTPUT SPECIFICATIONS

Refer to Fig. 43.

Line 010

Filename (Columns 7 through 14): When the programmer coded the File Description Specifications sheet, he determined that he was assigning the name of DATA-LINE to the Output file. The filename must be coded identically on the Output Specifications sheet as on the File Description Specifications. The field is left-justified.

Type (H/D/T/E) (Columns 15 through 15): The alphabetical letter D is coded in this column to show that the line of print is a detail print line.

150/10/6 PRINT CHART   PROG. ID _____ PAGE _____

(SPACING: 150 POSITION SPAN, AT 10 CHARACTERS PER INCH, 6 LINES PER VERTICAL INCH)   DATE _____

PROGRAM TITLE _____

PROGRAMMER OR DOCUMENTALIST: _____

CHART TITLE _____

Figure 40

Space After (Column 18 through 18): The digit 2 coded in this column indicates that the Output Report is to be double spaced. If the report were to be single spaced, the programmer would have coded a 1 in this column.

Output Indicators (Columns 23 through 31): The programmer used only the first section of this field. The coding 01 signifies that the detail line will print when the Record Identifying Indicator is ON. See Fig. 43.

Lines 020 through 060

Field Name (Columns 32 through 37): The names coded in this field are left-justified. The programmer assigned these names from the Input record. As noted, the names MUST be exactly as previously coded. However, they need not be coded strictly from a left-to-right alignment of the Input record. All that is required is that all fields necessary for the Output Report be present. The determining factor here is what the programmer diagrammed on the Print Chart.

End Position in Output Record (Columns 40 through 43): The field is right-justified. The numbers coded correspond directly to the end position of the field on the Print Chart. It is of extreme importance that the end position of each output field be properly coded in order to ensure that truncation (dropping off of characters) does not occur.

All the statements coded on the Specifications sheets of Project Two have now been explained. When you program the next Project, use the concepts learned from Projects One and Two.

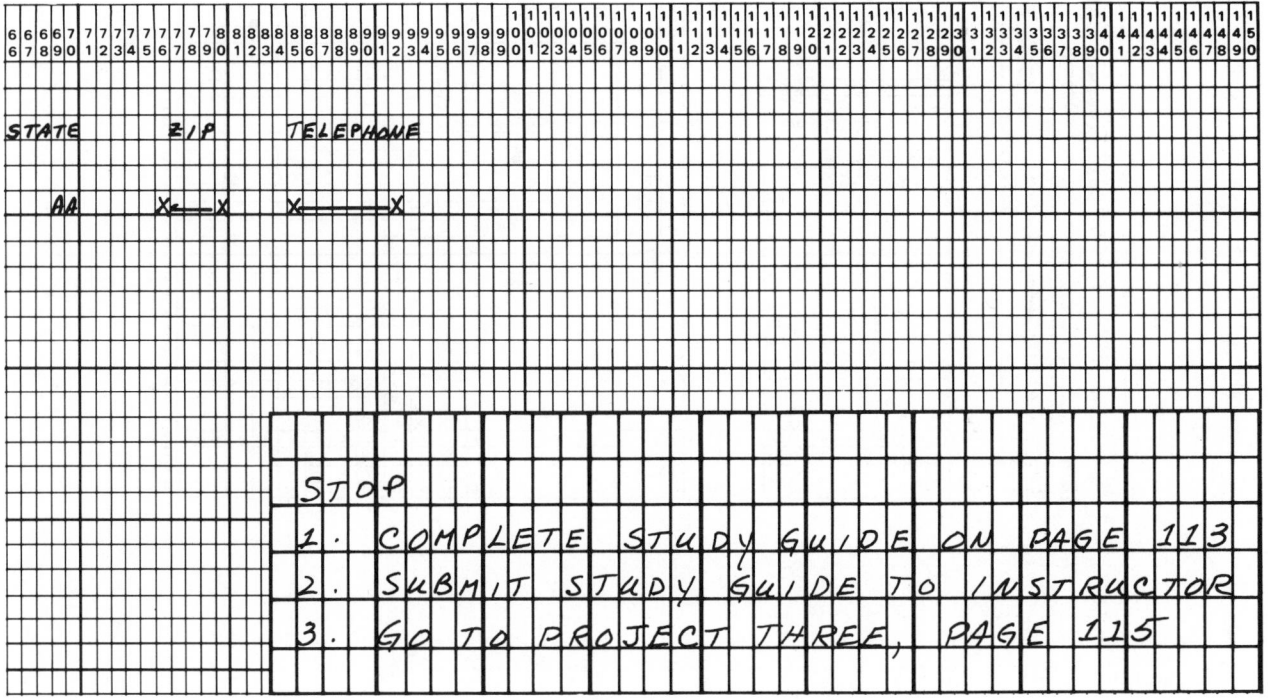

Figure 40 (cont.)

IBM International Business Machine Corporation

RPG CONTROL CARD AND FILE DESCRIPTION SPECIFICATIONS

GX21-9092-3 UM/050*
Printed in U.S.A.

Program	STUDENT NAME LISTING	Punching Instruction		Graphic		Card Electro Number				*No. of forms per pad may vary slightly

Programmer RPCB   Date 09/01/--   Punch

Page 01 of 3   1 2   Program Identification RPCB02

Card Electro Number 5081

Control Card Specifications

Line	Form Type					

0 1 H

File Description Specification

(see form image)

Figure 41

F-specification lines:

Line	Form Type	Filename		Device			Record Length	
0 2	F	*PROJECT TWO (YOUR NAME)						
0 3	F	*NAME LISTING						
0 4	F	CARDSIN	IPE	READ42			80	
0 5	F	DATALINED		PRINTER			120	
0 6	F							
0 7	F							
0 8	F							
0 9	F							
1 0	F							

Refer to the specific System Reference Library manual for actual entries.

RPG INPUT SPECIFICATIONS

IBM International Business Machines Corporation

GX21-9094-2 U/M 050*
Printed in U.S.A.

Program	STUDENT NAME LISTING	Punching Instruction	Graphic	Card Electro Number
Programmer	RPCB	Date ø9/ø1/--	Punch	5ø81

Page (1 2) ø2 of 3 — Program Identification (75–80): RPCBø2

Line (3–5)	Form Type (6)	Filename (7–14)	Sequence (15–16)	Number (1-N) (17)	Option (O) (18)	Record Identifying Indicator or ** (19–20)	Record Identification Codes 1 (21–27)	Record Identification Codes 2 (28–34)	Record Identification Codes 3 (35–41)	Stacker Select (42)	P/B/L/R (43)	Field Location From (44–47)	Field Location To (48–51)	Decimal Positions (52)	Field Name (53–58)	Control Level (L1-L9) (59–60)	Matching Fields or Changing Fields (61–62)	Field Record Relation (63–64)	Field Indicators Plus (65–66)	Minus (67–68)	Zero or Blank (69–70)	(71–74)
01ø	I	CARDSIN	AA			ø1																
02	I											1	18		NAME							
03	I											19	36		STREET							
04	I											37	54		CITY							
05	I											55	56		STATE							
06	I											57	61		ZIP							
07ø	I											74	8ø		TELPHN							
08	I																					
09	I																					
10	I																					
11	I																					
12	I																					
13	I																					
14	I																					
15	I																					
16	I																					
17	I																					
18	I																					
19	I																					
20	I																					
	I																					
	I																					
	I																					
	I																					
	I																					

Figure 42

RPG   OUTPUT   SPECIFICATIONS

IBM International Business Machine Corporation

GX21-9090-2 U/M 050*
Printed in U.S.A.

| Program | STUDENT NAME LISTING | | Card Electro Number | | Page 03 of 3 | Program Identification | RPCB02 |
| Programmer | RPCB | Date 09/01/-- | 5081 | | 1 2 | | 75 76 77 78 79 80 |

Punching Instruction / Graphic / Punch

Line	Form Type	Filename	Type (H/D/T/E)	Stacker #/Fetch(F)	Space Before/After	Skip Before/After	Output Indicators	Field Name *Auto	Edit Codes B/A/C/1-9/R	End Position in Output Record	P/B/L/R
01	O	DATALINED			2		01				
02	O							NAME		18	
03	O							STREET		44	
04	O							CITY		64	
05	O							STATE		70	
06	O							ZIP		80	
07	O							TELPHN		92	

Constant or Edit Word

Commas	Zero Balances to Print	No Sign	CR	-
Yes	Yes	1	A	J
Yes	No	2	B	K
No	Yes	3	C	L
No	No	4	D	M

X = Remove Plus Sign
Y = Date Field Edit
Z = Zero Suppress

Figure 43

STUDY GUIDE

Date _____ Name_____

DIRECTIONS: *Answer the following questions in the spaces provided. Your answers should indicate the depth of understanding that you have toward the concepts and definitions presented. If there is insufficient space provided for your answer, complete your answer on the reverse side of the Study Guide.*

1. Explain the purpose of comment cards in a program and how the compiler treats them.

2. Explain how the programmer uses various codes when developing the Print Chart.

3. Explain the relationship between the Output Indicators and the Field Names coded on the Output Specifications sheet.

4. List the coding specifications sheets and give short explanations of what is coded on each.

5. Explain the connection between the Output Indicators and the Record Identifying Indicator.

PROJECT THREE

SPECIFICATIONS: BUSINESS DIRECTORY

The object of this project is to print a business directory. Using the Source Document provided on page 117, collect the data required. Observe that some of the fields will be

1. Alphabetic

2. Alphabetic and numeric (alphameric)

3. Numeric

Using the concepts presented, developed, and discussed in Project Two, develop a program to produce the directory.

INPUT CARD FORMAT

The input data card format for Project Three is as follows:

Name	CC 1–23
Street	CC 24–41
City	CC 42–59
State	CC 60–61
Zip	CC 62–66
Telephone Number	CC 67–73

INPUT FILE

Filename	Develop your own
Record Length	80 Positions

115

OUTPUT FILE

Filename   Develop your own

Record Length   120 Positions

The following additional specifications should be taken into consideration before development of the program is begun.

- The coding sheets for this project are found on pages 118 through 120.
- Output data is to be double spaced.
- Develop a Print Chart for the output. Use the Print Chart on page 454–455 for the development of your output report for this project.
- Leave four spaces between each column of the printout.
- Keypunch the coded program.
- Assemble the Source Program in the sequence dictated by the computer configuration being used.
- Debug and compile the project.
- The Output Record should appear as illustrated on page 121.

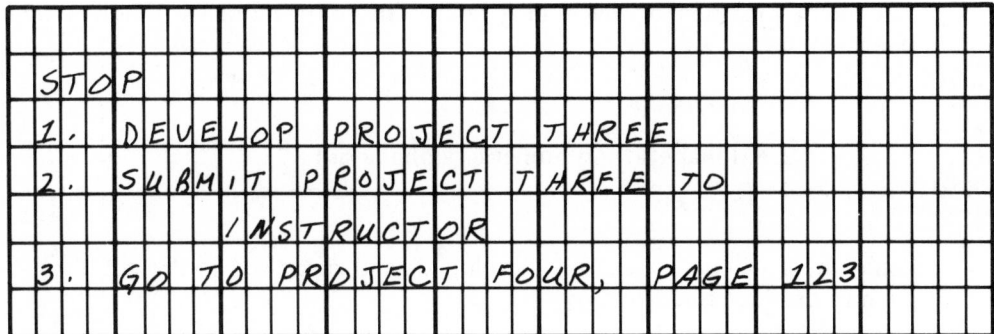

```
STOP
1.   DEVELOP PROJECT THREE
2.   SUBMIT PROJECT THREE TO
         INSTRUCTOR
3.   GO TO PROJECT FOUR, PAGE 123
```

BUSINESS DIRECTORY

NAME OF BUSINESS	STREET	CITY-STATE	ZIP	TEL. NUMBER

GX21-9092-3 UM/050°
Printed in U.S.A.

RPG CONTROL CARD AND FILE DESCRIPTION SPECIFICATIONS

IBM International Business Machine Corporation

Program

Programmer

Date

Punching Instruction

Graphic

Punch

Card Electro Number

*No. of forms per pad may very slightly

Page [ ] of [___]

Program Identification 75 76 77 78 79 80

Refer to the specific System Reference Library manual for actual entries.

Control Card Specifications

		Form Type
Line		H

Control card fields (columns 7–74):
- Core Size to Compile (7 8)
- Object Output (9 10)
- Listing Options (11 12 13 14)
- Core Size to Execute
- Debug (15)
- MFCM Stacking Sequence (16 17 18 19 20)
- Inverted Print (21)
- 360/20 2501 Buffer (22)
- Number Of Print Positions (23 24)
- Alternate Collating Sequence (25 26)
- Address to Start (27 28 29 30)
- Work Tapes (31)
- Overlay Open (32)
- Overlap Printer (33)
- Binary Search (34)
- Tape Error (35)
- 2152 Checking (36)
- Inquiry (37)
- Model 20 — Read/Write/Compute (38)
- Keyboard Output (39)
- Sign Handling (40)
- 1P Forms Position (41)
- Indicator Setting (42)
- File Translation (43)
- Punch MFCU Zeros (44)
- Nonprint Characters (45)
- Table Load Halt (47)
- Shared I/O (48)
- Field Print (49)
- Formatted Core Dump (50)
- RPG to RPG II Conversion (51)

File Description Specification

		Form Type
Line		F

Line numbers: 0 1, 0 2, 0 3, 0 4, 0 5, 0 6, 0 7, 0 8, 0 9, 1 0

File Description fields (columns 7–74):
- Filename (7–14)
- File Type (15)
- I/O/U/C/D (15)
- File Designation (16)
- P/S/C/R/T/D (16)
- End of File (17)
- E (17)
- Sequence (18)
- A/D (18)
- File Format (19)
- F/V/S/M/D (19)
- Block Length (20 21 22 23)
- Record Length (24 25 26 27)
- Mode of Processing (28)
- L/R (28 29)
- Length of Key Field or of Record Address Field (29 30)
- A/P/I/K (31)
- Record Address Type (31)
- Type of File Organization or Additional Area (32)
- I/D/T or 2 (32 33)
- Overflow Indicator (33 34)
- Key Field Starting Location (35 36 37 38)
- Extension Code E/L (39)
- Device (40–46)
- Symbolic Device (47–52)
- Labels S/N/E/M (53)
- Name of Label Exit (54–59)
- Continuation Lines
- K (53)
- Option (54–59)
- Entry (60–65)
- Extent Exit for DAM (60–65)
- Core Index (61–65)
- A/U (66)
- File Addition/Unordered (66)
- Number of Tracks for Cylinder Overflow (68 69)
- Number of Extents (68 69)
- Tape Rewind (70)
- File Condition U1-U8 (71 72)
- R/U/N (70)

75 118

RPG INPUT SPECIFICATIONS

IBM International Business Machine Corporation

GX21-9094-2 U/M 050*
Printed in U.S.A.

Program		Punching Instruction	Graphic	Card Electro Number
Programmer	Date		Punch	

Page (1 2) of ___ Program Identification (75 76 77 78 79 80)

I

Line (3–5)	Form Type (6)	Filename (7–13)	Sequence (14–16) OR / AND	Number (1–N) (17)	Option (O) (18)	Record Identifying Indicator or ** (19–20)	Record Identification Codes 1: Position (21–24)	Not (N) (25)	C/Z/D (26)	Character (27)	Record Identification Codes 2: Position (28–31)	Not (N) (32)	C/Z/D (33)	Character (34)	Record Identification Codes 3: Position (35–38)	Not (N) (39)	C/Z/D (40)	Character (41)	Stacker Select (42)	P/B/L/R (43)	Field Location: From (44–47)	Field Location: To (48–51)	Decimal Positions (52)	Field Name (53–58)	Control Level (L1–L9) (59–60)	Matching Fields or Changing Fields (61–62)	Field Record Relation (63–64)	Field Indicators: Plus (65–66)	Field Indicators: Minus (67–68)	Field Indicators: Zero or Blank (69–70)	(71–74)
01	I																														
02	I																														
03	I																														
04	I																														
05	I																														
06	I																														
07	I																														
08	I																														
09	I																														
10	I																														
11	I																														
12	I																														
13	I																														
14	I																														
15	I																														
16	I																														
17	I																														
18	I																														
19	I																														
20	I																														
	I																														
	I																														
	I																														
	I																														
	I																														

RPG OUTPUT SPECIFICATIONS

IBM International Business Machine Corporation

GX21-9090-2 U/M 050*
Printed in U.S.A.

Program

Programmer

Date

Punching Instruction

Graphic

Punch

Card Electro Number

Page 1 2 of

Program Identification 75 76 77 78 79 80

Commas	Zero Balances to Print	No Sign	CR	-
Yes	Yes	1	A	J
Yes	No	2	B	K
No	Yes	3	C	L
No	No	4	D	M

X = Remove Plus Sign
Y = Date Field Edit
Z = Zero Suppress

Constant or Edit Word

120

Name	Address	City	State	Zip	Number
STEVE BABKEY & CO.	1044 ALEXANDER DR	PRINTOWN	CA	97120	5768899
JANE BROWN GIFTS	761 STETSON BLVD	GRACIOUS	IL	15276	2143524
GARVEY CHIP & DIP	228 PROSPECT ST.	MAJOR	KY	12075	7521122
GIFTS AND THINGS	5 STUBENVILLE RD	COUNTY LINE	RI	03301	5011050
MCCARTHY GLASS	88 MORGAN ST.	FRYBURG	PA	09523	4569871
RON FRIEMAN SHOP	27 BALCOURT WAY	NEW PICKERTON	MA	68042	5220011
STRONG'S PARTS	351 WITHERSPOON DR	ROCKAWAY	VA	14553	2121199
SUPER ERIC'S	681 GUYOUT ST	AARNTOWNSVILLE	NY	01010	7523265
SHART'S NOVELTIES	744 TERHAUT PL	FINGERTON	NH	03524	7521358
SCOT TRAIN'S & HBS	414 SNOWDOWN ST	SAWER JUNCTION	NJ	08001	6644466
RUBLEV SKILL CTR	311 HUNT ST.	BUNINGTON	WV	15275	3510052
MOM'S PUTTERY	555 WEST STATE ST	MAKERVILLE	GA	22410	2001040
MAKING THINGS	EAST MAIN ST	DANDYTOWN	MN	62005	9981133
STACY'S	MARKET ST	HUBBER	PA	09552	4215577
GIFT SUPERMARKET	8 GROVER BLVD	GRANGEBURG	CT	04445	1237004
EDDIE'S	2222 GREAT TREE DR	MERSER	ND	78451	2561289
BILL BUXTON'S	11 FLAVER PLACE	WASHINGTON	PA	09002	4931319
DUDLEY'S PLANT CTR	668 DRIVEWAY RD	FLUGLETON	OH	42253	3337721

PROJECT FOUR

*SPECIFICATIONS: BUSINESS
DIRECTORY — HEADINGS*

It is easy to see that someone reading the output of Project Three would have a difficult time understanding the data of each of the columns of the Output Report. To make the Output Report more meaningful when programming this project, observe the following conditions.

1. The printing of the output should begin at the top of a new page of output stock paper.

2. Columnar headings of the source document, page 117, will be printed above each column of each sheet of the Output Report.

NEW CONCEPTS

Overflow   Constant or Edit Word

Heading Line

OVERFLOW

In order to position a clean sheet of output stock paper on the printer, the programmer codes for this condition in the following manner on two Specifications sheets — File Description Specifications and Output Specifications. In Fig. 44 note particularly the details listed below.

1. The Filename on both Specifications sheets is identical.

2. The Field Location — card columns — of Filename on both Specifications sheets is identical.

3. The Overflow coding is on both Specifications sheets.

4. The Overflow indication on the Output Specifications sheets requires a second line of coding.

123

HEADING LINE

The Output Specifications sheet of Fig. 44 indicates that

1. Line 010 through 070 is the coding needed for one line of printed output.

2. The line of print is a Heading line indicated by the H in column 15 of line 010.

3. The line will print on line number 6 of the output printer form indicated by the 06 coded in columns 19 and 20. The printer will skip to line 6 before printing the line. For carriage control printers, 01 would be coded in columns 19 and 20 and the printer would skip to the 01 punched in the carriage control tape.

4. After this line prints, the printer will space forward 3 lines indicated by the 3 coded in column 18 of line 010.

5. The line will print when the First Page indicator (1P) *or* the Overflow indicator (OF) is on. The 1P indicator will be on for the first RPG cycle only. The OF indicator will be on for one RPG cycle beginning when the overflow condition is detected at the bottom of the last page of print. Heading lines will output at the same time in the RPG cycle as Detail output. If the Overflow indicator is on during Detail output time of the RPG cycle, then the line will print.

6. The succeeding lines (030–070) have the data that will print on this heading line. The constants NAME, STREET, etc. will print on this line with the ending positions indicated in columns 40 through 43.

CONSTANT OR EDIT WORD

When developing the logic of the Output Report, keep in mind how and where each OUTPUT record is going to appear on the Output Report. Such being the case, the heading OUTPUT must be printed prior to the detail data output printing. The segment of the program containing the heading data must be placed before the segment containing the detail data.

The headings can be defined as constant data. The heading data is coded in the Constant or Edit Word field — columns 45 through 70. This data must be enclosed within literal marks. Everything within the literal marks will be printed exactly as coded except that the literal marks themselves will not be printed. Each field is left-justified. It is of great importance that the ending positions of each of the columnar headings be designated and coded in the End Position in Output Record field. These ending positions are obtained from the developed Print Chart.

Observe how the columnar headings are coded in Fig. 44.

The Constant or Edit Word columns can also edit a field coded in columns 32 to 37 of the Output Specifications. An example would be for a phone number. If, for example, a field called PHONE were included in the input and was ten positions in length and coded as 1234567890, the coding necessary for the hyphens to be properly placed between the area code and between the three-digit section and the four-digit section would be as shown in Fig. 44. The telephone number would be printed on the Output Report as 123–456–7890 with the last digit of the phone number being printed in the 90th print position of the Output Report.

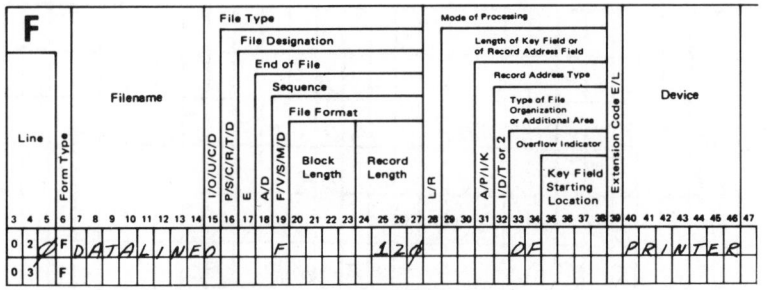

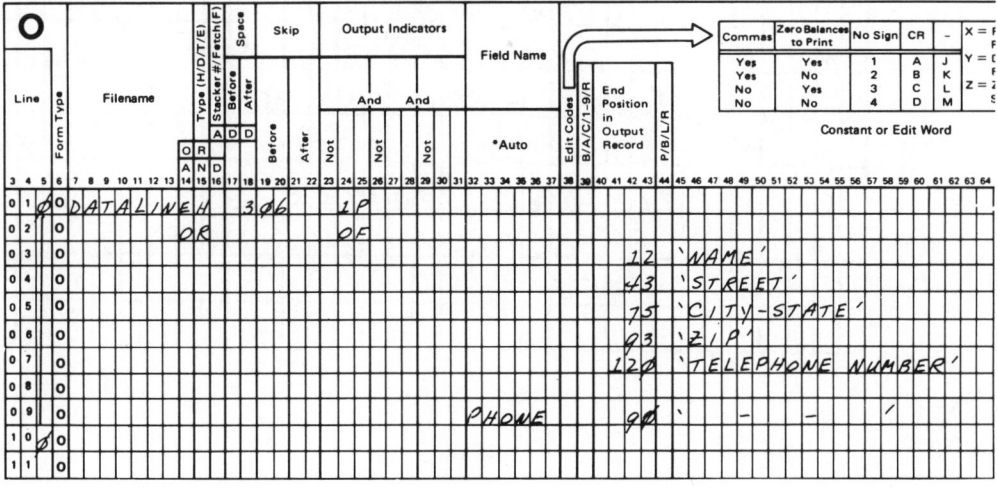

Figure 44

The following additional specifications should be considered in the development of this project.

- Develop a Print Chart for the Output Report. Use the Print Chart on page 454.

- Code the additional coding on the Specifications sheet on page 127.

- The detail lines of print are to be double spaced.

- The cards in which you punched the heading data must be inserted in the Source Program before the detail cards.

- Keypunch the additional coding.

- Assemble the Source Program in the sequence dictated by the Computer Configuration being used.

- Use the headings from Fig. 44 as the actual headings on your Output Report. However, you will need to change the ending print positions for each column in order that they conform to your Print Chart ending positions.

- Debug and compile the program.

- The Output Report should appear as illustrated on page 128.

125

```
STOP
1.   COMPLETE STUDY GUIDE ON PAGE 129
2.   SUBMIT STUDY GUIDE TO INSTRUCTOR
3.   DEVELOP PROJECT FOUR
4.   SUBMIT PROJECT FOUR TO
        INSTRUCTOR
5.   GO TO EXERCISE 13, PAGE 131
6.   COMPLETE EXERCISE 13
7.   SUBMIT EXERCISE TO INSTRUCTOR
8.   GO TO LINE COUNTER
        SPECIFICATIONS SHEET,
        PAGE 133
```

IBM

International Business Machine Corporation

RPG   OUTPUT   SPECIFICATIONS

GX21-9090-2 U/M 050*
Printed in U.S.A.

Program _____

Programmer _____   Date _____

Punching Instruction — Graphic / Punch

Card Electro Number

Page 1 2 of ___

Program Identification: 75 76 77 78 79 80

Commas	Zero Balances to Print	No Sign	CR	–
Yes	Yes	1	A	J
Yes	No	2	B	K
No	Yes	3	C	L
No	No	4	D	M

X = Remove Plus Sign
Y = Date Field Edit
Z = Zero Suppress

Constant or Edit Word

Line	Form Type	Filename	Type (H/D/T/E)	Stacker #/Fetch(F)	Space Before	Space After	Skip Before	Skip After	Output Indicators And Not	And Not	And Not	Field Name *Auto	Edit Codes B/A/C/1-9/R	End Position in Output Record	P/B/L/R	Constant or Edit Word

O

127

NAME	STREET	CITY-STATE		ZIP	TELEPHONE NUMBER
STEVE BABKEY & CO.	1044 ALEXANDER DR	PRINTOWN	CA	97120	576-8899
JANE BROWN GIFTS	761 STETSON BLVD	GRACIOUS	IL	15276	214-3524
GARVEY CHIP & DIP	228 PROSPECT ST.	MAJOR	KY	12075	752-1122
GIFTS AND THINGS	5 STUBENVILLE RD	COUNTY LINE	RI	03301	501-1050
MCCARTHY GLASS	88 MORGAN ST.	FRYBURG	PA	09523	456-9871
RON FRIEMAN SHOP	27 BALCOURT WAY	NEW PICKERTON	MA	68042	522-0011
STRONG'S PARTS	351 WITHERSPOON DR	ROCKAWAY	VA	14553	212-1199
SUPER ERIC'S	681 GUYOUT ST	AARNTOWNSVILLE	NY	01010	752-3265
SHART'S NOVELTIES	744 TERHAUT PL	FINGERTON	NH	03524	752-1358
SCOT TRAIN'S & HBS	414 SNOWDOWN ST	SAWER JUNCTION	NJ	08001	664-4466
RUBLEV SKILL CTR	311 HUNT ST.	BUNINGTON	WV	15275	351-0052
MOM'S POTTERY	555 WEST STATE ST	MAKERVILLE	GA	22410	200-1040
MAKING THINGS	EAST MAIN ST	DANDYTOWN	MN	62005	998-1133
STACY'S	MARKET ST	HUBBER	PA	09552	421-5577
GIFT SUPERMARKET	8 GROVER BLVD	GRANGEBURG	CT	04445	123-7004
EDDIE'S	2222 GREAT TREE DR	MERSER	ND	78451	256-1289
BILL BUXTON'S	11 FLAVER PLACE	WASHINGTON	PA	09002	493-1319
DUDLEY'S PLANT CTR	668 DRIVEWAY RD	FLUGLETON	OH	42253	333-7721

Date _____   Name _____

DIRECTIONS: *Answer the following questions in the spaces provided. Your answers should indicate the depth of understanding that you have toward the concepts and definitions presented. If there is insufficient space provided for your answer, complete your answer on the reverse side of the Study Guide.*

1. Explain all the coding necessary to have heading lines printed on the Output Report.

2. Explain the use of OVERFLOW. Why and when would a programmer use the concept?

3. List and explain the conditions that can cause heading lines to print.

4. Explain the coding used in the Constant or Edit Word Field.

Date _____   Name _____

TRUE–FALSE: *Each of the following statements is either true or false. Indicate your choice in the Answers column by encircling "T" for a true answer or "F" for a false answer.*

Answers

1. Specifications sheets have common fields   T   F

2. Sequencing of line numbers is in multiples of ten   T   F

3. The H in column 7 indicates that the card is a header control card   T   F

4. Comment cards are identified by an asterisk in column 7   T   F

5. Program Identification is punched into each card in card columns 75 through 80   T   F

6. A file is any number of like cards assembled in logical order   T   F

7. The P coded in the File Designation field on the File Description Specifications sheet indicates that the file is a Primary file   T   F

8. The Record Length field on the File Description Specifications sheet is left-justified   T   F

9. If the file does not require any particular sequencing of records, the Sequence Field can be coded with any two alphabetical characters   T   F

10. Fields of an Input record must be described in the exact order in which they appear on the input card   T   F

11. Field Definition Statement Lines are coded on lines by themselves   T   F

12. Comment identification cannot be written in control cards   T   F

13. The Print Chart is the tool used by the programmer to design the appearance of the Output Report   T   F

14. Truncation means the dropping off of characters of a field of print   T   F

15. In order to position a clean sheet of stock paper on the printer, the programmer codes an OF on both the File Specifications and Output Specifications sheets   T   F

16. Comment statements have an effect on the program or its compilation   T   F

17. Types of printed lines can be indicated as either H for Heading or D for Detail on the Print Chart   T   F

18. If the headings are to be printed only on the first sheet of the Output Report, the programmer codes an IP in the Output Indicators field   T   F

19. For printers that are not carriage tape controlled, the coding in columns 19 and 20 instructs the printing device to skip then print on the line   T   F

20. The OF indicator is an overflow indicator   T   F

21. Headings are defined as constant data   T   F

131

22. The numbers coded in the End Position in the Output Record field are obtained from the formatted card used as input   T   F

23. The Constant or Edit Word field can be used for coding of editing symbols   T   F

24. The Field Name field on the Output Specifications sheet is similar to the one on the Input Specifications sheet   T   F

25. The FROM field represents the beginning card columns and the TO field represents the ending card columns of the field on the Input card   T   F

COMPLETION: *Fill in the blank with the appropriate word or words.*

1, 2. The Overflow Condition must be coded on the _____ as well as the _____ Specifications sheets.

3. To leave spaces between print lines, the programmer codes the appropriate digit in the _____ field.

4. To print constant data on the output report, the programmer codes the constant in the _____ field.

MATCHING: *Match Column 1 to Column 2.*

COLUMN 1	COLUMN 2	*Answers*
A. 1P	1. Constant data	_____
B. 12		
C. Headings	2. Coding for headings to appear on first sheet of Output Report	
D. OF		_____
E. OR	3. Overflow punch in carriage control tape	_____
F. 01		
	4. Second condition that can cause a heading line to print	_____

LINE COUNTER SPECIFICATIONS SHEET

For printers that use line counting for carriage control instead of a carriage control tape, the Line Counter Specifications sheet may be required.

Most standard forms used on printers are 66 lines long. This number is considered standard because the printer generally prints 6 lines per vertical inch on an 11-inch-long form. Just as with any other printed page, printing does not consume the complete page. Therefore overflow will take place on line 60 of the standard form. If no Line Counter Specifications sheet is included in the RPG II Source Program, the Object Program will assume that there are 66 lines per printer page with overflow on line 60.

FIELDS

Filename (Columns 7 through 14)

The name coded in this field is the printer filename that was coded on the File Description Specifications sheet for the Output File. The field is left-justified. An L must also be coded in column 39, Extension Code E/L, of the File Description Specifications sheet for the printer file to make the Line Counter Specification effective.

There are 12 subdivisions to the Line Counter Specifications sheet. Each subdivision is further subdivided into two segments. Observe Fig. 45.

Subdivision 1 (Columns 15 through 19)

The purpose of this subdivision is to establish the length of the form that is to be used for printing the Output Report.

Line Number (Columns 15 through 17)

The number coded in this field represents the total length of the form being used by the printer. The length of the form, however, is expressed in lines instead of inches. The field is right-justified.

FL or Channel Number (Columns 18 through 19)

The characters are the abbreviation used for *Forms Length*.

Subdivision 2 (Columns 20 through 24)

This subdivision is used to establish when the overflow line is to be effective—that is, when the form will be ejected forward to begin printing from the beginning of the top of the page again.

Line Number (Columns 20 through 22)

The coding in this field signifies the last line of print of the Output Report. The field is right-justified.

OL or Channel Number (Columns 23 through 24)

The character OL are the abbreviation used for *Overflow Line*.

Subdivisions 3 through 12 will not be discussed in this text.

RPG EXTENSION AND LINE COUNTER SPECIFICATIONS

GX21-9091-2 UM/050*
Printed in U.S.A.

IBM International Business Machine Corporation

| Programmer | | Date | | Punching Instruction | Graphic | | | | | | Card Electro Number | | | | Page | | of | Program Identification | 75 76 77 78 79 80 |
| --- | | --- | | --- | Punch | | | | | | | | | | | | _ | | |

Extension Specifications

E	Line	Form Type	Record Sequence of the Chaining File / Number of the Chaining Field / From Filename	To Filename	Table or Array Name	Number of Entries Per Record	Number of Entries Per Table or Array	Length of Entry	P/B/L/R	Decimal Positions	Sequence (A/D)	Table or Array Name (Alternating Format)	Length of Entry	P/B/L/R	Decimal Positions	Sequence A/D)	Comments
3 4 5	6	7 8	9 10 11 12 13 14 15 16 17 18	19 20 21 22 23 24 25 26	27 28 29 30 31 32	33 34 35	36 37 38 39	40 41 42	43	44	45	46 47 48 49 50 51	52 53 54	55	56	57	58 59 60 61 62 63 64 65 66 67 68 69 70 71 72 73 74
0 1		E															
0 2		E															
0 3		E															
0 4		E															
0 5		E															
0 6		E															
0 7		E															
0 8		E															
		E															
		E															

Line Counter Specifications

L	Line	Form Type	Filename	1 Line Number	FL or Channel Number	2 Line Number	OL or Channel Number	3 Line Number	Channel Number	4 Line Number	Channel Number	5 Line Number	Channel Number	6 Line Number	Channel Number	7 Line Number	Channel Number	8 Line Number	Channel Number	9 Line Number	Channel Number	10 Line Number	Channel Number	11 Line Number	Channel Number	12 Line Number	Channel Number
3 4 5		6	7 8 9 10 11 12 13 14	15 16 17	18 19	20 21 22	23 24	25 26 27	28 29	30 31 32	33 34	35 36 37	38 39	40 41 42	43 44	45 46 47	48 49	50 51 52	53 54	55 56 57	58 59	60 61 62	63 64	65 66 67	68 69	70 71 72	73 74
1 1		L																									
1 2		L																									
		L																									

Figure 45

134

PROJECT FIVE

SPECIFICATIONS: ADDRESS LABELS
ONE CARD – ONE UP

Periodically a firm mails to its present and prospective customers sales promotional materials and information pertaining to price changes or other pertinent information. To facilitate the mailing of such materials, the departments responsible for preparing promotional materials request mailing labels. The names and addresses needed for printing the labels may be obtained from the accounts receivable ledger and from customer "leads" or salesmen's contact forms completed by the sales representatives and the sales department.

Address labels are pressure sensitive, for the mucilage or glue that holds them onto the backing paper allows each label to be stripped or peeled off and then attached to an envelope or their mailing containers. The backing paper has pinfeed holes along each side so that the strip of labels can be easily fed through the printer device. The size of individual labels may run from 3½ inches by $^{15}/_{16}$ inch to 5 inches by $3^{15}/_{16}$ inch. Labels can also be color coded as an additional distinguishing characteristic.

Address labels are often packaged 5000 to a box in a fanfold arrangement similar to the stock paper used on the printer or they can be on a continuous roll. The labels are so positioned on the backing paper that they fit the vertical printing of six spaces to a vertical inch. The height of the label used must be taken into account, for addresses may require three or four lines of print to make them complete.

Notice, in Fig. 46, how the labels are positioned on the backing paper.

It should be understood that when customer numbers are assigned, they are usually assigned so that the names will be alphabetically arranged when the input data cards are sorted on the customer number field. When the labels are printed, the customer number is not printed as a part of the label. This suppression of the customer number field is accomplished by not coding the number on the Input or Output Specifications sheets. For this project the printing of the labels will be on stock paper rather than on actual labels. Also, instead of developing an Accounts Receivable card format for this project, we will use the Name and Address card format that has been used in previous projects.

135

INPUT FILE

Filename	Develop your own
Record Length	80 columns

OUTPUT FILE

Filename	Develop your own
Record Length	120 print positions

The coding on the Output Specifications sheet must be such as to allow for three detail lines of print from one input record. See Fig. 47.

In Fig. 47 it should be noted that

1. After line 01 or the 01 punch is detected in the carriage control tape, the name line is printed. If the printer uses line control, code a Line Counter Specifications sheet to conform to the label length used.

2. The input Record Identifying Indicator was coded as the 01 Indicator and is used to print each line.

3. The printer was advanced one space after each line of print.

4. Three lines are printed for each input record. The printer will advance to line 1 or channel 1 on the first line of print.

The following additional specifications should be taken into account before development of this program is begun.

- The label length and height must be known for proper spacing.

- Develop a Print Chart for the output. Use the Print Chart on page 456.

- Code the program on the necessary coding sheets that are provided on pages 138 through 140.

- Keypunch the coded program.

- Assemble the Source Program in the sequence dictated by the computer configuration being used.

- Debug and compile the program.

- The Output Report should appear as illustrated in Fig. 46.

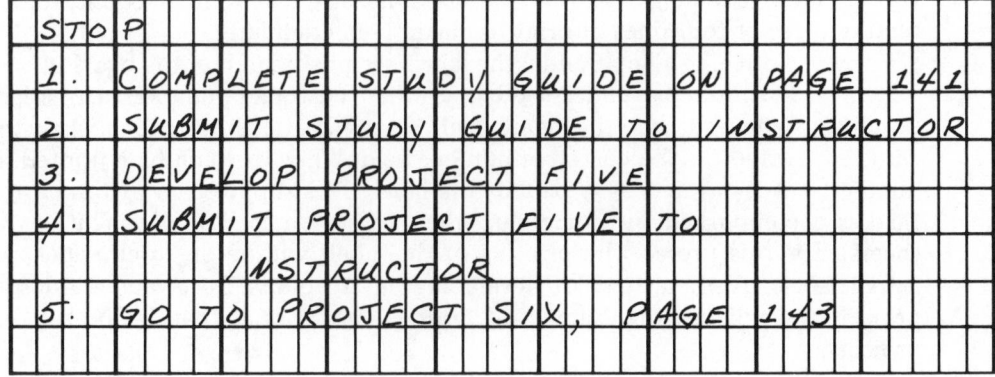

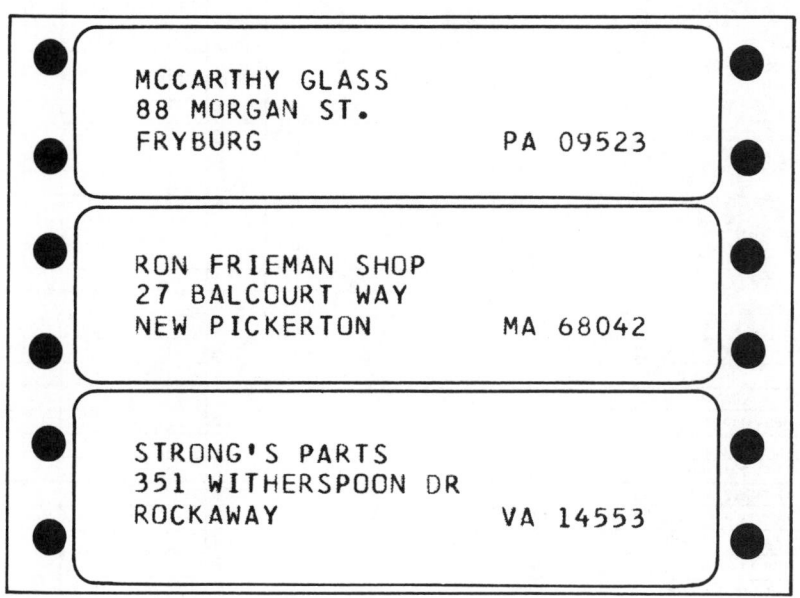

MCCARTHY GLASS
88 MORGAN ST.
FRYBURG   PA 09523

RON FRIEMAN SHOP
27 BALCOURT WAY
NEW PICKERTON   MA 68042

STRONG'S PARTS
351 WITHERSPOON DR
ROCKAWAY   VA 14553

Figure 46

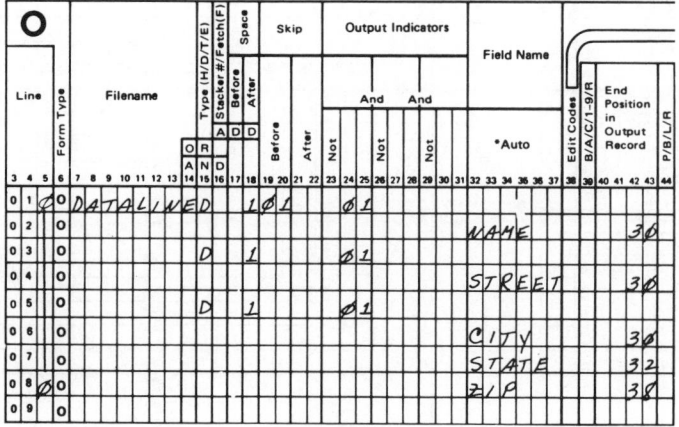

Figure 47

137

GX21-9092-3 UM/050*
Printed in U.S.A.

RPG CONTROL CARD AND FILE DESCRIPTION SPECIFICATIONS

IBM International Business Machine Corporation

Program		Punching Instruction	Graphic		Card Electro Number
			Punch		
Programmer	Date				

* No. of forms per pad may very slightly

Page [ ] of [ ] — Program Identification: 75 76 77 78 79 80

Control Card Specifications

Refer to the specific System Reference Library manual for actual entries.

H Form Type — Line

Control Card fields (columns 7–74):
Core Size to Compile, Object Output, Listing Options, Core Size to Execute, Debug, MFCM Stacking Sequence, Inverted Print, 360/20 2501 Buffer, Number Of Print Positions, Alternate Collating Sequence, Address to Start, Work Tapes, Overlay Open, Overlap Printer, Binary Search, Tape Error, 2152 Checking, Inquiry, Read/Write/Compute, Keyboard Output, Model 20, Sign Handling, 1P Forms Position, Indicator Setting, File Translation, Punch MFCU Zeros, Nonprint Characters, Table Load Halt, Shared I/O, Field Print, Formatted Core Dump, RPG to RPG II Conversion

File Description Specification

F Form Type — Line

File Description fields (columns 7–74):
Filename, File Type, File Designation, End of File, Sequence, File Format, Block Length, Record Length, Mode of Processing, Length of Key Field or of Record Address Field, Record Address Type, Type of File Organization or Additional Area, Overflow Indicator, Key Field Starting Location, Extension Code E/L, Device, Symbolic Device, Labels S/N/E/M, Name of Label Exit, Extent Exit for DAM, Core Index, Continuation Lines, Option, Entry, File Addition/Unordered, Number of Tracks for Cylinder Overflow, Number of Extents, Tape Rewind, File Condition U1-U8

I/O/U/C/D, P/S/C/R/T/D, E, A/D, F/V/S/M/D, L/R, A/P/I/K, I/D/T or 2, K, S/N/E/M, A/U, R/U/N

138

RPG INPUT SPECIFICATIONS

IBM International Business Machine Corporation

GX21-9094-2 U/M 050*
Printed in U.S.A.

| Program | | | | |
| Programmer | | | Date | |

Punching Instruction — Graphic / Punch

Card Electro Number

Page 1 2 of ___

Program Identification 75 76 77 78 79 80

Line	Form Type	Filename	Sequence	Number (1-N)	Option (O)	Record Identifying Indicator or **	Record Identification Codes 1 Position / Not (N) / C/Z/D / Character	Record Identification Codes 2 Position / Not (N) / C/Z/D / Character	Record Identification Codes 3 Position / Not (N) / C/Z/D / Character	Stacker Select	P/B/L/R	Field Location From / To	Decimal Positions	Field Name	Control Level (L1-L9)	Matching Fields or Changing Fields	Field Record Relation	Field Indicators Plus / Minus / Zero or Blank	
3 4	5 6	7 8 9 10 11 12	13 14(AND) 15(OR) 16	17	18	19 20	21 22 23 24 25 26 27	28 29 30 31 32 33 34	35 36 37 38 39 40 41	42	43	44 45 46 47 / 48 49 50 51	52	53 54 55 56 57 58	59 60	61 62	63 64	65 66 / 67 68 / 69 70	71 72 73 74
0 1	I																	
0 2	I																	
0 3	I																	
0 4	I																	
0 5	I																	
0 6	I																	
0 7	I																	
0 8	I																	
0 9	I																	
1 0	I																	
1 1	I																	
1 2	I																	
1 3	I																	
1 4	I																	
1 5	I																	
1 6	I																	
1 7	I																	
1 8	I																	
1 9	I																	
2 0	I																	

139

IBM   International Business Machine Corporation

GX21-9090-2 U/M 050*
Printed in U.S.A.

Program
Programmer
Date

Punching Instruction
Graphic
Punch

Card Electro Number

Page □ 1 □ 2 of ___

Program Identification
75 76 77 78 79 80

O

Line | Form Type | Filename | Type (H/D/T/E) | Stacker #/Fetch(F) | Space | Skip | Output Indicators | Field Name | Edit Codes | End Position in Output Record | P/B/L/R | Constant or Edit Word

	Commas	Zero Balances to Print	No Sign	CR	–
	Yes	Yes	1	A	J
	Yes	No	2	B	K
	No	Yes	3	C	L
	No	No	4	D	M

X = Remove Plus Sign
Y = Date Field Edit
Z = Zero Suppress

140

STUDY GUIDE

Date _____   Name_____

DIRECTIONS: *Answer the following questions in the spaces provided. Your answers should indicate the depth of understanding that you have toward the concepts and definitions presented. If there is insufficient space provided for your answer, complete your answer on the reverse side of the Study Guide.*

1. Explain the general makeup of a "one-up" label.

2. Explain the difference between a printer using a carriage control tape to govern form ejection as opposed to one using the Line Counter Specifications sheet entries form ejection.

3. Explain columns 7 through 24 of the Line Counter Specifications sheet.

PROJECT SIX

SPECIFICATIONS: ADDRESS LABELS
ONE CARD – THREE UP

Whenever labels are to be printed, it is advisable to print more than one set. This project is a slight modification of Project Five in that three sets of labels will be printed at one time. Therefore in computer language the project is known as a "Three-up" program.

Since only 35 print positions were used to print the One up label routine, this project will utilize another 73 positions of the printer. In other words, each label will utilize a column of 35 print positions in width. The placement of each of the columns will be governed by the placement of the label forms on the backing sheet.

Three-up labels are also pressure sensitive. The backing paper (in most cases) is approximately 11 inches wide between the pinwheel holes. Vertically, the backing paper allows for the placement of 12 complete labels (less if the label form is more than $15/16$ inch vertically). It should be noted that these calculations are approximate in that different label manufacturers allow for sizes that they specify. So as a programmer you will need to adjust the End Position in the Output Record in order to meet the specifications of the manufacturer whose labels you are using.

The size of individual labels may vary from 3½ inches by $15/16$ inch to 5 inches by $3\,15/16$ inch — three wide across the backing paper. Since they are three wide, they are usually packaged in amounts of 15,000 labels per box in a fanfold arrangement.

After the printing of the labels has been completed, the three sets can be easily separated because the backing paper is perforated between label columns one and two and between label columns two and three.

NEW CONCEPTS

✱PLACE

✱PLACE (Columns 32 through 37)

✱PLACE is a special reserved word that allows a programmer to have the same data of a record printed or written on several locations of the print line of the Output

Report. The controlling factor where the printing is to be placed is specified by the number coded in the End Position in the Output Record Field on the Output Specifications sheet.

The rules that govern the use of *PLACE are listed below.

1. *PLACE is coded after the field name that is going to be printed in different locations on the print line.

2. *PLACE must be coded for each print location of the data that is being printed.

3. When *PLACE is used, a specified end printing position must be coded in the End Position.

4. Whenever *PLACE is used, the leftmost position of the field being moved is always assumed to be position 1.

5. When using *PLACE, the programmer must be certain that the number coded in the End Position does not cause an overlapping of the printed data.

In Fig. 49, observe how the labels are positioned on the backing paper. Also notice how the programmer diagrammed the Print Chart by using the labels as a key for proper placement.

When developing the Print Chart layout, the programmer will allow for

1. One blank space between the ending print position of the CITY name and the two-letter STATE abbreviation.

2. One blank space between the ending print position of the abbreviated STATE name and the ZIP code number.

The object of this project is to

1. Print the NAME field of the input record in three different locations on the print line.

2. Advance the printer one line.

3. Print the STREET field of the input record directly beneath the NAME field in the three different locations on the print line.

4. Advance the printer one line.

5. Print the CITY-STATE-ZIP fields of the input record directly beneath the STREET field in the three different locations on the print line.

6. Advance the paper to the top of the next group of labels.

7. Repeat the process of instructions 1 through 6 as many times as necessary so as to produce the mailing labels for the user.

In order to have each field print in the three different locations, the coding must be in the following order.

1. The Print Chart indicates that the ending positions for the NAME fields will be 23, 60, and 96. Since this is the first detail line of the labels, the coding will be as shown in Fig. 48, lines 010–040.

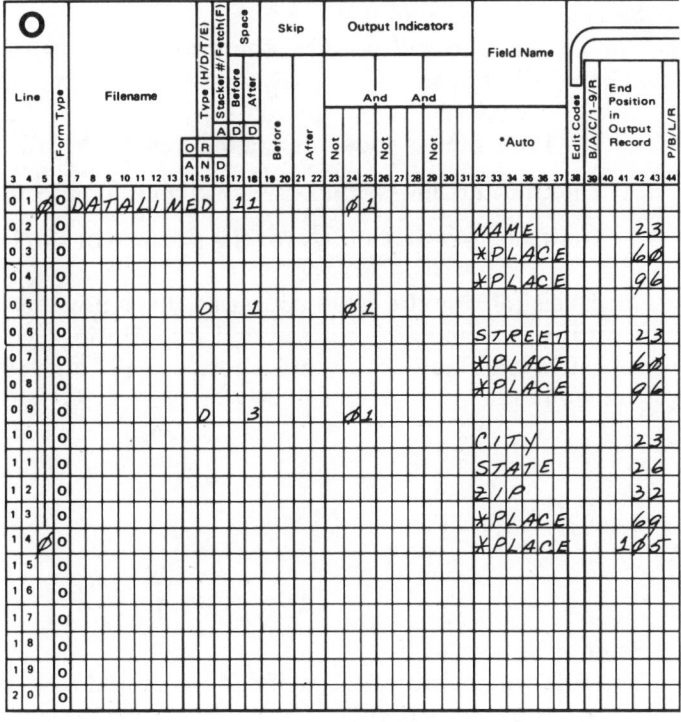

Figure 48

The coding of Fig. 48 will produce the first print line of each of the three labels — that is, the NAME of the addressee. Note that

a. The Print Line is coded as a detail line.

b. The Output Line is conditioned to print when the indicator is ON.

c. The spacing is coded to allow for advancement of a single space before and after the printing of the line.

2. The Print Chart also indicates that the ending print positions for the STREET fields will be 23, 60, and 96. Since this is the second detail line of the labels, the coding will be as shown in Fig. 48, lines 050–080.

Such coding will produce the second print line of each of the three labels — that is, the STREET of the addressee. Note that

1. The Print Line is coded as a detail line.

2. The Output Line is conditioned to print when the indicator is ON.

3. The spacing is coded to allow for advancement of a single space on the printer.

4. The Print Chart indicates that the ending positions for the CITY, STATE, and ZIP fields will be

a. 23, 60, and 96 for the City.

b. 26, 63, and 99 for the State.

c. 32, 69, and 105 for the Zip.

145

See Fig. 48, lines 090–140.

The coding here will produce the third print line of each of the three labels — that is, the CITY, STATE, and ZIP of the addressee. Observe that

1. The Print Line is coded as a detail line.

2. The Output Line is conditioned when the indicator is ON.

3. The spacing coded allows for the advance of three spaces.

Three sets of labels (all for the same addressee) have now been coded to be printed. The next detail card is positioned to be read and the printing cycle is again completed. The process is repeated again and again until all the detail cards for the addressees have been read by the computer.

INPUT FILE

Same as Project Five.

OUTPUT FILE

Same as Project Five.

The following additional specifications should be taken into account before development of this program is begun.

• Develop a Print Chart for the output. Use the Print Chart on page 456.

• Code the necessary additions on the coding sheet provided on page 148.

• Keypunch the coded data.

• Assemble the Source Program in the sequence dictated by the computer configuration being used.

• Use the detail cards punched for Project Five as the detail cards for this project.

• Debug and compile the program.

• The Output Report should appear as illustrated on page 147.

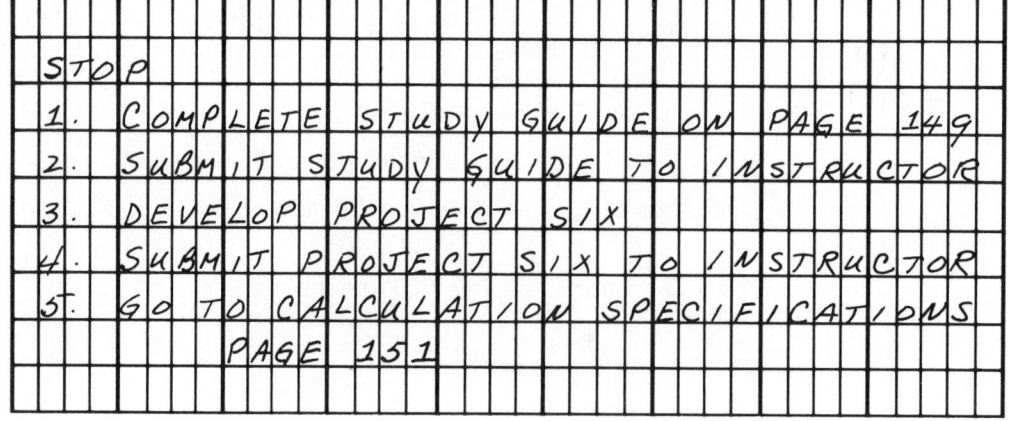

```
STOP
1.  COMPLETE STUDY GUIDE ON PAGE 149
2.  SUBMIT STUDY GUIDE TO INSTRUCTOR
3.  DEVELOP PROJECT SIX
4.  SUBMIT PROJECT SIX TO INSTRUCTOR
5.  GO TO CALCULATION SPECIFICATIONS
        PAGE 151
```

147

EDDIE'S
2222 GREAT TREE DR
MERSER   ND 78451

BILL BUXTON'S
11 FLAVER PLACE
WASHINGTON   PA 09002

DUDLEY'S PLANT CTR
668 DRIVEWAY RD
FLUGLETON   OH 42253

EDDIE'S
2222 GREAT TREE DR
MERSER   ND 78451

BILL BUXTON'S
11 FLAVER PLACE
WASHINGTON   PA 09002

DUDLEY'S PLANT CTR
668 DRIVEWAY RD
FLUGLETON   OH 42253

EDDIE'S
2222 GREAT TREE DR
MERSER   ND 78451

BILL BUXTON'S
11 FLAVER PLACE
WASHINGTON   PA 09002

DUDLEY'S PLANT CTR
668 DRIVEWAY RD
FLUGLETON   OH 42253

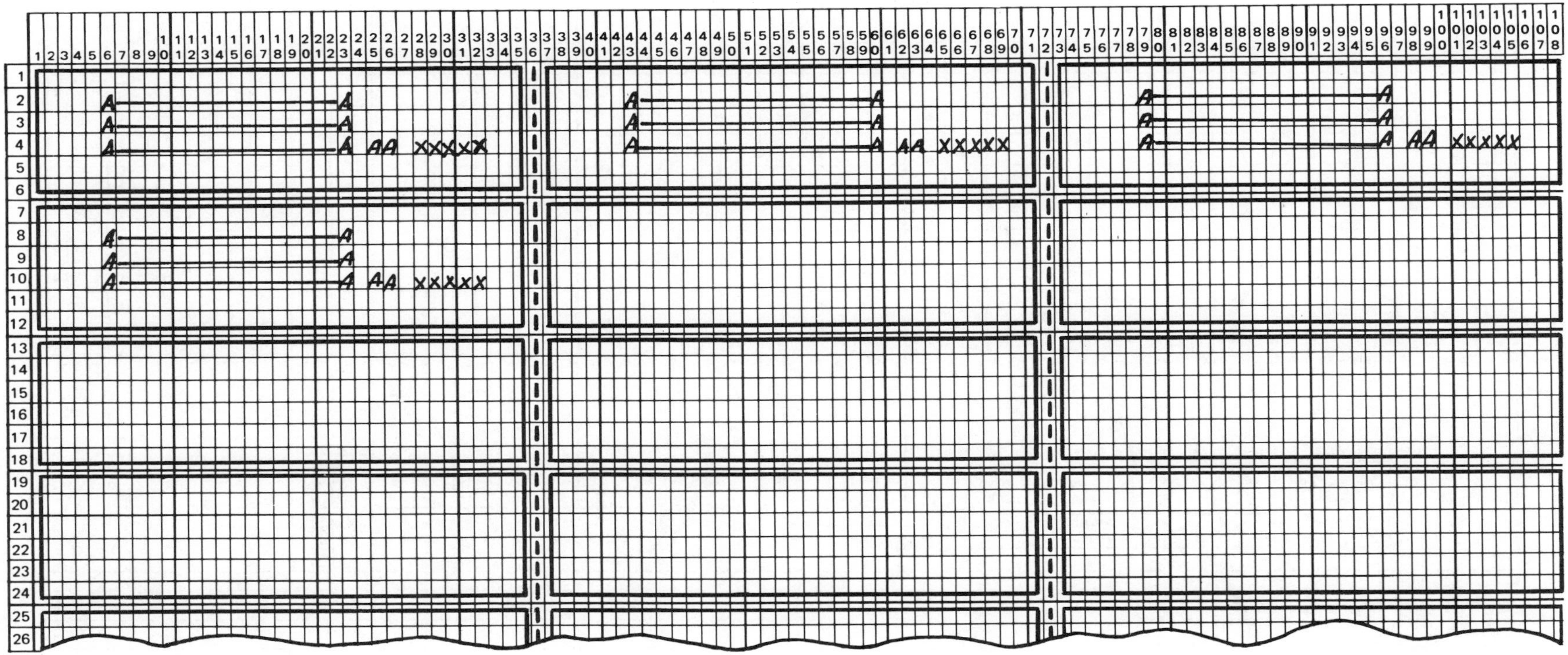

Figure 49

IBM

International Business Machine Corporation

RPG   OUTPUT   SPECIFICATIONS

GX21-9090-2 U/M 050*
Printed in U.S.A.

Program _____

Programmer _____   Date _____

Punching Instruction — Graphic / Punch

Card Electro Number

Page [1] of [2]

Program Identification: 75 76 77 78 79 80

Commas	Zero Balances to Print	No Sign	CR	−
Yes	Yes	1	A	J
Yes	No	2	B	K
No	Yes	3	C	L
No	No	4	D	M

X = Remove Plus Sign
Y = Date Field Edit
Z = Zero Suppress

Constant or Edit Word

Edit Codes

B/A/C/1-9/R

End Position in Output Record

P/B/L/R

Field Name   *Auto

Output Indicators — And — Not / And — Not / Not

Skip — After / Before

Space — After / Before

Stacker #/Fetch(F)

Type (H/D/T/E)   OR / AND

Filename

Form Type

Line

O

Date _____   Name_____

DIRECTIONS: *Answer the following questions in the spaces provided. Your answers should indicate the depth of understanding that you have toward the concepts and definitions presented. If there is insufficient space provided for your answer, complete your answer on the reverse side of the Study Guide.*

1. Explain the use of the reserved word *PLACE as a programming aid.

2. Explain why it is advisable to print more than one set of labels at a time.

3. Explain the layout of three-up labels on the backing paper.

CALCULATION SPECIFICATIONS

Calculations or operations coded on the CALCULATION SPECIFICATIONS sheet (see page 164) will perform manipulations of data during the execution of an RPG program. A detailed explanation of exactly when calculations are performed during the RPG cycle is explained in Appendix A.

Each calculation can be conditioned by indicators being set ON or OFF during the time when input is read into the computer. Also, calculations can be conditioned by the indicators set in other calculations.

Five basic types of operations can be performed in the RPG Language. They are ARITHMETICAL, MOVE, COMPARE, LOGICAL, and INPUT-OUTPUT. Each of these operations will be discussed in detail as they are needed in each project. However, a brief description of each follows.

ARITHMETICAL

This type of operation will perform arithmetic on numeric data. Add, subtract, multiply, and divide are the four operands covered by this basic type.

MOVE

This type of operation will cause data to be moved from one data field to another within the program.

COMPARE

Comparing two data fields will cause conditions that will set indicators On or Off. The indicators can then be used to perform other calculations or output to occur.

LOGICAL

An operation that will cause the program to branch around within the program itself is called logical operations.

INPUT-OUTPUT

These operations will perform the reading of input records or the writing of output records. The RPG cycle (Appendix A) determines when a record can be read or written under normal conditions. However, input–output operations can be used by the programmer to give added flexibility to RPG programming.

The coding of the Calculation Specifications sheet will be described along with the usage of the different types of operations. The relationships of the coding fields depend on the operation being performed.

FIELDS

Indicators (Columns 9 through 17)

This field is subdivided into three equal subfields. This field takes the same responsibility as the Output Indicators on the Output Specifications sheet.

Calculations need not be performed on every RPG cycle. Using the indicators to condition certain operations to occur can be coded for this purpose. Up to three different indicators can be used to condition an operation on one line of the Calculation Specifications sheet. In addition, columns 7 and 8 can be coded to cause an AND or OR relationship between indicators. See Fig. 50.

In Fig. 50, line 010, the coding states that when Indicator 01 is ON, perform the operation that is coded. That is, ADD Field B to Field A, giving the answer in Field C.

In Fig. 50, line 030, the coding states that when Indicators 01 and 03 but N (not) 02 are ON, perform the operation.

In Fig. 50, lines 050 and 060, the coding states that when Indicators 01, 02, 03, 04, and 05 are all ON, perform the operation.

In Fig. 50, lines 080 and 090, the coding states that when Indicators 01 and 02 OR 03 and 04 are ON, perform the operation.

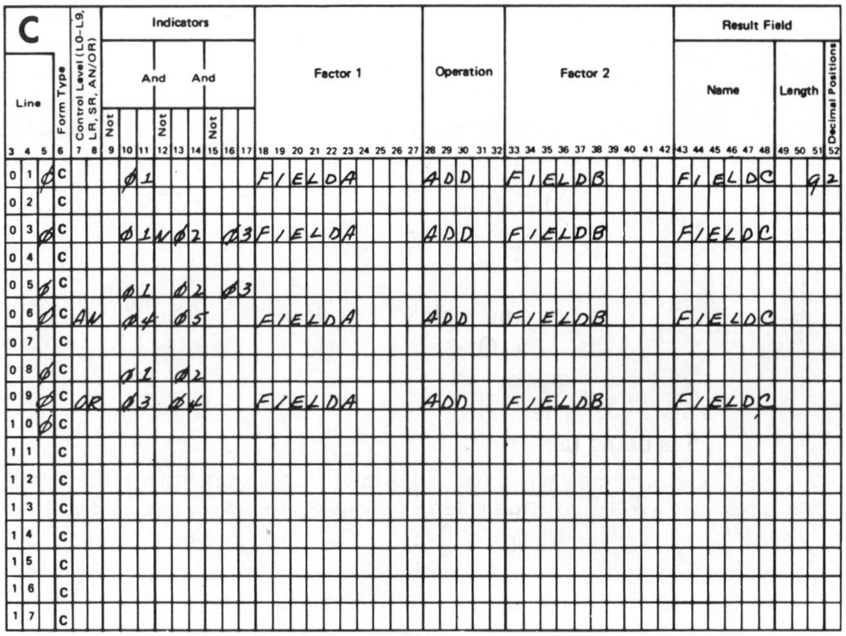

Figure 50

Operation (Columns 28 through 32)

The Operation field is the most important field of the Calculation Specifications sheet. It is ALWAYS coded. The operation to be performed on a line of calculation is coded in this field. The Operation field is left-justified. The coding must begin in column 28.

Factor (Columns 18 through 42)

There are two Factor fields.

Factor 1   Columns 18 through 27

Factor 2   Columns 33 through 42

The factors or data fields that will have operations performed on them or with them will be coded in FACTOR 1 and/or FACTOR 2. Data coded in the Factor fields is always left-justified. The data coded in Factor 1 or Factor 2 can be either a data field name or constant data. The constant data may be numeric or a literal. A literal is always coded between quote marks ('), commonly known as a literal sign.

Examples of correct data in Factor 1 or Factor 2 are shown in Fig. 51.

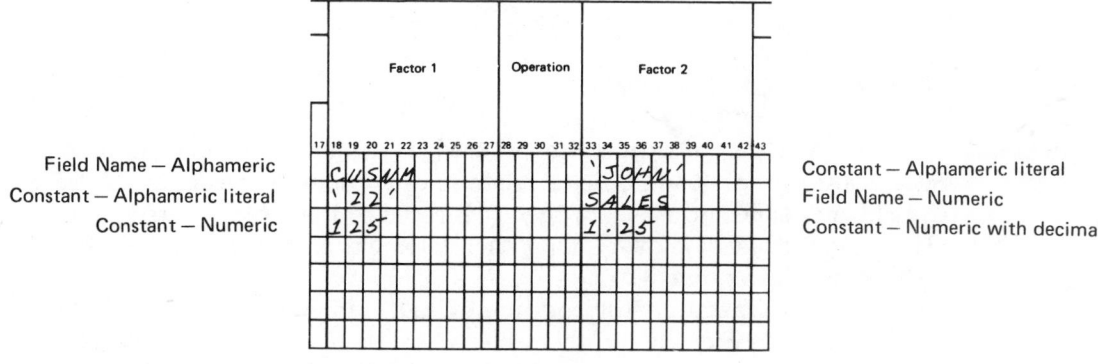

Figure 51

Result Field (This field is subdivided into two subfields.)

Name   Columns 43 through 48

Length   Columns 49 through 51

Name: The Name field is the field that will receive or hold the result of the operations specified in the Operation field. If it is used, it is ALWAYS a data field name, and the data field depends on the operation being performed. It can be alphameric or numeric. This field is left-justified and must begin with an alphabetic character. If the Result Field is being used for the first time in a program, its length must be defined.

Length: The purpose of the Length field is to specify the length of the field defined in the Result Field Name. If the Result Field is numeric, then the decimal positions must be defined in column 52. For example, a data field called FIELDC, defined as a result field for the first time, would have its length and number of decimal positions coded as shown in Fig. 50, line 010. Here we have a field with a length of nine-digit places, with two decimal positions to the right of a decimal point. It is a numeric field.

153

Resulting Indicators (Columns 54 through 59)

This field is subdivided into three subfields for arithmetic operations.

1. Plus

2. Minus

3. Zero

Checking the results of an operation could be important in determining which operation should be performed next. The results of an arithmetic operation could be positive, negative, or zero. To determine the condition of the result, the Resulting Indicators must be used. See Fig. 52, line 010. Here the coding shows that Field A is to be added to Field B, giving the result in Field C. The result in Field C would be checked further to determine whether it was a positive result. If so, Resulting Indicator 10 would be turned ON. Indicator 11 would be turned ON if the result were negative or minus. Indicator 12 would be turned ON if the result were zero.

All three Resulting Indicators, Plus, Minus or Zero, would not need to be coded as shown in Fig. 52. One field, or two fields in any combination, could be coded as needed. For instance, the addition of two positive fields together would never cause a minus condition; therefore indicator 11 in the minus column would not be coded.

CODING ARITHMETIC OPERATIONS

Algebraic notation can be used to advantage to explain how the Calculation Specifications sheet coding fields relate to each other. For example, A + B = C states that if Field A is added to Field B, then it is equal to Field C or, stated another way, Field A plus Field B equals Field C. Coding this statement on the Calculation Specifications sheet is shown in Fig. 52, line 010.

The Operation for addition is ADD. In Fig. 52, line 010, Field A would be added (ADD) to Field B and the result would be placed in a field called Field C. Remember that if Field C were being defined for the first time, its length and decimal positions MUST BE defined. Such was the case in Fig. 52, line 010.

In Fig. 52, line 030, A – B = C: Field A minus (SUB) Field B equals Field C.

The operation for Subtraction is (SUB). Fig. 52, line 030 shows that Field B is to be subtracted from Field A, giving the result in Field C. The operation SUB *always* causes Factor 2 to be subtracted from Factor 1.

Clearly, in Fig. 52, line 050, reversing the fields in the factor areas would produce a different result.

The operation for Multiplication is MULT. In the example shown in Fig. 52, line 070, A × B = C states that Field A times (multiplied) Field B equals Field C. The coding in Fig. 52, line 070 will cause Field A to be multiplied (MULT) by Field B and give the result to Field C.

The operation for Division is DIV. In Fig. 52, line 090, A ÷ B = C states that Field A is to be divided by Field B and that the quotient (answer) equals Field C. Factor 1 is ALWAYS divided by Factor 2.

The four basic arithmetic operations ADD, SUB, MULT, and DIV have now been discussed. In every case, we neglected to say what happened to Factor 1 and Factor 2 in these operations. NOTHING happens. In each case, Factor 1 and Factor 2 remain the same. That is, they do not change because of an arithmetic operation. In other words, the data represented by these fields did not change as the result of the operation coded in the Operation field.

154

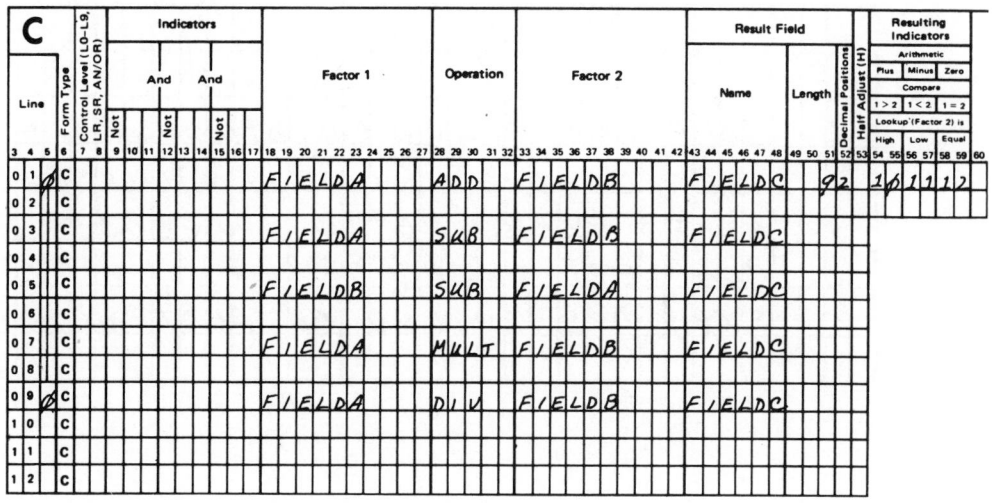

Figure 52

What would happen when the programmer coded the Calculation Specifications sheet as shown in Fig. 53? Here it states that Field A is to be added to Field B, thus giving Field A. This coding is correct. Field B is added to Field A and the result is placed in Field A. The contents of Field A before the operation is performed are replaced by new contents after the operation is performed.

If, for example, the programmer wished to add up the Field B's of each detail record read into the program, the coding shown in Fig. 53 would cause Field B to be added to the result of adding Field B to the result before it. Clear? Refer to the table below. After reading records 1, 2, 3, and 4, the result of adding Field B from each record to Field A is 5 + 2 + 8 + 7 = 22.

	Field B		Field A before Operation		Field A after Operation
Record 1	5	+	0	=	5
Record 2	2	+	5	=	7
Record 3	8	+	7	=	15
Record 4	7	+	15	=	22

The same method can be used for SUB, MULT, and DIV. On page 163 is an exercise that should be coded to see that the basics of the arithmetic operations are thoroughly understood. Remember, the results that the programmer desires in each case, are, of course, determined by the design of the overall program or application.

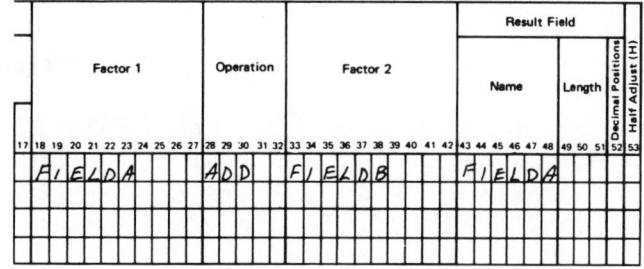

Figure 53

```
STOP
1.  COMPLETE STUDY GUIDE ON PAGE 157
2.  SUBMIT STUDY GUIDE TO INSTRUCTOR
3.  GO TO EXERCISE 14, PAGE 159
4.  COMPLETE EXERCISE 14
5.  SUBMIT EXERCISE TO INSTRUCTOR
```

STUDY GUIDE

Date _____   Name_____

DIRECTIONS: *Answer the following questions in the spaces provided. Your answers should indicate the depth of understanding that you have toward the concepts and definitions presented. If there is insufficient space provided for your answer, complete your answer on the reverse side of the Study Guide.*

1. Briefly explain the five basic types of operations that can be performed in the RPG language.

2. Explain the importance of the Factor fields on the Calculations Specifications sheet.

3. Explain the relationship between the Factor fields and each of the arithmetic coding operations.

4. Explain how the Resulting Indicators — Plus, Minus, and Zero — work.

EXERCISE 14

Date _____   Name_____

TRUE–FALSE: *Each of the following statements is either true or false. Indicate your choice in the Answers column by encircling "T" for a true answer or "F" for a false answer.*

Answers

1. Address labels are pressure sensitive   T   F

2. Labels come in only one standard size   T   F

3. The printing of labels is six lines to a vertical inch   T   F

4. Customer numbers must be printed on each label   T   F

5. The Output Indicator coded on the Output Specifications sheet must be ON to condition the output of a Detail line.   T   F

6. Calculations can be conditioned by indicators being set On or Off   T   F

7. The five basic types of operations that can be performed in RPG language are Arithmetical, Move, Compare, Logical, and Input-Output   T   F

8. The RPG cycle determines when a record can be read or written   T   F

9. The Operation field on the Calculation Specifications sheet need not always contain an operand   T   F

10. Data coded in either Factor 1 or Factor 2 can be either a data name field or constant data   T   F

11. A literal need not be coded within quotes   T   F

12. The Result field holds the results of the operation specified in the Operation Field   T   F

13. The data field coded in Factor 2 is added to the data field coded in Factor 1   T   F

14. The operand for multiplication is MUL   T   F

15. Whenever an arithmetical operation is performed, the data in Factor 1 is unchanged but the data in Factor 2 is changed   T   F

16. The results of an arithmetic operation could be positive, zero, or negative   T   F

17. Calculations must be performed on every RPG cycle   T   F

18. Up to three different indicators can be used to condition an operation on one line of the Calculation Specifications sheet   T   F

19. The maximum number of print lines or spaces that the printer can be advanced at one time is three   T   F

20. Three separate data cards must be used to print one "three-up" label   T   F

COMPLETION: *Fill in the blank with the appropriate word or words.*

1, 2. Name and address for printing labels are obtained from the _____ _____ ledger or from salesmen's contacts called _____ .

3. Label forms are fed through the printing device with the aid of _____ _____ .

4. The vertical print spacing of labels is usually _____ lines per vertical inch.

5. Overflow will take place on line _____ of a standard sheet of stock paper.

6. The Object Program assumes that there are _____ lines per printer page if no Line Counter Specifications sheet is included in the Source Program.

7. There are _____ subdivisions to the Line Specifications sheet.

8, 9. When the Line Counter Specifications sheet is used, the length of the form is expressed in _____ rather than _____ .

10. When the programmer desires the same data to be printed or written in several locations of the print line, _____ is coded in the Field Name of the Output Specifications sheet.

11. The controlling factor of where the printing of the field is to be placed on the print line is specified by the number coded in the _____ .

12, 13. Subdivision 1 of the Line Counter Specifications sheet is used to signify the _____ , whereas Subdivision 2 is used to signify _____ _____ .

```
STOP
1.   GO TO CALCULATION SPECIFICATIONS
        SHEET TEST, PAGE 161
2.   COMPLETE CALCULATION
        SPECIFICATIONS SHEET TEST
3.   SUBMIT TEST TO INSTRUCTOR
4.   GO TO PROJECT SEVEN, PAGE 169
```

CALCULATION SPECIFICATIONS SHEET TEST

Date _____   Name _____

PART I. *True or False (5 points each). Write the letter "T" for a true answer and the letter "F" for a false answer.*

Answers

1. Calculations can be conditioned by indicators being set ON or OFF _____

2. The operand for Division is DIVIS _____

3. The operation field is always coded on the Calculation Specifications sheet _____

4. In the division operation, Factor 2 is divided by Factor 1 _____

5. In the operation below, Factor 2 will be subtracted from Factor 1.

Factor 1	*Operation*	*Factor 2*	*Result*
AMOUNT	SUB	TAX	NETPAY

   _____

6. In the operation below using MULT, Factor 1 and Factor 2 can be interchanged.

Factor 1	*Operation*	*Factor 2*	*Result*
HOURS	MULT	RATE	PAY

   _____

7. The five basic types of operations that can be performed in the RPG language include Arithmetic, Move, Compare, Input-Output, and Replace _____

8. The data coded in the factor fields can be either a field name or a constant _____

9. The coding below is a sample of accumulative addition.

Factor 1	*Operation*	*Factor 2*	*Result*
SOCTAX	ADD	FEDTAX	TOTTAX

   _____

10. The data coded in the Result field can be either a field name or a constant _____

PART II. *Application problem (50 points). Using the following data, code the problem on the specifications sheets on pages 165–168. Use the Print Chart on page 456 to diagram the output.*

1. A report is to be printed with the information from the following formatted data.

2. Code   CC 1–1

Employee Name	CC 2–20
Employee Code	CC 21–25
Rate	CC 26–30 (two decimal positions)
Hours	CC 40–41
Taxes	CC 56–60 (two decimal positions)

3. The input file name will be developed by you.

4. The output file name will be developed by you.

5. The input file has 80 positions, the output file has 120 positions.

6. Use the appropriate Overflow Indicators.

161

7. Include the following calculations in the program:

   a. Rate MULT Hours = Gross Pay

   b. Gross Pay SUB Taxes = Net Pay

   c. Produce an accumulated Total Net Pay (use the net pay field).

8. Design a Printer Spacing Chart, using the necessary information from your Input and Calculation Specifications sheets. The major heading should read

BRASS TACKS INC.

WEEKLY PAYROLL REPORT

9. Provide appropriate columnar headings, detail line, editing symbols, and total lines of print.

ARITHMETIC EXERCISE

DIRECTIONS: *Use the coding sheet on page 164 to code the necessary statements to solve each of the equations.*

1. $A + B - C = D$

2. $A + B + C = D$

3. $(A \times B) - C = D$

4. $A + B (A + B) = D$

5. $C - A - B = C$

6. $D + A = D$

7. $(A \div A) \times (D \times A) = D$

8. $(A \times B) + (A \times B) = C$

9. $((A \times B) - C) - C = D$

10. $(A + B) \div (A - B) \times 100 = D$

IBM International Business Machine Corporation

GX21-9093-2 UM/050* Printed in U.S.A.
*No. of forms per pad may vary slightly

RPG CALCULATION SPECIFICATIONS

Program			
Programmer		Date	

Punching Instruction: Graphic | Punch

Card Electro Number

Page □ 1 □ 2 of __

Program Identification: 75 76 77 78 79 80

Line	Form Type	Control Level (L0-L9, LR, SR, AN/OR)	Indicators (And, Not, And, Not, And, Not)	Factor 1	Operation	Factor 2	Result Field (Name, Length, Decimal Positions, Half Adjust (H))	Resulting Indicators (Arithmetic: Plus, Minus, Zero; Compare 1>2, 1<2, 1=2; Lookup (Factor 2) is High, Low, Equal)	Comments
0 1	C								
0 2	C								
0 3	C								
0 4	C								
0 5	C								
0 6	C								
0 7	C								
0 8	C								
0 9	C								
1 0	C								
1 1	C								
1 2	C								
1 3	C								
1 4	C								
1 5	C								
1 6	C								
1 7	C								
1 8	C								
1 9	C								
2 0	C								

RPG CONTROL CARD AND FILE DESCRIPTION SPECIFICATIONS

IBM International Business Machine Corporation

GX21-9092-3 UM/050*
Printed in U.S.A.

No. of forms per pad may very slightly

| Program | | Punching | Graphic | | | Card Electro Number | |
| Programmer | Date | Instruction | Punch | | | | |

Page [ ] 1 2 of [ ] [ ]

Program Identification [75 76 77 78 79 80]

Control Card Specifications

Refer to the specific System Reference Library manual for actual entries.

H	Form Type		Core Size to Compile	Object Output	Listing Options	Core Size to Execute	Debug	MFCM Stacking Sequence		Inverted Print	360/20 2501 Buffer	Number Of Print Positions	Alternate Collating Sequence	Model 20	Address to Start	Work Tapes	Overlay Open	Overlay Printer	Binary Search	Tape Error	2152 Checking	Inquiry	Read/Write/Compute	Keyboard Output	Sign Handling	1P Forms Position	Indicator Setting	File Translation	Punch MFCU Zeros	Nonprint Characters	Table Load Halt	Shared I/O	Field Print	Formatted Core Dump	RPG to RPG II Conversion
Line	3 4 5	6	7 8 9	10	11 12	13 14	15	16 17	18 19 20	21	22	23 24	25	26 27	28 29 30	31	32	33 34	35	36	37	38 Model 20	39	40	41	42	43	44	45	46 47	48	49	50	51 52 ... 74
0 1		H																																

File Description Specification

F	Form Type	Filename	File Type	File Designation	End of File	Sequence	File Format	Block Length	Record Length	Mode of Processing	Length of Key Field or of Record Address Field	Record Address Type	Type of File Organization or Additional Area	Overflow Indicator	Key Field Starting Location	Extension Code E/L	Device	Symbolic Device	Name of Label Exit		Extent Exit for DAM	Core Index	Continuation Lines		File Addition/Unordered	Number of Tracks for Cylinder Overflow	Number of Extents	Tape Rewind	File Condition U1-U8	
Line	3 4 5	6 7...14	15 I/O/U/C/D	16 P/S/C/R/T/D	17 E	18 A/D	19 F/V/S/M/D	20 21 22 23	24 25 26	27 28 L/R	29 30	31 A/P/I/K	32 I/D/T or 2	33 34	35 36 37 38	39	40...46	47...52	53 Labels S/N/E/M	54...58 K	59...65 A/U	66	Option	Entry	70 N/U/R	71...74
0 2	F																													
0 3	F																													
0 4	F																													
0 5	F																													
0 6	F																													
0 7	F																													
0 8	F																													
0 9	F																													
1 0	F																													

165

RPG INPUT SPECIFICATIONS

IBM International Business Machine Corporation

GX21-9094-2 U/M 050*
Printed in U.S.A.

Program		Punching Instruction	Graphic		Card Electro Number	Page 1 2 of	Program Identification 75 76 77 78 79 80
Programmer	Date		Punch				

A form showing columns for:

- Line (3-5)
- Form Type (6) — all rows marked **I**
- Filename (7-14)
- Sequence (7-13)
- OR / AND (14-16)
- Number (1-N) (17)
- Option (O) (18)
- Record Identifying Indicator or ** (19-20)
- Record Identification Codes:
  - 1: Position (21-24), Not (N) (25), C/Z/D (26), Character (27)
  - 2: Position (28-31), Not (N) (32), C/Z/D (33), Character (34)
  - 3: Position (35-38), Not (N) (39), C/Z/D (40), Character (41)
- Stacker Select (42)
- P/B/L/R (43)
- Field Location: From (44-47), To (48-51)
- Decimal Positions (52)
- Field Name (53-58)
- Control Level (L1-L9) (59-60)
- Matching Fields or Changing Fields (61-62)
- Field Record Relation (63-64)
- Field Indicators: Plus (65-66), Minus (67-68), Zero or Blank (69-70)
- (71-74)

Line numbers 01 through 20 listed in the Line column.

166

No. of forms per pad may vary slightly.

IBM International Business Machine Corporation

GX21-9093-2 UM/050* Printed in U.S.A.
*No. of forms per pad may vary slightly

RPG CALCULATION SPECIFICATIONS

Program

Programmer

Date

Punching Instruction

Graphic

Punch

Card Electro Number

Page [1] [2] of —

Program Identification   75 76 77 78 79 80

C																																									
Line	Form Type	Control Level (L0-L9, LR, SR, AN/OR)	Not	And	Not	And	Not	Indicators	Factor 1	Operation	Factor 2	Name	Length	Decimal Positions	Half Adjust (H)	Resulting Indicators	Comments

RPG OUTPUT SPECIFICATIONS

GX21-9090-2 U/M 050*
Printed in U.S.A.

IBM International Business Machine Corporation

Program		Punching Instruction	Graphic	Card Electro Number
Programmer	Date		Punch	

Page 1 2 of ___ Program Identification 75 76 77 78 79 80

O

Line (3 4 5)	Form Type (6)	Filename (7–13)	OR / AND (14–16)	Type (H/D/T/E) (15)	Stacker #/Fetch(F) (16)	Space Before (17)	Space After (18)	Skip Before (19 20)	Skip After (21 22)	Output Indicators: Not (23–25)	And: Not (26–28)	And: Not (29–31)	Field Name / *Auto (32–37)	Edit Codes (38)	B/A/C/1-9/R (39)	End Position in Output Record (40–43)	P/B/L/R (44)	Constant or Edit Word (45–70)	(71–74)
0 1	O																		
0 2	O																		
0 3	O																		
0 4	O																		
0 5	O																		
0 6	O																		
0 7	O																		
0 8	O																		
0 9	O																		
1 0	O																		
1 1	O																		
1 2	O																		
1 3	O																		
1 4	O																		
1 5	O																		
1 6	O																		
1 7	O																		
1 8	O																		
1 9	O																		
2 0	O																		
	O																		
	O																		
	O																		
	O																		
	O																		

Space: A D D

Commas	Zero Balances to Print	No Sign	CR	-
Yes	Yes	1	A	J
Yes	No	2	B	K
No	Yes	3	C	L
No	No	4	D	M

X = Remove Plus Sign
Y = Date Field Edit
Z = Zero Suppress

PROJECT SEVEN

Much insight pertinent to the buying habits of the customer can be obtained from an analysis of his purchase orders. The amount of credit extended is in direct relationship to his ability to pay and the promptness with which payment is made. Therefore an Invoice Register is produced periodically so that the sales of all customers for a given time period can be analyzed. In the process of analyzing a customer's account, the relationship of the selling date (date of invoice) to the date of the analysis statement is examined; the total amount of sales sold to each customer and the amount of State Tax, Shipping Charges, and Special Charges of each invoice are recorded.

A customer's purchase order is the source document used to generate a Sales Invoice. Each item of merchandise requested is listed on the invoice. Each invoice is then totaled. During any particular fiscal period a customer can generate several invoices. The formatted input card to be used for this project is shown in Fig. 54.

DETAIL CARD FIELDS

The Record Code IS field
(Columns 1 through 2)

This field is punched into the invoice summary card by the output of the invoice program. The field identifies this card as an *Invoice Summary* record. It is a constant; that is, it will be punched into all cards of this type.

The INVOICE NUMBER field
(Columns 3 through 8)

This is the preprinted number of the sales invoice. These numbers are in sequential order. The invoice number was assigned by the invoice program and is the same number printed on the actual invoices.

169

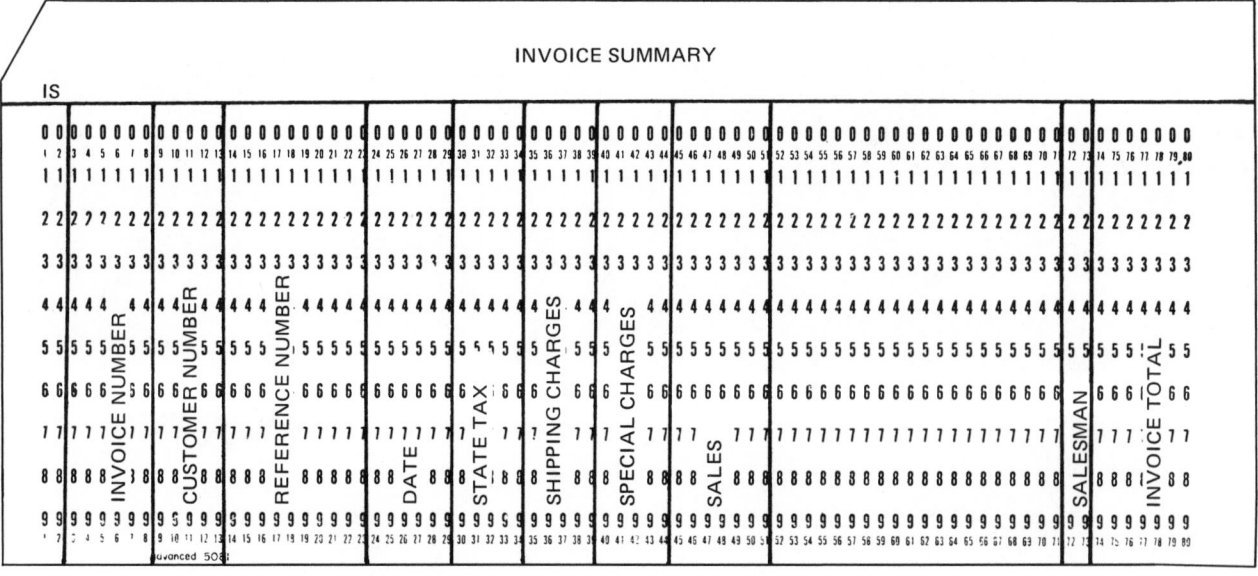

Figure 54

The CUSTOMER NUMBER field
(Columns 9 through 13)

This is the number assigned to a particular customer. If the customer purchases merchandise several times during the fiscal period or year, this same number is always used. It is the method used to alphabetize or to identify the customer name in the Accounts Receivable Ledger.

The REFERENCE NUMBER field
(Columns 14 through 23)

This is the number obtained from the purchase order submitted by the customer. This is the field that ties together the purchase order and the invoice of the seller. Since it is an alphabetic field, all punching should start in column 14.

The DATE field
(Columns 24 through 29)

This is the date that the invoice was issued. If any sales discount is to be given, this date is the one used for the necessary calculations.

The STATE TAX field
(Columns 30 through 34)

The data in this field represents the amount of tax that must be calculated on the Sales. The percentage used for this project is at the rate of 5%.

The SHIPPING CHARGES field
(Columns 35 through 39)

The data in this field represents the fee that is paid by the customer (buyer) to get the merchandise he purchased from the seller to his place of business. Another common term used for this field is Transportation Charges.

170

The SPECIAL CHARGES field
(Columns 40 through 44)

The data in this field represents the fee that is paid by the customer for special handling of merchandise, such as those items that would be breakable or perishable.

The SALES field (Columns 45 through 51)

The data in this field represents the actual selling price of the merchandise sold.

The SALESMAN field (Columns 72 through 73)

The number punched into this field is the number that has been assigned to the salesman who sold the merchandise for the PRINTREN GIFT SHOP.

The INVOICE TOTAL field
(Columns 74 through 80)

The data in this field represents the total amount of the invoice. The amount in this field represents the Sales amount added to any or all of the STATE TAX, SHIPPING CHARGES, and SPECIAL CHARGES fields.

NEW CONCEPTS

Input Specifications sheet
        Record Identification Codes

Output Specifications sheet
Y	Edit Code
L	Edit Code
J	Edit Code
T	Type Print Line
LR	Last Record

Calculation Specifications sheet
        Factor 1
        Operation
        Factor 2
        Result Field
        Name
        Length

INPUT SPECIFICATIONS
Record Identification Codes
(Columns 21 through 41)

This field is subdivided into three equal subfields: Subfield 1 - card columns 21 through 27. Subfield 2 - card columns 28 through 34; and Subfield 3 - card columns 35 through 41.

To ensure that all the detail cards are of the correct type, the identifying code punched into each card must be present in order to turn on the Record Identifying Indicator coded in columns 19 and 20. The special coding used for this check process is illustrated in Fig. 55.

The C's coded in columns 26 and 33 direct the computer to check the punching of the complete character in columns 15 and 16 of the input card. Indicator 09 will turn ON if the input card has an A and a B in columns 15 and 16, respectively.

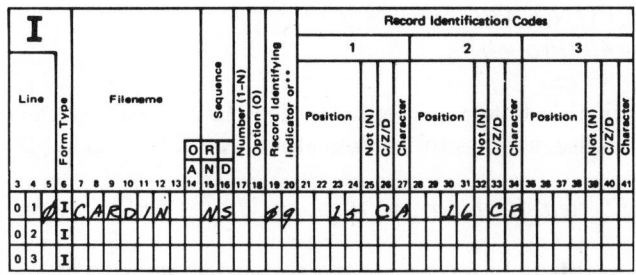

Figure 55

OUTPUT SPECIFICATIONS

Y Edit Code (Columns 38 through 38)

The Y Edit Code enables the programmer to code in editing symbols on the date field so that the results are easier to read. The Y must be coded in column 38. For example, one of the invoices of this project has the date of November 18, 19--. When coding with Y, the date would be printed out on the output report as 11/18/--. The two hyphens represent the current year.

On the Print Chart, the DATE field would need to be considered as an eight-position field because of the added slashes between the month-day and the day-year portion of the date. In Fig. 56, notice how the Y code is coded on the Output Specifications sheet to obtain the editing for the DATE field.

L Edit Code (Column 38 through 38)

The L Edit Code enables the programmer to have no commas with zero balances printed on the Output Report for numeric fields. This is indicated by an L being coded in column 38.

Note in Fig. 56 how the L code is coded on the Output Specifications sheet to obtain the editing for the STTAX field.

J Edit Code (Columns 38 through 38)

The J Edit Code enables the programmer to have comma(s) (correctly positioned), and the zero balance being printed.

In Fig. 56, note how the J code is coded on the Output Specifications sheet to obtain the editing for the SALES field.

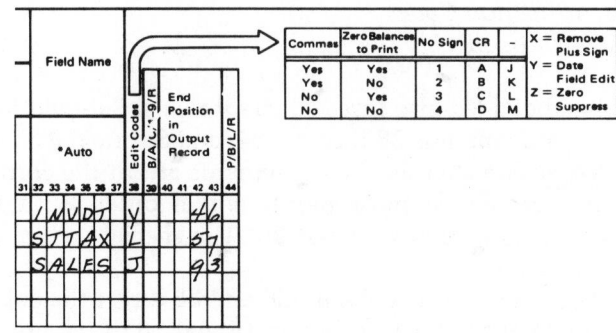

Figure 56

Type (H/D/T/E) (Columns 15 through 15)

Type T line is an Output Record type that describes total records. The type or classification of data contained in this total record is the result of a specific calculation(s) on detail record(s). After all the input records have been processed, totals need to be printed. In order to print a total line, the Output Specifications sheet must be coded with the proper instruction. Total lines are only printed at specified times. This step is accomplished by coding a T in column 15 on the Output Specifications sheet. Total lines should have additional spaces before and after them for better clarity. If the detail lines are single spaced, the printer is usually spaced forward two spaces or lines before the total line is printed. If the detail lines are double spaced, the printer is usually spaced forward three spaces of lines. Spacing before printing is accomplished by coding the digit (spaces to be skipped) in column 17.

Last Record (LR) (Columns 23 through 31)

If a total line is to be printed after all the input records have been processed, the coding of LR (last record) in one of the subfields of the Output Indicators field is necessary. Observe, in Fig. 57, how a total line is coded for printing on the same file as the detail line of printing. Notice that the Filename need not be coded again. This situation occurs because all the types of printing lines (Heading, Detail and Total) are on the Output printer file.

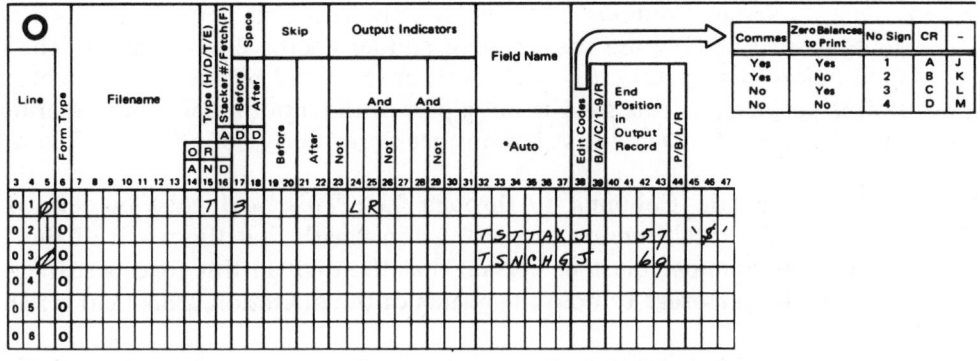

Figure 57

Editing $ Sign (Columns 45 through 70)

Dollar signs can be printed in a fixed position (same print column each time it is printed) or in a floating position. When the dollar sign ($) is coded to float, it will automatically be positioned to print in the print position IMMEDIATELY to the left of the high-order significant digit. In Fig. 57, line 020, observe how the $ is coded to float.

CALCULATION SPECIFICATIONS

Factor 1 (Columns 18 through 27)

In Fig. 58 the field name entered into this field by the programmer represents the total amount of State Taxes that has accumulated from each of the detail cards. The field name data coded in Factor 2 is added to this field. The field is left-justified.

173

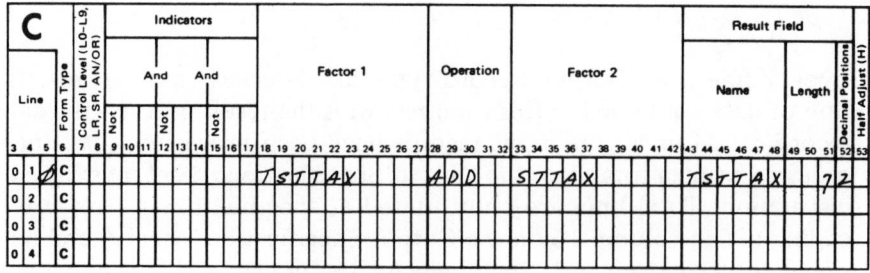

Figure 58

Operation (Columns 28 through 32)

The field must ALWAYS be coded. It is coded with an abbreviation of the operation to be performed. The field is left-justified. This field is illustrated in Fig. 58.

Factor 2 (Columns 33 through 42)

In Fig. 58 the field name entered into this field by the programmer represents the amount of the State Tax. This tax was calculated at the rate of 5% of the Total Sales. The field is also left-justified.

Result Field (Columns 43 through 52)

Name (Columns 43 through 48): This field must be defined as numeric. The contents of this field are the result of adding Factor 2 to Factor 1. The contents of the field before the operation is performed are replaced by the new contents after the operation is performed. This field is not a part of the input record (not described on the Input Specifications sheet) and thus has not been previously defined. The field is left-justified.

Length (Columns 49 through 51): This field must be defined as numeric. It represents the total number of positions in length that the result of the operation could be. The programmer must be certain that the digit in this field is sufficient to allow for enough area in storage to hold the results of the operation. This field is right-justified.

Decimal Positions (Columns 52 through 52): The digit coded in this field designates the number of positions to be assumed to the right of the decimal point. All the rules applied to the Decimal Position of the Input Specifications Sheet are applicable to this field. Observe how the result field is coded in Fig. 58.

Here the State Tax will be accumulated and stored in TSTTAX of the Result Field as each record is read. The length of the field is seven positions with a decimal point two places from the right.

INPUT FILE

Filename	INVSUMCD
Record Length	80 Columns

OUTPUT FILE

Filename	REPORT
Record Length	120 Print Positions

174

The following additional specifications should be taken into account before development of the program is begun.

- Develop a Print Chart for the Output Report. Use the Print Chart on page 458–459.

- Code the program on the necessary coding sheets that are provided on pages 179 through 184.

- No sequence checking of the file is necessary.

- Have a triple space between the main heading and the columnar headings. Have a triple space between the columnar headings and the detail lines.

- The detail data lines are to be double spaced.

- Code the Invoice Date and Salesman fields on the Input Specifications Sheets so that these fields are numeric and do not have any decimal position allotment.

- Code the State Tax, Shipping Charges, Special Charges, Sales, and Invoice Total fields on the Input Specifications sheets, for two decimal positions.

- Code the Invoice Date field on the Output Specifications sheets so that the field will be edited with "/'s."

- The Record Identification Codes are to be IS in columns 1 and 2 of the input record.

- Code the State Tax, Shipping Charges, and Special Charges fields so that the editing on the Output Report will print a zero balance if warranted.

- Code so that the Constant or Edit Word FINAL TOTALS will be printed on the same line as the totals of the various columns are printed.

- Keypunch the coded source program.

- The detail data necessary for the completion of this project is provided on the Source Document on page 176 and are to be keypunched.

- Sort the detail cards in ascending order on the INVOICE NUMBER field. The first detail card should be 532450, followed by 532451, until all the detail cards are in sequence.

- Assemble the Source Program in the sequence dictated by the computer configuration being used.

- Compile and debug the program.

The Output Report should appear as illustrated on page 178.

IS	Invoice Number	Cus- tomer Number	Ref- erence Number	Date	Tax	Ship- ping Charge	Special Charge	Sales	Sales- man Number	Invoice Total
	532468	3824	A0528	1117--	19.78	1.50		395.72	24	417.00
	532450	4597	BK1526J	1113--	262.29	7.75	20.00	5245.75	27	5535.79
	532457	4902	516	1114--	139.29	1.50		2785.89	25	2926.68
	532453	7120	123A2	1114--	50.40	1.50		1007.94	24	1059.84
	532473	8839	56723	1118--	46.53	2.25		930.57	27	979.35
	532465	50389	126422H	1116--	3.45	.50		69.00	21	72.95
	532451	9353	160	1113--	128.37	3.75	6.00	2567.42	23	2705.54
	532469	10357	IRC1067	1117--	29.18	1.00		583.55	27	613.73
	532460	1854	2629JHN	1115--	.68	.50		13.54	27	14.72
	532463	50389	SP106	1116--	192.68	5.75	15.00	3853.52	24	4066.95
	532456	68935	5987-01	1114--	152.84	5.50		3056.73	21	3215.07
	532458	32943	16A029B	1114--	22.93	1.00		458.50	25	482.43
	532470	34982	00517	1118--	2.80	.50		56.09	21	59.39
	532452	10357	IRC2016	1113--	18.73	.75		374.50	24	393.98
	532461	39673	MK-013878	1115--	5.00	.50	.50	100.00	27	106.00
	532459	45276	220011	1115--	2.75	.50		54.90	23	58.15
	532462	50389	325122H	1115--	2.45	.50		49.03	25	51.98
	532474	53898	789	1117--	147.19	3.75	2.00	2943.89	24	3096.83
	532472	68935	7929-01	1118--	15.23	1.00		304.59	21	320.82
	532454	7120	9860A3	1114--	28.44	1.00		568.75	21	598.19
	532467	69451	0047AD8	1117--	98.17	1.50		1963.45	27	2063.12
	532471	9353	197	1118--	201.19	6.00	24.00	4023.85	24	4255.04
	532464	83959	PO-12890	1116--	29.67	1.25		593.40	27	624.32
	532455	3824	A0966	1114--	17.45	1.00		348.90	25	367.35
	532466	68935	8011-01	1116--	44.72	2.00		894.28	24	941.00
			FINAL TOTAL		$1,662.21	$52.75	$67.50	$33,243.76		$35,026.22

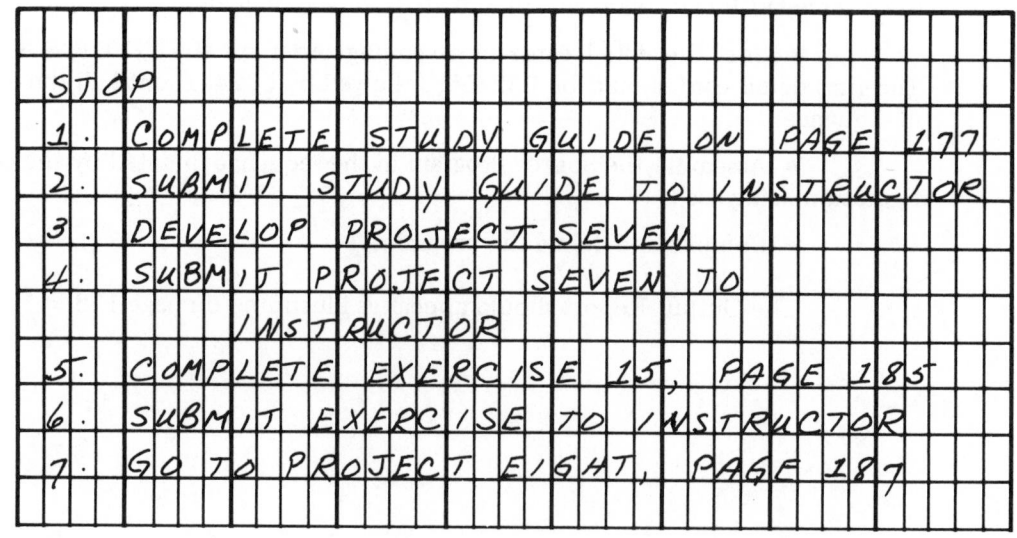

STOP
1. COMPLETE STUDY GUIDE ON PAGE 177
2. SUBMIT STUDY GUIDE TO INSTRUCTOR
3. DEVELOP PROJECT SEVEN
4. SUBMIT PROJECT SEVEN TO
   INSTRUCTOR
5. COMPLETE EXERCISE 15, PAGE 185
6. SUBMIT EXERCISE TO INSTRUCTOR
7. GO TO PROJECT EIGHT, PAGE 187

Date ———————————————   Name———————————————

   DIRECTIONS: *Answer the following questions in the spaces provided. Your answers should indicate the depth of understanding that you have toward the concepts and definitions presented.*

1. Explain the types of data that can be obtained from the buying habits of a customer. How can the data be put to use?

2. Explain the purpose of Record Identification Codes.

3. Explain the uses of the Y, L, and J Edit Codes.

4. Explain the reasoning behind the coding used with the printing of a Total Line.

5. Explain the two methods used to print dollar ($) signs. What is the advantage of one method over the other?

PRINTREN INVOICE REGISTER

INVOICE NUMBER	CUSTOMER NUMBER	REFERENCE NUMBER	INVOICE DATE	STATE TAX	SHIPPING CHARGE	SPECIAL CHARGE	SALES	SALESMAN	INVOICE TOTAL
532450	04597	BK1526J	11/13/76	262.29	7.75	20.00	5,245.75	27	5,535.79
532451	09353	160	11/13/76	128.37	3.75	6.00	2,567.42	23	2,705.54
532452	10357	IRC2016	11/13/76	18.73	.75	.00	374.50	24	393.98
532453	07120	123A2	11/14/76	50.40	1.50	.00	1,007.94	24	1,059.84
532454	07120	9860A3	11/14/76	28.44	1.00	.00	568.75	21	598.19
532455	03824	A0966	11/14/76	17.45	1.00	.00	348.90	25	367.35
532456	68935	5987-01	11/14/76	152.84	5.50	.00	3,056.73	21	3,215.07
532457	04902	516	11/14/76	139.29	1.50	.00	2,785.89	25	2,926.68
532458	32943	16A029B	11/14/76	22.93	1.00	.00	458.50	25	482.43
532459	45276	220011	11/15/76	2.75	.50	.00	54.90	23	58.15
532460	01854	2629JHN	11/15/76	.68	.50	.00	13.54	27	14.72
532461	39673	MK-013878	11/15/76	5.00	.50	.50	100.00	27	106.00
532462	50389	325122H	11/15/76	2.45	.50	.00	49.03	25	51.98
532463	50389	SP106	11/16/76	192.68	5.75	15.00	3,853.52	24	4,066.95
532464	83959	PO-12890	11/16/76	29.67	1.25	.00	593.40	27	624.32
532465	50389	126422H	11/16/76	3.45	.50	.00	69.00	21	72.95
532466	68935	8011-01	11/16/76	44.71	2.00	.00	894.28	24	940.99
532467	69451	0047AD8	11/17/76	98.17	1.50	.00	1,963.45	27	2,063.12
532468	03824	A0528	11/17/76	19.79	1.50	.00	395.72	24	417.01
532469	10357	IRC1067	11/17/76	29.18	1.00	.00	583.55	27	613.73
532470	34982	00517	11/18/76	2.80	.50	.00	56.09	21	59.39
532471	09353	197	11/18/76	201.19	6.00	24.00	4,023.85	24	4,255.04
532472	68935	7929-01	11/18/76	15.23	1.00	.00	304.59	21	320.82
532473	08839	56723	11/18/46	46.53	2.25	.00	930.57	27	979.35
532474	53898	789	11/17/76	147.19	3.75	2.00	2,943.89	24	3,096.83
FINAL TOTAL				$1,662.21	$52.75	$67.50	$33,243.76		$35,026.22

RPG CONTROL CARD AND FILE DESCRIPTION SPECIFICATIONS

IBM International Business Machine Corporation

GX21-9092-3 UM/050*
Printed in U.S.A.

*No. of forms per pad may very slightly

Program			Punching Instruction	Graphic		Card Electro Number
Programmer		Date		Punch		

Page [1] [2] of ___

Program Identification 75 76 77 78 79 80

Control Card Specifications

Refer to the specific System Reference Library manual for actual entries.

Form Type H

Line

Columns: Form Type 6, Core Size to Compile 7 8, Object Output 9, Listing Options 10 11, Core Size to Execute 12 13 14, Debug 15, MFCM Stacking Sequence 16, 17 18 19 20, Inverted Print 21, 360/20 2501 Buffer 22, Number Of Print Positions 23 24 25, Alternate Collating Sequence 26 27 28 29, Address to Start 30, Work Tapes 31, Overlay Open 32, Overlap Printer 33, Binary Search 34, Tape Error 35, 2152 Checking 36, Inquiry 37, Read/Write/Compute 38, Keyboard Output 39, Sign Handling 40, 1P Forms Position 41, Indicator Setting 42, File Translation 43, Punch MFCU Zeros 44, Nonprint Characters 45, Table Load Halt 46, Shared I/O 47, Field Print 48, Formatted Core Dump 49, RPG to RPG II Conversion 50, 51, 52 53 54 55 56 57 58 59 60 61 62 63 64 65 66 67 68 69 70 71 72 73 74

Model 20

File Description Specification

Form Type F

Line

Columns: Form Type 6, Filename 7–14, File Type (I/O/U/C/D) 15, (P/S/C/R/T/D) 16, E 17, File Designation (A/D) 18, End of File 19, Sequence (F/V/S/M/D) 20, File Format 21, Block Length 22 23 24, Record Length 25 26 27, Mode of Processing (L/R) 28 29, (A/P/I/K) 30, Length of Key Field or of Record Address Field 31, (I/D/T or 2) 32, Record Address Type 33, Type of File Organization or Additional Area 34, Overflow Indicator 35 36, Key Field Starting Location 37, Extension Code E/L 38 39, Device 40–46, Symbolic Device 47–52, Labels (S/N/E/M) 53, K 54, Name of Label Exit 55 56 57 58 59, Continuation Lines, Option 60 61, Entry 62 63, Extent Exit for DAM 64 65, Core Index 66, A/U 67, Number of Extents 68, File Condition U1-U8 69 70, (R/U/N) 71, Number of Tracks for Cylinder Overflow 72, Tape Rewind 73, File Addition/Unordered 74

IBM International Business Machine Corporation

GX21-9094-2 U/M 050*
Printed in U.S.A.

RPG INPUT SPECIFICATIONS

Program

Programmer

Date

Punching Instruction

Graphic

Punch

Card Electro Number

Page 1 2 of

75 76 77 78 79 80

Program Identification

Line	Form Type	Filename	Sequence	Number (1-N)	Option (O)	Record Identifying Indicator or **	Record Identification Codes															Stacker Select	P/B/L/R	Field Location		Decimal Positions	Field Name	Control Level (L1-L9)	Matching Fields or Changing Fields	Field Record Relation	Field Indicators		

The form is numbered 180 at the bottom. Column positions run 3 through 74 across the top, and 1 through 72 down the right side. The Form Type column is filled with the letter "I" (H shown rotated) for each line numbered 01 through 20.

IBM International Business Machine Corporation

GX21-9093-2 UM/050* Printed in U.S.A.
*No. of forms per pad may vary slightly

RPG CALCULATION SPECIFICATIONS

Program				Punching Instruction	Graphic			Card Electro Number			Page 1 2 of ___
Programmer		Date			Punch						Program Identification 75 76 77 78 79 80

C	Line	Form Type	Control Level (L0-L9, LR, SR, AN/OR)	Indicators			Factor 1	Operation	Factor 2	Result Field				Resulting Indicators		Comments

Column reference: 3 4 5 6 7 8 9 10 11 12 13 14 15 16 17 18 19 20 21 22 23 24 25 26 27 28 29 30 31 32 33 34 35 36 37 38 39 40 41 42 43 44 45 46 47 48 49 50 51 52 53 54 55 56 57 58 59 60 61 62 63 64 65 66 67 68 69 70 71 72 73 74

Indicators: And / Not, And / Not, And / Not

Result Field: Name, Length, Decimal Positions, Half Adjust (H)

Resulting Indicators: Arithmetic — Plus, Minus, Zero; Compare — 1 > 2, 1 < 2, 1 = 2; Lookup (Factor 2) is — High, Low, Equal

Line numbers: 01 02 03 04 05 06 07 08 09 10 11 12 13 14 15 16 17 18 19 20

Right margin columns: 1 2 3 4 5 6 7 8 9 10 11 12 13 14 15 16 17 18 19 20 21 22 23 24 25 26 27 28 29 30 31 32 33 34 35 36 37 38 39 40 41 42 43 44 45 46 47 48 49 50 51 52 53 54 55 56 57 58 59 60 61 62 63 64 65 66 67 68 69 70 71 72

181

RPG OUTPUT SPECIFICATIONS

IBM International Business Machine Corporation

GX21-9090-2 U/M 050*
Printed in U.S.A.

Program		Punching Instruction	Graphic		Card Electro Number
Programmer	Date		Punch		Program Identification
					75 76 77 78 79 80

Page [ ] of [ ]
(1 2)

Commas / Zero Balances to Print / No Sign / CR / – Edit Codes

Commas	Zero Balances to Print	No Sign	CR	–	
Yes	Yes	1	A	J	X = Remove Plus Sign
Yes	No	2	B	K	Y = Date Field Edit
No	Yes	3	C	L	Z = Zero Suppress
No	No	4	D	M	

Constant or Edit Word

Edit Codes — B/A/C/1-9/R (38-39)

End Position in Output Record (40 41 42 43)

P/B/L/R (44)

Field Name / *Auto (32-37)

Output Indicators — And (23) N, And (26-27) N, And (29-30) N

Skip — Before (20), After (21 22)

Space — Before (17), After (18)

Stacker #/Fetch(F) (16)

Type (H/D/T/E) (15) — OR / AND (14)

Filename (7-12)

Form Type (6) — O

Line (3 4 5)

01 02 03 04 05 06 07 08 09 10 11 12 13 14 15 16 17 18 19 20

Column numbers: 1–74

182

IBM International Business Machine Corporation

RPG   OUTPUT   SPECIFICATIONS

GX21-9090-2 U/M 050*
Printed in U.S.A.

Program			Punching Instruction	Graphic		Card Electro Number		Page	1 2 of _	Program Identification	75 76 77 78 79 80
Programmer		Date		Punch							

O

Form Type (6)

Line (3-5)

Filename (7-14)

Type (H/D/T/E) — O/A/R (14), O/A/N (15)

Stacker #/Fetch(F) — A/R/D (16)

Space: Before (17), After (18)

Skip: Before (19-20), After (21-22)

Output Indicators: Not (23), And (24-25), Not (26), And (27-28), Not (29-30), And (31)

Field Name (32-37) — *Auto

Edit Codes (38)

B/A/C/1-9/R (39)

End Position in Output Record (40-43)

P/B/L/R (44)

Constant or Edit Word (45-70)

Commas	Zero Balances to Print	No Sign	CR	-
Yes	Yes	1	A	J
Yes	No	2	B	K
No	Yes	3	C	L
No	No	4	D	M

X = Remove Plus Sign
Y = Date Field Edit
Z = Zero Suppress

183

IBM

International Business Machine Corporation

RPG   OUTPUT   SPECIFICATIONS

GX21-9090-2 U/M 050*
Printed in U.S.A.

Program		Punching	Graphic			Card Electro Number	
		Instruction	Punch				
Programmer		Date					

Page [1][2] of ____

Program Identification [75 76 77 78 79 80]

Constant or Edit Word

Commas	Zero Balances to Print	No Sign	CR	-
Yes	Yes	1	A	J
Yes	No	2	B	K
No	Yes	3	C	L
No	No	4	D	M

X = Remove Plus Sign
Y = Date Field Edit
Z = Zero Suppress

Output form

Line	Form Type	Filename	Type (H/D/T/E)	AND OR	Stacker #/Fetch(F)	Space Before After	Skip Before After	Output Indicators And Not And Not	Field Name *Auto	Edit Codes B/A/C/1-9/R	End Position in Output Record	P/B/L/R

Column numbers:
3 4 5 6 7 8 9 10 11 12 13 14 15 16 17 18 19 20 21 22 23 24 25 26 27 28 29 30 31 32 33 34 35 36 37 38 39 40 41 42 43 44 45 46 47 48 49 50 51 52 53 54 55 56 57 58 59 60 61 62 63 64 65 66 67 68 69 70 71 72 73 74

Lines: 01 02 03 04 05 06 07 08 09 10 11 12 13 14 15 16 17 18 19 20

184

Date _____   Name _____

TRUE–FALSE: *Each of the following statements is either true or false. Indicate your choice in the Answers column by encircling "T" for a true answer or "F" for a false answer.*

		Answers	
1.	Analysis of purchase orders shows very little about the customer	T	F
2.	The Sales Invoice is the first document of a business transaction	T	F
3.	The IS of columns 1 and 2 of the detail cards is a constant	T	F
4.	When preparing invoices, Invoice Numbers are assigned in sequential order	T	F
5.	The Reference Number Field is the field that ties together the Purchase Order and the Invoice	T	F
6.	The Identifying Record Code C is used to check the complete field of the Input card	T	F
7.	The Y Edit Code enables the date to be automatically edited	T	F
8.	The input of the date field and the output of the date field have the same number of positions after editing	T	F
9.	The L code will automatically allow for zero balances to print when used on a numeric field.	T	F
10.	A zero balance prints out as the word "zero"	T	F
11.	Editing codes are coded in column 37 of the Output Specifications sheet	T	F
12.	The letters LR represent last record	T	F
13.	To have the printer triple space after printing a line, the programmer codes a 3 column 18 on the Output Specifications sheet.	T	F
14.	In addition, the operation ADD adds Factor 2 to Factor 1	T	F
15.	Three types of printing lines are H, D, and T	T	F
16.	The Operation code for multiplication is MUL	T	F
17.	In any arithmetical operation the Result Field must be defined as being numeric	T	F
18.	The Result Field of a calculation must have been previously defined in another calculation	T	F
19.	Dollar sign editing symbols can be either floated or fixed as far as the printing position is concerned	T	F
20.	For the Edit Code Y to be effective, the Input field must be coded as numeric	T	F

COMPLETION: *Fill in the blank with the appropriate word or words.*

1. The fee paid by a customer to get merchandise from the seller's place of business is known as _____ .

2. A total line can be printed after all the Input records have been processed by coding _____ in the Output Indicators field.

3. Whenever there is coding in either Factor 1 or Factor 2, there must always be coding in the _____ .

4, 5. The two methods of printing dollar signs are _____ and _____ .

6. To have the total or complete character used as a checking code, the programmer codes a _____ in column 26 on the Input Specifications sheet.

7. The _____ field need not be defined on the Input record or be previously defined as a result of other calculations.

8. The digit coded in the Decimal Position field determines the number of positions to be assumed to the _____ .

MATCHING: *Match Column 1 to Column 2.*

COLUMN 1	COLUMN 2	Answers
A. Invoice Register	1. Automatic printing of zero balances	_____
B. Source Document	2. Analyzing sales of customers	_____
C. Transportation Charges		
D. Y	3. Automatic printing of commas and zero balances	_____
E. L	4. Purchase Order	_____
F. J	5. Date Edit Code	_____

PROJECT EIGHT

Whenever input data is to become a part of future projects or the data is to be stored in primary or secondary storage, its accuracy must be as close to 100% as possible.

In order to check the extreme accuracy of the input data of Project Seven before it is put to further use, a program must be written to check each field of the input data for accuracy. Such is the object of Project Eight. The Output Report should be such that only those Summary Records containing an error(s) will be printed. Those records that are completely correct should flush through the reading device of the computer configuration in use.

NEW CONCEPTS

1. Operation Codes

   Logical Operation

   a. SETOF

   b. SETON

   Compare Operation

   COMP

   Arithmetic Operation

   a. MULT

   b. SUB

   Move Operation

   a. MOVE

   b. MOVEL

2. Half Adjust (H)

3. Comment Field (Calculation Specifications)

SETOF (Set Off)

This operation code or instruction will cause any Resulting Indicators that are coded in the Resulting Indicators Field (columns 54 through 59) to be turned OFF if certain conditions are met. See Fig. 59. In Fig. 59, line 010 the instruction will SETOF (Set Off) the indicators 10, 11, and 12 unconditionally. However, observe Fig. 59, line 020. The instruction in Fig. 59, line 020 will SETOF the indicators 15 and 16 *only* if indicators 13 and 14 are ON. If 15 and 16 are ON before this instruction, they will remain ON if 13 and 14 are NOT both ON.

SETON (Set On)

This operation code or instruction will cause a Resulting Indicator(s) that is/are coded in the Resulting Indicator Field (columns 54 through 59) to be turned ON if certain conditions are met. See Fig. 59, line 030. Here the instruction will SETON Indicators 10, 11, and 12. If they were ON before the operation, they will remain ON.

In Fig. 59, line 040 the instruction states that if indicators 13 and 14 were both ON, this instruction will SETON 15, 16, and 17.

Another use of the SETON or SETOF is to set an indicator for more than one pass through the RPG cycle as in Fig. 59, line 050 and 060. In this figure Indicator 25 conditions the initial value of CONTR to 1. The very next instruction turns Indicator 25 ON. There is no other instruction in the program to affect Indicator 25. Therefore since 25 is ON and remains ON for the duration of program execution, the instruction conditioned by 25 will not occur again.

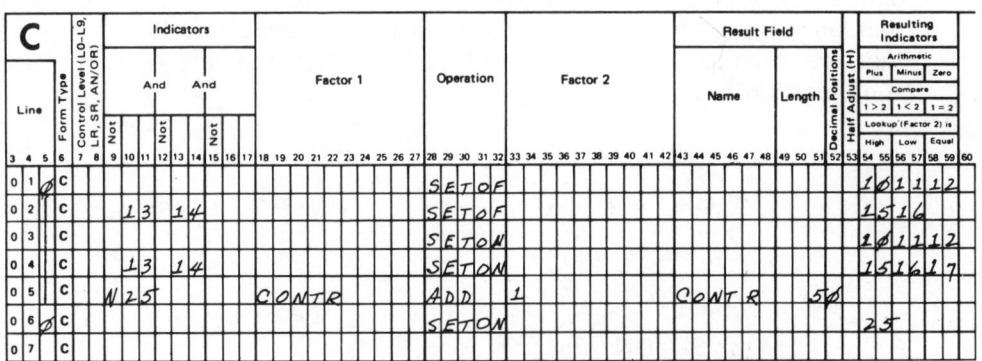

Figure 59

TIP TO PROGRAMMER

Indicators, of course, are used to control the logical operation of the program. Arithmetic and Compare operations can turn indicators ON and OFF under conditions established for that operation. The use of SETON and SETOF operations can turn indicators ON or OFF conditionally or unconditionally through the use of indicators in columns 9 through 17. SETON or SETOF operation codes are used to control the setting of indicators when there is more than one condition that will control one other condition or, when there is one condition that will control more than one condition.

COMP (Compare)

The data contained in Factor 1 is compared against the data in Factor 2. The Result Field is not used in a compare operation. The following rules should be observed when using the COMP operation.

1. When comparing numeric fields, the shorter field will be filled with zeros to the left or right of the decimal point so that the fields become equal in length for the comparison.

2. When comparing alphameric fields, the shorter field is filled with blank characters to the right so that the fields become equal in length for the comparison.

3. Numeric comparisons are accomplished algebraically.

4. Embedded blanks within a numeric field are considered as zeros.

5. Numeric fields CANNOT be compared to alphameric fields.

When COMP is used in the Operation Field of the Calculation Specifications sheet, the programmer is seeking alternatives for processing the data. He is, in effect, coding to see if the results of the comparison of the data in Factor 1 is greater than, less than, or equal to the data in Factor 2. See Fig. 60, line 010.

Referring to Fig. 60, line 010, note that

1. If the value in Factor 1 is greater than the value in Factor 2, Indicator 10 will be turned ON.

2. If the value in Factor 1 is less than the value in Factor 2, Indicator 15 will be turned ON.

3. If the value in Factor 1 is equal to the value in Factor 2, Indicator 20 will be turned ON.

Depending on the comparison, an indicator will be turned ON or OFF to allow for different types of processing of data within the program. The indicators can, of course, be coded on the Output Specifications when a data line is to be printed.

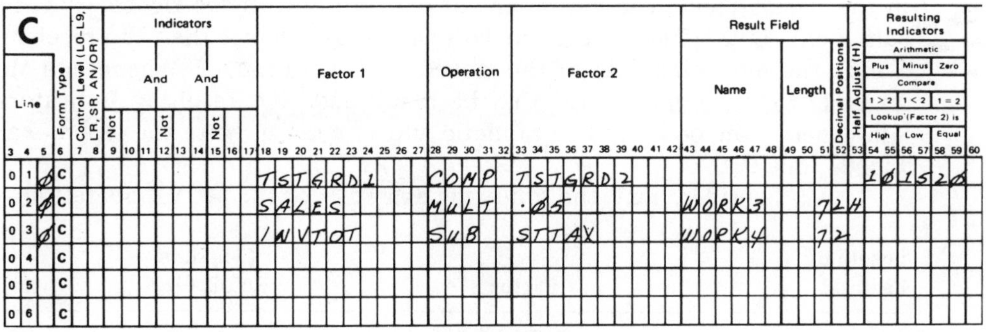

Figure 60

MULT (Multiply)

The contents of the field or literal coded in Factor 1 are multiplied by the contents of the field or literal coded in Factor 2. The result of this operation is placed in the Result Field.

189

Since the amount of the sale is being multiplied by a 5% tax, the rounding-off principle must be considered. This topic is discussed in the paragraph on HALF ADJUST (H). See Fig. 60, line 020.

SUB (Subtraction)

The data coded in Factor 2 is subtracted from the data coded in Factor 1. The difference is placed in the area coded in the Result Field. See Fig. 60, line 030.

HALF ADJUST (H) (Columns 53 through 53)

The rounding principle involves arithmetic operations that have decimal positions within the data coded in Factor 1 and Factor 2. If the third digit to the right of the decimal point is 5 or greater, the second digit to the right of the decimal point is raised to the next higher digit. If the third digit to the right of the decimal point is less than 5, the second digit to the right of the decimal point remains as printed. See the table below.

Factor 1 Sales	Factor 2	Result Work 03	Before Half Adjust
123.45	.05	6.17	6.1725
56.78	.05	2.84	2.839

As can be seen the coding in Fig. 60, line 020 illustrates the following facts.

1. The data coded in Factor 2 is a constant numeric.

2. The length of the Result Field is seven positions. There is a decimal point two places from the rightmost position.

3. The final result will be half-adjusted (H in column 53).

MOVE

This operation will cause the data specified in Factor 2 to be moved to the field coded in the Result Field. The movement of data starts with the rightmost position in the Result Field. If the field being moved (Factor 2) is larger than the receiving field (Result Field), the remaining data of the moved field is not moved. Whenever a MOVE operation is used, Factor 1 must ALWAYS be blank and NO Resulting Indicators can be used. Alphameric can be moved to numeric and vice versa. Note the alpha example shown in Fig. 61, line 010.

Consider, next, the following examples of the MOVE operation.

Length of Factor 2	Factor 2	Length of Result Field	Result of MOVE
10	ABCDEFGHIJ	5	FGHIJ
5	ABCDE	5	ABCDE
5	ABCDE	10	ƀƀƀƀƀABCDE
10	ABCDEƀƀƀƀƀ	10	ABCDEƀƀƀƀƀ

MOVEL (Move Left)

This operation will cause the leftmost data specified in Factor 2 to be moved to the leftmost position in the Result Field. If the field being moved (Factor 2) is larger than the receiving field (Result Field), the remaining data of the moved field (Factor 2) are not moved.

The table below illustrates the MOVEL operation.

Length of Factor 2	Factor 2	Length of Result Field	Result of MOVEL
10	ABCDEFGHIJ	5	ABCDE
5	ABCDE	5	ABCDE
5	ABCDE	10	ABCDEþþþþþ
10	ABCDEþþþþþ	10	ABCDEþþþþþ

Figure 61 depicts both the MOVE and the MOVEL operations. Once again, in Fig. 61 nothing was coded in Factor 1.

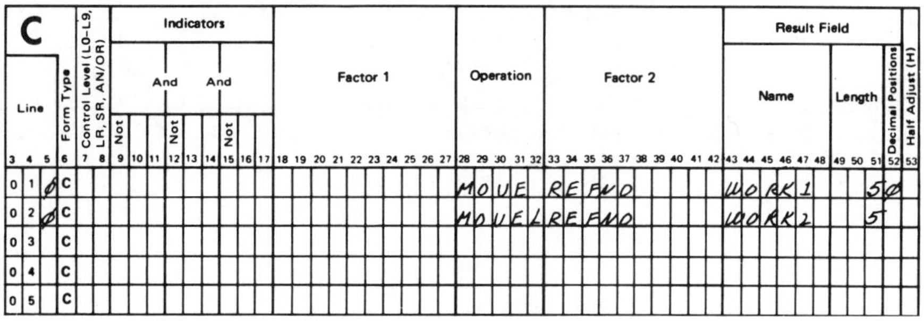

Figure 61

COMMENTS (Columns 60 through 74)

The coding in this field serves to clarify the processing that is to take place as a result of the operation. Here the coding has no effect on the compilation of the program. The programmer enters information (statement) in this field that will enable him to remember what he was doing with each specification line. Comments need NOT tie in with any other Specifications sheet. See the example later in this project in Figures 63 and 65.

INPUT SPECIFICATIONS

The detail card illustrated in Fig. 54 (page 170) is to be coded on the Input Specifications sheet provided. In particular, be sure that the Record Identification Code IS is coded in the appropriate Record Identification Codes field. Also, pay strict attention to those fields that need decimal positions.

INPUT FILE

Filename	INVSUMCD
Record Length	80 Positions

PRINT CHART

When development of the Print Chart is in process, consider a logical meaningful message that will, when printed on the Output Report, tell precisely which field(s) is/are in error. See Fig. 62.

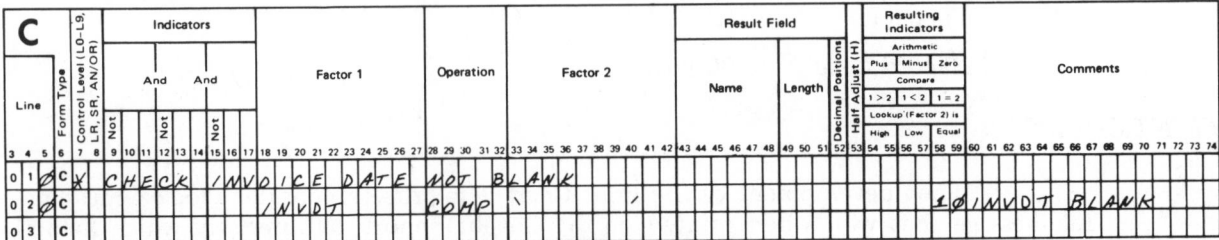

INVOICE SUMMARY RECORD EDIT

INVOICE
NUMBER   RECORDS PRINTED ONLY IF IN ERROR

XXXXXX   INVOICE SUMMARY RECORD IN ERROR

                INVOICE DATE COLUMNS 24 TO 29 IS ZERO

                CUSTOMER NUMBER COLUMNS 9 TO 13 IS BLANK

                CUSTOMER REFERENCE NUMBER COLUMNS 14 TO 23 IS BLANK

                SALESMAN NUMBER COLUMNS 72 TO 73 IS BLANK

                SALES TAX NOT 5 PERCENT, SHOULD BE XX,XXX.XX-

                INVOICE TOTAL INCORRECT-TOTAL IS IN ERROR BY XX,XXX.XX-

Figure 62

CALCULATION SPECIFICATIONS AND OUTPUT SPECIFICATIONS

As stated in the Specification section of this project, it is extremely important to see that each field of the detail card has been properly and accurately punched. Each field check should be coded with a *prior* comment specification line. (See Fig. 63.) The coding ascertains if the Invoice Date is blank.

In Fig. 63 notice that

1. The Field Name INVDT was coded on the Input Specifications when the detail card was defined.

2. The INVDT (invoice date in Factor 1) is being compared (tested against) to a six-position blank field in Factor 2. If the Invoice Date has NOT been punched into the detail card(s), then the Resulting Indicator 10 would be turned ON. The only way Indicator 10 can be turned ON is if there is an equal compare. If the Invoice Date was punched into the card(s), the comparison would be unequal and Indicator 10 would be OFF.

3. The coding in the COMMENTS field INVDT BLANK merely reinforces the type of checking that the programmer is doing by coding the specification in this manner.

Line	Form Type	Control Level (L0-L9, LR, SR, AN/OR)	Indicators Not	And Not	And Not	Factor 1	Operation	Factor 2	Result Field Name	Length	Decimal Positions	Half Adjust (H)	Resulting Indicators Arithmetic Plus 1>2 / High	Minus 1<2 / Low	Zero 1=2 / Equal	Comments
0 1	0	C	X			CHECK INVOICE DATE NOT BLANK										
0 2	0	C				INVDT	COMP	' '							10	INVDT BLANK
0 3		C														

Figure 63

192

The necessary coding on the Output Specifications sheet if the Invoice Date has not been punched into the detail card(s) is illustrated in Fig. 64.

If the Output Indicator 10 is ON in Fig. 64, the coding in the Constant or Edit Word Field would be printed on the Output Report. The Output Indicator on the Output Specifications sheet has a direct relationship to the Resulting Indicators 10 of the Calculation Specifications sheet. In other words, if the *Invoice Date* is blank, Output Indicator 10 would be ON, thereby printing the message coded in the Comment or Edit Word Field on the Output Report. The same type of coding should be considered when checking the *Customer Number* and *Salesman Number* Fields. However, each field must be assigned its own *Indicator* number. The message coded in the Constant or Edit Word Field is similar or equal to the one that would be coded on the Print Chart shown in Fig. 62. Remember that, whatever the message, its meaning corresponds to what is actually being processed.

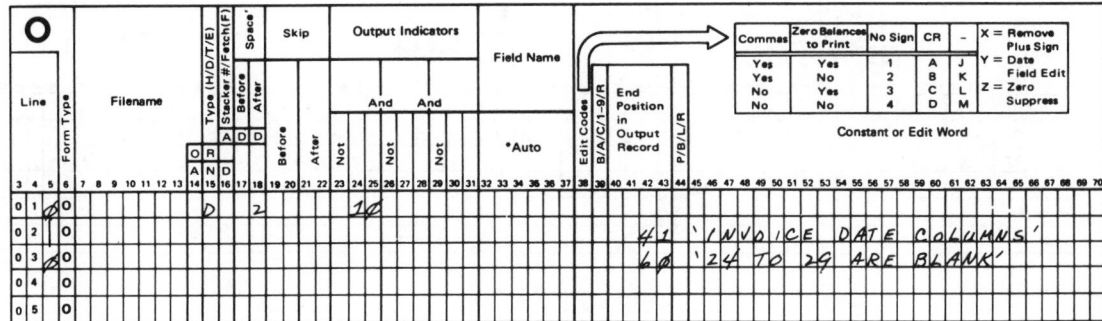

Figure 64

When checking to see if the Reference Number Field of the detail card(s) is blank, the programmer coded this area to check for the following points.

1. Is the left portion of the field blank?

2. Is the right portion of the field blank?

3. Or is the complete field blank?

The field was divided into two equal parts. The second five-position section or portion was moved to an area created by the programmer called WORK1. The data was moved

Figure 65

into WORK1 by the rightmost position first. Remember that when the MOVE operation is used, Factor 1 MUST be blank. Next, the first five-position portion was moved to an additional work area called WORK2 by using the MOVEL operation. When this operation is used, the data is moved by the leftmost position first.

In the next two specification lines, WORK1 and WORK2 become Factor 1. Factor 1 can now be compared to the five blank positions in Factor 2. If the comparison shows that Factor 1 is blank, then Indicator 12 or 13 would be ON. Both Indicators, 12 and 13, are used to SETON Indicator 14, which would print out the message coded on the Output Specifications sheet. Notice in Figs. 65 and 66 how the coding is on both Specifications sheets.

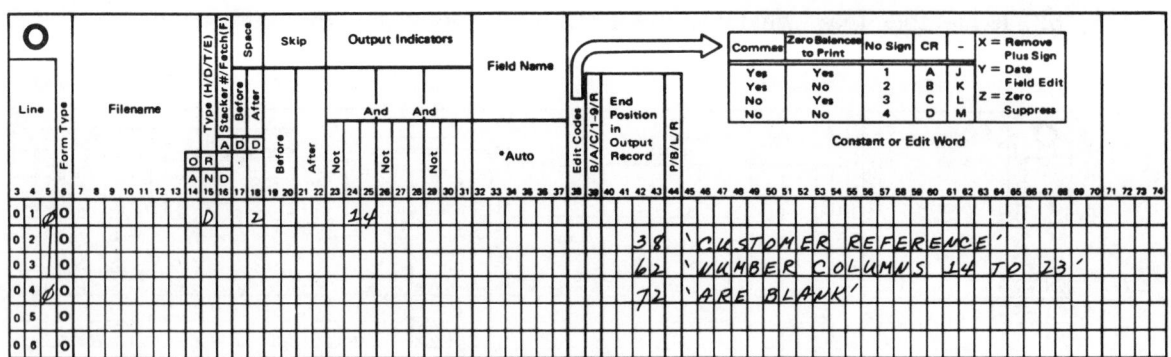

Figure 66

OUTPUT FILE

Filename	REPORT
Record Length	120 Positions

The additional specifications listed below should be considered before development of this program is begun.

● Check each invoice summary card to see if the STTAX (State Tax) is 0.05% of the SALES field. Print a message if not true and print the correct tax.

● Check each invoice summary card to see if STTAX, SHCHG, SPCHG, and SALES add to equal INVOT. Print a message if the totals are not equal and print the correct total.

● Develop a Print Chart for the Output. Use the Print Chart on page 458–459.

● Code the program on the coding sheets provided on pages 196–201.

● Keypunch the coded data.

● Assemble the Source Program in the sequence dictated by the computer configuration being used.

● Use the detail cards used in Project Seven as the data.

● Take ten detail cards and deliberately punch errors into reproductions of them. In punching the errors, make sure that there is at least one error in each card. This does not mean that some of the cards cannot have more than one error in them. Each one of the error cards should contain some identifying mark so that at the end of the successful compilation they can be extracted from the data deck easily.

Example: In one data card make the Customer Number Field blank.

In the next data card make the Invoice Number Field blank.

Change an amount field.

- Compile and debug the program.
- The Output Report should be similar to the one illustrated below.

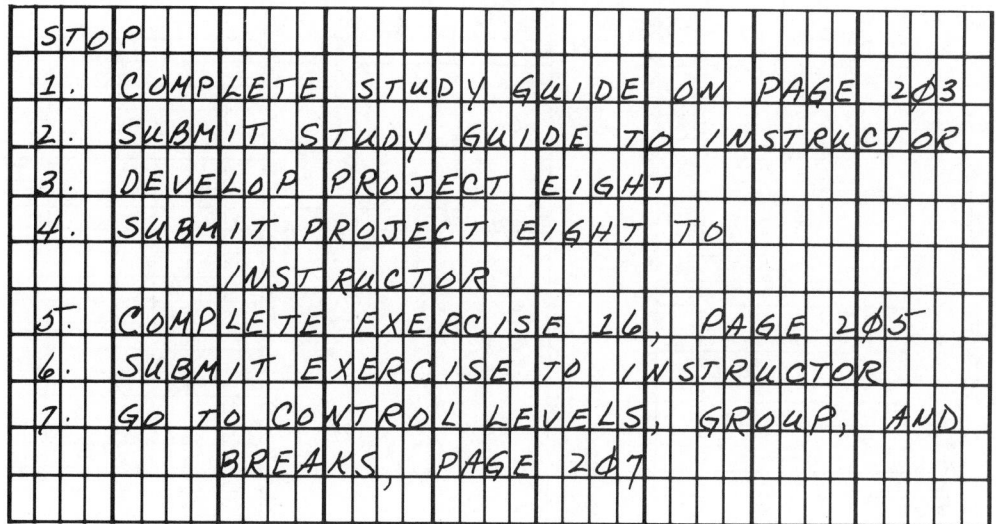

```
STOP
1.  COMPLETE STUDY GUIDE ON PAGE 203
2.  SUBMIT STUDY GUIDE TO INSTRUCTOR
3.  DEVELOP PROJECT EIGHT
4.  SUBMIT PROJECT EIGHT TO
        INSTRUCTOR
5.  COMPLETE EXERCISE 16, PAGE 205
6.  SUBMIT EXERCISE TO INSTRUCTOR
7.  GO TO CONTROL LEVELS, GROUP, AND
        BREAKS, PAGE 207
```

```
                              INVOICE SUMMARY  RECORD EDIT

INVOICE          RECORDS PRINTED ONLY IF IN ERROR
NUMBER
532451           INVOICE SUMMARY RECORD IN ERROR

                 CUSTOMER NUMBER COLUMNS 9 TO 13 IS BLANK

532452           INVOICE SUMMARY RECORD IN ERROR

                 CUSTOMER REFERENCE NUMBER COLUMNS 14 TO 23 IS BLANK

532453           INVOICE SUMMARY RECORD IN ERROR

                  INVOICE DATE COLUMNS  24 TO 29 IS ZERO

532454           INVOICE SUMMARY RECORD IN ERROR

                 SALES TAX NOT 5 PERCENT, SHOULD BE    28.44

                 INVOICE TOTAL INCORRECT   -TOTAL IS IN ERROR BY       28.44

532455           INVOICE SUMMARY RECORD IN ERROR

                 INVOICE TOTAL INCORRECT   -TOTAL IS IN ERROR BY        1.00

532457           INVOICE SUMMARY RECORD IN ERROR

                 SALES TAX NOT 5 PERCENT, SHOULD BE     .00

                 INVOICE TOTAL INCORRECT   -TOTAL IS IN ERROR BY    2,785.89

532458           INVOICE SUMMARY RECORD IN ERROR

                 SALESMAN NUMBER COLUMNS 72 TO 73 IS BLANK

532459           INVOICE SUMMARY RECORD IN ERROR

                 INVOICE TOTAL INCORRECT   -TOTAL IS IN ERROR BY       58.15-
```

GX21-9092-3 UM/050*
Printed in U.S.A.

RPG CONTROL CARD AND FILE DESCRIPTION SPECIFICATIONS

IBM International Business Machine Corporation

Program

Programmer

Date

Punching Instruction

Graphic

Punch

Card Electro Number

*No. of forms per pad may very slightly

Page 1 2 of ___

Program Identification

75 76 77 78 79 80

Control Card Specifications

Refer to the specific System Reference Library manual for actual entries.

H

Line

Form Type

Core Size to Compile

Object Output

Listing Options

Core Size to Execute

Debug

MFCM Stacking Sequence

Inverted Print

360/20 2501 Buffer

Number Of Print Positions

Alternate Collating Sequence

Address to Start

Work Tapes

Model 20

Overlay Open

Overlap Printer

Binary Search

Tape Error

2152 Checking

Inquiry

Read/Write/Compute

Keyboard Output

Model 20

Sign Handling

1P Forms Position

Indicator Setting

File Translation

Punch MFCU Zeros

Nonprint Characters

Table Load Halt

Shared I/O

Field Print

Formatted Core Dump

RPG to RPG II Conversion

File Description Specification

F

Line

Form Type

Filename

File Type

File Designation

End of File

Sequence

File Format

Block Length

Record Length

Mode of Processing

Length of Key Field or of Record Address Field

Record Address Type

Type of File Organization or Additional Area

Overflow Indicator

Key Field Starting Location

Extension Code E/L

Device

Symbolic Device

Name of Label Exit

Labels S/N/E/M

Continuation Lines

Option

Entry

Extent Exit for DAM

Core Index

File Addition/Unordered

Number of Tracks for Cylinder Overflow

Number of Extents

Tape Rewind

File Condition U1-U8

I/O/U/C/D

P/S/C/R/T/D

E

A/D

F/V/S/M/D

L/R

A/P/I/K

I/D/T or 2

O/I

U/M/E/N/S

K

U/N/R

U/A

196

RPG INPUT SPECIFICATIONS

IBM International Business Machine Corporation

GX21-9094-2 U/M 050*
Printed in U.S.A.

Program			
Programmer		Date	

Punching Instruction — Graphic / Punch

Card Electro Number

Page 1 2 of ___

Program Identification: 75 76 77 78 79 80

This is a blank IBM RPG Input Specifications coding form (Form Type **I**). The column headers across the form include:

- Line (3–5)
- Form Type (6)
- Filename (7–14)
- Sequence (15–16), AND / OR (14–15)
- Number (1-N) (17)
- Option (O) (18)
- Record Identifying Indicator or ** (19–20)
- Record Identification Codes:
  - 1: Position (21–24), Not (N) (25), C/Z/D (26), Character (27)
  - 2: Position (28–31), Not (N) (32), C/Z/D (33), Character (34)
  - 3: Position (35–38), Not (N) (39), C/Z/D (40), Character (41)
- Stacker Select (42)
- P/B/L/R (43)
- Field Location: From (44–47), To (48–51)
- Decimal Positions (52)
- Field Name (53–58)
- Control Level (L1-L9) (59–60)
- Matching Fields or Changing Fields (61–62)
- Field Record Relation (63–64)
- Field Indicators: Plus (65–66), Minus (67–68), Zero or Blank (69–70)
- (71–74)

Line numbers 01 through 20 are printed with Form Type **I**. Column numbers 1–72 run across the grid.

197

IBM

International Business Machine Corporation

RPG CALCULATION SPECIFICATIONS

GX21-9093-2 UM/050* Printed in U.S.A.
*No. of forms per pad may vary slightly

Program			
Programmer		Date	

Punching Instruction: Graphic / Punch

Card Electro Number

Page 1 2 of ___

Program Identification 75 76 77 78 79 80

C Form Type (6)

Line	Control Level (L0-L9), LR, SR, AN/OR	Indicators (And / Not / And / Not / Not)	Factor 1	Operation	Factor 2	Result Field (Name / Length)	Decimal Positions	Half Adjust (H)	Resulting Indicators	Comments

Resulting Indicators:
- Arithmetic: Plus / Minus / Zero
- Compare: 1 > 2 / 1 < 2 / 1 = 2
- Lookup (Factor 2) is: High / Low / Equal

Column headers: 3 4 5 6 7 8 9 10 11 12 13 14 15 16 17 18 19 20 21 22 23 24 25 26 27 28 29 30 31 32 33 34 35 36 37 38 39 40 41 42 43 44 45 46 47 48 49 50 51 52 53 54 55 56 57 58 59 60 61 62 63 64 65 66 67 68 69 70 71 72 73 74

Line numbers: 01 02 03 04 05 06 07 08 09 10 11 12 13 14 15 16 17 18 19 20

Right margin column numbers: 1 2 3 4 5 6 7 8 9 10 11 12 13 14 15 16 17 18 19 20 21 22 23 24 25 26 27 28 29 30 31 32 33 34 35 36 37 38 39 40 41 42 43 44 45 46 47 48 49 50 51 52 53 54 55 56 57 58 59 60 61 62 63 64 65 66 67 68 69 70 71 72

198

GX21-9093-2 UM/050* Printed in U.S.A.
*No. of forms per pad may vary slightly

IBM International Business Machine Corporation

RPG CALCULATION SPECIFICATIONS

Program			Punching	Graphic			Card Electro Number	
Programmer		Date	Instruction	Punch				

Page [1] [2] of [ ]

Program Identification [ ] 75 76 77 78 79 80

GX21-9090-2 U/M 050*
Printed in U.S.A.

IBM International Business Machine Corporation

RPG   OUTPUT   SPECIFICATIONS

Program		Punching Instruction	Graphic		Card Electro Number
			Punch		
Programmer	Date				

Page ☐ 1   of ☐ 2

Program Identification

75 76 77 78 79 80

Commas	Zero Balances to Print	No Sign	CR	−
Yes	Yes	1	A	J
Yes	No	2	B	K
No	Yes	3	C	L
No	No	4	D	M

X = Remove Plus Sign
Y = Date Field Edit
Z = Zero Suppress

Constant or Edit Word

Field Name
*Auto

Output Indicators
And   Not   And   Not   Not

Edit Codes
B/A/C/1-9/R
End Position in Output Record
P/B/L/R

Skip — After / Before
Space — After / Before
Stacker #/Fetch(F)
Type (H/D/T/E)

Filename

Line   Form Type

GX21-9090-2 U/M 050*
Printed in U.S.A.

IBM International Business Machine Corporation

RPG   OUTPUT   SPECIFICATIONS

Program

Programmer

Date

Punching Instruction

Graphic

Punch

Card Electro Number

Page [1] [2] of ___

Program Identification [ ]

Commas	Zero Balances to Print	No Sign	CR	−
Yes	Yes	1	A	J
Yes	No	2	B	K
No	Yes	3	C	L
No	No	4	D	M

X = Remove Plus Sign
Y = Date Field Edit
Z = Zero Suppress

Constant or Edit Word

Field Name

*Auto

Output Indicators

And   Not   And   Not   And   Not

Skip   After   Before

Space   After   Before

Stacker #/Fetch(F)

Type (H/D/T/E)

Filename

Line   Form Type

Edit Codes
B/A/C/1-9/R
End Position in Output Record
P/B/L/R

O

STUDY GUIDE

Date ——————————————   Name ——————————————————

DIRECTIONS: *Answer the following questions in the spaces provided. Your answers should indicate the depth of understanding that you have toward the concepts and definitions presented. If there is insufficient space provided for your answer, complete your answer on the reverse side of the Study Guide.*

1. Explain the use of SETON or SETOF Operations codes.

2. Explain the rules of the COMP Operation code.

3. Explain the MULT Operation and its connection to the HALF ADJUST code.

4. Explain and give an illustration of the MOVE Operation code.

5. Explain and give an illustration of the MOVEL Operation code.

6. Explain the use of the Comments Field on the Calculations Specifications sheet.

Date _____   Name _____

TRUE–FALSE: *Each of the following statements is either true or false. Indicate your choice in the Answers column by encircling "T" for a true answer or "F" for a false answer.*

		Answers	
1.	There are six basic types of operations in RPG	T	F
2.	The Half Adjust Operation can turn on indicators	T	F
3.	There can be more than one condition to turn ON indicators	T	F
4.	Indicators can be turned ON or OFF conditionally or unconditionally	T	F
5.	Resulting Indicators are coded on the Output Specifications sheet	T	F
6.	The data of Factor 2 is compared to the data of Factor 1	T	F
7.	Result Field must be coded for each operation	T	F
8.	Comparing fields must be identical in length	T	F
9.	Embedded blanks are allowable in the Compare Operation	T	F
10.	Numeric fields can be compared to Alphanumeric fields	T	F
11.	The Compare sign > means greater than	T	F
12.	Comparison allows for different types of processing to go on within the program	T	F
13.	The data of Factor 1 is multiplied by the data in Factor 2	T	F
14.	The MOVE Operation moves data specified in Factor 2	T	F
15.	If the Receiving Field is smaller than the Sending Field, in a MOVE Operation the field will be truncated	T	F
16.	The MOVEL Operation moves data to the leftmost position in the Result Field	T	F
17.	When the MOVE Operation is used, data is coded in Factor 1	T	F
18.	In a field with two decimal positions the rounding principle is based on the digit that is the third position to the right of the decimal	T	F
19.	Half Adjust does not have a direct relationship with the Decimal Position Field of the Input Specifications sheet	T	F
20.	Comments field has a direct bearing on the compilation	T	F
21.	Comments do not have a tie-in with any other Specifications sheet	T	F
22.	Successive subtractions are limited to three specifications statements	T	F
23.	Field mode in the MOVE Operation can be changed	T	F
24.	All records are not checked to see if the data is accurately punched in each of the fields. That is why some of the data cards flush	T	F
25.	The SETON and SETOF Operations fall under the Compare Operation	T	F

COMPLETION: *Fill in the blank with the appropriate word or words.*

1-5. The five basic types of operation codes are _____ , _____ _____ , _____ , _____ , and _____ _____ .

6. The logical operation of a program is controlled by the use of _____ _____ .

7, 8. Operation codes can be used to turn indicators ON or OFF _____ or _____ through the use of indicators.

9. When the Compare Operation is used, the _____ contains no coding.

10. During a Compare Operation, embedded blanks within a numeric field are considered to be _____ .

11, 12. Whenever a MOVE Operation is used, Factor _____ must always be blank and Resulting Indicators _____ be used.

13. The coding in the _____ field has no effect on the compilation of the program.

14. Data is moved by the _____ position first when the MOVEL Operation Code is used.

15. The rounding-off principle is taken into account by using the _____ _____ column.

CONTROL LEVELS, GROUPS, AND BREAKS

NEW CONCEPTS

Control Level (L1–L9)

Blank After

CONTROL LEVELS, GROUPS, BREAKS
AND FIELDS INPUT SPECIFICATIONS
COLUMNS 59 THROUGH 60

Business reports require totals of figures that they contain. Such figures as invoice amount or quantity sold are added together from the Input Detail Record. Not only are Final Totals, which are written at the end of the report required, but Intermediate Totals are needed as well.

In order to control the writing of totals, Control Fields are necessary. In the following example the requirement is to write a total for each group of items.

Customer

Salesman

Division

Region

Company

This example illustrates how a company would organize its sales force. Each group increases in importance within the organization. The Control Field for each group would be the Customer Number, Salesman Number, and so on. Each group is known as a Control Group. When a Control Field changes from one group to the next, a total is written; then the next group is processed and a total is written. The concept is repeated as often as necessary through the coding in the program. When a Control Field changes as records are read into the program, it is called a Control Break.

The RPG indicator assigned to detect a Control Break is the Control Level Indicator (L1–L9). The Control Level Indicators are assigned a hierarchy. The higher the level number, the greater its importance.

207

In the previous example the Level Indicators would be assigned with Customer Number having L1 and Region Number having L4. Company would not need a Level Indicator because, when all records were processed, LR (Last Record) would be used to control the Company Total.

When a Level Indicator turns ON due to a Control Break, all lower Level Indicators go ON. If L3 goes ON for Division, the Division, Salesman, and Customer totals would be written. Level Indicators may be turned ON as a resulting indicator in Calculations. In this case, all lower level indicators do not turn ON also.

Refer to Appendix A on the RPG cycle. A Control Break causes the RPG cycle to pass through the Total Calculations and Total Output before Detail Calculations and Detail Output. Notice also that the fields from the last Input Record read are not available for processing until Total Output is complete. The last Input Record caused the Control Break because the Control Field changed. The total on the last Control Group is written before the next Control Group is processed.

In Fig. 67 the CUSNR field is the Control Field. Observe how it is coded.

Line (3–5)	Form Type (6)	Filename (7–14)	Sequence (15–16)	Record Identifying Indicator (19–20)	Position 1 (21–24)	C/Z/D (26)	Character (27)	Position 2 (28–31)	C/Z/D (33)	Character (34)	From (44–47)	To (48–51)	Field Name (53–58)	Control Level (59–60)
01Ø	I	INVSUMCD	NS	Ø1	1	C	I	2	C	S				
02	I										3	8	INVNR	
03Ø	I										9	13	CUSNR	L1
04	I													
05	I													
06	I													

Figure 67

Control Level Calculation Specifications (Columns 7 through 8)

If a Control Level is indicated in this field, any operation described on the same specification line as the indicator is done only when the indicated Control Level Indicator is ON. This signifies that the data in the Control Field has changed. These indicators are in conjunction with a Total Calculation.

In Fig. 68 notice how the Control Level Indicator is coded on the Calculation Specifications sheet. Tax and Special Charge are added to a field at L1 time. These total fields will be available for use in additional calculations at the next level up or at LR time.

Line (3–5)	Form Type (6)	Control Level (7–8)	Indicators (9–17)	Factor 1 (18–27)	Operation (28–32)	Factor 2 (33–42)	Result Field Name (43–48)	Length (49–51)	Decimal Positions (52)	Half Adjust (53)
01Ø	C	L1		TSTTAX	ADD	DSTTAX	TSTTAX	7	2	
02Ø	C	L1		TSHCHG	ADD	DSHCHG	TSHCHG	7	2	
03	C									
04	C									

Figure 68

Control Level
Output Specifications
(Columns 23 through 31)

The fields coded in Fig. 69 will be printed when L1 Output Indicator comes ON. Note that it is a total line of print. This fact is evident by the T being coded in column 15.
Control Level Indicators can be coded on three different Specifications sheets. Referring to Figs. 67, 68, and 69, Control Level indicators are

Input   The field(s) that is the Control Field — columns 59 through 60.

Calculation The field(s) that is to amass the data as totals — columns 7 through 8.

Output   When the total line is to be printed — columns 23 through 31.

Blank After (Columns 39 through 39)

The coding of this field resets the fields to zeros or blanks. This code is used when a field serves to accumulate totals for groups of data. Blank After is used when a total field is to be initialized before it starts to accumulate data for the next Control Group. Observe the coding in Fig. 69.

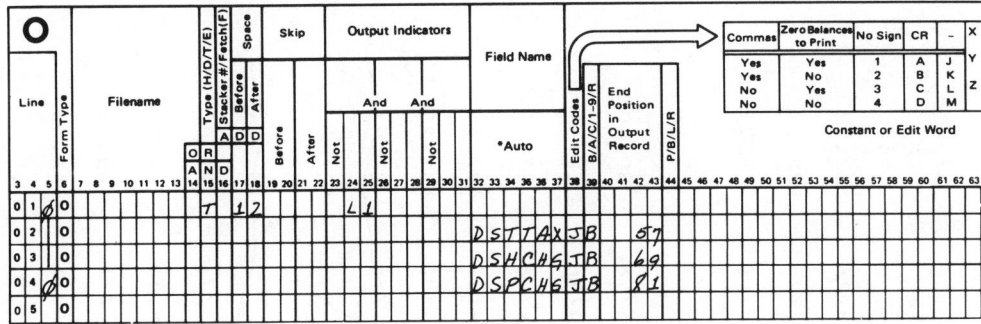

Figure 69

TIP TO PROGRAMMER

A timesaver: correct ALL diagnostic messages in Compile Listing before attempting next compilation.

PRENTREN INVOICE REGISTER BY DATE

INVOICE NUMBER	CUSTOMER NUMBER	REFERENCE NUMBER	INVOICE DATE	STATE TAX	SHIPPING CHARGE	SPECIAL CHARGE	SALES	INVOICE TOTAL
532450	04597	BK1526J	11/13/76	262.29	7.75	20.00	5,245.75	5,535.79
532451	09353	160	11/13/76	128.37	3.75	6.00	2,567.42	2,705.54
532452	10357	IRC2016	11/13/76	18.73	.75	.00	374.50	393.98
TOTAL INVOICES FOR - 11/13/76				409.39	12.25	26.00	8,187.67	8,635.31 *
532453	07120	123A2	11/14/76	50.40	1.50	.00	1,007.94	1,059.84
532454	07120	9860A3	11/14/76	28.44	1.00	.00	568.75	598.19
532455	03824	A0966	11/14/76	17.45	1.00	.00	348.90	367.35
532456	68935	5987-01	11/14/76	152.84	5.50	.00	3,056.73	3,215.07
532457	04902	516	11/14/76	139.29	1.50	.00	2,785.89	2,926.68
532458	32943	16A029B	11/14/76	22.9?	1.00	.00	458.5?	48?.?
...OICES FOR - 11/17/76				?.14	4.00	.??	2,94?	3?.?? *
532470	34982	00517	11/18/76	2.80	.50	.00	56.09	59.39
532471	09353	197	11/18/76	201.19	6.00	24.00	4,023.85	4,255.04
532472	68935	7929-01	11/18/76	15.23	1.00	.00	304.59	320.82
532473	08839	56723	11/18/76	46.53	2.25	.00	930.57	979.35
532474	53898	789	11/18/76	147.19	3.75	2.00	2,943.89	3,096.83
TOTAL INVOICES FOR - 11/18/76				412.94	13.50	26.00	8,258.99	8,711.43 *
FINAL TOTALS				1,662.21	52.75	67.50	33,243.76	35,026.22 **

PROJECT NINE

SPECIFICATIONS:
INVOICE REGISTER BY DATE
DAILY TOTAL – FINAL TOTAL

In Project Seven all the input records were added together to give a final total. In this project there will be a total for each day's invoices as well as a final total.

INPUT SPECIFICATIONS

Since the same Detail Cards used in Project Seven and Project Eight are to be used in this project, definition of the fields will be identical with one exception — the specification line of the Invoice Date Field.

As noted earlier, records having the same data in a Control Field are known as the Control Group; the Control Group field for this project is the Invoice Date Field. Whenever the date of a record is different from that of the previous record(s), a Level Break will occur. This Level Break will indicate that the data that was added from the previous records (all containing the same date) will have the totals of the State Tax, Shipping Charges, Special Handling Charges, Sales, and Invoice Total fields printed.

INPUT FILE

Filename	INVSUMCD
Record Length	80 Positions

PRINT CHART

The Invoice Number, Customer Number, Reference Number, and Invoice Date fields need not be diagrammed to be printed when the Daily Totals and Final Totals are printed for the above-mentioned fields. However, when developing the complete Print Chart, be sure to include all the output fields that are to be printed on the Output Report.

CALCULATIONS SPECIFICATIONS

In this project the data from the Invoice Summary Card must be accumulated and totals printed for each date. One level of totals plus final totals are required. Detail additions are required to accumulate daily totals. Total calculations are needed for final totals. Calculations must be written to accumulate daily totals and final totals for Tax, Shipping Charge, Special Handling, Sales (invoice amount), and Invoice Totals.

OUTPUT SPECIFICATIONS

When there is a change in the Date Control Group, a total must be written that indicates the amounts of the different fields for that date. In order that the total field be reinitialized before the next Control Group starts accumulating, the Blank After concept is used. The final total line should be printed when the Last Record (LR) has been processed.

Editing $ Sign (Columns 45 through 70)

In Project Seven the floating dollar sign method was used. In this project, use the fixed method of printing dollar signs. The zero to the left of the decimal point is the character that suppresses leading zeros. When using this method to print the dollar sign, there are often many blank spaces between the dollar sign and the first significant digit. Notice also that there are NO editing symbols for the field (column 38) when the fixed dollar sign is used. See Fig. 70.

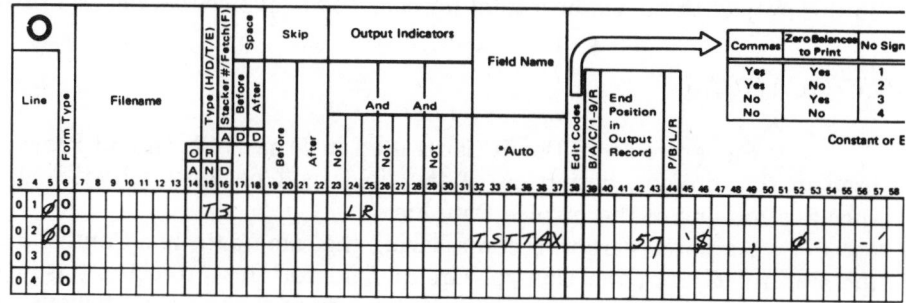

Figure 70

OUTPUT FILE

Filename	REPORT
Record Length	120 Positions

The following additional specifications should be considered before development of the program is begun.

- Extract the detail error cards of Project Eight from the data deck. They may be discarded.

- Develop a Print Chart for the Output Report. Use the Print Chart on page 460–461.

● Code the program on the necessary coding sheets that are provided on pages 214 through 219.

● There is no sequence checking necessary of the file.

● Be sure to allow for proper decimal positions and editing features of the money amounts.

● Code the appropriate headings. You must allow for the skipping or spacing between major and columnar headings as well as between the columnar headings and the detail lines of print.

● Code so that the Constant or Edit Word TOTAL INVOICES FOR- and FINAL TOTALS will be printed.

● Keypunch the coded Source Program.

● Assemble the Source Program in the sequence dictated by the computer configuration being used.

● Compile and debug the program.

● Sort the Invoice Summary cards into invoice date sequence. The earliest date first, the latest date last.

● Use the sorted data to test the program.

● The Output Report should appear as illustrated on page 210.

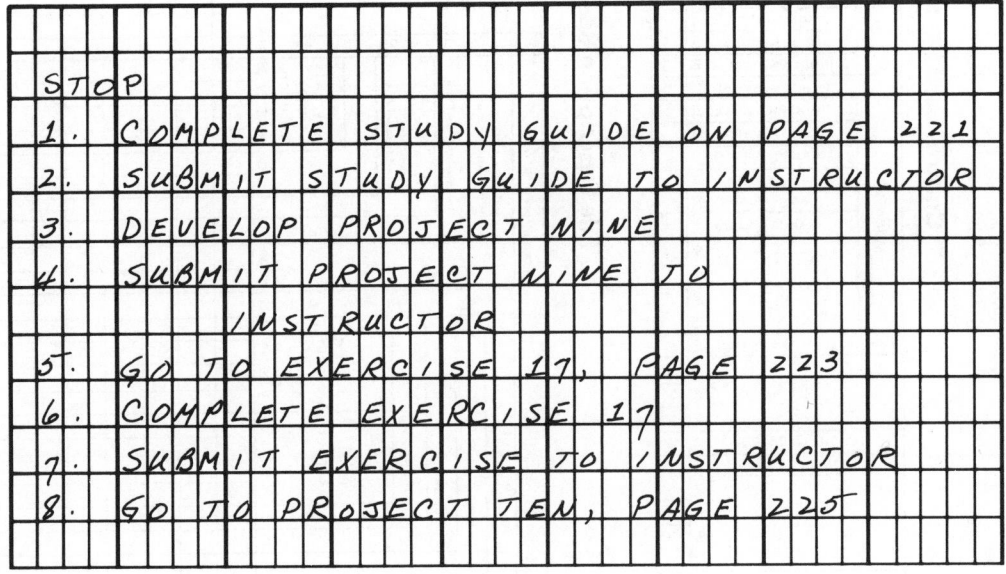

```
STOP
1.  COMPLETE STUDY GUIDE ON PAGE 221
2.  SUBMIT STUDY GUIDE TO INSTRUCTOR
3.  DEVELOP PROJECT NINE
4.  SUBMIT PROJECT NINE TO
        INSTRUCTOR
5.  GO TO EXERCISE 17, PAGE 223
6.  COMPLETE EXERCISE 17
7.  SUBMIT EXERCISE TO INSTRUCTOR
8.  GO TO PROJECT TEN, PAGE 225
```

RPG CONTROL CARD AND FILE DESCRIPTION SPECIFICATIONS

IBM International Business Machine Corporation

GX21-9092-3 UM/050*
Printed in U.S.A.

*No. of forms per pad may very slightly

Program

Programmer

Date

Punching Instruction

Graphic

Punch

Card Electro Number

Program Identification

75 76 77 78 79 80

Page [ ] of [ ] 1 2

Control Card Specifications

Refer to the specific System Reference Library manual for actual entries.

H

Form Type — 6

Line — 3 4 5

0 1 — H

Core Size to Compile — 7 8

Object Output — 9 10

Listing Options — 11

Core Size to Execute — 12 13 14

Debug — 15

MFCM Stacking Sequence — 16 17

Model 20:
- Inverted Print — 20 21
- 360/20 2501 Buffer — 22
- Number Of Print Positions — 23 24 25
- Alternate Collating Sequence — 26 27
- Address to Start — 28 29 30
- Work Tapes — 31
- Overlay Open — 32
- Overlap Printer — 33
- Binary Search — 34
- Tape Error — 35
- 2152 Checking — 36
- Inquiry — 37
- Read/Write/Compute — 38
- Keyboard Output — 39
- Sign Handling — 40
- 1P Forms Position — 41
- Indicator Setting — 42
- File Translation — 43
- Punch MFCU Zeros — 44
- Nonprint Characters — 45
- Table Load Halt — 46 47
- Shared I/O — 48
- Field Print — 49
- Formatted Core Dump — 50
- RPG to RPG II Conversion — 51

File Description Specification

F

Form Type — 6

Line — 3 4 5

Filename — 7 8 9 10 11 12 13 14

File Type (E) — 15

File Designation (P/S/C/R/T/D) — 16

End of File (I/O/U/C/D) — 17

Sequence (A/D) — 18

File Format (F/V/S/M/D) — 19

Block Length — 20 21 22 23

Record Length — 24 25 26 27

Mode of Processing (L/R) — 28

Length of Key Field or of Record Address Field (A/P/I/K) — 29 30 31

Record Address Type (I/D/T or 2) — 32

Type of File Organization or Additional Area — 33

Overflow Indicator — 34 35

Key Field Starting Location — 36 37 38

Extension Code E/L — 39

Device — 40 41 42 43 44 45 46

Symbolic Device — 47 48 49 50 51 52

Labels S/N/E/M (K) — 53

Name of Label Exit — 54 55 56 57 58 59

Extent Exit for DAM — 60 61 62 63 64 65

Core Index — 66

Continuation Lines:
- Option — 53 54
- Entry — 55 56 57 58 59 60 61 62 63 64 65

File Addition/Unordered (A/U) — 66

Number of Tracks for Cylinder Overflow — 67 68 69

Number of Extents — 70

Tape Rewind (R/U/N) — 70 71

File Condition U1-U8 — 72 73 74

Lines: 0 2, 0 3, 0 4, 0 5, 0 6, 0 7, 0 8, 0 9, 1 0

Column numbers: 1 2 3 4 5 6 7 8 9 10 11 12 13 14 15 16 17 18 19 20 21 22 23 24 25 26 27 28 29 30 31 32 33 34 35 36 37 38 39 40 41 42 43 44 45 46 47 48 49 50 51 52 53 54 55 56 57 58 59 60 61 62 63 64 65 66 67 68 69 70 71 72 73 74

RPG INPUT SPECIFICATIONS

IBM International Business Machine Corporation

GX21-9094-2 U/M 050*
Printed in U.S.A.

Program		Punching Instruction	Graphic		Card Electro Number
Programmer	Date		Punch		

Page (1 2) of ___ Program Identification (75 76 77 78 79 80)

Line	Form Type	Filename	OR / AND	Sequence	Number (1-N)	Option (O)	Record Identifying Indicator or**	Record Identification Codes 1: Position	Not (N)	C/Z/D	Character	2: Position	Not (N)	C/Z/D	Character	3: Position	Not (N)	C/Z/D	Character	Stacker Select	P/B/L/R	Field Location: From	To	Decimal Positions	Field Name	Control Level (L1-L9)	Matching Fields or Changing Fields	Field Record Relation	Field Indicators: Plus	Minus	Zero or Blank	
3 4 5	6	7 8 9 10 11 12 13	14 15	15 16	17	18	19 20	21 22 23 24	25	26	27	28 29 30 31	32	33	34	35 36 37 38	39	40	41	42	43	44 45 46 47	48 49 50 51	52	53 54 55 56 57 58	59 60	61 62	63 64	65 66	67 68	69 70	71 72 73 74
0 1	I																															
0 2	I																															
0 3	I																															
0 4	I																															
0 5	I																															
0 6	I																															
0 7	I																															
0 8	I																															
0 9	I																															
1 0	I																															
1 1	I																															
1 2	I																															
1 3	I																															
1 4	I																															
1 5	I																															
1 6	I																															
1 7	I																															
1 8	I																															
1 9	I																															
2 0	I																															
	I																															
	I																															
	I																															
	I																															
	I																															

1 2 3 4 5 6 7 8 9 10 11 12 13 14 15 16 17 18 19 20 21 22 23 24 25 26 27 28 29 30 31 32 33 34 35 36 37 38 39 40 41 42 43 44 45 46 47 48 49 50 51 52 53 54 55 56 57 58 59 60 61 62 63 64 65 66 67 68 69 70 71 72

GX21-9093-2 UM/050* Printed in U.S.A.
*No. of forms per pad may vary slightly

IBM International Business Machine Corporation

RPG CALCULATION SPECIFICATIONS

Program		Punching Instruction	Graphic	Card Electro Number
Programmer	Date		Punch	

Page (1 2) [ ] of ___ Program Identification (75 76 77 78 79 80) [ ]

Line (3–5)	Form Type (6)	Control Level (L0–L9, LR, SR, AN/OR) (7–8)	Indicators: Not (9), 10–11	And: Not (12), 13–14	And: Not (15), 16–17	Factor 1 (18–27)	Operation (28–32)	Factor 2 (33–42)	Result Field: Name (43–48)	Result Field: Length (49–51)	Decimal Positions (52)	Half Adjust (H) (53)	Resulting Indicators: Arithmetic Plus / Compare 1 > 2 / Lookup (Factor 2) is High (54–55)	Minus / 1 < 2 / Low (56–57)	Zero / 1 = 2 / Equal (58–59)	Comments (60–74)
01	C															
02	C															
03	C															
04	C															
05	C															
06	C															
07	C															
08	C															
09	C															
10	C															
11	C															
12	C															
13	C															
14	C															
15	C															
16	C															
17	C															
18	C															
19	C															
20	C															
	C															
	C															
	C															
	C															
	C															

IBM International Business Machine Corporation

RPG   OUTPUT   SPECIFICATIONS

GX21-9090-2 U/M 050*
Printed in U.S.A.

Program
Programmer
Date
Punching Instruction
Graphic
Punch
Card Electro Number
Page 1 2 of ___
Program Identification 75 76 77 78 79 80

Commas	Zero Balances to Print	No Sign	CR	–
Yes	Yes	1	A	J
Yes	No	2	B	K
No	Yes	3	C	L
No	No	4	D	M

X = Remove Plus Sign
Y = Date Field Edit
Z = Zero Suppress

Constant or Edit Word

O

Line — Form Type — Filename — Type (H/D/T/E) — Stacker #/Fetch(F) — Space Before/After — Skip Before/After — Output Indicators (And / Not) — Field Name — *Auto — Edit Codes — B/A/C/1-9/R — End Position in Output Record — P/B/L/R

RPG   OUTPUT   SPECIFICATIONS

Program

Programmer

Date

Punching Instruction

Graphic

Punch

Card Electro Number

GX21-9090-2 U/M 050*
Printed in U.S.A.

Program Identification 75 76 77 78 79 80

Commas	Zero Balances to Print	No Sign	CR	−
Yes	Yes	1	A	J
Yes	No	2	B	K
No	Yes	3	C	L
No	No	4	D	M

X = Remove Plus Sign
Y = Date   Field Edit
Z = Zero Suppress

Constant or Edit Word

Field Name

Output Indicators

Filename

Type (H/D/T/E)

Stacker #/Fetch (F)

Space — Before / After

Skip — Before / After

And — Not

*Auto

Edit Codes

B/A/C/1-9/R

End Position in Output Record

P/B/L/R

Line

Form Type

IBM International Business Machine Corporation

RPG   OUTPUT   SPECIFICATIONS

GX21-9090-2 U/M 050*
Printed in U.S.A.

Program
Programmer
Date

Punching Instruction: Graphic / Punch

Card Electro Number

Page [1] [2] of [ ]

75 76 77 78 79 80
Program Identification

Commas	Zero Balances to Print	No Sign	CR	-
Yes	Yes	1	A	J
Yes	No	2	B	K
No	Yes	3	C	L
No	No	4	D	M

X = Remove Plus Sign
Y = Date Field Edit
Z = Zero Suppress

Constant or Edit Word

Form Type O — Output

Columns:
- Line (3,4,5)
- Form Type (6)
- Filename (7-14)
- Type (H/D/T/E) (15)
- Stacker #/Fetch(F) (16)
- Space — Before/After (17,18)
- Skip — Before/After (19,20,21,22)
- Output Indicators — And/Not (23-30)
- Field Name / *Auto (32-37)
- Edit Codes (38)
- B/A/C/1-9/R (39)
- End Position in Output Record (40,41,42,43)
- P/B/L/R (44)
- Constant or Edit Word (45-70)

Lines: 01 02 03 04 05 06 07 08 09 10 11 12 13 14 15 16 17 18 19 20

Date_____   Name _____

      DIRECTIONS: *Answer the following questions in the spaces provided. Your answers should indicate the depth of understanding that you have toward the concepts and definitions presented. If there is insufficient space provided for your answer, complete your answer on the reverse side of the Study Guide.*

1. Explain why input data must be sorted for the proper use of Level Indicators in RPG.

2. Explain the hierarchy of Control Level Indicators.

3. Explain why Blank After is necessary.

4. Explain the interworkings of the Control Level Indicators on the Input, Calculation, and Output Specifications sheets.

5. Explain the fixed method of printing the dollar sign.

EXERCISE 17

Date _____   Name _____

TRUE–FALSE: *Each of the following statements is either true or false. Indicate your choice in the Answers column by encircling "T" for a true answer or "F" for a false answer.*

Answers

1. Control Level Indicators can be used to specify when a specific operation is to be done   T   F

2. Level Indicators are assigned where the data is in constant change   T   F

3. A Control Field can be known as the Control Group   T   F

4. There is no hierarchy in Control Level Indicators   T   F

5. Whenever an indicator is used for printing, it must always be in the ON condition   T   F

6. A control break signifies that the data has changed in the control fields   T   F

7. On the Calculation Specifications sheet, the indicators in columns 9 through 17 are used in conjunction with detail calculations   T   F

8. Control Level Indicators can be coded on three different Specifications sheets   T   F

9. To reinitialize a field, the Blank After concept is used   T   F

10. All fields that were defined on the Input Specifications sheet must be diagrammed on the Print Chart   T   F

11. The names coded in the Factor 1 Field and the Result Field cannot be identical   T   F

12. The necessary coding for the printing of fixed editing symbols must be coded within literal signs in the Constant or Edit Word Field of the Calculation Specifications sheet   T   F

13. When coding for the fixed dollar sign, the editing symbol is coded in column 38 of the Output Specifications sheet   T   F

14. Whenever a higher-ranked Level indicator is ON, all lower-ranked Level indicators are also turned ON   T   F

15. Indicators must be assigned in ascending order in increments of one   T   F

COMPLETION: *Fill in the blank with the appropriate word or words.*

1. A change in the data of a field used to govern when totals will be printed is known as a _____ .

2. Control Level Indicators are assigned a hierarchy from _____ .

3, 5. Control Level Indicators can be coded on the _____ , _____ _____ , and _____ Specifications sheets.

6. Reinitialization of a counter is accomplished by using _____ .

7, 8. When using the fixed dollar sign method of printing $ signs, the coding is accomplished in the _____ field. Furthermore, there is no coding in the _____ field.

9. To control when to write a total, coding is required in a _____ field.

10. Any indicators coded within the Indicators Field of the Calculation Specifications are in conjunction with _____ line of print.

MATCHING: *Match Column 1 to Column 2.*

COLUMN 1	COLUMN 2	Answers
A. Control Group	1. Column 38 of Output Specification	_____
B. Blank After		
C. Print Chart	2. Resetting fields to zeros or blanks	_____
D. Suppression of	3. Zero coded to left of a decimal point in a	
Leading Zeros	Constant or Edit Word Field	_____
E. Edit Codes		
F. Fixed $	4. Same data in a given field	_____
G. Intermediate Total	5. Output fields diagrammed on a working tool	_____

PROJECT TEN

Periodically, usually on a monthly basis, management must be given a report that indicates

1. The type and quantity of merchandise being sold to each customer.

2. The salesperson selling the merchandise to each particular customer.

3. The frequency of sales to each customer.

4. The total amount of sales to each customer.

5. The total amount of sales of each salesperson per the given fiscal period.

NEW CONCEPTS

PAGE

UDATE, UMONTH, UDAY, UYEAR

PAGE

PAGE is a special word or field name used in RPG II. This field is always four numeric characters in length. The page number will automatically increment by one when a skip to the top of a new page is performed. However, if the constant PAGE is to be printed in addition to the particular page number on successive pages of the Output Report, the coding shown in Fig. 71 should be noted. Here the constant PAGE will be printed as a heading line on each page of the Output Report. The Z coded in column 38 specifies that the leading zeros will be suppressed on successive page numbers.

UDATE, UMONTH, UDAY, UYEAR

UDATE is a special word or field name used in RPG II. Its function is to provide the date when the Output Report is being printed. This date is taken from the CPU

225

memory of the computer configuration. It is a six-position field. However, the Y Edit Code, column 38 of the Output Specifications sheet, is generally used in conjunction with it. This factor, of course, allows for editing on the Output Report. See Fig. 71.

UMONTH, UDAY, and UYEAR are two-position numeric fields. In addition, they are reserved fields. UMONTH, UDAY, and UYEAR are available to the program. Each reserved date field may be referenced in Calculation Specifications. It may not be used as a Result Field.

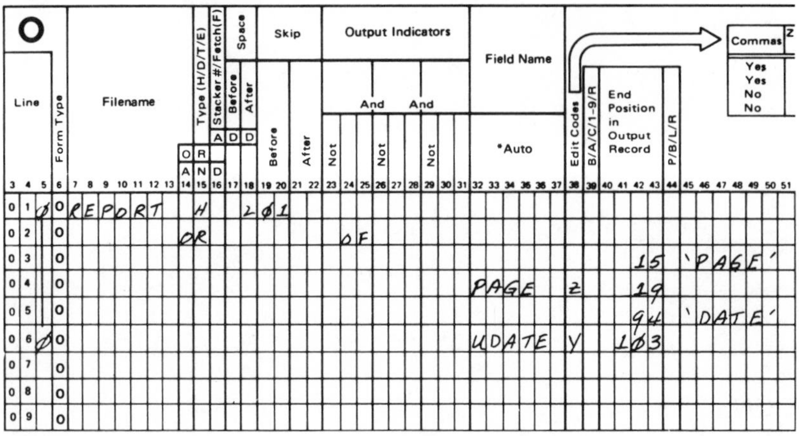

Figure 71

INPUT SPECIFICATIONS

The type of data to be accumulated controls the level number that is to be assigned. That is, the data of least significance is assigned the lowest-level number. The data of greatest significance is assigned the highest-level number. After the first record of a control group is read, the level number assigned will be turned ON. It will remain ON throughout the cycle. Control level numbers DO NOT have to be assigned sequentially in an ascending order.

Once a level number is assigned to a control group on the Input Specifications sheet, it must also be assigned each time that control group is used within the program. Level numbers are also used on the Calculation Specifications sheet and Output Specifications sheets.

When the Invoice Summary card fields are defined, control level numbers must be taken into account for group indication. To obtain the Total Sales for each customer

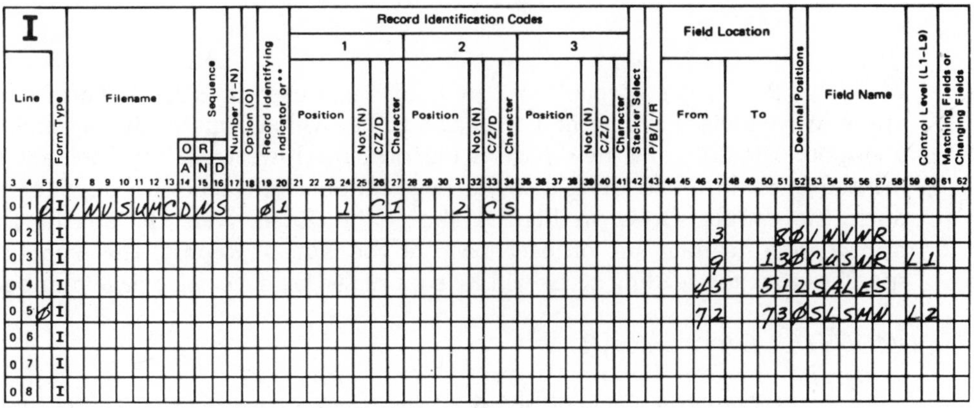

Figure 72

group, control level L1 is assigned to the Customer Number Field. To obtain the Total Sales for each salesman group, control level L2 is assigned to the Salesman Field. See Fig. 72.

In Fig. 72, each time that there is a change in the Customer Number group (Control break), a total will be printed for that customer. Also, each time that there is a change in the Salesman Number (Control break), a total will be printed for that Salesman.

INPUT FILE

Filename	INVSUMCD
Record Length	80 columns

CALCULATIONS SPECIFICATIONS

In this project the data from the Invoice Summary Card must be accumulated and totals printed for each customer and each salesman. Two levels of totals plus final totals are required. Detail additions are required to accumulate customer totals. Total calculations are needed for salesman and final totals. Calculations must be written to accumulate intermediate totals and final totals for Tax, Shipping Charge, Special Handling, Sales (invoice amount), and Invoice Totals.

PRINT CHART

The Print Chart should be diagrammed so that when the Customer Total is printed, a single asterisk will be printed to the right of the Invoice Total column. When the Salesman Total is printed, have two asterisks print to the right of the Invoice Total Field. When the Company Total is printed, three asterisks should be printed to the right of the Invoice Total Field. Asterisks used in this manner automatically give importance to the total level and make the report easier to read.

OUTPUT SPECIFICATIONS

From the Print Chart that you develop, code in the appropriate headings. However, it is suggested that the special words PAGE and UDATE be printed on the same header line along with the name of the report "SALESMAN SALES REPORT." Your Print Chart layout will dictate the end print positions for the Output Specifications sheets.

There need be no spacing after the printing of the LR Total lines.

OUTPUT FILE

Filename	REPORT
Record Length	120 positions

The following additional specifications should be considered before development of this program is begun.†

- Develop a Print Chart for the Output. Use the Print Chart on page 460–461.

- Code the program on the coding sheets provided on pages 229 through 234.

†Upon a successful compilation, reserve the detail cards for use in future programs.

- Keypunch the coded data.

- Assemble the Source Program in the sequence dictated by the computer configuration being used.

- Use the detail cards used in Project Seven as the data. These cards should be sorted in the sequence of Customer Number within Salesman Number.

- Compile and debug the program.

- The Output Report should appear as illustrated on page 236.

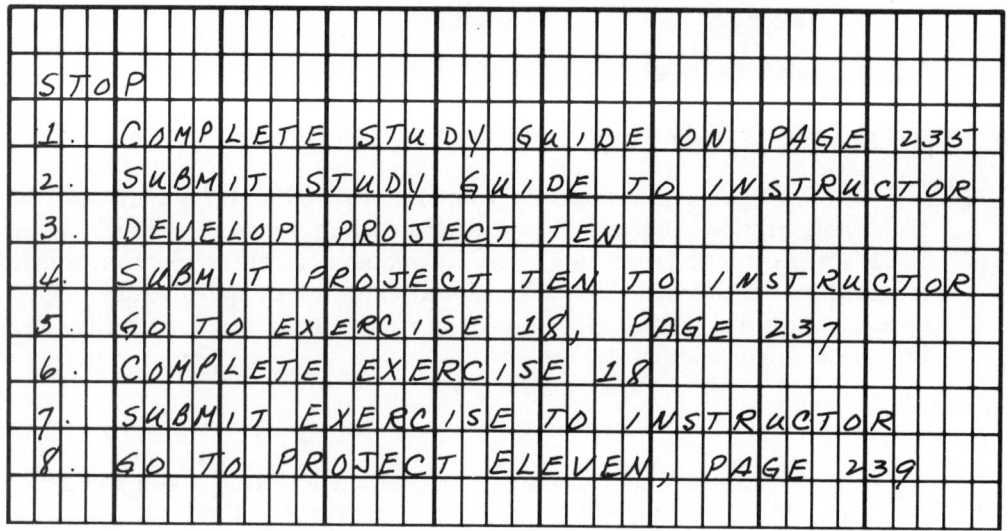

```
STOP
1.  COMPLETE STUDY GUIDE ON PAGE 235
2.  SUBMIT STUDY GUIDE TO INSTRUCTOR
3.  DEVELOP PROJECT TEN
4.  SUBMIT PROJECT TEN TO INSTRUCTOR
5.  GO TO EXERCISE 18, PAGE 237
6.  COMPLETE EXERCISE 18
7.  SUBMIT EXERCISE TO INSTRUCTOR
8.  GO TO PROJECT ELEVEN, PAGE 239
```

RPG CONTROL CARD AND FILE DESCRIPTION SPECIFICATIONS

IBM International Business Machine Corporation

GX21-9092-3 UM/050*
Printed in U.S.A.

*No. of forms per pad may very slightly

75 76 77 78 79 80
Program Identification

Program
Programmer
Date

Punching Instruction
Graphic
Punch

Card Electro Number

Page 1 2 of ___

Control Card Specifications

Model 20

Refer to the specific System Reference Library manual for actual entries.

Form Type
Line

Core Size to Compile
Object Output
Listing Options
Core Size to Execute
Debug
MFCM Stacking Sequence
Inverted Print
360/20 2501 Buffer
Number Of Print Positions
Alternate Collating Sequence
Address to Start
Work Tapes
Overlay Open
Overlay Printer
Binary Search
Tape Error
2152 Checking
Inquiry
Read/Write/Compute
Keyboard Output
Sign Handling
1P Forms Position
Indicator Setting
File Translation
Punch MFCU Zeros
Nonprint Characters
Table Load Halt
Shared I/O
Field Print
Formatted Core Dump
RPG to RPG II Conversion

H

File Description Specification

Form Type
Line
Filename
File Type
File Designation
End of File
Sequence
File Format
Block Length
Record Length
Mode of Processing
Length of Key Field or of Record Address Field
Record Address Type
Type of File Organization or Additional Area
Overflow Indicator
Key Field Starting Location
Extension Code E/L
Device
Symbolic Device
Name of Label Exit
Extent Exit for DAM
Core Index
Continuation Lines
Option
Entry
File Addition/Unordered
Number of Tracks for Cylinder Overflow
Number of Extents
Tape Rewind
File Condition U1-U8

I/O/U/C/D
E
A/D
F/V/S/M/D
L/R
A/P/I/K
I/D/T or 2
A/U
Labels S/N/E/M
K
R/U/N

P/S/C/R/T/D

F

1 2 3 4 5 6 7 8 9 10 11 12 13 14 15 16 17 18 19 20 21 22 23 24 25 26 27 28 29 30 31 32 33 34 35 36 37 38 39 40 41 42 43 44 45 46 47 48 49 50 51 52 53 54 55 56 57 58 59 60 61 62 63 64 65 66 67 68 69 70 71 72 73 74

RPG INPUT SPECIFICATIONS

IBM International Business Machine Corporation

GX21.9094.2 U/M 050*
Printed in U.S.A.

Program

Programmer

Date

Punching Instruction

Graphic

Punch

Card Electro Number

Page 1 2 of ___

Program Identification 75 76 77 78 79 80

Line	Form Type	Filename	Sequence	Number (1-N)	Option (O)	Record Identifying Indicator or **	Record Identification Codes																				Stacker Select	P/B/L/R	Field Location			Decimal Positions	Field Name	Control Level (L1-L9)	Matching Fields or Changing Fields	Field Record Relation	Field Indicators				
			AND / OR				1 Position	Not (N)	C/Z/D	Character	2 Position	Not (N)	C/Z/D	Character	3 Position	Not (N)	C/Z/D	Character			From	To							Plus	Minus	Zero or Blank		

Record Identification Codes 1, 2, 3

Field Indicators: Plus, Minus, Zero or Blank

230

IBM International Business Machine Corporation

RPG   CALCULATION SPECIFICATIONS

Program			Punching	Graphic		Card Electro Number	
Programmer		Date	Instruction	Punch			

Page [1] [2] of ___

Program Identification: [75] [76] [77] [78] [79] [80]

C	Line	Form Type	Control Level (L0-L9, LR, SR, AN/OR)	Indicators						Factor 1	Operation	Factor 2	Result Field					Resulting Indicators				Comments
				Not	And	Not	And	Not				Name	Length	Decimal Positions	Half Adjust (H)		Arithmetic	Compare	Lookup (Factor 2) is	
	3 4 5	6	7 8	9 10	11 12	13 14	15 16 17		18-26	27 28 29 30 31 32	33-42	43-48	49 50 51	52	53		Plus 54	Minus 55	Zero 56		
	0 1	C																		
	0 2	C																		
	0 3	C																		
	0 4	C																		
	0 5	C																		
	0 6	C																		
	0 7	C																		
	0 8	C																		
	0 9	C																		
	1 0	C																		
	1 1	C																		
	1 2	C																		
	1 3	C																		
	1 4	C																		
	1 5	C																		
	1 6	C																		
	1 7	C																		
	1 8	C																		
	1 9	C																		
	2 0	C																		

231

IBM International Business Machine Corporation

GX21-9090-2 U/M 050*
Printed in U.S.A.

Program
Programmer
Date

Punching
Instruction

Graphic
Punch

Card Electro Number

Page ___ of ___

1 2

Program
*Identification

75 76 77 78 79 80

Commas	Zero Balances to Print	No Sign	CR	–
Yes	Yes	1	A	J
Yes	No	2	B	K
No	Yes	3	C	L
No	No	4	D	M

X = Remove Plus Sign
Y = Date Field Edit
Z = Zero Suppress

Constant or Edit Word

Edit Codes 38
B/A/C/1-9/R 39
End Position in Output Record 40 41 42 43
P/B/L/R 44

Field Name
*Auto

Output Indicators
And And
Not Not Not

Skip
After Before

Space
After Before

Stacker #/Fetch(F)
Type (H/D/T/E)

Filename

Form Type

Line

O

O

232

RPG OUTPUT SPECIFICATIONS

IBM International Business Machine Corporation

GX21-9090-2 U/M 050*
Printed in U.S.A.

Program _____
Programmer _____ Date _____

Punching Instruction — Graphic ___ Punch ___

Card Electro Number _____

Page [1] [2] of ___

Program Identification — 75 76 77 78 79 80

Commas	Zero Balances to Print	No Sign	CR	-
Yes	Yes	1	A	J
Yes	No	2	B	K
No	Yes	3	C	L
No	No	4	D	M

X = Remove Plus Sign
Y = Date Field Edit
Z = Zero Suppress

Constant or Edit Word

Edit Codes — B/A/C/1-9/R — P/B/L/R

End Position in Output Record

Field Name — *Auto

Output Indicators — And — And — Not

Skip — Before — After
Space — Before — After
Stacker #/Fetch(F)
Type (H/D/T/E)

Filename

Form Type — Line

O

233

IBM International Business Machine Corporation

GX21-9090-2 U/M 050°
Printed in U.S.A.

Program ____
Programmer ____ Date ____

Punching Instruction — Graphic / Punch

Card Electro Number

Page [1] [2] of ____

Program Identification [75 76 77 78 79 80]

Commas	Zero Balances to Print	No Sign	CR	–
Yes	Yes	1	A	J
Yes	No	2	B	K
No	Yes	3	C	L
No	No	4	D	M

X = Remove Plus Sign
Y = Date Field Edit
Z = Zero Suppress

Constant or Edit Word

Date _____   Name _____

DIRECTIONS: *Answer the following questions in the spaces provided. Your answers should indicate the depth of understanding that you have toward the concepts and definitions presented.*

1. Explain the use of the reserved word PAGE.

2. Explain the use of the reserved word UDATE.

3. Explain the use of Control Level Indicators within a program. Use your own example to explain how Level Indicators would be used to solve a business problem.

SALESMAN SALES REPORT

SALESMAN NUMBER	CUSTOMER NUMBER	INVOICE NUMBER	REFERENCE NUMBER	INVOICE DATE	STATE TAX	SHIPPING CHARGE	SPECIAL CHARGE	SALES	INVOICE TOTAL	
21	07120	532454	9860A3	11/14/76	28.44	1.00		568.75	598.19	
	CUSTOMER TOTAL				28.44	1.00		568.75	598.19	*
	34982	532470	00517	11/18/76	2.80	.50		56.09	59.39	
	CUSTOMER TOTAL				2.80	.50		56.09	59.39	*
	50389	532465	126422H	11/16/76	3.45	.50		69.00	72.95	
	CUSTOMER TOTAL				3.45	.50		69.00	72.95	*
	68935	532456	5987-01	11/14/76	152.84	5.50		3,056.73	3,215.07	
		532472	7929-01	11/18/76	15.23	1.00		304.59	320.82	
	CUSTOMER TOTAL				168.07	6.50		3,361.32	3,535.89	*
	SALESMAN TOTAL				202.76	8.50		4,055.16	4,266.42	**
23	09353	532451	160	11/13/76	128.37	3.75	6.00	2,567.42	2,705.54	
	CUSTOMER TOTAL				128.37	3.75	6.00	2,567.42	2,705.54	*
	45276	532459	220011	11/15/76	2.75	.50		54.90	58.15	
	CUSTOMER TOTAL				2.75					
	83959	532464	PO-12890	11/16/76	29.67	1.25		593.40	624.32	
	CUSTOMER TOTAL				29.67	1.25		593.40	624.32	*
	SALESMAN TOTAL				471.52	14.75	20.50	9,430.26	9,937.03	**
	COMPANY TOTAL				1662.21	52.75	67.50	33,243.76	35,026.22	***

Date_____   Name_____

       TRUE–FALSE: *Each of the following statements is either true or false. Indicate your choice in the Answers column by encircling "T" for a true answer or "F" for a false answer.*

Answers

1. It is not important to know how much merchandise is being sold by each salesman   T   F

2. The page number will automatically increment by one when a Skip to the Top of a New Page is performed   T   F

3. If the word PAGE is to be printed as a constant on each page of the Output Report, it must be coded as a heading on the Output Specifications sheet   T   F

4. The reserved word PAGE is always four numeric characters in length   T   F

5. The reserved word UDATE obtains the actual date from the CPU memory of the computer   T   F

6. In order to have the date edited on the Output Report, the Y Edit Code must be coded on the Output Specifications sheet   T   F

7. The data of least significance of importance is assigned the highest control level number   T   F

8. After the first record of a control group is read, the level number assigned will be turned ON   T   F

9. Once a level number has been assigned to an input control group, it must be used each time that control group is used within the program   T   F

10. Control Level indicators are not used on the Calculation Specifications sheet   T   F

11. Asterisks are automatically printed to indicate degrees of importance assigned to total levels   T   F

12. Each time a different customer's invoice total is printed, the accumulator is reinitialized by using the Blank After concept   T   F

13. The ending position of the field on the detail card determines the printing position on the Output Report   T   F

14. The sorting of the detail cards has little if no effect on the results of the Output Report   T   F

15. All computers support the reserve words PAGE and UDATE   T   F

COMPLETION: *Fill in the blank with the appropriate word or words.*

1. The first record of a control group must be read before the _____ _____ assigned will be turned ON.

2. The page number of the Output Report will automatically increment by _____ _____ when the skip to the top of a new page is performed.

3. The symbol that can be used to give additional importance to a printed total is the number of _____ used.

4. There need be no spacing after the printing of the _____ total line.

MATCHING: *Match Column 1 to Column 2. Give all correct answers.*

COLUMN 1	COLUMN 2	Answers
A. PAGE	1. A two-position numeric field	_____
B. Z		
C. UDATE	2. Coded in Column 38 for editing date field	_____
D. Y	3. Special field in RPG	_____
E. Reserved date field		
F. UYEAR	4. Suppresses leading zeros	_____
G. Asterisk	5. May not be used as a Result Field	_____
H. Print Chart	6. Taken from CPU memory	_____

PROJECT ELEVEN

SPECIFICATIONS:
PRODUCT SUMMARY CARD LIST

The merchandise sold to each customer must be accounted for. That is, each time that a product is sold to a customer, it must be subtracted from the amount on hand in the stockroom. When the number on hand reaches a predetermined number, management must make the decision to reorder the particular product. The reordering process is determined by how fast the product sells. This is known as product turnover. If the turnover rate is extremely slow, the product will not be reordered. Merchandise sitting on shelves in the storeroom represents money. Therefore management must be given accurate, up-to-date data that will be the determining factor for merchandising the products.

PRODUCT SUMMARY CARD

The new card format illustrated in Fig. 73 is for Inventory Products. Each time that a product is sold to a customer, a detail card must be punched. One card is punched for each line item on an invoice. This card is punched along with the Invoice Summary card during invoicing. Several of these cards would be necessary to make up a complete Sales Invoice. However, a customer may purchase just one product. In this case, a single card would make up the Sales Invoice. The formatted input card to be used for this project is also explained below.

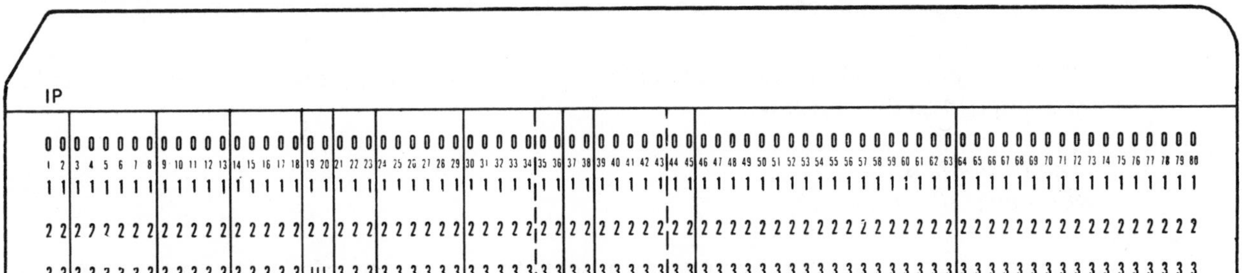

Figure 73

The Record Code IP Field
(Columns 1 through 2)

This constant is punched into each of the Product Summary cards. This field identifies the card as an *Invoice Product Record*.

The Invoice Number Field
(Columns 3 through 8)

This is the number of the Sales Invoice. These numbers are assigned in sequential order.

The Customer Number Field
(Columns 9 through 13)

This is the number assigned to a particular customer. If the customer purchases merchandise several times during the fiscal period or year, this same number is always used. It is the method used to identify the customer name in the Accounts Receivable Ledger.

The Product Code Field
(Columns 14 through 18)

Each product that is purchased for resale is assigned a five-digit numeric code by an employee of PRINTREN GIFT SHOP. This code will appear on each line item of the invoice.

The Product Group Code Field
(Columns 19 through 20)

Each product is classified when it is purchased. Similar product groups are compared for the purpose of product profit and sales analysis.

The Quantity Field
(Columns 21 through 23)

Products are sold in base amounts. That is, some are sold as single units and/or multiple units, such as dozen(s), pounds, and ounces.

The Date Field
(Columns 24 through 29)

The date punched into this field represents the business day on which the merchandise was shipped to the customer.

The Price Field
(Columns 30 through 36)

The amount punched into this field represents the cost of the product(s) to the customer.

The Unit of Measure Field
(Columns 37 through 38)

This field determines the packaging requirements of the product. For example, candles may be sold in single units, by the dozen, gross, or case.

The Cost Field (Columns 39 through 45)

The amount punched into this field represents the price that we paid for the product when it was purchased from one of our vendors. The difference between the Cost field and the Price field represents anticipated profit on the product.

The Description Field (Columns 46 through 63)

This field is used to give a limited explanation of the product being sold.

> *Note:* In previous projects you were provided with the necessary instructions for the flowcharting, coding, keying, and compiling of each project. However, starting with this project, only limited instructions will be given for the completion of each project.

COMPILATION INSTRUCTIONS

1. You are to flowchart, code, key, and compile this project to the satisfaction of your instructor.

2. Code this project to list the data as it is shown on page 243. You are to show a total of each invoice and a final total. Invoice totals should agree with the invoice sales totals in Project Nine.

3. Develop a Print Chart for the ouput. Use the Print Chart on page 460–461.

4. The input data necessary for execution of this project is found on page 242.

5. Coding specifications sheets are found on pages 244 through 248.

6. Reserve detail cards for use in future projects.

7. The Output Report should appear as illustrated on page 243.

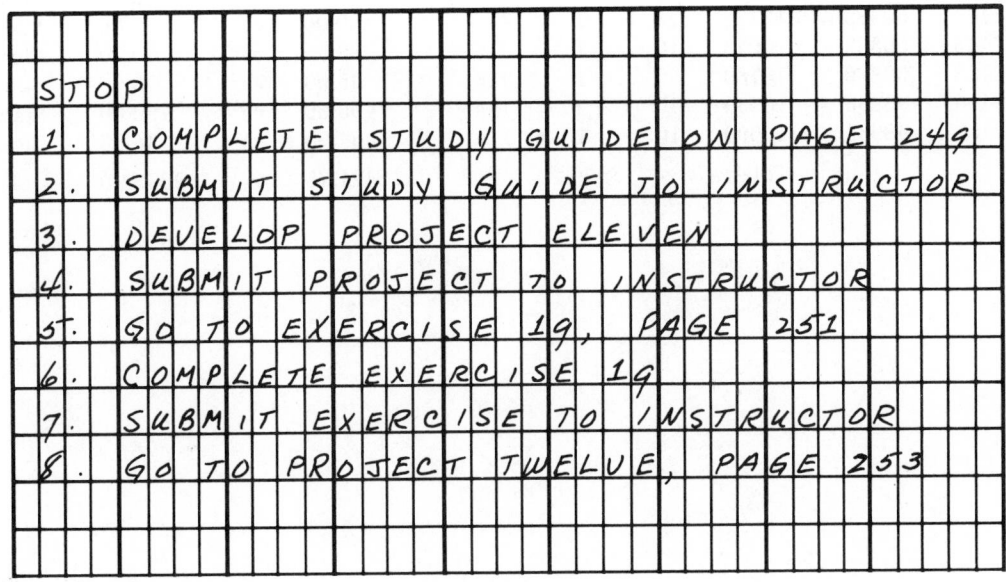

```
     STOP
  1. COMPLETE  STUDY  GUIDE  ON  PAGE  249
  2. SUBMIT  STUDY  GUIDE  TO  INSTRUCTOR
  3. DEVELOP  PROJECT  ELEVEN
  4. SUBMIT  PROJECT  TO  INSTRUCTOR
  5. GO  TO  EXERCISE  19,  PAGE  251
  6. COMPLETE  EXERCISE  19
  7. SUBMIT  EXERCISE  TO  INSTRUCTOR
  8. GO  TO  PROJECT  TWELVE,  PAGE  253
```

IP	Invoice Number	Customer Number	Product Code	Product Group	Qty	Date	Price	U/M	Cost	Description
	532468	3824	10040	10	1	1117--	395.72	ea	260.00	Clock, Marble
	532450	4597	10060	10	1	1113--	4195.00	ea	3000.00	Clock, Grand, No. 5
	532450	4597	10140	20	2	1113--	500.00	ea	250.00	Figurine, Silver
	532450	4597	10100	20	1	1113--	50.75	ea	30.00	Figurine, Ceramic
	532457	4902	10230	30	1	1114--	1495.89	ea	790.00	Statue, 50 inch
	532457	4902	10150	20	1	1114--	1290.00	ea	700.00	Figurine, Gold
	532453	7120	10130	20	2	1114--	250.00	ea	150.00	Figurine, Pewter
	532453	7120	10200	30	3	1114--	195.00	ea	105.00	Statue, 14 inch
	532453	7120	10270	40	1	1114--	117.95	ea	60.00	Vase, Silver
	532473	8839	10320	50	4	1118--	45.00	ea	30.00	Plant, Potted, Floor
	532473	8839	10330	50	8	1118--	60.00	ea	45.00	Plant, Potted, Floor
	532473	8839	10310	50	6	1118--	25.00	ea	15.00	Plant, Potted
	532473	8839	10280	50	3	1118--	30.00	ea	18.00	Plant, Hanging
	532473	8839	10250	40	1	1118--	30.57	ea	17.00	Vase, Ceramic
	532465	50389	10110	20	1	1116--	60.00	ea	36.00	Figurine, Ceramic
	532451	9353	10050	10	1	1113--	1995.00	ea	1000.00	Clock, Grand #1
	532451	9353	10080	10	1	1113--	112.00	ea	62.00	Clock, Wall, Elect
	532451	9352	10220	30	1	1113--	460.42	ea	260.00	Statue, 30 inch
	532469	10357	10170	30	1	1117--	99.55	ea	48.00	Statue, Bronze
	532469	10357	10240	40	4	1117--	36.00	ea	19.00	Vase, Crystal
	532469	10357	10200	30	1	1117--	195.00	ea	105.00	Statue, 14 inch
	532469	10357	10070	10	1	1117--	145.00	ea	80.00	Clock, Wall, Gold
	532460	1854	10030	10	1	1117--	13.54	ea	7.90	Clock, Table, Wood
	532463	50389	10150	20	2	1116--	1290.00	ea	700.00	Figurine, Gold
	532463	50389	10140	20	2	1116--	500.00	ea	250.00	Figurine, Silver
	532463	50389	10120	20	1	1116--	150.00	ea	90.00	Figurine, Pewter
	532463	50389	10020	10	1	1116--	88.52	ea	60.00	Clock, Table, Gold
	532463	50389	10180	30	1	1116--	35.00	ea	20.00	Statue, Ceramic,
	532456	68935	10230	30	2	1114--	1495.89	ea	790.00	Statue, 50 inch
	532456	68935	10090	10	1	1114--	64.95	ea	38.00	Clock, Wall, Batt
			Totals				15421.75		9035.90	

PRODUCT SUMMARY CARD LIST

INVOICE NUMBER	CUSTOMER NUMBER	PRODUCT CODE-DESC	GROUP CODE	QUANTITY SOLD	DATE SOLD	PRICE	EXTENDED PRICE	UNIT OF MEASURE	COST
532450	04597	10060 CLOCK GRAND NO 5	10	1	11/13/76	4,195.00	4,195.00		3,000.00
532450	04597	10140 FIGURINE	20	2	11/13/76	500.00	1,000.00		250.00
532450	04597	10100 FIGURINE CERAMIC	20	1	11/13/76	50.75	50.75		30.00
						INVOICE TOTAL	5,245.75		
532451	09353	10050 CLOCK, GRAND NO 1	10	1	11/13/76	1,995.00	1,995.00		1,000.00
532451	09353	10080 CLOCK, WALL ELECT	10	1	11/13/76	112.00	112.00		62.00
532451	09353	10220 STATUE, 30 INCHES	30	1	11/13/76	460.42	460.42		260.00
...473		...020 PLANT, POTTED, FLO		4	.../18/76	45.00	180.00		30.00
532473	08839	10330 PLANT, POTTED, FLO	50	8	11/18/76	60.00	480.00		45.00
532473	08839	10310 PLANT, POTTED	50	6	11/18/76	25.00	150.00		15.00
532473	08839	10280 PLANT, HANGING	50	3	11/18/76	30.00	90.00		18.00
532473	08839	10250 VASE, CEREMIC	40	1	11/18/76	30.57	30.57		17.00
						INVOICE TOTAL	930.57		
						FINAL TOTAL	20,509.64		

GX21-9092-3 UM/050*
Printed in U.S.A.

RPG CONTROL CARD AND FILE DESCRIPTION SPECIFICATIONS

IBM   International Business Machine Corporation.

*No. of forms per pad may very slightly

Program

Programmer   Date

Punching Instruction

Graphic   Punch

Card Electro Number

Page [1] of ___   Program Identification [75 76 77 78 79 80]

Control Card Specifications

Refer to the specific System Reference Library manual for actual entries.

H Control Card

- Form Type
- Line
- Core Size to Compile
- Object Output
- Listing Options
- Core Size to Execute
- Debug
- MFCM Stacking Sequence
- Inverted Print
- 360/20 2501 Buffer
- Number Of Print Positions
- Alternate Collating Sequence
- Address to Start
- Work Tapes
- Overlay Open
- Overlap Printer
- Binary Search
- Tape Error
- 2152 Checking
- Inquiry
- Read/Write/Compute (Model 20)
- Keyboard Output (Model 20)
- Sign Handling
- 1P Forms Position
- Indicator Setting
- File Translation
- Punch MFCU Zeros
- Nonprint Characters
- Table Load Halt
- Shared I/O
- Field Print
- Formatted Core Dump
- RPG to RPG II Conversion

File Description Specification

F File Description

- Form Type
- Line
- Filename
- File Type (I/O/U/C/D)
- File Designation (P/S/C/R/T/D)
- End of File (E)
- Sequence (A/D)
- File Format (F/V/S/M/D)
- Block Length
- Record Length
- Mode of Processing (L/R)
- Length of Key Field or of Record Address Field (A/P/I/K)
- Record Address Type (I/D/T or 2)
- Type of File Organization or Additional Area
- Overflow Indicator
- Key Field Starting Location
- Extension Code E/L
- Device
- Symbolic Device
- Labels S/N/E/M (K)
- Name of Label Exit
- Extent Exit for DAM
- Continuation Lines (K: Option / Entry)
- Core Index
- File Addition/Unordered (A/U)
- Number of Tracks for Cylinder Overflow
- Number of Extents
- Tape Rewind (R/U/N)
- File Condition U1-U8

244

RPG INPUT SPECIFICATIONS

IBM International Business Machine Corporation

GX21-9094-2 U/M 050*
Printed in U.S.A.

Program _____

Programmer _____   Date _____

Punching Instruction — Graphic ___ Punch ___

Card Electro Number ___

Page [1] [2] of ___

Program Identification [75 76 77 78 79 80]

Line	Form Type	Filename	Sequence	Number (1-N)	Option (O)	Record Identifying Indicator or **	Record Identification Codes													Field Location		Decimal Positions	Field Name	Control Level (L1-L9)	Matching Fields or Changing Fields	Field Record Relation	Field Indicators			
							1 Position	Not (N)	C/Z/D	Character	2 Position	Not (N)	C/Z/D	Character	3 Position	Not (N)	C/Z/D	Character	Stacker Select	P/B/L/R	From	To						Plus	Minus	Zero or Blank

IBM

International Business Machine Corporation

RPG CALCULATION SPECIFICATIONS

GX21-9093-2 UM/050* Printed in U.S.A.
*No. of forms per pad may vary slightly

| Program | | |
| Programmer | | Date |

Punching Instruction — Graphic / Punch

Card Electro Number

Page [ ] of [ ]   1 2

Program Identification [75 76 77 78 79 80]

Line	Form Type	Control Level (L0-L9, LR, SR, AN/OR)	Indicators						Factor 1	Operation	Factor 2	Result Field				Resulting Indicators	Comments
			And Not	And Not	And Not						Name Length Decimal Positions Half Adjust (H)				Arithmetic / Compare / Lookup (Factor 2) is	
3 4 5	6	7 8	9 10	11 12	13 14	15 16 17	18 19 20 21 22 23 24 25 26 27	28 29 30 31 32	33 34 35 36 37 38 39 40 41 42	43 44 45 46 47 48	49 50 51	52	53	Plus 54 55 / High / 1>2 / Minus 56 57 / Low / 1<2 / Zero 58 59 / Equal / 1=2	60 61 ... 74
0 1	C														
0 2	C														
0 3	C														
0 4	C														
0 5	C														
0 6	C														
0 7	C														
0 8	C														
0 9	C														
1 0	C														
1 1	C														
1 2	C														
1 3	C														
1 4	C														
1 5	C														
1 6	C														
1 7	C														
1 8	C														
1 9	C														
2 0	C														

246

RPG   OUTPUT   SPECIFICATIONS

IBM International Business Machine Corporation

GX21-9090-2 U/M 050*
Printed in U.S.A.

Program
Programmer
Date
Punching Instruction
Graphic
Punch
Card Electro Number

Page [1] [2] of [ ]

Program Identification 75 76 77 78 79 80

Commas	Zero Balances to Print	No Sign	CR	−
Yes	Yes	1	A	J
Yes	No	2	B	K
No	Yes	3	C	L
No	No	4	D	M

X = Remove Plus Sign
Y = Date Field Edit
Z = Zero Suppress

Constant or Edit Word

Field Name *Auto

Output Indicators
And   And
Not   Not   Not

Skip
After   Before

Space
After   Before

Stacker #/Fetch(F)

Type (H/D/T/E)

Filename

Form Type

Line

Edit Codes
B/A/C/1-9/R
End Position in Output Record
P/B/L/R

247

RPG OUTPUT SPECIFICATIONS

IBM International Business Machine Corporation

Program
Programmer
Date

Punching
Instruction

Graphic
Punch

Card Electro Number

Page [1] [2] of ___

GX21-9090-2 U/M 050*
Printed in U.S.A.

75 76 77 78 79 80
Program Identification

Output

Commas	Zero Balances to Print	No Sign	CR	-
Yes	Yes	1	A	J
Yes	No	2	B	K
No	Yes	3	C	L
No	No	4	D	M

X = Remove Plus Sign
Y = Date Field Edit
Z = Zero Suppress

Constant or Edit Word

Filename

Type (H/D/T/E)
Stacker #/Fetch(F)
Space Before/After
Skip Before/After
Output Indicators
And / Not

Field Name
*Auto

Edit Codes
End Position in Output Record
P/B/L/R
B/A/C/1-9/R

248

Date _____   Name_____

DIRECTIONS: *Answer the following questions in the spaces provided. Your answers should indicate the depth of understanding that you have toward the concepts and definitions presented. If there is insufficient space provided for your answer, complete your answer on the reverse side of the Study Guide.*

1. Explain how a company keeps track of the merchandise that it purchases.

2. Explain how a programmer can use the Invoice Number and Customer Number fields to obtain corresponding totals.

3. What is the purpose of a constant identifying code in data cards?

4. Explain how and why a programmer would assign Control Level Indicators in the project.

5. Explain how a control tape would be used for the Price and Cost fields.

Date _____   Name_____

TRUE–FALSE: *Each of the following statements is either true or false. Indicate your choice in the Answers column by encircling "T" for a true answer or "F" for a false answer.*

Andwers

1. There is no need to account for merchandise sold to customers   T   F

2. The reordering process of products is determined by how rapidly the product sells   T   F

3. Merchandise sitting on the shelves in the stockroom does not represent money   T   F

4. An invoice total can be the result of a single item of merchandise being sold to a customer   T   F

5. The record code must be punched into every detail card   T   F

6. Invoice numbers are not assigned in sequential order   T   F

7. The Accounts Receivable Ledger is an alphabetical arrangement of the names of the customers   T   F

8. Products need not be classified when they were purchased   T   F

9. Products are usually sold in base amounts   T   F

10. The difference between the cost and the selling price represents profits   T   F

COMPLETION: *Fill in the blank with the appropriate word or words.*

1. When a particular product sells rapidly, it must be reordered to keep it in stock. This is known as _____ .

2. The IP punched into each record in the program is known as a _____ _____ because it identifies each record as an Invoice Product Record.

3. The method used to identify a customer in the Accounts Receivable Ledger in this project is by assignment of a _____ .

4. A Product Profit and Sales Analysis report can be obtained when like_____ _____ are compared.

5. The_____ field is used when it is necessary to have a limited explanation of the product being sold.

PROJECT TWELVE

PRODUCT SUMMARY RECORD EDIT

The object of this project is to check the accuracy of the punched data in the Product Summary card illustrated in Fig. 73. The importance of editing input data cannot be overstressed. Accurate record keeping depends on thorough editing programs.

In Project Eight a different definitive message was printed for each field of the Invoice Summary card when the data was found to be incorrect. In this project the same definitive message can be printed each time that a field is found to be blank. However, there should be some indication as to the specific field being referenced. In order to obtain this special referencing, it is suggested that an asterisk be printed next to the high-order position of the field containing the incorrect data or the lack of data.

NEW CONCEPTS

1. Type of File Organization or Additional Area (I/D/T or 2) Columns 32 through 32 of the File Description Specifications sheet.

2. Field Indicators Columns 65 through 70 of the Input Specifications sheet.

TYPE OF FILE ORGANIZATION OR ADDITIONAL AREAS (I/D/T OR 2)

Placing a 2 in column 32 of the File Specifications sheet will assign to this program an additional input or output buffer. With no entry in column 32, one input or output buffer is assigned to a file. Improved processing times can be realized by the use of two buffers. The only disadvantage is that more computer memory is used. The programmer should be aware of this fact and ensure that enough memory is available for the compilation of the program.

The two assigned buffers are filled alternately by the input device or written from alternately to the output device. Processing is also done alternately. If, for instance, the input device is filling one buffer, the processor can be performing data manipulation on the other buffer. This situation is termed input/output processor overlap.

253

This field is subdivided into three separate subfields.

Plus (Columns 65 through 66)

A valid indicator coded in this subfield will be turned ON if the numeric field coded in FIELD NAME contains a value greater than zero.

Minus (Columns 67 through 68)

A valid indicator coded in this subfield will be turned ON if the numeric field coded in FIELD NAME contains a value less than zero.

Zero or Blank (Columns 69 through 70)

A valid indicator coded in this subfield will be turned ON if the numeric field coded in FIELD NAME contains zeros or if an alphameric field contains all blanks.

Indicators can be assigned the numbers 01 through 99. Field Indicators are used to test a field of an input record to see if its condition is

1. Plus

2. Minus

3. Zero or Blank

The number assigned to a Field Indicator on the Input Specifications sheet is used to control Calculation Specifications or Output Specifications.

The programmer must thoroughly understand when the assigned indicators will be turned ON and when they will be OFF. The indicators of this field are OFF at the beginning of the program. They are turned ON when the condition being tested is present in the record (card) being read. It is turned OFF after the card has been completely processed, just before another record is read.

INPUT SPECIFICATIONS

Each field of the input record should be checked to see if it is blank or zero. The indicator will be used on output to print an asterisk below the high-order position of the field in error and to print an appropriate message. Note this coding in Fig. 74.

In Fig. 74 the Level One (L1) Control Break will occur when the Invoice Number changes. If the Invoice Number Field contains zeros or is blank, Indicator 10 will be turned ON. Whenever the testing field condition is NOT met, the appropriate indicator will be turned ON and the asterisk can be printed in the designated position. Observe how the coding is done on the Output Specifications sheet of Fig. 77, line 140 and 190.

The printing positions for the Output Specifications are obtained from the Print Chart. Note the diagramming of the Print Chart in Fig. 76. Note also how the asterisks are positioned. If the completely coded Output Specifications sheet were illustrated, the printing positions for each of the asterisks would be coded as on the partial Output Specifications sheet shown in Fig. 77, lines 170 to 190.

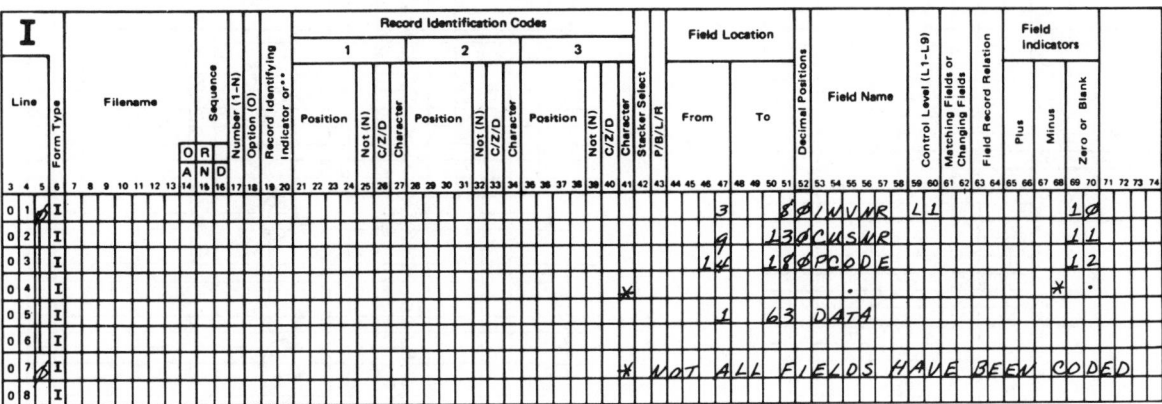

Figure 74

CALCULATION SPECIFICATIONS

Each Product Summary card must be checked for the following items.

1. Each Product Summary card of the same invoice has the same Customer Number.

2. Selling Price must be GREATER than Purchase Price.

3. Extension of Unit Prices to obtain Invoice Total.

4. Individual invoice totals accumulated into Final Total for all invoices.

Same Customer Number for Each Invoice

This is done here as an audit of whether the customer is being charged for the correct product on a given invoice. See Fig. 75, lines 010 to 040.

     In Fig. 75 notice that

1. The use of the Level Indicator is placed so it will have effect during the detail calculation phase of the RPG cycle (Appendix A).

2. The Level Indicators turned ON during the last Control Break will remain ON during the detail calculation phase.

3. The Level Indicator will be ON for only the first record of the control group.

255

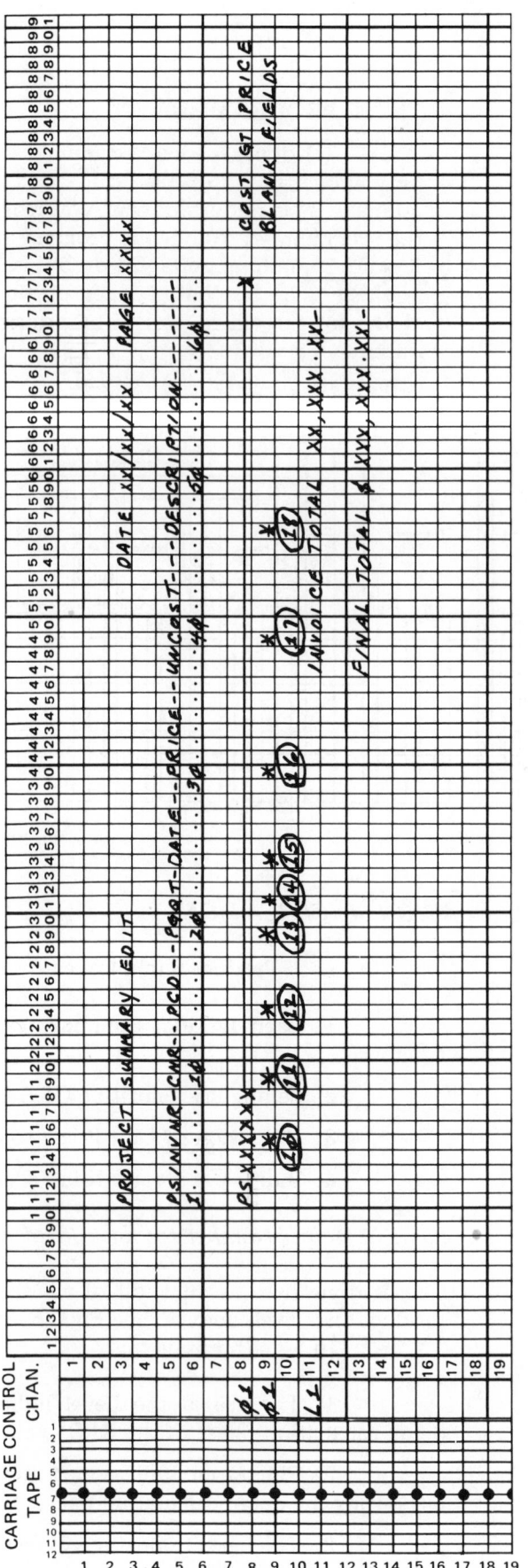

Figure 75

Figure 76

256

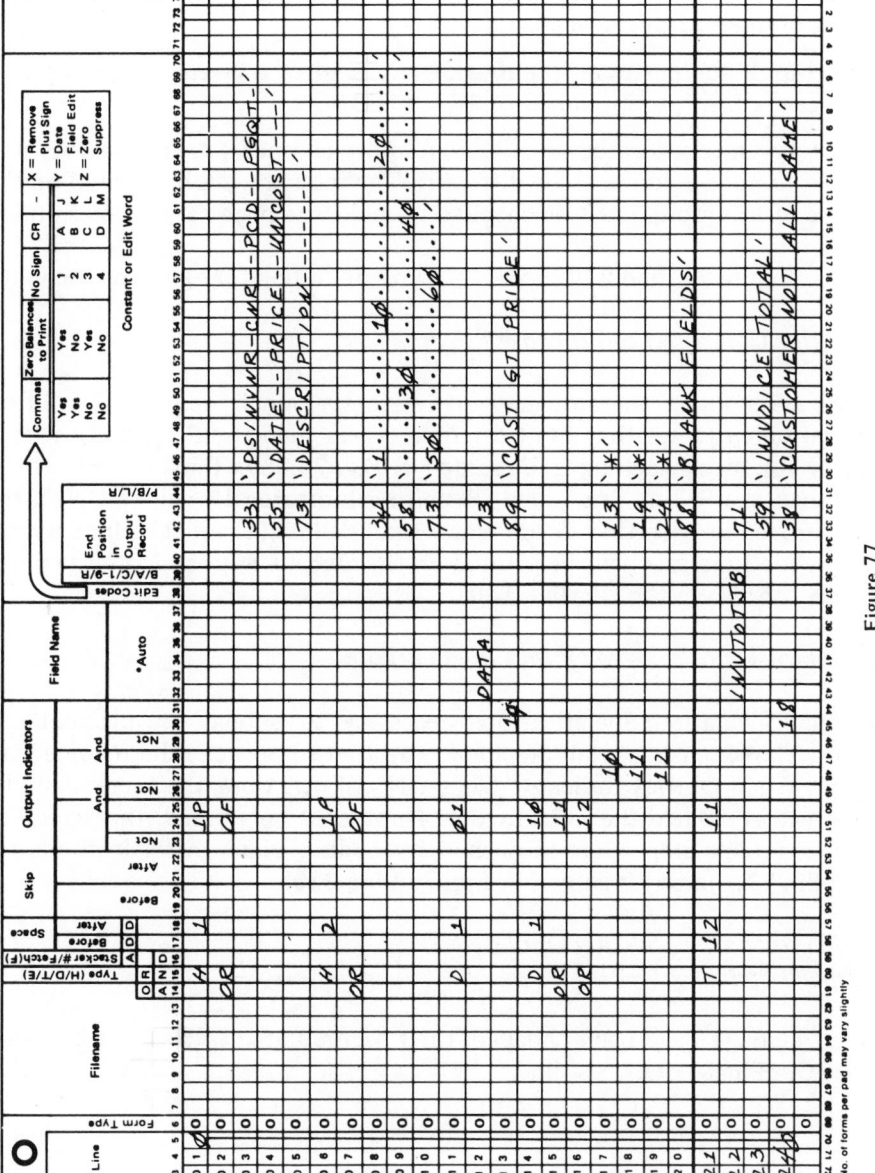

Figure 77

257

Therefore Statement 020 and 030 will only execute for the first card of a level group.

       1. Statement 020 will turn indicator 18 OFF on reading the first level group card.

       2. Statement 030 will move the first level group card's customer number to a field used as a hold area.

       Statement 040 will then compare each card's customer number to the first customer number of the level group.

       3. If the customer number of any card of a given level group is different than the first card of the group, indicator 18 turns ON.

       4. Once indicator 18 is ON, no more compares are needed because at least one customer number is found to be different. The message will be printed on the edit report. The cards of this group must be checked to make the necessary correction(s).

       Figure 77, line 240 shows the type of coding that governs the Output Indicator.

Selling Price Compared to Purchase Price

At times a keypunch operator may inadvertently punch incorrect data into a field. Steps should be taken to see that the Cost field is less than the Selling Price field. The coding necessary for such checking is illustrated in Fig. 75, lines 050 and 060. If the Cost field is greater than the Selling Price field, Resulting Indicator 19 will be ON. If the situation of Fig. 75 proves correct (Cost field greater than Selling Price field), Indicator 19 will be ON and the coded message will be printed on the Output Report. Note the Output Specifications sheet shown in Fig. 77, line 130.

Extension of Unit Prices to Obtain Invoice Total

Code the Calculation Specifications necessary to extend the product price times the quantity. The extension totals are added together to produce the Invoice Total.

       When Output Indicator L1 is ON at Total time, the accumulated Invoice Total will be printed. Since the next Invoice Number is being read, the accumulator must be reinitialized. This step is accomplished by coding Blank After in the appropriate field, column 39. The coding is shown in Fig. 77, line 220.

Individual Invoice Totals Accumulated
into Final Total

When all invoices have been checked, their accumulated totals must be added together to produce the Final Total.

OUTPUT SPECIFICATIONS

       Because each field that is blank will have an asterisk printed in the high order position, a heading should be printed at the top of each page to indicate the name of the field as well as the card column number. See the coding of Fig. 77, lines 010 to 050.

       The coding in this figure signifies the field headings as well as the unused portion of the Print Chart field that is not consumed by the heading. Example: Customer Number is a five-position field. The heading is CNR--. This places the heading directly over the column in the printed line that is the card image. In Fig. 77, lines 060 to 100, on the other hand, the field columns are specified in the coding.

Here the coding illustrates the use of column numbers in multiples of ten. These indicators give direction to the card columns of the input record. Note that there are 63 positions that represent the total number of columns of the input cards that were punched.

The Print Chart shown in Fig. 76 demonstrates that the ending print position of the detail data is print position 73. Also, notice that the field asterisks are indicated by individual Output Indicator numbers that will be turned ON if the particular field is blank. The coding to turn ON any one or all of the Output Indicators if the field(s) is/are blank is illustrated in Fig. 74.

If one or several Output Indicators are turned ON because the field(s) is/are blank, the asterisk(s) is/are printed to indicate this fact. The coding necessary for the printing of the asterisk(s) is/are, as well as the message of that fact, is shown in Fig. 77, lines 140 to 200.

Project Eight and this project represent two methods that can be used to verify the input data of records. However, verification can be accomplished in many ways. These two methods, are certainly not to be construed as the only two available to programmers.

The additional specifications given below should be taken into account before development of this program is begun.

- Use the Print Chart of Fig. 76 as the Print Chart for the output of this program. Remember to use the Print Chart as your programming guide.

- Code the program on the coding sheets provided on pages 261 through 266.

- Keypunch the coded data.

- Take a sufficient number of detail cards and deliberately punch errors into the fields or leave them blank.

a. To indicate that the fields are blank, print an asterisk in the high-order position of each field in error.

b. Print a message to indicate when customer number is not the same for each invoice.

c. Indicate that the cost is greater than the selling price.

d. Print the invoice totals and final total.

- Develop the program so that each time there is a change in the control field, Invoice Number, there will be a control level L1 indicator break signifying that an invoice total must be printed.

- Cards must be sorted on the following fields in the following order:

1. Customer Number — Card columns 13-9.

2. Invoice Number — Card Columns 8-3.

- Code so that the page numbers will be printed at the top of each output page.

- Code so that the date of the output will be printed at the top of each page.

- Compile the program.

The Output Report should appear as illustrated on page 260.

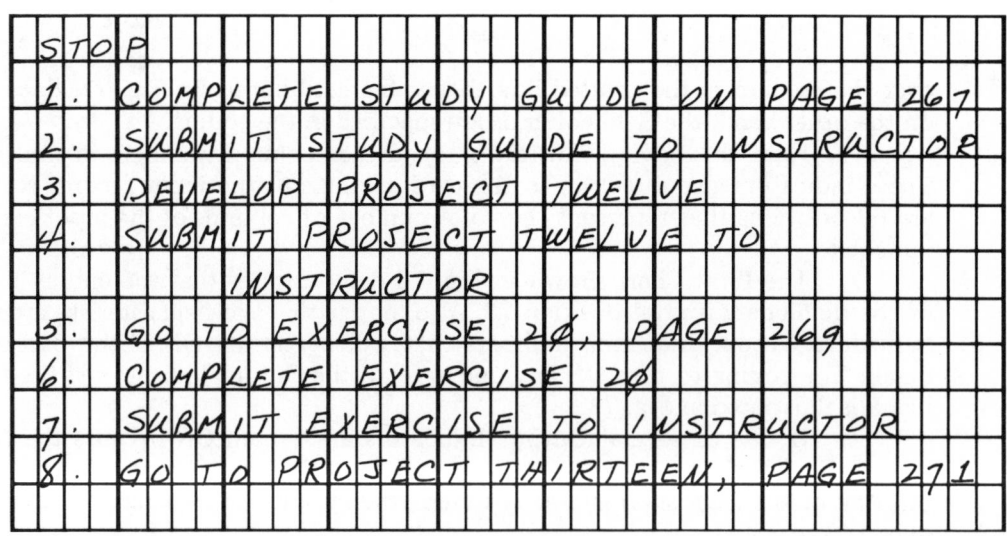

STOP
1. COMPLETE STUDY GUIDE ON PAGE 267
2. SUBMIT STUDY GUIDE TO INSTRUCTOR
3. DEVELOP PROJECT TWELVE
4. SUBMIT PROJECT TWELVE TO INSTRUCTOR
5. GO TO EXERCISE 20, PAGE 269
6. COMPLETE EXERCISE 20
7. SUBMIT EXERCISE TO INSTRUCTOR
8. GO TO PROJECT THIRTEEN, PAGE 271

PRODUCT SUMMARY EDIT

```
PSINVNR-CNR--PCD--PGQT-DATE--PRICE--UMCOST---DESCRIPTION-------
1........10........20........30........40........50........60...

IP532450045971006010   11113760419500   0300000CLOCK GRAND NO 5

                               INVOICE TOTAL    4,195.00

IP      045971006010   11113760419500   0300000CLOCK GRAND NO 5
   *                                                                BLANK FIELDS

                               INVOICE TOTAL    4,195.00

IP532450045971014020   21113760050000   0025000FIGURINE
IP532450045971010020   11113760005075   0003000FIGURINE CERAMIC

                               INVOICE TOTAL    1,050.75

IP532451093531005010   11113760199500   0100000CLOCK, GRAND NO 1
IP532451    1005010    11113760199500   0100000CLOCK, GRAND NO 1
        *                                                           BLANK FIELDS
IP532451093531008010   11113760011200   0006200CLOCK, WALL ELECT
IP532451093531022030   11113760046042   0026000STATUE, 30 INCHES

     CUSTOMER NOT ALL SAME          INVOICE TOTAL    4,562.42

IP532453071201013020   21114760025000   0015000FIGURINE, PEWTER
IP53245307120      20  21114760025000   0015000FIGURINE, PEWTER
        *                                                           BLANK FIELDS
IP532453071201010030   21114760019500   0010500STATUE, 14 INCHES
IP532453071201027040   11114760011795   0006000VASE, SILVER

                               INVOICE TOTAL    1,507.95


IP532473088391032050   41118760004500   0003000PLANT, POTTED, FLO
IP532473088391033050   81118760006000   0004500PLANT, POTTED, FLO
IP532473088391031050   61118760002500   0001500PLANT, POTTED
IP532473088391028050   31118760003000   0001800PLANT, HANGING
IP532473088391025040   11118760003057   0001700VASE, CEREMIC

                               INVOICE TOTAL     930.57

                                 FINAL TOTAL    $33,167.14
```

RPG CONTROL CARD AND FILE DESCRIPTION SPECIFICATIONS

IBM International Business Machine Corporation

GX21-9092-3 UM/050*
Printed in U.S.A.

*No. of forms per pad may very slightly

| Program | | Punching Instruction | | Graphic | | Card Electro Number |
| Programmer | Date | | | Punch | | |

Page [1] [2] of ___

Program Identification

75 76 77 78 79 80

Control Card Specifications

Refer to the specific System Reference Library manual for actual entries.

Control Card fields (columns):
- Form Type (6) — H
- Line (3 4 5)
- Core Size to Compile (7 8 9)
- Object Output (10)
- Listing Options (11)
- Core Size to Execute (12 13 14)
- Debug (15)
- MFCM Stacking Sequence (16 17)
- Inverted Print (21)
- 360/20 2501 Buffer (22)
- Number Of Print Positions (23 24 25)
- Alternate Collating Sequence (26)
- Address to Start (27 28 29 30)
- Work Tapes (31)
- Overlay Open (32)
- Overlap Printer (33)
- Binary Search (34)
- Tape Error (35)
- 2152 Checking (36)
- Inquiry (37)
- Read/Write/Compute (38)
- Keyboard Output (39)
- Sign Handling (40)
- 1P Forms Position (41)
- Indicator Setting (42)
- File Translation (43)
- Punch MFCU Zeros (44)
- Nonprint Characters (45)
- Table Load Halt (47)
- Shared I/O (48)
- Field Print (49)
- Formatted Core Dump (50)
- RPG to RPG II Conversion (51)

Model 20 (38 39) — Model 20

File Description Specification

File Description fields (columns):
- Form Type (6) — F
- Line (3 4 5)
- Filename (7–14)
- File Type (15) — I/O/U/C/D
- File Designation (16) — P/S/C/R/T/D
- End of File (17) — E
- Sequence (18) — A/D
- File Format (19) — F/V/S/M/D
- Block Length (20 21 22 23)
- Record Length (24 25 26)
- Mode of Processing (28) — L/R
- Length of Key Field or of Record Address Field (29 30)
- Record Address Type (31) — A/P/I/K
- Type of File Organization or Additional Area (32) — I/D/T or 2
- Overflow Indicator (33 34)
- Key Field Starting Location (35 36 37 38)
- Extension Code E/L (39)
- Device (40–46)
- Symbolic Device (47–52)
- Labels S/N/E/M (53)
- Name of Label Exit (54–59) — K (53)
- Extent Exit for DAM (60–65)
- Core Index (64 65)
- Continuation Lines
- Option (57 58)
- Entry (60–65)
- File Addition/Unordered (66) — A/U
- Number of Tracks for Cylinder Overflow (68 69)
- Number of Extents (70 71) — R/U/N
- Tape Rewind
- File Condition U1-U8 (73 74)

Line numbers: 0 2, 0 3, 0 4, 0 5, 0 6, 0 7, 0 8, 0 9, 1 0

261

RPG INPUT SPECIFICATIONS

IBM International Business Machine Corporation

GX21-9094-2 U/M 050*
Printed in U.S.A.

Program

Programmer

Date

Punching Instruction

Graphic

Punch

Card Electro Number

Page __ of __

Program Identification

Line	Form Type	Filename	Sequence		Number (1-N)	Option (O)	Record Identifying Indicator or **	Record Identification Codes																					Field Location		Decimal Positions	Field Name	Control Level (L1-L9)	Matching Fields or Changing Fields	Field Record Relation	Field Indicators		
			OR	AND				1					2					3					Stacker Select	P/B/L/R	From	To						Plus	Minus	Zero or Blank
								Position	Not (N)	C/Z/D	Character	Position	Not (N)	C/Z/D	Character	Position	Not (N)	C/Z/D	Character												

Record Identification Codes

Field Location

GX21-9093-2 UM/050* Printed in U.S.A.
*No. of forms per pad may vary slightly

IBM International Business Machine Corporation

RPG CALCULATION SPECIFICATIONS

Program		Punching Instruction	Graphic		Card Electro Number	
Programmer	Date		Punch			

Page [ ] of ___

Program Identification: 75 76 77 78 79 80

Line	Form Type	Control Level (L0-L9, LR, SR, AN/OR)	Indicators									Factor 1	Operation	Factor 2	Result Field					Resulting Indicators							Comments
			Not	And	Not	And	Not								Name	Length	Decimal Positions	Half Adjust (H)		Arithmetic			Compare				
																			Plus	Minus	Zero	1>2	1<2	1=2		
																						Lookup (Factor 2) is				
																						High	Low	Equal		

(Column numbers: 3 4 5 6 7 8 9 10 11 12 13 14 15 16 17 18 19 20 21 22 23 24 25 26 27 28 29 30 31 32 33 34 35 36 37 38 39 40 41 42 43 44 45 46 47 48 49 50 51 52 53 54 55 56 57 58 59 60 61 62 63 64 65 66 67 68 69 70 71 72 73 74)

Lines: 01, 02, 03, 04, 05, 06, 07, 08, 09, 10, 11, 12, 13, 14, 15, 16, 17, 18, 19, 20 (all Form Type C)

IBM International Business Machine Corporation

RPG   OUTPUT   SPECIFICATIONS

GX21-9090-2 U/M 050*
Printed in U.S.A.

Program

Programmer

Date

Punching
Instruction

Graphic

Punch

Card Electro Number

Page ___ of ___

Program
Identification

75 76 77 78 79 80

Form Type

Line

Filename

Type (H/D/T/E)

Stacker #/Fetch(F)

Space

Before / After

Skip

Before / After

Output Indicators

And / And

Not / Not / Not

Field Name

*Auto

Edit Codes

B/A/C/1-9/R

End Position in Output Record

P/B/L/R

Constant or Edit Word

Commas	Zero Balances to Print	No Sign	CR	-
Yes	Yes	1	A	J
Yes	No	2	B	K
No	Yes	3	C	L
No	No	4	D	M

X = Remove Plus Sign
Y = Date Field Edit
Z = Zero Suppress

RPG OUTPUT SPECIFICATIONS

IBM International Business Machine Corporation

GX21-9090-2 U/M 050*
Printed in U.S.A.

Program		Punching Instruction	Graphic	Card Electro Number
Programmer	Date		Punch	

Page (1 2) of ___ Program Identification (75 76 77 78 79 80)

Commas	Zero Balances to Print	No Sign	CR	-
Yes	Yes	1	A	J
Yes	No	2	B	K
No	Yes	3	C	L
No	No	4	D	M

X = Remove Plus Sign
Y = Date Field Edit
Z = Zero Suppress

Line (3–5)	Form Type (6)	Filename (7–13)	OR / AND (14)	Type (H/D/T/E) (15)	Stacker #/Fetch(F) (16)	Space Before (17)	Space After (18)	Skip Before (19–20)	Skip After (21–22)	Output Indicators: Not (23)	(24–25)	And: Not (26)	(27–28)	And: Not (29)	(30–31)	Field Name / *Auto (32–37)	Edit Codes (38)	B/A/C/1–9/R (39)	End Position in Output Record (40–43)	P/B/L/R (44)	Constant or Edit Word (45–70)	(71–74)
01	O																					
02	O																					
03	O																					
04	O																					
05	O																					
06	O																					
07	O																					
08	O																					
09	O																					
10	O																					
11	O																					
12	O																					
13	O																					
14	O																					
15	O																					
16	O																					
17	O																					
18	O																					
19	O																					
20	O																					
	O																					
	O																					
	O																					
	O																					
	O																					

IBM

International Business Machine Corporation

RPG   OUTPUT   SPECIFICATIONS

| Program | | |
| Programmer | | Date |

Punching Instruction

Graphic / Punch

Card Electro Number

Page ☐ of ___

GX21-9090-2 U/M 050*
Printed in U.S.A.

75 76 77 78 79 80

Program Identification

O

| Line | Form Type | Filename | Type (H/D/T/E) | Stacker #/Fetch(F) | Space Before/After | Skip Before/After | Output Indicators | Field Name *Auto | Edit Codes | End Position in Output Record | Constant or Edit Word |

Commas	Zero Balances to Print	No Sign	CR	-
Yes	Yes	1	A	J
Yes	No	2	B	K
No	Yes	3	C	L
No	No	4	D	M

X = Remove Plus Sign
Y = Date Field Edit
Z = Zero Suppress

STUDY GUIDE

Date _____   Name _____

DIRECTIONS: *Answer the following questions in the spaces provided. Your answers should indicate the depth of understanding that you have toward the concepts and definitions presented. If there is insufficient space provided for your answer, complete your answer on the reverse side of the Study Guide.*

1. Explain how an additional input buffer allows faster program execution.

2. Explain how the Field Indicators work in the testing procedure of an input record.

3. Explain why it is important to check the relationship between the Customer Number and the Invoice Number.

4. Explain why it is important to test the relationship between the Purchase and Selling Price fields of the input record.

5. Explain an alternate method by which a program can be used to edit and check the accuracy of data.

Date_____   Name_____

TRUE–FALSE: *Each of the following statements is either true or false. Indicate your choice in the Answers column by encircling "T" for a true answer or "F" for a false answer.*

Answers

1. When using an editing program to edit detail cards, it is not necessary to be concerned about the accuracy of the data punched into the cards .... T   F

2. Any of the computer-supported symbols can be coded by the programmer to signify that a field(s) contains incorrectly punched data ... T   F

3. Improved processing time can be realized by the use of two buffers ... T   F

4. Additional storage is automatically allocated by the computer when more than one buffer is required by the Source Program ... T   F

5. The term "input/output processor overlap" signifies that the input device is filling one buffer while the processor is performing data manipulation on the other buffer ... T   F

6. Field Indicators are used to test a field of the input record to see if its condition is only plus or minus ... T   F

7. Operations cannot be conditioned by Field Indicators ... T   F

8. Field Indicators have a numbering system whereby they only run from 01 throuh 49 ... T   F

9. It makes little if any difference when Field Indicators are ON or OFF ... T   F

10. Field Indicators can be used to condition any type of output data ... T   F

11. Whatever the programmer diagrams on the Print Chart will be printed on the Output Report ... T   F

12. The Print Chart is not a formality but a tool to be used by the programmer ... T   F

13. Care should be taken to see that the cost field data is less than the selling price field data ... T   F

14. Accumulators can be reinitialized to zero by moving the constant zero into the accumulator ... T   F

15. When coding comment statements, every consecutive card column must contain a character ... T   F

16. No additional coding is necessary if additional buffers are to be used ... T   F

17. The filling and processing of buffers is done alternately ... T   F

18. Zero and Blank are valid for checking by a Field Indicator ... T   F

19. A Field Indicator is OFF at the beginning of the program and just before the next record is read. ... T   F

20. The sequencing of the detail cards must be in a prescribed order ... T   F

COMPLETION: *Fill in the blank with the appropriate word or words.*

1, 2. When additional buffers are used in a program, improved_____ _____ time can be realized. However, the disadvantage of using additional buffers is that more _____ _____ will be used.

3, 4. The term input/output processor overlap refers to when one buffer is being filled by the_____ _____ and the processor is performing_____ _____ on the other buffer.

5, 7. Field Indicators test fields of an input record to see if the condition is_____ _____ or _____ and/or_____ _____ .

8, 9. The number assigned to a Field Indicator on the Input Specification Sheet is used to control _____ or _____ .

10, 12. Field Indicators are_____ at the beginning of the program. However, they are turned_____when the condition being tested is present in the record being read. They are again turned_____ immediately after the record has been completely processed.

13. A Print Chart is not a formality but a_____to be used by the programmer.

14. An asterisk placed in column 7 indicates that the card is a_____ _____ card.

MATCHING: *Match Column 1 to Column 2.*

COLUMN 1	COLUMN 2	Answers
A. Reinitialize	1. Product price times the quantity	_____
B. "2" in column 32		
C. Field Indicators	2. Coding of a B in column 39 of the Output Specifications	_____
D. Level Indicators		
E. MOVE	3. Numbers L1 through L9	_____
F. Extension	4. Assignment of additional buffers	_____
G. Total Time		
	5. Nothing coded in Factor 1 when used	_____
	6. Numbers 01 through 99	_____

PROJECT THIRTEEN

The main reason for the PRINTREN GIFT SHOP, or your business, being in business is to make a profit. By listing all income and expenses on an Income Statement, it is possible to determine how much profit was made over a fiscal period. The profit made during one fiscal period can be applied to the next fiscal period for growth and expansion, or it can be used to reduce or completely pay off debts of the business or to pay the stockholders a dividend.

The income of the PRINTREN GIFT SHOP can be shown by listing the monies that have been collected from the sale of merchandise. The expenses involved in running the business are many. Some are rent, light, heat, water, custodial services, wages, salaries paid to the employees, and short-term and long-term loan repayments.

This project will determine the profit percentages of each product, product group, and total profit for the business. The percentage established on this report is called Product Profit Contribution. In other words, how much does each product contribute to the final profit of the company? To find this percentage, a simple formula is used.

$$\frac{\text{Selling price} - \text{cost}}{\text{Selling price}} \times 100 = \text{percent of profit}$$

EXAMPLE

Selling Price = $160.00

Cost Price   =   80.00

$$\frac{160.00 - 80.00}{160.00} \times 100 = 50\%$$

In this example it can readily be seen that the amount of profit is computed by dividing the selling price of the product into the difference between the cost price and the selling price of the product.

The products or merchandise that a business sells is obtained through one of two processes: (1) the products are manufactured from raw materials for resale or, (2) the finished products are purchased for resale. Your business purchases the finished products for resale.

271

NEW CONCEPTS

Division

Half Adjust

DIVISION (DIV)

The Operation Code for Division is DIV. When using the DIV operation, the data in Factor 1 is ALWAYS divided by the data in Factor 2. The result of the division (the Quotient) is placed in the Result Field. Half Adjust (H) should be taken into consideration when division is coded on the Calculation Specifications sheet. See Fig. 78.

In Fig. 78 notice that

1. TPCST (Total Product Cost) coded in Factor 2 is the divisor.

2. TPSAL (Total Product Sales) coded in Factor 1 is the dividend.

3. WRK1 (Work 1) coded in the Result Field is the quotient.

4. The length of the quotient is four positions with a decimal point three positions from the right.

5. The quotient will be half-adjusted (rounded off) by coding in the Half Adjust (H) Field—column 53.

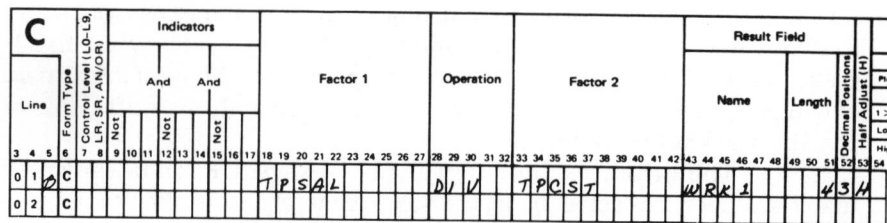

Figure 78

HALF ADJUST

Half Adjust (Rounding Off) should be considered when

1. The number of decimal positions of the Result Field is less than the number of decimal positions in Factor 1 or Factor 2 of an ADD or SUBTRACT operation.

2. The number of decimal positions is less than the combined number of decimal positions of Factor 1 and Factor 2 in MULTIPLY operation.

3. A DIVIDE operation is used.

An H coded in column 53 of the Calculation Specifications sheet causes the process of Half Adjust. Half Adjust causes the value of 5 to be added to the right of the last position of the Result Field. Note the following examples.

ADD	123.567	Factor 1	MULT	1.36	Factor 1
	+ 2.1	Factor 2		X 0.27	Factor 2
	125.667	Intermediate Result		0.3672	Intermediate Result
	+ 5	Half Adjust		+ 5	Half Adjust
	125.7	Result		0.37	Result

272

INPUT SPECIFICATIONS

As noted, not all the fields of the input record are necessary for the compilation of this project. However, of the ones that must be used, special consideration should be given to the Product Code and Product Group fields.

To ensure a total for each Product Code as well as for each Product Group, level breaks should be assigned. A Level 1 control break should be placed on the Product Code Field. A Level 2 Control Break should be placed on the Product Group field. Fig. 79 shows the coding of the level breaks.

Control level breaks will occur each time the Product Code changes. Each time the Product Group changes, a total will be indicated for it as well as for Product Code. Remember that each time a higher-level control break occurs, all lesser control breaks also occur.

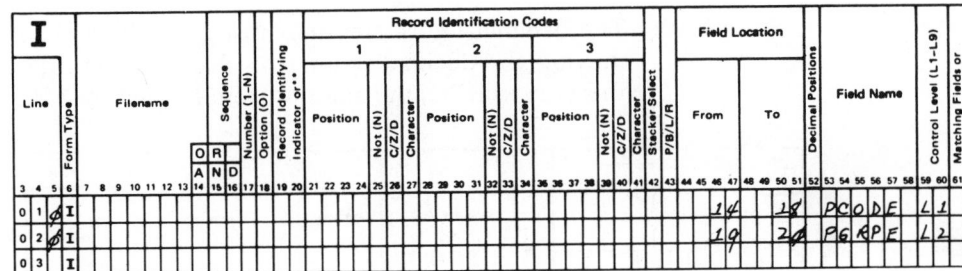

Figure 79

INPUT FILE

Filename   PRODSUM

Record Length   80 Positions

CALCULATION SPECIFICATIONS

For this project the coding on the Calculation Specifications sheet can be divided into four specific areas.

1. Product Level Data Accumulation (Detail Time)

2. Product Profit Calculations and Group Total Accumulation (L1 Time)

3. Group Profit Calculations and Final Total Accumulations (L2 Time)

4. Final Profit Calculation (LR Time)

Product Level Data Accumulation
(Detail Time)

Each detail card is utilized so that all like products are added together. The cost price of each product is multiplied by the quantity purchased to establish the cost of purchases. The quantity sold is multiplied by the selling price to establish the total amount of sales.

Product Profit Calculation and Group Total
Accumulation (L1 Time)

Management must be informed as to how much profit is made on a particular product

273

purchased from the group. As stated earlier, the profit is determined by subtracting the cost price from the selling price. This amount is then divided by the selling price. The figure will be a decimal amount. In order to convert the decimal amount into a percentage amount (moving the decimal point two places to the right), the decimal amount is multiplied by 100. Note the coding of Fig. 80.

Referring to Fig. 80, note that

Line 010   The Cost of the Product is subtracted from the Selling Price. A field WRK1 was created in the Result Field to store the difference.

Line 020   The amount (difference) stored in WRK1 is divided by the Total Product Sales (TPSAL) and the minuend is stored in WRK2 of the Result Field.

Line 030   The decimal figure amount must be converted to a percentage by moving the decimal point two places to the right. To accomplish this step in RPG, the amount is multiplied by 100.

Figure 80

Group Profit Calculation and Final Total Accumulation (L2 Time)

The next step in the sequence is to determine specific group profit. It should be understood that while profit is being figured, a total must be given sufficient consideration in that it, too, must be accumulated.

Final Profit Calculation (LR Time)

The final totals being accumulated for the Cost and Selling fields must now be considered for the amount of profit that has been generated.

In Fig. 80 special attention should be paid to how WRK1 and WRK2 were used in the Result Field. Each time that data was placed in either or both fields, it destroyed the data that was previously stored in the field. This replacement is known as destructive readin. The ability of destructive readin allows the same field position in core storage to be used again and again in many different ways.

When the Product Code changes (at L1 Total Time), it will be necessary to print out the following fields:

1. Product Code

2. Product Description

3. Number Sold

4. Total Sales

5. Total Cost

6. Percent of Profit

When the Group Code changes (at L2 Total Time), it will be necessary to print only those fields that have been accumulating. These fields are

1. Product Group

2. Total Sales

3. Total Cost

4. Percent of Profit

These fields should contain the necessary editing codes that will allow the printout to have user readability. Proper care should also be taken so that the accumulators are reinitialized at the various total levels. Finally, when the last record has been processed, the Grand Total must also be printed.

OUTPUT FILE

Filename   REPORT

Record Length   120 Print Positions

COMPILATION INSTRUCTIONS

1. Develop a Print Chart for the Output Report. Use the Print Chart on page 462-463.

2. Code, keypunch, and compile this project to the satisfaction of your instructor.

3. Coding Specifications sheets are on pages 277 through 282.

4. The Output Report should appear as illustrated on page 276.

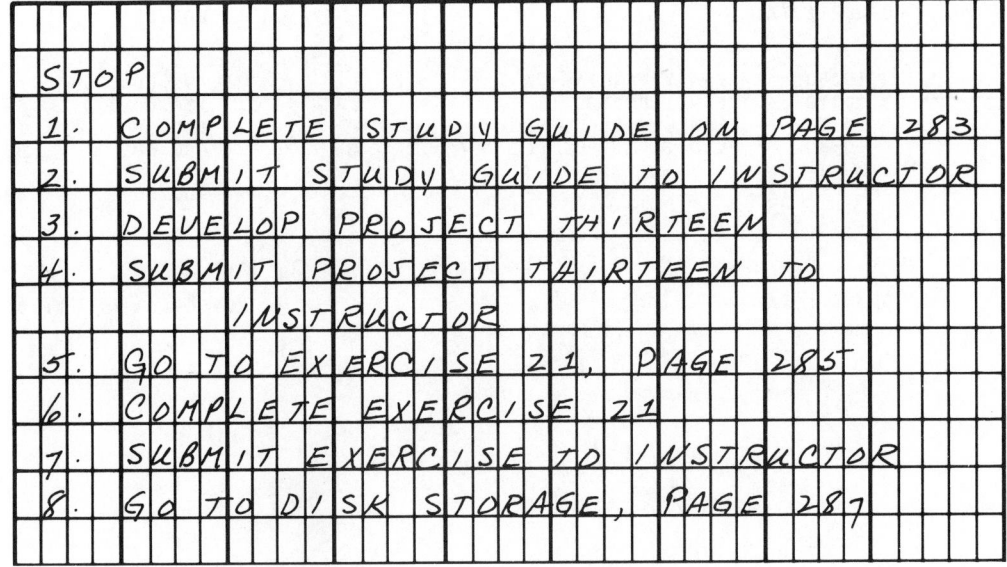

```
STOP
1. COMPLETE STUDY GUIDE ON PAGE 283
2. SUBMIT STUDY GUIDE TO INSTRUCTOR
3. DEVELOP PROJECT THIRTEEN
4. SUBMIT PROJECT THIRTEEN TO
   INSTRUCTOR
5. GO TO EXERCISE 21, PAGE 285
6. COMPLETE EXERCISE 21
7. SUBMIT EXERCISE TO INSTRUCTOR
8. GO TO DISK STORAGE, PAGE 287
```

PRODUCT PROFIT ANALYSIS

| ----------PRODUCT-------------------- | | | TOTAL | TOTAL | TOTAL | PERCENT |
GROUP	CODE	DESCRIPTION	SALES QTY.	SALES	COST	PROFIT
	10020	CLOCK, TABLE, GOLD	1	88.52	60.00	32.2
	10030	CLOCK, TABLE, WOOD	1	13.54	7.90	41.7
	10040	CLOCK MARBLE	1	395.72	260.00	34.3
	10050	CLOCK, GRAND NO 1	1	1,995.00	1,000.00	49.9
	10060	CLOCK GRAND NO 5	1	4,195.00	3,000.00	28.5
	10070	CLOCK, WALL, GOLD	1	145.00	80.00	44.8
	10080	CLOCK, WALL ELECT	1	112.00	62.00	44.6
	10090	CLOCK, WALL, BAT	1	64.95	38.00	41.5
10	GROUP TOTAL			7,009.73	4,507.90	35.6
	10100	FIGURINE CERAMIC	1	50.75	30.00	40.9
	10110	FIGURINE, CERAMIC	1	69.00	36.00	47.8
	10120	FIGURINE, PEWTER	1	150.00	90.00	40.0
	10130	FIGURINE, PEWTER	2	500.00	300.00	40.0
	10140	FIGURINE	4	2,000.00	1,000.00	50.0
	10150	FIGURINE, GOLD	3	3,870.00	2,100.00	45.7
20	GROUP TOTAL			6,639.75	3,556.00	46.4
	10100	STATUE, 14 INCHES	2	390.00	210.00	46.2
	10170	STATUE, BRONZE	1	99.55	48.00	51.8
	10180	STATUE, CERAMIC	1	35.00	20.00	42.9
	10200	STATUE 14 INCHES	1	195.00	105.00	46.2
	10220	STATUE, 30 INCHES	1	460.42	260.00	43.5
	10230	STATUE, 50 INCHES	3	4,487.67	2,370.00	47.2
30	GROUP TOTAL			5,667.64	3,013.00	46.8
	10240	VASE, CRYSTAL	4	144.00	76.00	47.2
	10250	VASE, CEREMIC	1	30.57	17.00	44.4
	10270	VASE, SILVER	1	117.95	60.00	49.1
40	GROUP TOTAL			292.52	153.00	47.6
	10280	PLANT, HANGING	3	90.00	54.00	40.0
	10310	PLANT, POTTED	6	150.00	90.00	40.0
	10320	PLANT, POTTED, FLO	4	180.00	120.00	33.3
	10330	PLANT, POTTED, FLO	8	480.00	360.00	25.0
50	GROUP TOTAL			900.00	624.00	30.6
	GRAND TOTAL			20,509.64	11,853.90	42.2

RPG CONTROL CARD AND FILE DESCRIPTION SPECIFICATIONS

IBM International Business Machine Corporation

GX21-9092-3 UM/050*
Printed in U.S.A.

*No. of forms per pad may very slightly

Program		Punching Instruction	Graphic		Card Electro Number
Programmer	Date		Punch		

Page [1] [2] of ____

Program Identification 75 76 77 78 79 80

Control Card Specifications

H

Line — Form Type (6) — H

Columns: 7 8 9 10 11 12 13 14 15 16 17 18 19 20 21 22 23 24 25 26 27 28 29 30 31 32 33 34 35 36 37 38 39 40 41 42 43 44 45 46 47 48 49 50 51 52 53 54 55 56 57 58 59 60 61 62 63 64 65 66 67 68 69 70 71 72 73 74

- Core Size to Compile (7 8)
- Object Output (9)
- Listing Options (11)
- Core Size to Execute (12 13 14)
- Debug (15)
- MFCM Stacking Sequence (16 17)
- Inverted Print (20)
- 360/20 2501 Buffer (21 22)
- Number Of Print Positions (23 24 25)
- Alternate Collating Sequence (26 27)
- Address to Start (28 29 30)
- Work Tapes (31) — Model 20
- Overlay Open (32)
- Overlap Printer (33)
- Binary Search (34)
- Tape Error (35)
- 2152 Checking (36)
- Inquiry (37)
- Read/Write/Compute (38) — Model 20
- Keyboard Output (39) — Model 20
- Sign Handling (40)
- 1P Forms Position (41)
- Indicator Setting (42)
- File Translation (43)
- Punch MFCU Zeros (44)
- Nonprint Characters (45)
- Table Load Halt (46)
- Shared I/O (48)
- Field Print (49)
- Formatted Core Dump (50)
- RPG to RPG II Conversion (51)

Refer to the specific System Reference Library manual for actual entries.

Line				
0 1				

File Description Specification

F

Line — Form Type (6) — F

Columns: 7 8 9 10 11 12 13 14 15 16 17 18 19 20 21 22 23 24 25 26 27 28 29 30 31 32 33 34 35 36 37 38 39 40 41 42 43 44 45 46 47 48 49 50 51 52 53 54 55 56 57 58 59 60 61 62 63 64 65 66 67 68 69 70 71 72 73 74

- Filename (7–14)
- File Type (15) — I/O/U/C/D
- File Designation (16) — P/S/C/R/T/D
- End of File (17) — E
- Sequence (18) — A/D
- File Format (19) — F/V/S/M/D
- Block Length (20 21 22 23)
- Record Length (24 25 26 27)
- Mode of Processing (28) — L/R
- Length of Key Field or of Record Address Field (29 30) — A/P/I/K
- Record Address Type (31) — I/D/T or 2
- Type of File Organization or Additional Area (32)
- Overflow Indicator (33 34)
- Key Field Starting Location (35 36 37 38)
- Extension Code E/L (39)
- Device (40–46)
- Symbolic Device (47–52)
- Labels S/N/E/M (53) — K
- Name of Label Exit (54–59) — Continuation Lines — Option (54 55 56 57 58)
- Extent Exit for DAM (60–65) — Entry (59 60 61 62 63 64)
- Core Index (61–65)
- A/U (66)
- File Addition/Unordered (66)
- Number of Tracks for Cylinder Overflow (67 68 69)
- Number of Extents (70 71)
- Tape Rewind (72)
- File Condition U1-U8 (73 74)
- R/U/N (70)

Line				
0 2	F			
0 3	F			
0 4	F			
0 5	F			
0 6	F			
0 7	F			
0 8	F			
0 9	F			
1 0	F			
	F			
	F			

277

RPG INPUT SPECIFICATIONS

IBM International Business Machine Corporation

GX21-9094-2 U/M 050*
Printed in U.S.A.

Program						
Programmer		Date				

Punching Instruction — Graphic / Punch

Card Electro Number

Page ☐ ☐ of ___

Program Identification (75 76 77 78 79 80)

This page is a blank IBM RPG Input Specifications coding form (Form Type I), containing a printed grid with column headings including: Line, Form Type, Filename, Sequence, Number (1-N), Option (O), Record Identifying Indicator or **, Record Identification Codes (Position, Not (N), C/Z/D, Character for codes 1, 2, 3), Stacker Select, P/B/L/R, Field Location (From, To), Decimal Positions, Field Name, Control Level (L1-L9), Matching Fields or Changing Fields, Field Record Relation, Field Indicators (Plus, Minus, Zero or Blank). Column numbers run 1–80 across and line numbers 01–20 down.

278

RPG CALCULATION SPECIFICATIONS

IBM International Business Machine Corporation

GX21-9093-2 UM/050* Printed in U.S.A.
*No. of forms per pad may vary slightly

Program

Programmer

Date

Punching Instruction — Graphic — Punch

Card Electro Number

Page 1 2 of __

Program Identification 75 76 77 78 79 80

C

Line	Form Type	Control Level (L0-L9, LR, SR, AN/OR)	Indicators							Factor 1	Operation	Factor 2	Result Field				Resulting Indicators	Comments

Indicators: And — Not, And — Not, And — Not

Result Field: Name, Length, Decimal Positions, Half Adjust (H)

Resulting Indicators — Arithmetic: Plus, Minus, Zero — Compare (Factor 2) is: 1 > 2, 1 < 2, 1 = 2 — Lookup (Factor 2) is: High, Low, Equal

Column numbers: 3 4 5 6 7 8 9 10 11 12 13 14 15 16 17 18 19 20 21 22 23 24 25 26 27 28 29 30 31 32 33 34 35 36 37 38 39 40 41 42 43 44 45 46 47 48 49 50 51 52 53 54 55 56 57 58 59 60 61 62 63 64 65 66 67 68 69 70 71 72 73 74

Line
0 1
0 2
0 3
0 4
0 5
0 6
0 7
0 8
0 9
1 0
1 1
1 2
1 3
1 4
1 5
1 6
1 7
1 8
1 9
2 0

279

IBM International Business Machine Corporation

RPG CALCULATION SPECIFICATIONS

GX21-9093-2 UM/050* Printed in U.S.A.
*No. of forms per pad may vary slightly

Program

Programmer

Date

Punching Instruction

Graphic

Punch

Card Electro Number

Page ___ of ___

Program Identification

75 76 77 78 79 80

C

IBM International Business Machine Corporation

GX21-9090-2 U/M 050*
Printed in U.S.A.

Program				Punching Instruction	Graphic		Card Electro Number		
Programmer		Date			Punch				

Page [ ][1] [2] of ___

Program Identification

75 76 77 78 79 80

Commas	Zero Balances to Print	No Sign	CR	–
Yes	Yes	1	A	J
Yes	No	2	B	K
No	Yes	3	C	L
No	No	4	D	M

X = Remove Plus Sign
Y = Date Field Edit
Z = Zero Suppress

Constant or Edit Word

Field Name
*Auto

Output Indicators
And And
Not   Not   Not

Skip
Before After

Space
Before After

Stacker #/Fetch(F)
Type (H/D/T/E)

Filename

Form Type

Line

Edit Codes
B/A/C/1-9/R
End Position in Output Record
P/B/L/R

O

Line	Form Type
0 1	O
0 2	O
0 3	O
0 4	O
0 5	O
0 6	O
0 7	O
0 8	O
0 9	O
1 0	O
1 1	O
1 2	O
1 3	O
1 4	O
1 5	O
1 6	O
1 7	O
1 8	O
1 9	O
2 0	O

Program
Programmer
Date

Punching Instruction
Graphic
Punch

Card Electro Number

Page [1] [2] of ___

Program Identification
75 76 77 78 79 80

O Output Specifications form (blank grid)

Commas	Zero Balances to Print	No Sign	CR	-
Yes	Yes	1	A	J
Yes	No	2	B	K
No	Yes	3	C	L
No	No	4	D	M

X = Remove Plus Sign
Y = Date Field Edit
Z = Zero Suppress

Constant or Edit Word

Field Name / *Auto

Edit Codes B/A/C/1-9/R End Position in Output Record P/B/L/R

Output Indicators — And / Not / And / Not / Not

Skip — Before / After

Space — Before / After D D

Stacker #/Fetch(F) A D

Type (H/D/T/E) OR AND

Filename

Form Type

Line

282

Date _____   Name_____

DIRECTIONS: *Answer the following questions in the spaces provided. Your answers should indicate the depth of understanding that you have toward the concepts and definitions presented. If there is insufficient space provided for your answer, complete your answer on the reverse side of the Study Guide.*

1. Explain how Net Profit is obtained.

2. Explain how Percent of Profit is determined.

3. When should Half Adjust be considered?

4. Explain how the hierarchy of the Control Level field works.

5. List and explain the four specific areas of coding for this project on the Calculation Specifications sheet.

Date _____   Name_____

TRUE–FALSE: *Each of the following statements is either true or false. Indicate your choice in the Answers column by encircling "T" for a true answer or "F" for a false answer.*

		Answers

1. The Income Statement has listed on it all incomes and expenses — T F

2. The profit of each fiscal period is always completely consumed within that fiscal period — T F

3. Commissions paid to employees are considered an expense to PRINTREN GIFT SHOP — T F

4. The profit of a business can only be shown at an individual product level — T F

5. The profit that each product contributes to the final profit of PRENTREN GIFT SHOP is called Product Profit Contribution — T F

6. The percent of profit is found by dividing the selling price into the cost of the product — T F

7. The percentage routine automatically transfers the percentage of profit into the decimal equivalent of profit — T F

8. The amount of profit is computed by dividing the selling price into the difference between the cost price and the selling price of the product — T F

9. To change a decimal amount to a percentage amount, the quotient must be multiplied by 100 — T F

10. All fields of an input record must be coded on an Input Specifications sheet — T F

11. When using the division operation, Factor 1 is always divided by Factor 2 — T F

12. The Half Adjust is another way of saying rounding off — T F

13. The name coded in the Result Field of the Calculation Specifications sheet receives the quotient of a division problem — T F

14. The coding of length of the Result Field must be adequate to accept the quotient — T F

15. The Decimal Positions Field of the Calculation Specifications sheet indicates the number of positions from the right for rounding-off purposes — T F

16. It is possible to obtain a total of all like products — T F

17. The higher the control level number assigned to control field, the more important the total is if there are level numbers assigned to other fields — T F

18. There can be several total levels within a program — T F

285

19. The selling price of a product can be established by adding the markup
of PRINTREN GIFT SHOP to the cost price of the product   T   F

20. A decimal amount is converted into a percentage amount by moving
the decimal point two places to the right   T   F

21. The concept of destructive readin does not allow the same field
position in core storage to be used again and again in many different
ways   T   F

22. Every program must contain heading, detail, and total level lines of
printing   T   F

23. Y Edit Codes are automatic on date field output   T   F

24. Accumulators must be reinitialized in order for them to show correct
amounts   T   F

25. It is unnecessary to reinitialize accumulators that were used for
Grand Totals   T   F

COMPLETION: *Fill in the blank with the appropriate word or words.*

1, 2. When using the Operation Code DIV, the data of Factor_____ is
always divided by the data in Factor _____ .

3. Half Adjust should be taken into consideration on the _____spec-
ifications when division is involved in a problem.

4, 5. Profit is determined by subtracting the _____ from the _____
_____ .

6. To convert a decimal amount to a percentage amount, the _____
amount is multiplied by 100.

7. Each time that new data is added to an existing field, it replaces the data that was
previously stored. This replacement of data is known as _____ .

8. Reinitialization of accumulators is accomplished by coding the letter_____
_____ in column 39 of the Output Specifications.

DISK STORAGE

PHYSICAL ARRANGEMENT OF DISK

What Is Disk Storage?

A disk is a magnetically coated metallic platter mounted on a spindle that revolves at high speed. The platter or disk, while spinning, is magnetically encoded with information (data) that, when subsequently read by read/write heads, allows for input or output data to enter or exit the computer. The read/write heads act like the heads on a tape recorder except that, unlike the tape heads, the read/write heads on a disk storage device do not come in contact with the platter. They actually fly! The disk read/write heads are aerodynamically designed to fly just millionths of an inch above the disk or platter surface. Consequently, there is no wear on the disk surface or the read/write heads.

There are as many designs of disk storage devices as there are manufacturers of such devices. Some of the more common terms to describe the disk device can be defined by looking at a typical disk device. A disk device can have one or more platters, as in Figs. 81 and 82.

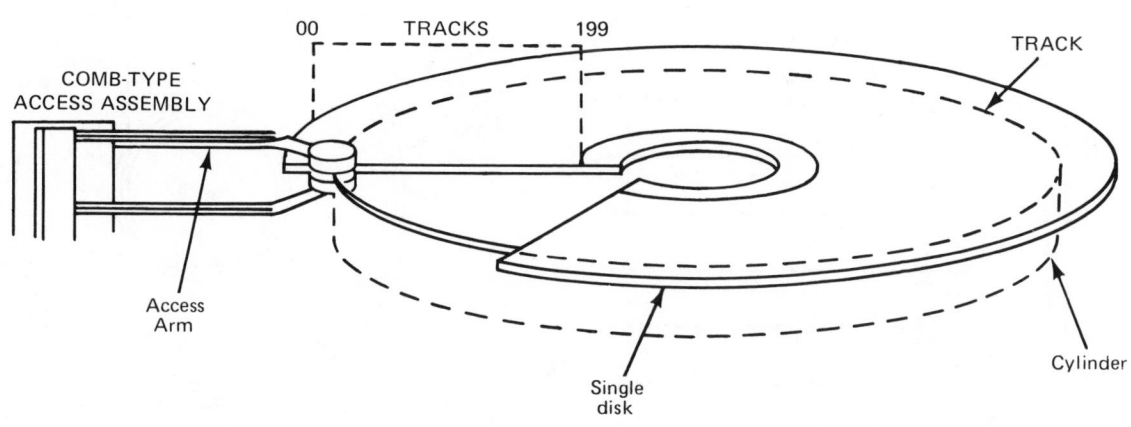

Figure 81

If the disk cartridge contains six platters or disks, data is recorded on only 10 of the possible 12 sides. The reason is that the top side of the first disk is not capable of being used because of the physical proximity to the cartridge cover. The same applies to the bottom side of the sixth disk. Another reason is to protect the recording surfaces against damage when handling. Observe Fig. 83.

Both sides of a platter can be used for reading or writing. The recording surface of a platter is divided into segments. Common forms of segments are tracks, cylinders, and sectors.

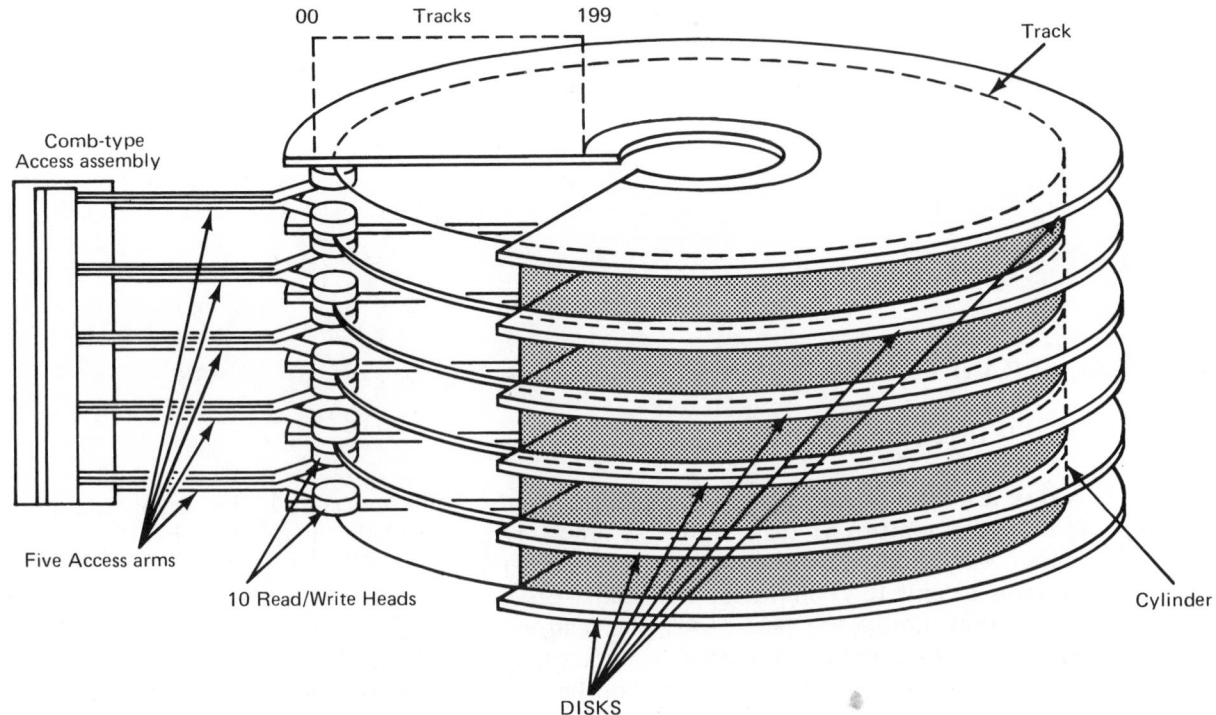

Figure 82. This Disk Cartridge contains six platters or disks.

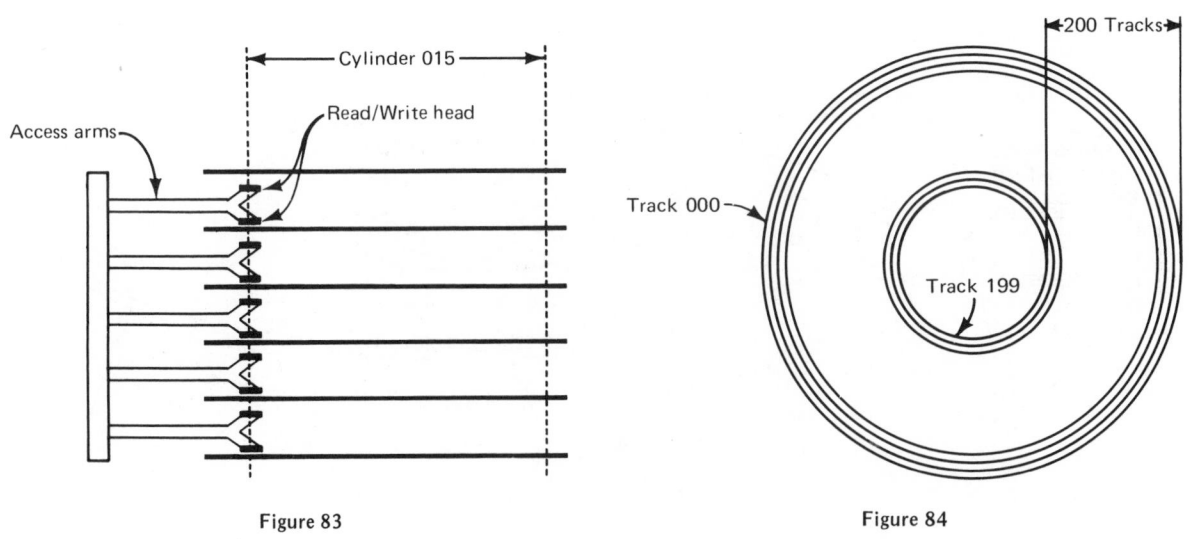

Figure 83

Figure 84

Tracks

Tracks are segments of the recording surface that are one continuous circuit around the disk platter. Figure 84 illustrates tracks.

In Fig. 84 there are 200 concentric strips or tracks on the disk or platter. Tracks are one continuous circuit, NOT spirals as on a phonograph record. The number of tracks per surface of a disk or platter depends on the manufacturer. The number of characters stored on each track (recording density) is also dependent on the configuration and/or the model number of the configuration being used. Technology has continuously improved recording density.

Sectors

Each track is divided into segments called sectors. Depending on the manufacturer of the equipment, there can be any number of sectors per track. Some manufacturer's disks have no sectors at all. Each track has a recorded mark and a physical mark called a home address. The sectors are numbered starting at the home address as illustrated in Fig. 85.

In Fig. 85 there are eight sectors following the home address. On disks that have no sectors, the records of a file are recorded one after the other following the home address. The computer uses record number instead of sector number to get the required data from a track. The number of characters recorded on each sector is also dependent on the manufacturer.

Cylinders

Cylinders are an imaginary line of tracks from surface to surface of each platter. In one platter each cylinder is composed of two tracks—one track on top of the platter and one track on the bottom of the platter. See Fig. 86.

There would be the same number of cylinders on the disk device as there are tracks on one surface of a platter. When more than one platter makes up the cartridge, each two-track combination—top and bottom—makes up a cylinder. Figure 86 has ten tracks per cylinder.

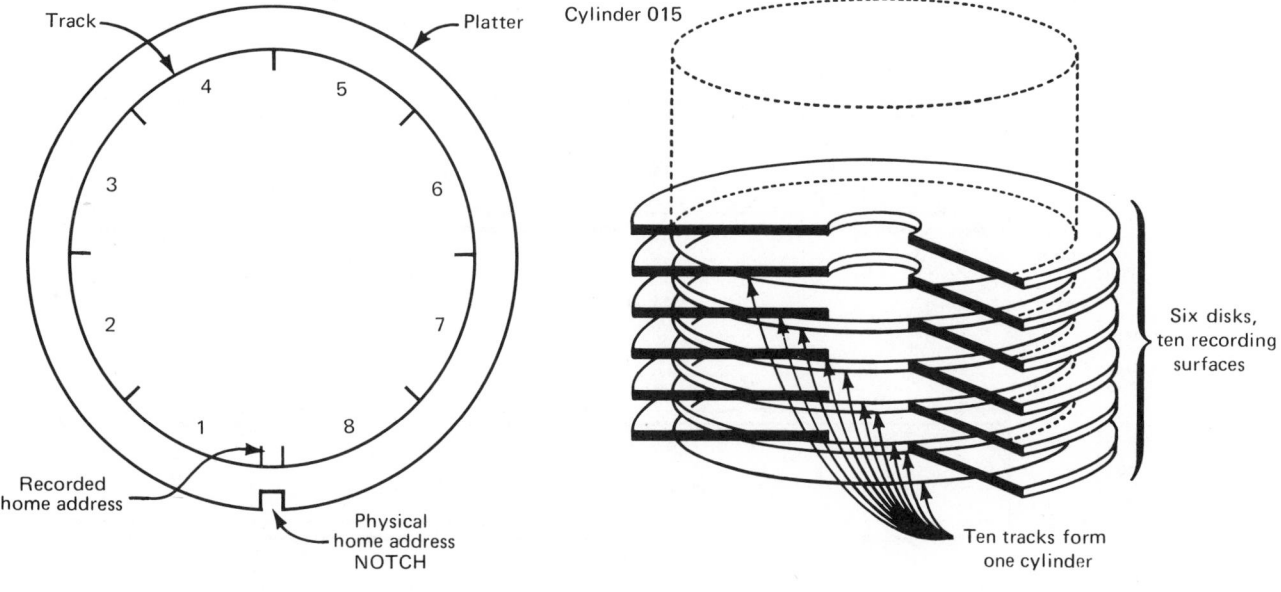

Figure 85

Figure 86

Like a Street Address, the Disk Address directs the read/write head to the proper segment where the data is to be written or read. An address of 010,05,02 would instruct the read/write head to seek the tenth cylinder from the edge of the platter, turn on the 5th read/write head, scan the track for the home address marker and count to the second sector, and then read or write the data as the program instructions indicate. All this activity takes place in a 1000th of a second.

DISK PROGRAMMING CONCEPTS

Block Length

When the program instructs the disk to read or write data, the computer configuration will read or write data in certain segment sizes. If the disk device, for example, was designed by the manufacturer to have a sector length of 256 characters, then on each read operation 256 characters of data would be transferred to the computer buffer with each read, regardless of the actual record length in the program. Knowing this fact, the programmer can make the record length in the program multiples of 256 characters and make the block length 256 characters or multiples greater than 256 characters. Note the examples of block length shown in Fig. 87.

In this figure the sector length is 256 characters and the record length is 200 characters. When the program instruction causes a read of the first record, the first sector is read. But when the second record is read, both the first and second sectors are physically read by the disk device in order to read the second record into the computer buffer. More time is taken to read records 2, 3, and 4 than is necessary. This example also assumes that the disk device is designed to allow records to span sector boundaries. On some manufacturer's disk devices, the spanning of sectors is NOT allowed as Fig. 88 demonstrates.

As can be seen, the problem discussed for Fig. 87 relating to the utilization of disk storage does not occur. The problem here, however, is that, for every record that is 200 characters in length, 256 characters are used up. So it can easily be seen that 56 characters of space of each sector are not being used.

In Fig. 89 the record length was determined by the application design to be 128 characters. Clearly there will be two records per each 256-character sector. If the

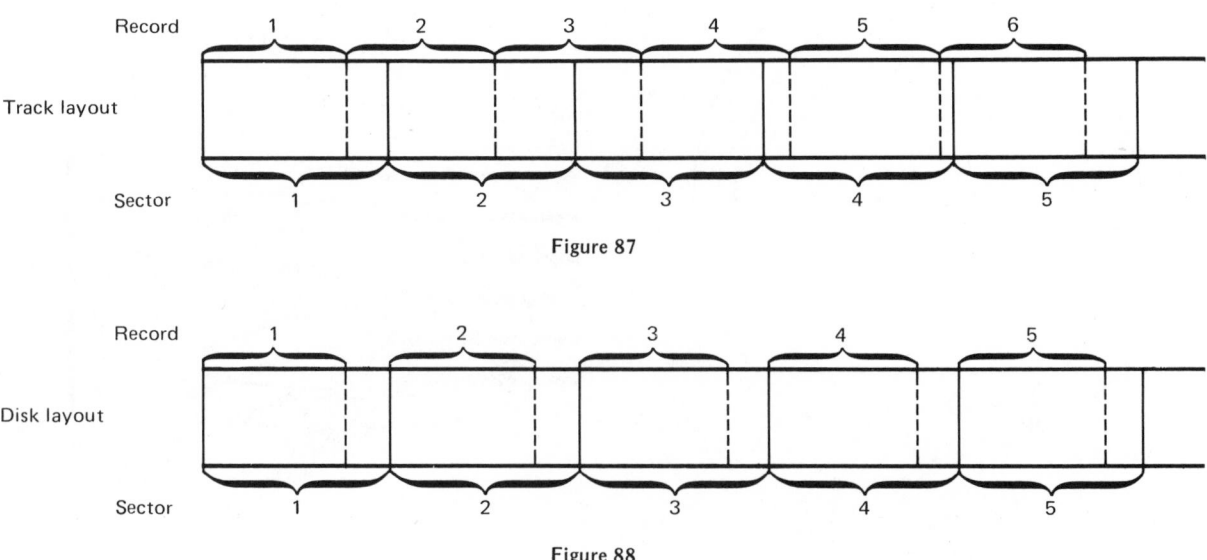

Figure 87

Figure 88

290

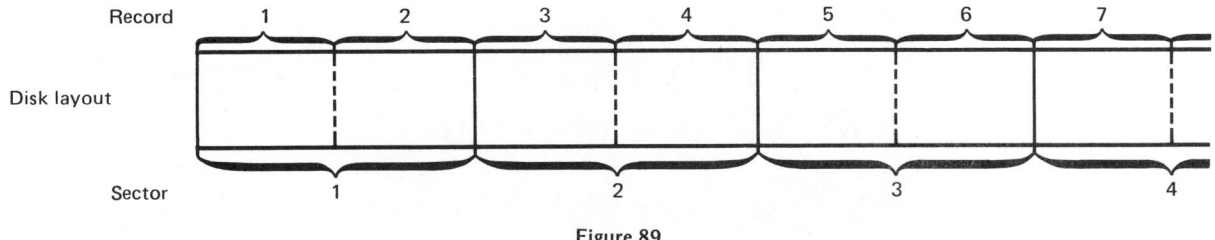

Figure 89

program read each record in turn, each sector would be read by the configuration reading device twice. However, if the programmer made the block length in the program 256 characters, a buffer would be reserved in computer storage for two records. As the program processed each record, the disk device would need to read once for each two records. The programmer could also make the block length a larger multiple of 256. The length could be 512, 1024, or 4096 if the computer configuration being used possessed the storage-capacity capability. By making the block length as large as the storage capability, large amounts of data could be read by the hardware with each seek and more efficient and faster program processing would occur.

TIP TO PROGRAMMER

The amount of information that can be stored on one disk device varies according to the manufacturer and the price paid for the disk. With today's technology one device can store the white pages of the telephone directory of Philadelphia, Pennsylvania — that is, approximately 100 million characters. This disk module is approximately 16 inches in diameter and 12 inches high.

MAJOR ORGANIZATION METHODS OF DISK STORAGE

There are three major types of disk storage, each with its own advantages and disadvantages. The main factor that a programmer should remember concerns the type of storage best suited to the type of programming needed to produce the Output Report desired. The types of disk storage are

1. Consecutive Storage

2. Direct Storage Organization

3. Indexed File Organization

Consecutive Storage

Methods of storing information on disk storage can be the same as cards — one record after another. This process is called consecutive storage. The method is used to store data that will be read or accessed consecutively. Generally the data is sorted into sequential order before it is written to disk. An invoice summary file would be an example of a consecutive file — that is, the records being sorted in invoice number sequence before they are written to the disk file.

291

Figure 90

Direct Storage Organization

It will be easier to understand Direct Storage File if you visualize a section of mailboxes in a post office. The idea is shown in Fig. 90. When mail is sorted into boxes at a post office, a certain procedure is followed. Similarly, three steps are involved in a Direct Access File.

       1. *Design.* The programmer must decide how many holes or slots there will be for records and how large each hole or slot will be. This factor relates to file size — that is, number of records and record length.

       2. *Build or Create.* Building the mailboxes provides the slots for the mail. Creating a direct file provides the slots for each record. When the mailboxes are built, a number is assigned to each box. When the direct file is created, a number is assigned to each slot. On a direct file, these numbers will be used by the program to get the required information or specific record.

       3. *Add and Retrieve.* The postal clerk will add mail to the proper box. He mentally converts the address on the letter to the number on the mailbox. When adding records to a direct file, the program converts the record-identifying information to a number that corresponds to the proper slot in the direct file. The programmer will write this conversion routine. These conversion routines are called ALGORITHMS. To retrieve the record, the same routine or Algorithm is used again in the retrieval program.

Indexed File Organization

Indexed files have two file areas:

    1. Data Area

    2. Index Area

    Data Area: The data area contains records that are consecutively organized either in sequential or nonsequential order.

292

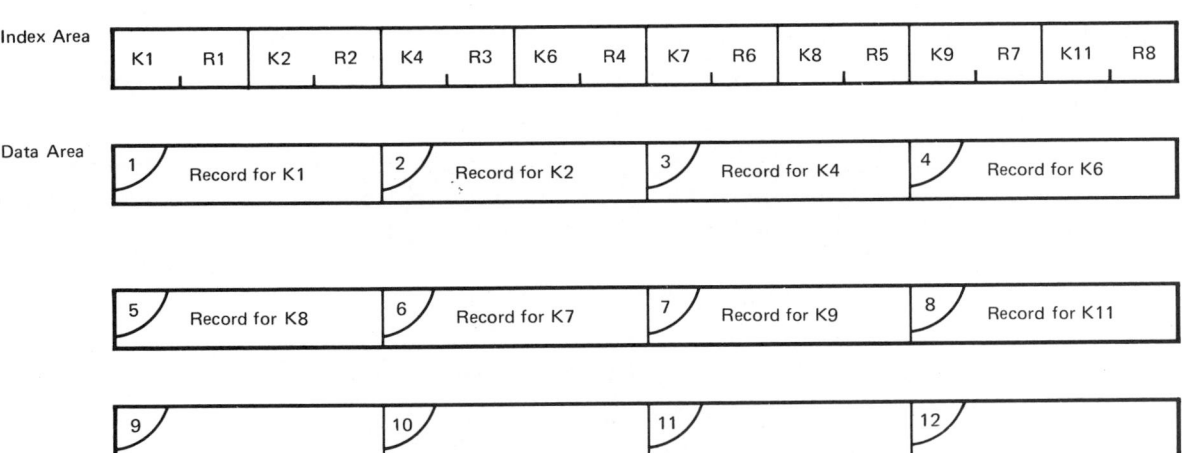

Figure 91

Index Area: The index area is made up of records, the contents of which are the data record key and the relative record number or physical disk address of the data record. Use of relative record number (RRN) or physical disk address in the record depends on the computer manufacturer or the model of the computer configuration being used. The difference is unimportant here.

Some manufacturers' index areas are split into hierarchal levels with a small index pointing to an intermediate index that points to a large index that finally points to the data area. In Fig. 91 a simple one-index area is used. Note that K1, K9, etc. represent record keys. An example would be the Customer Number of a Customer Master Record. R1, R2, etc. represent the relative record number or physical disk address. For clarity, the little number in the upper left corner of each data record represents the relative record number.

As can be seen, if the index area is scanned for the key and the key is found, the relative record number is then used to address the data record directly, thereby saving considerable time. Every record does not need to be read by the program in a search for the right one. It is true, however, that each index record would need to be read until the correct one was found, but the index area is physically located on the disk in a small number of segments. The read/write heads need not move a great distance to scan the index. The entire index could be read into computer memory where the index would be scanned at computer speed. Records in the data area do not need to be sequentially organized. The index, however, must be sequentially organized. Some manufacturers call index files the Indexed Sequential Access Organization or Method.

TIP TO PROGRAMMER

The main factor to be remembered when designing disk files is access time. Access time is the amount of time that it takes from the read instruction start in the program to the completion of a full buffer in computer memory. The major portion of disk access time is taken by read/write head movement. If *Direct Access Organization* is used, the record is located with one head movement. If *Indexed File Organization* is used, the record is located with a minimum of two head movements — one or more to the index and one to the data area. Both organizations have advantages and disadvantages. It is up to the programmer to decide which is better.

CREATING DISK FILES

Using Disk Files

Certain terms or functions will appear when using disk files. These terms or functions are *Create*, *Load*, *Add*, *Update*, and *Retrieve*. The following considerations should be studied when performing each function. The functions may vary with file organization.

Create

a. Setting aside or allocating space on a disk device.

b. Specifying the file size — number of records.

c. Specifying the record length.

d. Defining the method of file organization.

Load

a. Defining the record identification or key of each record.

b. Organizing the record into proper sequence.

c. Filling the disk file with new records.

d. Providing a list of records loaded (audit trail).

Add

a. Defining the record identification or key of each to be added.

b. Checking or editing each record for proper content.

c. Checking for records that may exist on the disk file.

d. Add the new record to the disk file.

e. Provide a list of added records (audit trail).

Update

a. Check or edit each input record for proper data.

b. Find the record to be changed on the disk file; then read the record into computer memory.

c. Replace the data in the record with new data.

d. Write the updated record to the disk file, replacing the old record.

Retrieve

a. Determine which records from the disk file are wanted.

b. Determine in which order the records are to be read.

c. Read the desired records.

Methods Used for Creation of Disk Files

Three methods are used to create disk files. Each has advantages and disadvantages.

1. Consecutive File Organization

2. Direct File Organization

3. Indexed File Organization

Consecutive File Organization: Creating or loading a consecutive disk file is simply a matter of reading a record from one file and writing the record consecutively to a disk file. One record after another is placed into the disk file, just like a line of print on the printer.

Direct File Organization: A number of methods exist to create a Direct File. The best one is to write a program that will create the file with the number of records desired along with the proper record length. Then a second program must be written that will update each record as required with input data. The first program is used only once — to create or load the file with blank records. The second program can be used any number of times both to ADD new records and to UPDATE old ones. The second program would have several routines — for example, one to edit the incoming data, one for the algorithm, one to check for an existing record in that address created by the algorithm routine, and one to update the existing record or add a new record.

> **TIP TO PROGRAMMER**
>
> Direct files sound like a great deal of work — they are. But it must be remembered that direct access files give the best performance from a speed of retrieval point of view.

Indexed File Organization: Creating an indexed file is very simple with RPG. The File Specifications Sheet describes the indexed file. The main consideration in creating indexed files is to define the key length and key location. RPG takes care of the routines that will properly format the file into the proper areas.

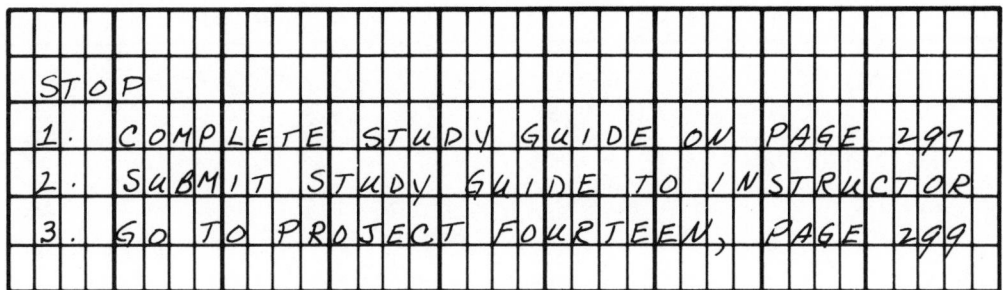

```
STOP
1.  COMPLETE STUDY GUIDE ON PAGE 297
2.  SUBMIT STUDY GUIDE TO INSTRUCTOR
3.  GO TO PROJECT FOURTEEN, PAGE 299
```

Date _____   Name _____

Directions: *Answer the following questions in the spaces provided. Your answers should indicate the depth of understanding that you have toward the concepts and definitions presented. If there is insufficient space provided for your answer, complete your answer on the reverse side of the Study Guide.*

1. Define Disk Storage.

2. Explain the relationship of track, cylinders and sectors.

3. Explain Block Length as it relates to Track Layout.

4. Explain Block Length as it relates to Disk Layout.

5. Explain the Consecutive Storage method of storing data on a disk.

6. Explain the Direct Storage method of storing data on a disk.

7. Explain the Indexed File Organization method of storing data on a disk.

8. List and explain the functions of the term CREATE as it relates to a disk file.

9. List and explain the functions of the term LOAD as it relates to a disk file.

10. List and explain the functions of the term ADD as it relates to a disk file.

11. List and explain the functions of the term UPDATE as it relates to a disk file.

12. List and explain the functions of the term RETRIEVE as it relates to a disk file.

PROJECT FOURTEEN

TIP TO PROGRAMMER

       The Master File of our customers has been in card format. Some of the disadvantages of having a file on cards are listed below.

    1. Cards are difficult to handle.

    2. Cards are difficult to store.

    3. Cards become lost or damaged.

    4. Cards may become out of proper order or sequence.

    5. Cards are difficult to sort.

However, all the disadvantages of cards (listed above) become advantages when files are on disk.

SPECIFICATIONS:
DISK STORAGE

       Project Fourteen will consist of two programs that will:

    (14A) Load Customer File Cards to Disk Storage, creating a Customer Master File.

    (14B) List the Disk Customer Master File verifying that the Customer Master File was loaded correctly.

Specifications
Creation of an Indexed Sequential File

This project illustrates how to create an Indexed Sequential File on a disk.

299

NEW CONCEPTS

Length of Key Field or of Record Address Field

Record Address Type ($A/P/J/K$)

Type of File Organization or Additional Area ($I/D/T$ or 2)

Key Field Starting Location

Length of Key Field or Record Address Field
(Columns 29 through 30)

This field is used when the file being created is to be an Indexed Sequential File. Within each record of an Indexed Sequential File is a Key Field. A Key Field contains the code that will identify the data being entered into the indexed file. The Key Field is not only part of the data record but is also part of the index entry for the file. In Fig. 92, the Key Field is the Customer Number Field of the data cards. The Key Field is five characters in length. Coding 05 in columns 29 and 30 specifies the length of the key.

Record Address Type A/P/I/K
(Columns 31 through 31)

This field has a direct relationship to the Key Field. The coding of the key field is as follows:

        1. If the file is to be processed by alphameric keys, the letter A is coded in this field.

        2. P/I/K will not be covered at this time.

Note, in Fig. 92, that the letter A is coded in this field, signifying that the file will be processed by alphameric keys.

Type of File Organization or Additional Area (I/D/T or 2)
(Columns 32 through 32)

The entry coded in this field indicates the file organization type. That is,

        1. If the Output File is Indexed Sequential, the letter I must be coded in this field.

        2. D/T—These two concepts are not to be considered at this time.

Observe the coding of Fig. 92. The letter I coded in this field signifies that the Output File will be an Indexed File.

Key Field Starting Location
(Columns 35 through 38)

The beginning column in which the key field will start in the disk record is specified in this field. In Fig. 92 note that the key begins in column 1 of the record. Of particular note in this figure is the Device Field. All the previous projects had the Output Device "Printer" coded in this field. Notice that the Output Device in this program is DISK. Check your manufacturer's reference manual for the proper device name.

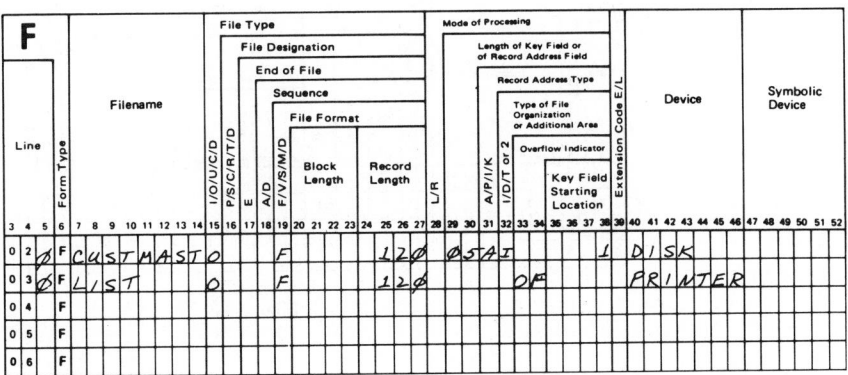

Figure 92

Symbolic Device

Some computers require a Symbolic Device. The manufacturer's manual must be consulted for the requirements of this field.

File Description Specifications

Whenever an Indexed Sequential File is being created, the programmer must make certain that the data being used to create the file is accurate. One way to ascertain the accuracy of the data (besides having it verified on a verifying machine) is to have two Output Files. The data of the first Output File will be used for the creation of the Indexed Sequential File on the disk. The purpose and function of the second Output File are to print on the printing device the exact data that has been loaded or created on the disk by the first Output File. Figure 92 illustrates the concept.

SPECIFICATIONS:
PROJECT FOURTEEN-A

Input Specifications

In this project the image of the customer master card will be loaded to disk. Observe the coding in Fig. 93.

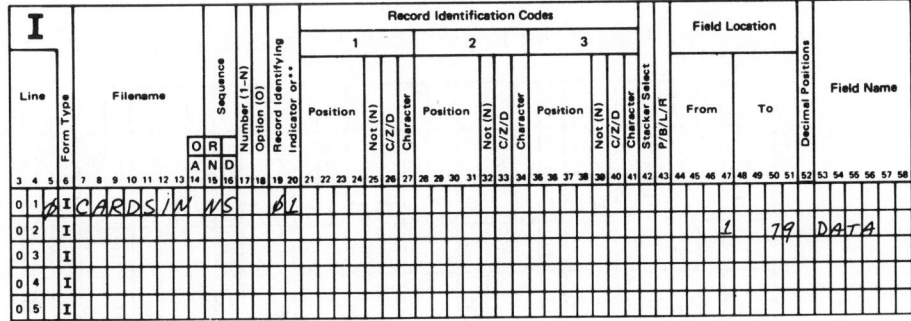

Figure 93

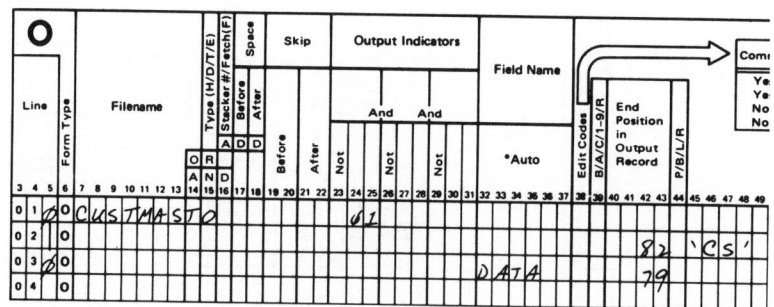

Figure 94A

Output Specifications

The complete CARDSIN record is written into the file on the disk. It is also important to add a code identifying the record as a Customer Summary Record. (See Fig. 94A). The Customer Summary Code "CS" is not a part of the input record. Consequently, the code will not be represented on the Output Report of this program. However, when Program 14B is written to show what data exists in the Indexed Sequential File (as a result of Program 14A), the Customer Summary Code "CS" will be on the Output Report.

Audit Trail

A printed record of all the activity associated with the Disk File must be maintained. Its purpose is to trace the activity of a Disk File, such as records loaded, records added, records deleted, or records changed. This printed record is called an Audit Trail and is required by auditors when auditing a business. It is the function of auditors to check the business's record-keeping practices to ensure that they are accurate.

On the completion of a successful compilation of this program, the attention of the programmer must be directed to the second program of this project. The second program (14B) must be so constructed as to print out exactly what had been created on the DISK by Program 14A.

Compilation Instructions

1. Develop a Print Chart for the Output Report. Use the Print Chart on page 462–463.

2. Code, keypunch, and compile this program to the satisfaction of your instructor.

3. Coding Specifications sheets are on pages 305 through 307.

4. The Input Records for this program will be those created on page 117.

5. The Output Report should appear as illustrated on page 304.

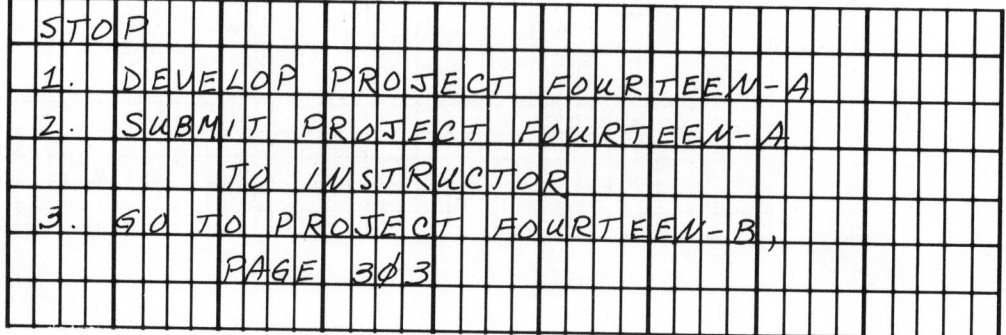

PROJECT FOURTEEN-B

Specifications Printing of Loaded Disk

The object of this program is to have the data stored by Program 14A printed on the printing device. This program represents an additional step taken by the programmer to make certain that the data stored in the Disk File is accurate.

File Description Specifications

The Output Disk File of Program 14A becomes the input to this program.

Input Specifications

Since this file was created as an Output File in Program 14A, the Customer Summary Code must be used as a Record Identification code.

Output Specifications

In order to find the stored data more easily, the programmer has an additional heading line printed on the Output Report. The heading line will indicate the disk record position numbers from which the input data was read. The necessary coding for this type of heading is depicted in Fig. 94B. The dots in some of the columns serve merely as indicators to columnar numbers.

Finally, the detail line of print representing the stored data is to be coded.

The area of greatest importance on the compilation of this program (14B) is to make certain that the Output Report is identical to the Output Report of Program 14A with the exception of CS in print positions 81 and 82. If the two printouts are identical, the data has been stored correctly on the disk in the file called CUSTMAST. However, if some of the data of the two Output Reports is dissimilar, then the programmer must check to see why and make the necessary corrections.

Compilation Instructions

1. Code, keypunch, and compile this program to the satisfaction of your instructor.

2. Use the same coding sheets from FOURTEEN-A.

3. The Output Report should appear as illustrated on page 304.

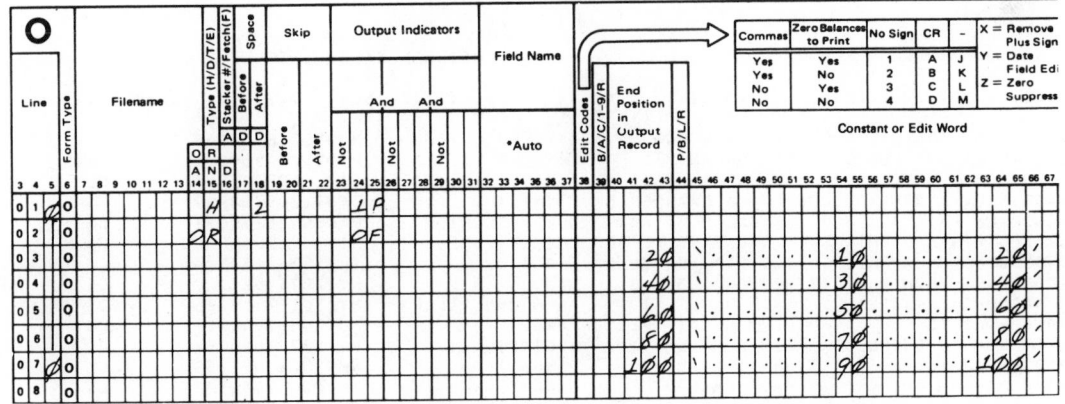

Figure 94B

303

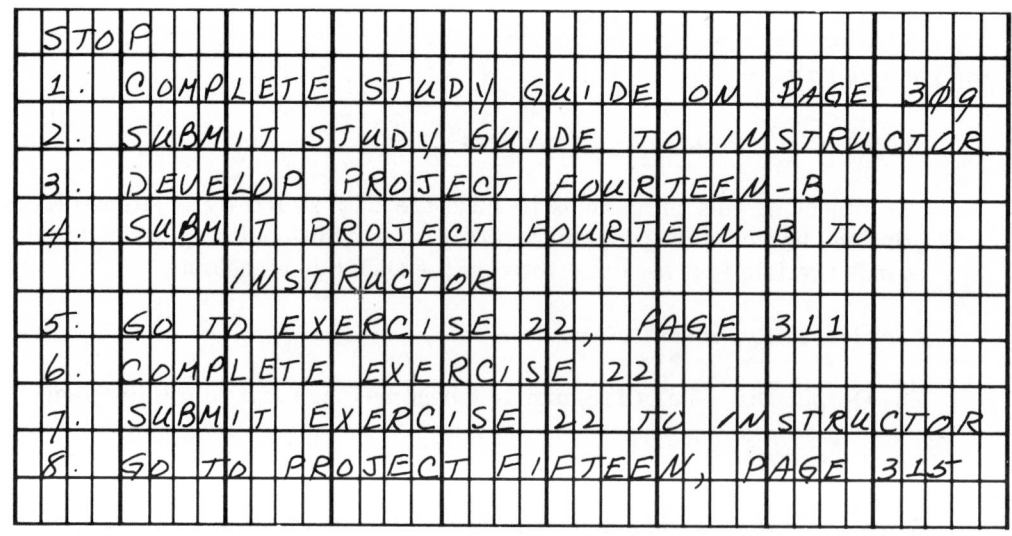

```
STOP
1. COMPLETE STUDY GUIDE ON PAGE 309
2. SUBMIT STUDY GUIDE TO INSTRUCTOR
3. DEVELOP PROJECT FOURTEEN-B
4. SUBMIT PROJECT FOURTEEN-B TO
   INSTRUCTOR
5. GO TO EXERCISE 22, PAGE 311
6. COMPLETE EXERCISE 22
7. SUBMIT EXERCISE 22 TO INSTRUCTOR
8. GO TO PROJECT FIFTEEN, PAGE 315
```

CUSTOMER LOAD LIST

```
01854SCOT TRAIN'S & HBS414 SNOWDOWN ST    SAWER JUNCTION    NJ080016644466

03824MCCARTHY GLASS      88 MORGAN ST.     FRYBURG           PA095234569871

03893MOM'S POTTERY       555 WEST STATE ST MAKERVILLE        GA224102001040

04597STEVE BABKEY & CO.1044 ALEXANDER DR PRINTOWN           CA971205768899

04902RON FRIEMAN SHOP    27 BALCOURT WAY   NEW PICKERTON     MA680425220011

07120GIFTS AND THINGS    5 STUBENVILLE RD  COUNTY LINE       RI033015011050

09353JANE BROWN GIFTS    761 STETSON BLVD  GRACIOUS          IL152762143524

09353JANE BROWN GIFTS    761 STETSON BLVD  GRACIOUS          IL152762143524

10357GARVEY CHIP & DIP 228 PROSPECT ST.   MAJOR             KY120757521122

32943SUPER ERIC'S        681 GUYOUT ST     AARNTOWNSVILLE    NY010107523265

34982EDDIE'S             2222 GREAT TREE DRMERSER           ND784512561289

39673RUBLEV SKILL CTR    311 HUNT ST.      BUNINGTON         WV152753510052

45276SHART'S NOVELTIES 744 TERHAUT PL      FINGERTON         NH035247521358

50389MAKING THINGS       EAST MAIN ST      DANDYTOWN         MN620059981133

53898DUDLEY'S PLANT CTR668 DRIVEWAY RD     FLUGLETON         OH422533337721

68935STRONG'S PARTS      351 WITHERSPOON DRROCKAWAY         VA145532121199

69451GIFT SUPERMARKET    8 GROVER BLVD     GRANGEBURG        CT044451237004

83959STACY'S             MARKET ST         HUBBER            PA095524215577
```

14A Output Report

CUSTOMER FILE LIST

```
1........10........20........30........40........50........60........70........80........90.......100
01854SCOT TRAIN'S & HBS414 SNOWDOWN ST    SAWER JUNCTION    NJ080016644466       CS
03824MCCARTHY GLASS      88 MORGAN ST.     FRYBURG           PA095234569871       CS
03893MOM'S POTTERY       555 WEST STATE ST MAKERVILLE        GA224102001040       CS
04597STEVE BABKEY & CO.1044 ALEXANDER DR PRINTOWN           CA971205768899       CS
04902RON FRIEMAN SHOP    27 BALCOURT WAY   NEW PICKERTON     MA680425220011       CS
07120GIFTS AND THINGS    5 STUBENVILLE RD  COUNTY LINE       RI033015011050       CS
09353JANE BROWN GIFTS    761 STETSON BLVD  GRACIOUS          IL152762143524       CS
10357GARVEY CHIP & DIP 228 PROSPECT ST.   MAJOR             KY120757521122       CS
32943SUPER ERIC'S        681 GUYOUT ST     AARNTOWNSVILLE    NY010107523265       CS
34982EDDIE'S             2222 GREAT TREE DRMERSER           ND784512561289       CS
39673RUBLEV SKILL CTR    311 HUNT ST.      BUNINGTON         WV152753510052       CS
45276SHART'S NOVELTIES 744 TERHAUT PL      FINGERTON         NH035247521358       CS
50389MAKING THINGS       EAST MAIN ST      DANDYTOWN         MN620059981133       CS
53898DUDLEY'S PLANT CTR668 DRIVEWAY RD     FLUGLETON         OH422533337721       CS
68935STRONG'S PARTS      351 WITHERSPOON DRROCKAWAY         VA145532121199       CS
69451GIFT SUPERMARKET    8 GROVER BLVD     GRANGEBURG        CT044451237004       CS
83959STACY'S             MARKET ST         HUBBER            PA095524215577       CS
```

14B Output Report

IBM International Business Machine Corporation

RPG CONTROL CARD AND FILE DESCRIPTION SPECIFICATIONS

GX21-9092-3 UM/050*
Printed in U.S.A.

*No. of forms per pad may very slightly

Program

Programmer

Date

Punching Instruction — Graphic / Punch

Card Electro Number

Program Identification

Page 1 of 2

Control Card Specifications

Refer to the specific System Reference Library manual for actual entries.

Column labels (H — Control Card):
- Form Type
- Core Size to Compile
- Object Output
- Listing Options
- Core Size to Execute
- Debug
- MFCM Stacking Sequence
- Inverted Print
- 360/20 2501 Buffer
- Number Of Print Positions
- Alternate Collating Sequence
- Address to Start
- Work Tapes
- Overlay Open
- Overlay Printer
- Binary Search
- Tape Error
- 2152 Checking
- Inquiry
- Read/Write/Compute (Model 20)
- Keyboard Output (Model 20)
- Sign Handling
- 1P Forms Position
- Indicator Setting
- File Translation
- Punch MFCU Zeros
- Nonprint Characters
- Table Load Halt
- Shared I/O
- Field Print
- Formatted Core Dump
- RPG to RPG II Conversion

File Description Specification

Column labels (F — File Description):
- Form Type
- Filename
- File Type
- File Designation
- End of File
- Sequence
- File Format
- Block Length
- Record Length
- Mode of Processing
- Length of Key Field or of Record Address Field
- Record Address Type
- Type of File Organization or Additional Area
- Overflow Indicator
- Key Field Starting Location
- Extension Code E/L
- Device
- Symbolic Device
- Name of Label Exit
- Extent Exit for DAM
- Core Index
- Continuation Lines
- Option
- Entry
- File Addition/Unordered
- Number of Tracks for Cylinder Overflow
- Number of Extents
- Tape Rewind
- File Condition U1-U8

IBM International Business Machine Corporation

RPG INPUT SPECIFICATIONS

GX21-9094-2 U/M 050*
Printed in U.S.A.

Program					
Programmer		Date			

Punching Instruction

Graphic	
Punch	

Card Electro Number

Page [ ] of [ ]

Program Identification 75 76 77 78 79 80

I

Line	Form Type	Filename	Sequence	Number (1-N)	Option (O)	Record Identifying Indicator or **	Record Identification Codes																Field Location			Decimal Positions	Field Name	Control Level (L1-L9)	Matching Fields or Changing Fields	Field Record Relation	Field Indicators			

(blank form grid)

IBM
International Business Machine Corporation

GX21-9090-2 U/M 050*
Printed in U.S.A.

RPG   OUTPUT   SPECIFICATIONS

Program
Programmer   Date

Punching
Instruction   Graphic
               Punch

Card Electro Number

Page 1 of 2 ____

Program
Identification
75 76 77 78 79 80

Commas	Zero Balances to Print	No Sign	CR	-
Yes	Yes	1	A	J
Yes	No	2	B	K
No	Yes	3	C	L
No	No	4	D	M

X = Remove Plus Sign
Y = Date Field Edit
Z = Zero Suppress

Constant or Edit Word

International Business Machine Corporation

Program
Programmer   Date

Punching
Instruction

Graphic
Punch

Card Electro Number

Page ___ of ___

GX21-9090-2 U/M 050*
Printed in U.S.A.

Program
Identification

75 76 77 78 79 80

Commas	Zero Balances to Print	No Sign	CR	-
Yes	Yes	1	A	J
Yes	No	2	B	K
No	Yes	3	C	L
No	No	4	D	M

X = Remove Plus Sign
Y = Date Field Edit
Z = Zero Suppress

Constant or Edit Word

Form Type
Line
Filename
Type (H/D/T/E)
Stacker #/Fetch(F)
Space
Skip
Output Indicators
Field Name
*Auto
Edit Codes
End Position in Output Record
P/B/L/R
B/A/C/1-9/R

And Or And
Not Not Not
After Before
Before After

Date _____   Name_____

DIRECTIONS: *Answer the following questions in the spaces provided. Your answers should indicate the depth of understanding that you have toward the concepts and definitions presented. If there is insufficient space provided for your answer, complete your answer on the reverse side of the Study Guide.*

1. Explain the significance of the length of the Key Field.

2. Explain how two different output devices can be used in the same program.

3. Explain how a constant can be added to a file.

4. Explain the purpose of an Audit Trail.

5. Explain the reason for printing the data of the Disk File that has just been created.

6. Explain how the special coding in Fig. 94B will enable the programmer to locate any errors in the data.

Date _____   Name _____

TRUE–FALSE: *Each of the following statements is either true or false. Indicate your choice in the Answers column by encircling "T" for a true answer or "F" for a false answer.*

Answers

1. One of the disadvantages of having files on cards is that cards can become out of proper order and sequence   T   F

2. All the disadvantages of cards become the advantages when files are on disk   T   F

3. A disk pack must always contain four platters even though only one platter is used at a time   T   F

4. The read head and the write head are two individual heads used for reading and/or writing the data of a platter   T   F

5. The heads of a disk pack very lightly touch the platter surface when reading or writing data   T   F

6. Both sides of every platter of a disk pack are used for storage of data   T   F

7. The recording surface of a platter is divided into segments   T   F

8. Segments are further broken down into tracks, cylinders, and sectors   T   F

9. A track is a spiral circuit around the disk platter   T   F

10. The number of concentric tracks around a platter is dependent on the manufacturer of the platter   T   F

11. The density of the characters stored on each track depends on the configuration   T   F

12. Cylinders are imaginary lines of tracks from surface to surface of each platter   T   F

13. There are the same number of cylinders on the disk device as there are tracks on one surface of a platter   T   F

14. Each track is divided into segments called sectors   T   F

15. The possibility exists whereby some disks have no sectors at all   T   F

16. The track home address is both physical and recorded   T   F

17. Some computers use record number instead of sector number to get the required data from a track   T   F

18. Sector lengths are designed by the manufacturer of the configuration being used   T   F

19. Record lengths cannot span sector boundaries   T   F

20. Records are a part of sectors that are a part of a track   T   F

21. All disk devices have the same storage capacity   T   F

22. Consecutive storage is when records are recorded one after the other on the disk   T   F

23. Data is usually sorted into sequential order before it is written to disk if direct storage is being used   T   F

24. Three steps are utilized when using a Direct Access File   T   F

25. Indexed Files have two file areas known as data and index areas   T   F

26. An index area is made up of records   T   F

27. Records are placed on the disk by either the Direct Access Method or the Index File Access Organization Method   T   F

28. The record is located with one movement of the read/write head if the data was stored using the Direct Access Organization Method   T   F

29. Access time is the amount of time that it takes from the READ instruction start in the program, to the completion of a full buffer in computer memory   T   F

30. Create, Load, Add, Update, and Retrieve are functions associated with file organization   T   F

31. Defining of the method of file organization is a Create function   T   F

32. Defining the record identification or key of each record is a Load function   T   F

33. Replacing data in the record with new data is a Load function   T   F

34. The Length of the Key Field on the File Description Specifications sheet must be used if the file being created is to be an Indexed Sequential File   T   F

35. A Key Field contains the code that will give the necessary identification to the data being entered onto the indexed file   T   F

36. The data being used as the Key Field must be defined with the letter A if the data being retrieved is to be processed by alphameric keys   T   F

37. If the Output File is Indexed Sequential, the letter I need not be coded in the Type of File Organization or Additional Area Field   T   F

38. The beginning column in which the Key Field starts need not be coded on the File Specifications, but the ending position must be   T   F

39. The disk is an input/output device   T   F

40. One method used to determine the accuracy of the data loaded onto the disk is to have the data that was loaded be printed out on the printing device of the configuration being used   T   F

41. It is possible to write data on the disk that is not part of the input record   T   F

42. A printed record of all the activity associated with the disk file is maintained. This activity is known as the Audit Trail   T   F

43. It is not possible to have a file that was an Output file in one program become an Input file of another program   T   F

44. Data stored on a disk during testing should always be double checked
    to see if it was stored exactly as intended   T   F

45. The difficulty of handling and storing or damaging and losing cards
    are some of the disadvantages of having a file on cards   T   F

46. The read/write head actually flies approximately a millionth of an inch
    above the platter surface, thereby causing no surface damage
    to the platter   T   F

47. If a platter has 200 tracks, track 199 is on the outer rim of the platter   T   F

48. The number of characters stored per inch of recording surface is known
    as recording density   T   F

49. The number of characters storable in a sector length is determined by
    the manufacturer   T   F

50. The program used to Create a Direct File is used only one time   T   F

COMPLETION: *Fill in the blank with the appropriate word or words.*

1, 5. Five disadvantages of having a Master File on cards are _____
       _____ , _____ , _____
       _____ , and _____ .

6. Read/write heads are aerodynamically designed to _____ just
   above the platter, thereby eliminating damage to the platter surface.

7. If the disk cartridge contains six platters, data is recorded on only _____
   sides.

8, 10. The recording surface of a platter is divided into segments of _____ ,
        _____ , and _____ .

11. On each platter, the cylinder is composed of _____ tracks.

12. The recorded mark and the physical mark of a track are known as its _____
    _____ _____ .

13. On disks having no sectors, the computer uses the _____
    _____ to get the required data.

14. On disks having sectors, the computer uses the _____ _____
    to get the required data.

15, 16. The two home addresses of a platter are _____ and _____
         _____ .

17, 19. The three major types of disk storage are _____ _____ ,
         _____ _____ and _____ _____ .

20, 21. The two file areas of Indexed Files are the _____ _____ and
         the _____ _____ .

22, 26. Five functional terms employed when using disk files are _____ ,
         _____ , _____ , _____ , and _____ .

MATCHING: *Match Column 1 to Column 2*

COLUMN 1

A. Disk
B. Read/Write Heads
C. Track
D. Recording Density
E. Cylinder
F. Sector
G. Consecutive Storage
H. Index File
I. Load
J. Audit Trail

COLUMN 2   *Answers*

1. Division of a track into segments   _____

2. Filling the disk file with new records   _____

3. Printed record of all activity associated with a file   _____

4. Magnetically coated metallic platter   _____

5. Imaginary line of tracks from surface to surface of each
   platter   _____

6. Allows for input or output data to enter or exit the computer   _____

7. Storing one record after another   _____

8. One continuous circuit around the platter   _____

9. Number of characters stored on each track   _____

PROJECT FIFTEEN

As your business grows, you will acquire new customers, and these customer records must be added to your Customer Master File. The computer manufacturer and the model of the configuration being used will determine how records will physically be added to a Disk File. Disk File Organization also determines how additional records are handled.

CONSECUTIVE FILE ORGANIZATION

Some computer models will allow record additions directly to a consecutive file. The records are physically added to the end of the data area of the file. If the application requires these additional records to be sequenced along with the records already in the file, then the file must be sorted. Manufacturers supply sort programs for this purpose.

Where it is not possible to add records directly to a consecutive file, a merge program must be written. Figure 95 illustrates how records are added by the use of a merge program. As can be seen, when the merge program is complete, the Input File may be deleted.

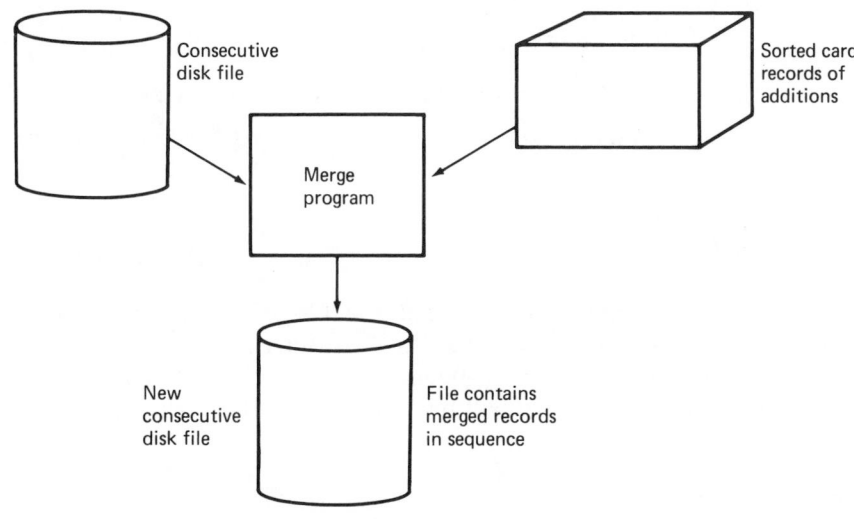

Figure 95

DIRECT FILE ORGANIZATION

In Project 14 the post office mailbox was used to describe how a Direct File was created and loaded. Using the same example, the mailbox, you should remember that a record slot was created for every possible record address within the file boundaries. To describe how records are added to a direct file would be incorrect. It is more correct to say update. New records would update the record located in the slot for the new record's record address. The program to update (add) records to a Direct File would include the following routines.

1. Convert the mailbox number to the record address, using an algorithm.

2. Read the record at the record address to make sure that it is empty. (No one else's mail in the mail slot.)

3. Write the new record into the record slot.

INDEXED FILE ORGANIZATION

Physically, an indexed file can have many forms, depending, again, on the computer model and manufacturer. Adding records to an indexed file can be simple with RPG. The manufacturer's supplied RPG Indexed File Routines will do most of the work. The routine will add the record in the proper file location, add the indexed record, and put everything in the proper sequence.

> **TIP TO PROGRAMMER**
>
> If an attempt is made to add to the Master File a record that already exists, the computer will stop and give a message. To make the program more complete, the file should first be checked to see if the record to be added already exists. If it does, then have a message printed by the printer stating this fact.
>
> In a business application, it is important to provide a trail of activity on the Master Files. Therefore in an ADD program the added records should be printed and kept by the person responsible for maintaining the accuracy of the file. Any data that represents additions, corrections, updating, and/or deletions of a file is then known as an Audit Trail.

NEW CONCEPTS

File Type I/O/U/C/D	File Addition/Unordered A/U
File Description P/S/C/R/T/D	Chain Operation Code
Mode of Processing L/R	ADD (Add a Record)

File Type I/O/U/C/D
(Columns 15 through 15)

The U in the column indicates that the file will be both Input and Output within the same RPG cycle. In this project the Customer File will be read as input to verify that the Customer Number that is being added is not already in existence on the file. After verification, the new record will be added to the file. (See Fig. 97)

316

File Description P/S/C/R/T/D
(Columns 16 through 16)

The C in this column indicates that the CHAIN Operation Code will be used in the Calculation Specifications to read the file. (See Fig. 97).

Mode of Processing L/R
(Columns 28 through 28)

The R in this column indicates that the file will be read randomly. If the CHAIN operation is used, the file is processed randomly. The file must be an Input or an Update File. (See Fig. 97).

File Addition/Unordered A/U
(Columns 66 through 66)

When new records are to be added to an already existing Sequential or Indexed Sequential File, an A is coded in column 66 of the File Specifications Sheet. The file must be an Output or an Update File. (See Fig. 97).

Chain Operation Code
(Columns 28 through 32)

The Chain Operation Code is used to read a file within the Calculation Specifications. The file is processed by a relative record number or by key. Sequential, Direct, and Indexed files can be processed by relative record number. Only Indexed files can be processed by key. If a relative record number is used, it must be coded in Factor 1 of the Calculation Specifications and must be numeric. In order for the proper record to be read, the programmer must know or be able to calculate the position of the record relative to the first record in the file.

For processing by key, Factor 1 must contain the proper key of the record to be read. This can be a numeric constant, alphameric literal, or a field name. It must be the same length as the key described for the file in the File Description Specifications.

Factor 2 must be the filename described on the File Description Specifications sheet.

A Resulting Indicator may or may not be required, depending on the computer involved. Refer to the RPG Manual for the RPG Compiler under the CHAIN Operation Code for this requirement. The purpose of the Resulting Indicator is to indicate the success of the CHAIN operation. In Fig. 96, Indicator 10 will turn ON if the CHAIN operation is NOT successful or if the Record with the KEY specified in Factor 1 is not found.

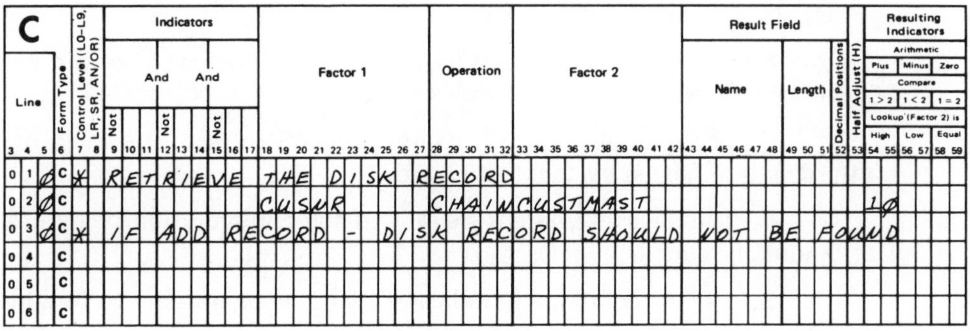

Figure 96

ADD (Add a Record) (Columns 16 through 18)
(Output Specifications)

This group heading (of the Output Specifications sheet) is used to specify that a record(s) is to be added to an Output or an Update File. When the ADD concept is used, the Output device for the file must be a DISK. The A must be specified in column 66 of the File Description Specifications sheet when this concept is used in a program.

FILE SPECIFICATIONS

Since new records are to be added to the existing Customer Master File, the statement illustrated in Fig. 97 should be coded.

Referring to Fig. 97, note the following on line 030.

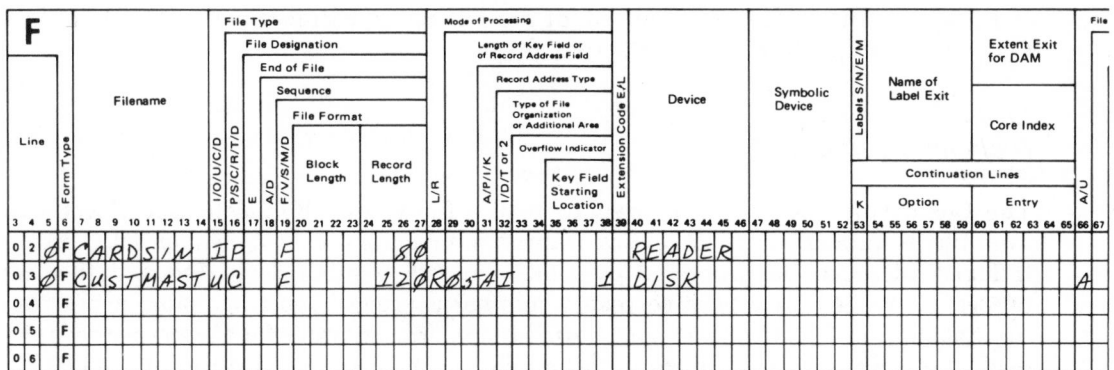

Figure 97

1. The CUSTMAST File is defined as an UPDATE (U in column 15) File and a CHAIN (C in column 16) File. In this way, the file may be read in the Calculations to check for duplicate Customer Numbers.

2. The R (column 28) indicates that the file will be read randomly.

3. The length of the Key Field (columns 29–30) is five positions. This is the Customer Number Field of the Record.

4. The A (column 31) indicates that the records of the file will be processed by using the alphameric record key.

5. Since the records will be processed by the use of record keys, an I (column 32) must be coded to indicate an Indexed File.

6. The starting position (columns 35–38) of the Key Field of the data record on the disk is indicated by the digit coded.

7. The device (columns 40–46) of the configuration being used as the Output Device must be coded.

8. The A (column 66) indicates that new records are to be added to an Output File.

9. Check your Reference Manual for Symbolic Device.

INPUT SPECIFICATIONS

The new records must be added in their entirety. Therefore all 80 columns must be coded in such a manner that the entire card is added to the file. An A should be punched in column 80 of the input record to indicate an Add Transaction.

INPUT FILE

Filename	CARDSIN
Record Length	80 Positions

CALCULATION SPECIFICATIONS

The specifications for the calculations are

1. Use the Customer Number as the record key chain to the Customer Master File.

2. On a record-not-found condition, set an indicator.

3. With the record-not-found indicator and the proper input record-identifying indicator, set an indicator to be used to print a message, such as DUPLICATE RECORD.

OUTPUT SPECIFICATIONS

The coding of the Output Specifications should be such that no matter what data was added to the Customer Master File, the input record will be printed.

OUTPUT FILE

Filename	CUSTMAST
Record Length	120 Positions

Also, on Output, the message DUP RECORD should be printed if the Customer Number is already encoded on the file.

TO TEST PROGRAM

To ADD a new customer,

1. Make up a new Customer Number, such as 99999. The card layout is the same as the load card with an A punched in column 80.

2. Add this new customer card to the Customer Master File.

To Test DUPLICATE RECORD Message,

1. Select one of the existing Customer cards and punch an A in column 80 of the card.

2. Attempt to add this record to the Customer Master File.

3. Use Program 14B to print the file to check the results.

319

When completed, your program should ADD a new record in the same Input and Output format described in Project Fourteen-A. The Disk Output should also be the same as Project Fourteen. The Output listing of the program should print the card image, and the message RECORD ADDED or DUP RECORD should be printed.

COMPILATION INSTRUCTIONS

1. Develop a Print Chart for the Output Record. Use the Print Chart on page 462–463.

2. Code, keypunch, and compile this project to the satisfaction of your instructor.

3. Coding Specifications sheets are on pages 321 through 324.

4. A sample of the output from this project appears below.

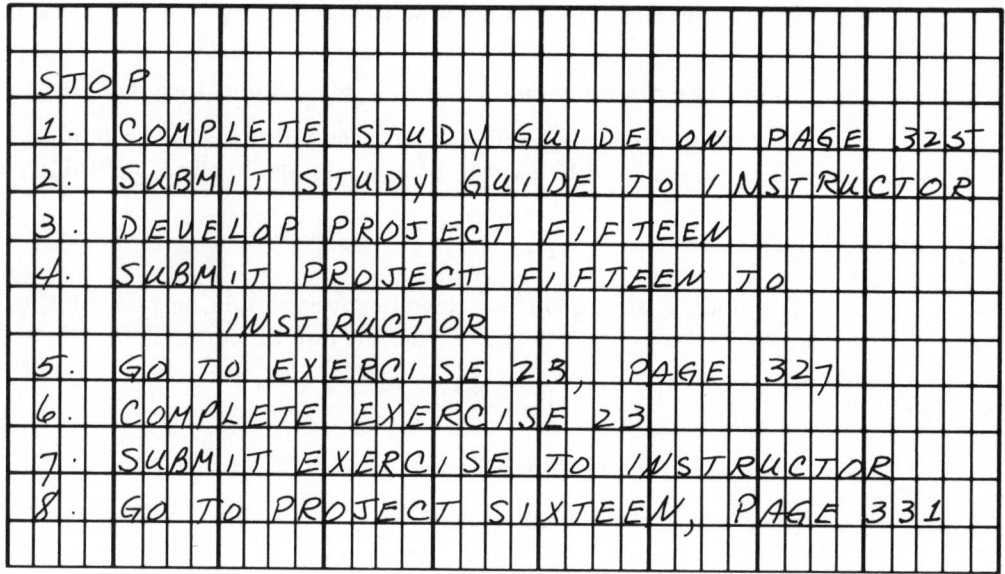

```
STOP
1.  COMPLETE STUDY GUIDE ON PAGE 325
2.  SUBMIT STUDY GUIDE TO INSTRUCTOR
3.  DEVELOP PROJECT FIFTEEN
4.  SUBMIT PROJECT FIFTEEN TO
       INSTRUCTOR
5.  GO TO EXERCISE 23, PAGE 327
6.  COMPLETE EXERCISE 23
7.  SUBMIT EXERCISE TO INSTRUCTOR
8.  GO TO PROJECT SIXTEEN, PAGE 331
```

```
                          CUSTOMER FILE MAINTENANCE--ADD
DUP RECORD          01854SCOT TRAIN'S & HBS414 SNOWDOWN ST     SAWER JUNCTION       NJ080016644466
RECORD ADDED        88888CUSTOMER ADD     TEST                 CARD                 SS111112222222
```

IBM International Business Machine Corporation

RPG CONTROL CARD AND FILE DESCRIPTION SPECIFICATIONS

GX21-9092-3 UM/050*
Printed in U.S.A.

*No. of forms per pad may very slightly

Program		Punching	Graphic		Card Electro Number	
Programmer	Date	Instruction	Punch			

Page [ ] of ___

Program Identification 75 76 77 78 79 80

Control Card Specifications

Refer to the specific System Reference Library manual for actual entries.

File Description Specification

RPG INPUT SPECIFICATIONS

IBM International Business Machine Corporation

GX21-9094-2 U/M 050*
Printed in U.S.A.

Program		Punching Instruction	Graphic							Card Electro Number
Programmer	Date		Punch							

Page 1 2 of ___ Program Identification 75 76 77 78 79 80

Line (3–5)	Form Type (6)	Filename (7–13)	OR / AND (14–16)	Sequence (15–16)	Number (1–N) (17)	Option (O) (18)	Record Identifying Indicator or** (19–20)	Record Identification Codes 1: Position (21–24)	1: Not (N) (25)	1: C/Z/D (26)	1: Character (27)	2: Position (28–31)	2: Not (N) (32)	2: C/Z/D (33)	2: Character (34)	3: Position (35–38)	3: Not (N) (39)	3: C/Z/D (40)	3: Character (41)	Stacker Select (42)	P/B/L/R (43)	Field Location From (44–47)	Field Location To (48–51)	Decimal Positions (52)	Field Name (53–58)	Control Level (L1–L9) (59–60)	Matching Fields or Changing Fields (61–62)	Field Record Relation (63–64)	Field Indicators Plus (65–66)	Field Indicators Minus (67–68)	Field Indicators Zero or Blank (69–70)	71–74
01	I																															
02	I																															
03	I																															
04	I																															
05	I																															
06	I																															
07	I																															
08	I																															
09	I																															
10	I																															
11	I																															
12	I																															
13	I																															
14	I																															
15	I																															
16	I																															
17	I																															
18	I																															
19	I																															
20	I																															
	I																															
	I																															
	I																															
	I																															
	I																															

GX21-9093-2 UM/050* Printed in U.S.A.
*No. of forms per pad may vary slightly

IBM International Business Machine Corporation

RPG CALCULATION SPECIFICATIONS

Program				Punching Instruction	Graphic		Card Electro Number	
Programmer		Date			Punch			

Page ☐ 1 2 of ☐

| Program Identification | 75 76 77 78 79 80 |

C

Line	Form Type	Control Level (L0-L9, LR, SR, AN/OR)	Indicators						Factor 1	Operation	Factor 2	Result Field					Resulting Indicators				Comments
			And		And							Name	Length	Decimal Positions	Half Adjust (H)	Arithmetic Plus / Minus / Zero; Compare 1>2 / 1<2 / 1=2; Lookup (Factor 2) is High / Low / Equal				
3 4 5	6	7 8	9 10N	11 12 13N	14 15N	16 17	18 19 20 21 22 23 24 25 26 27	28 29 30 31 32	33 34 35 36 37 38 39 40 41 42	43 44 45 46 47 48	49 50 51	52	53	54 55 56 57	58 59	60 61 62 63 64 65 66 67 68 69 70 71 72 73 74
0 1	C															
0 2	C															
0 3	C															
0 4	C															
0 5	C															
0 6	C															
0 7	C															
0 8	C															
0 9	C															
1 0	C															
1 1	C															
1 2	C															
1 3	C															
1 4	C															
1 5	C															
1 6	C															
1 7	C															
1 8	C															
1 9	C															
2 0	C															

323

IBM International Business Machine Corporation

RPG   OUTPUT   SPECIFICATIONS

Program			Punching Instruction	Graphic			Card Electro Number	
Programmer		Date		Punch				

Page [1] [2] of ___

GX21-9090-2 U/M 050*
Printed in U.S.A.

Program Identification
75 76 77 78 79 80

Commas	Zero Balances to Print	No Sign	CR	-	
Yes	Yes	1	A	J	X = Remove Plus Sign
Yes	No	2	B	K	Y = Date Field Edit
No	Yes	3	C	L	Z = Zero Suppress
No	No	4	D	M	

Constant or Edit Word

Edit Codes

B/A/C/1-9/R

End Position in Output Record

P/B/L/R

Field Name

*Auto

Output Indicators — And / Not / And / Not / Not

Skip — Before / After

Space — Before / After

Stacker #/Fetch(F)

Type (H/D/T/E)

Filename

Form Type

Line

O

Date _____ Name_____

DIRECTIONS: *Answer the following questions in the spaces provided. Your answers should indicate the depth of understanding that you have toward the concepts and definitions presented. If there is insufficient space provided for your answer, complete your answer on the reverse side of the Study Guide.*

1. Explain how new records can be readily added to or merged with an existing file when using Consecutive File Organization.

2. Explain how new records can be readily added to or merged with an existing file when using Direct File Organization.

3. Explain the process of trying to add a record to a file with an already existing record on the file.

4. Explain how the CHAIN Operation Code works.

5. What is random processing?

Date _____   Name_____

TRUE–FALSE: *Each of the following statements is either true or false. Indicate your choice in the Answers column by encircling "T" for a true or "F" for a false answer.*

Answers

1. Individual fields within a record or the complete record can be changed by an updating process   T   F

2. To delete a record from a file, a delete code must be built into the program and record   T   F

3. It is generally accepted that an Audit Trail should be printed of all changes to a file   T   F

4. Column 80 of an input record always contains specific codes   T   F

5. Records cannot be added to Direct Organization Files   T   F

6. Disk File Organization determines how record additions are handled   T   F

7. When direct files are created, a record is created for every possible address within the file boundaries   T   F

8. At least three major steps must be considered when adding records to a file   T   F

9. An identical record can be added any number of times to a consecutive file   T   F

10. Any listing that represents additions, corrections, updating, and/or deletions of a file is known as an Audit Trail   T   F

11. If the Chain Operation Code is to be used in a program, it must be so indicated by a C in column 15 on the File Description Specifications sheet   T   F

12. The U in column 15 of the File Description Specifications sheet shows that the File type is an update file   T   F

13. The coding of an R in column 28 and the coding of an A in column 66 of the File Specifications sheet are necessary if the file is to be read randomly and at the same time have new records added   T   F

14. The C in column 15 of the File Description Specifications sheet has a direct relationship to the Operation Code of the Calculation Specifications sheet   T   F

15. Sequential, Direct, and Indexed files can be processed by a key   T   F

16. The Relative Record Number must be coded as Factor 1 in the Calculation Specifications sheet, and it must be numeric   T   F

17. It is not necessary for the programmer to calculate the position of the record relative to the first record of a Direct File   T   F

18. Processing records by key necessitates that the proper key of the record be used   T   F

19. The length of the key described for the file is of little significance   T   F

20. Resulting Indicators must be coded when the Chain Operation
Code is used   T   F

21. Audit Trail information is automatically printed from each program.   T   F

22. It is not necessary to show whether a record was found on the file   T   F

23. Factor 1 of the Calculations Specifications sheet is the Filename
for a Chain Operation   T   F

24. Before any Resulting Indicators are used in a program, they should
always be associated with a SETOF operation   T   F

25. The A coded in column 66 of the File Description Specifications
sheet is used in conjunction with the ADD concept of the Output
Specifications   T   F

26. Records can be added to a file at any time   T   F

27. Whenever a new record is added to a file, its format need not correspond
to those records already existing in the file   T   F

28. A file within a program can be defined or used only one time on output   T   F

29. An indicator can be set on a record-not-found condition   T   F

30. When adding a record to a Direct File it replaces a record that
already exists in the file   T   F

COMPLETION: *Fill in the blank with the appropriate word or words.*

1. The file should be checked to see if a record to be added already exists within the
_____ .

2. A programmer provides a trail of activity on the master files by the use of a/an
_____ .

3. A file can be both input and output within the same RPG cycle. In order that
the computer realizes this fact, a _____ is coded in column 15
of the File Description Specifications.

4. When the CHAIN operation is used, the file is processed _____ .

5, 7. The three types of files that can be processed by relative record number are _____
_____ , _____ , and _____ .

8. Only _____ files can be processed by key.

9. Adding records to a direct file is really an _____ operation.

10. When the ADD concept is used, the Output device for the file must be a _____
_____ .

MATCHING: *Match Column 1 to Column 2*

COLUMN 1	COLUMN 2	Answers

COLUMN 1

A. Consecutive File
B. Merge Program
C. Update
D. C
E. A
F. U

COLUMN 2   Answers

1. Records in a direct sequence   _____

2. The character coded in column 66 of the File
   Description Specifications for a file add   _____

3. The character that must be coded in column 16 of
   the File Description Specifications to indicate that
   the CHAIN Operation Code is being used.   _____

4. When records cannot be added directly to a consecutive file, they are added by use of a   _____

5. Another name for adding records to a direct file is   _____

PROJECT SIXTEEN

The next step in disk file maintenance is changing or updating a Disk Master Record. In prior projects the Master File was loaded and listed; then new records were added. In this project you will change the information within a record of the Master File or update the fields within a record.

The information or fields that are changed in a master file update program are those fields that are primarily static or indicative. The Customer Master File will again be used. The fields that should be in the update program are

1. Customer Name

2. City, State, and Zip Code

3. Telephone Number

One additional field will be added — a delete code field. To delete a customer, a code will be placed in this field. The code will indicate to all applications using the customer file that the customer is inactive and will soon be purged from the file.

The program from Project Fifteen will be added to and altered to complete this project. The function of this project will be

1. To change any one field in the customer file.

2. To change any field to blanks.

3. To delete or place a delete code in the file.

4. To print an audit trail of all changes made to the file.

Figure 98 illustrates the logic necessary for this project. In reference to Fig. 98, note the following points.

1. The CARDIN file will have two additional record types added to Project Fifteen.

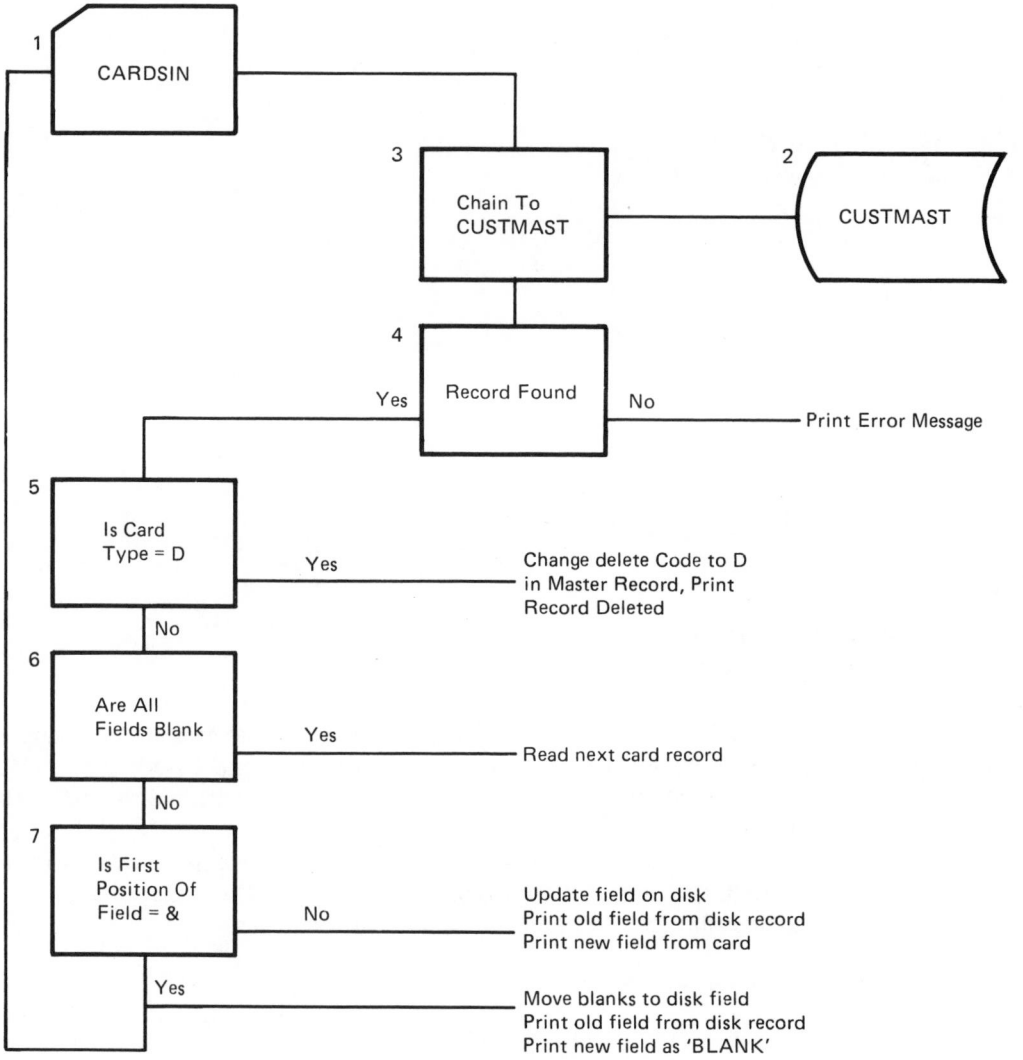

Figure 98

a. A C in column 80 will indicate a change transaction.

b. A D in column 80 will indicate a delete transaction.

2. All fields to be changed will be coded on input so that they can be printed.

3. The CHAIN operation is directly from Project Fifteen.

4. In Project Fifteen the programmer was asked to indicate DUP RECORD when a record was being added and the Customer Record was found. In this project the error condition is RECORD NOT FOUND when a record is to be changed and it is not an existing Customer Record.

5. If CARDIN column 80 is a D, it will indicate that the Customer Record should be coded with a D in the delete code field of the master record.

6. Each field will have a zero or blank indicator assigned to it on the input specifications. If all fields are blank, do nothing with this input card. Of course, if the record type were a D, then the prior step would have taken place and it would be valid to have all the input fields blank.

332

7. To blank a field on disk requires some indication to the program that the field would be blanked. One method would be to put a code in the first position of the card field to indicate this. An ampersand is a good choice because it will probably not be the first character of any input field. Each nonblank input field is checked in this step for an ampersand in the first position. If there is an ampersand in the first position, turn ON an indicator to be used in Output.

NEW CONCEPTS

File Type U	More Than One Record Type
Field Record Relation Indicators	Handling Blank Numeric Fields
GOTO Operation Code	

File Type I/O/U/C/D (Columns 15 through 15)

The type of file being used is defined in this field. When using a single input disk in which both reading and writing are needed, the coding of a U in this field is required. The updating process is such that the record is read, the field(s) of the record is updated, and then the record is written back in the same location on the disk from which it was read.

Field Record Relation (Columns 63 through 64)

When some of the fields of a record are not common to all records being used, this particular field must contain an appropriate indicator. This field is used in conjunction with the Record Identifying Indicator Field (columns 19–20). For those fields that are not common to all records, the same appropriate indicator number is used in both fields. See Fig. 99, line 060.

More Than One Record Type
(Columns 27, 34, 41)

In Fig. 99 CARDIN has three record types. Column 80 can have an A, a C, or a D punched into it. If an A is punched into column 80, the record is an ADD record. If a C is punched into column 80, the record is a change or update record. Finally, if a D is punched into column 80, the record is to be deleted. Notice that each record type will turn on a different Record Identifying Indicator.

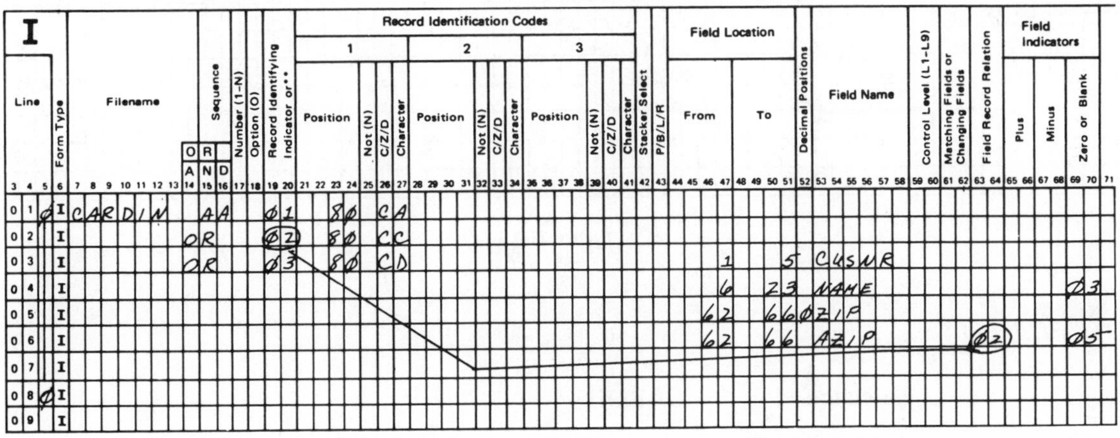

Figure 99

In Fig. 99 it can be seen that Indicator 02 is coded in the Record Identifying Indicator Field and the Field Record Relation Field. Also, notice that the fields defined in columns 62 through 66 of the Input Record have two different field names. The purpose is to code the field coded ZIP both as a numeric field, as in the first case, and as an alphabetic field AZIP in the second case.

Handling Blank Numeric Fields

All numerically defined input fields are converted to zeros if they are blank when read into an RPG program. Therefore special handling of numeric fields is necessary to indicate whether they are blank or zero. In Fig. 99 the ZIP code field is defined two times, once as a numeric field and once as an alphameric field. The Zero or Blank Indicator 05 will come ON if the field AZIP is zero or blank. The field called ZIP is numeric and will be used in the Output Specifications for file update and printing on the report.

GOTO Tag (Columns 28 through 32)

If the condition being tested has been met, there is no need to execute unnecessary code in the program. Therefore the GOTO operation allows for bypassing instructions in the program from one point in the program to another point in the program known as a TAG. All the statements between the GOTO Statement and the TAG Statement are skipped or branched over. The Coding Name in Factor 2 of the GOTO Statement must also be used in the TAG Statement except that the Coding Name is in Factor 1 of the TAG Statement. This type of coding is shown in Fig. 100. The instructions between statements 010 and 040 of Fig. 100 will not be executed if Indicator 10 is NOT ON and 02 is ON.

The GOTO operation may cause some unpredictable results. Notice that in the coding used in Fig. 100 Indicator 11 could remain ON if the GOTO was conditioned to occur. The proper type of programming necessitates that Indicator 11 would be SETOF at the beginning of the Calculation Specifications.

C

Line (3–5)	Form Type (6)	Control Level (L0–L9, LR, SR, AN/OR) (7–8)	Indicators: Not / And Not / And Not (9–17)	Factor 1 (18–27)	Operation (28–32)	Factor 2 (33–42)	Result Field Name (43–48)	Result Field Length (49–51)	Decimal Positions (52)	Half Adjust (H) (53)	Resulting Indicators: Arithmetic Plus / Compare 1 > 2 / Lookup (Factor 2) is High (54–55)	Resulting Indicators: Minus / 1 < 2 / Low (56–57)	Resulting Indicators: Zero / 1 = 2 / Equal (58–59)	Comments (60–70)
01Ø	C		N1Ø Ø2		GOTO	UPDOK								
02	C	*	ERROR CONDITIONS											
03	C		N1Ø Ø1		SETON						11			ADD ERROR
04Ø	C			UPDOK	TAG									
05	C													
06	C													
07	C													

Figure 100

INPUT FILE

Filename CARDIN

Record Length 80 Positions

CALCULATION SPECIFICATIONS

One technique that will be needed in this project is the ability to check a single position of a field for a specific character. By using a series of MOVE or MOVEL operations with the Result Field Length different from the moved field, it is possible to isolate any position within a field for comparison purposes. See Fig. 101 for example.

C	Form Type	Control Level (L0-L9, LR, SR, AN/OR)	Indicators			Factor 1	Operation	Factor 2	Result Field		Decimal Positions	Half Adjust (H)	Resulting Indicators
Line			And Not	And Not	Not	Factor 1	Operation	Factor 2	Name	Length			Arithmetic / Compare / Lookup
01	C		*			FIELDA INITIALLY IS ZYZXABCDEF							
02	C						MOVE	FIELDA	TEST1	7			
03	C		*			TEST1 IS NOW XABCDEF							
04	C						MOVEL	TEST1	TEST2	1			
05	C		*			TEST2 IS NOW X							
06	C					TEST2	COMP	'X'					10 10 11
07	C		*			10 IS ON IF NOT X, 11 IS ON IF X							
08	C												
09	C												

Figure 101

OUTPUT SPECIFICATIONS

With each field change of a customer record, a line of print should be printed, indicating the customer number of the record effected, the contents of the field before the change, and the contents of the field after the change has been made. If the field is to be blanked, indicate this fact also. See Fig. 102.

The coding of statement 010 will cause printing at detail time on an Indicator 02, which is a change transaction, and N10, which says that the disk record was not found, and N03, which says that the Name Field is not blank. The first item that will be printed on the line is Customer Number. The second item that will be printed is the

O	Form Type	Filename	Type (H/D/T/E)	Stacker#/Fetch(F)	Space Before/After	Skip Before/After	Output Indicators And Not / And Not / Not	Field Name *Auto	Edit Codes B/A/C/1-9/R	End Position in Output Record P/B/L/R	Constant or Edit Word
01	O	PRINT	D		2		02 N10 N03				
02	O									8	'CUST NO-'
03	O							CUSNR		13	
04	O									30	'NAME BEFORE'
05	O							DNAME		48	
06	O									58	'AFTER'
07	O						N13	NAME		68	
08	O								13	64	'BLANK'
09	O										
10	O										

Figure 102

contents of the field called DNAME from the disk record plus the contents of the field NAME from the card record. The field described as DNAME is from the disk record; the field described as NAME comes from the card record. Therefore DNAME is the Name Field before the change, and the field name NAME is the one used after the change has been made.

Figure 102 illustrates that when Indicator 13 is ON, the NAME field has an & in the first position and the word BLANK is printed.

The CUSTMAST Record should be defined an additional time on the Output Specifications in this project. Project Fifteen has the CUSTMAST record described for ADD on Output. Observe the necessary coding to accomplish this step in Fig. 103.

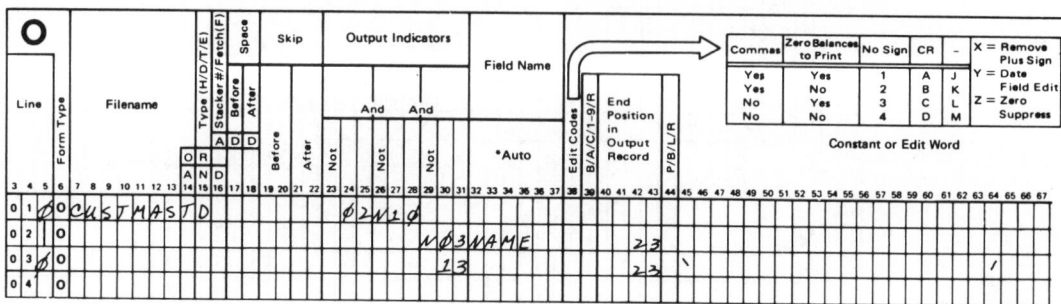

Figure 103

The record will be updated at detail time. Indicator 02 is ON when it is a change transaction-type record. Indicator 10 is *not* ON when the CUSTMAST record is found. Each field to be changed must be conditioned by its respective zero or blank indicator, and the field is to be blanked if there is an ampersand (&) in its first position.

Remember to output the delete code if the input transaction was a delete transaction. It should be located in the last position of the CUSTMAST record (position 128).

OUTPUT FILE

Filename   List

Record Length   120 Positions

TO TEST THE PROGRAM

The program that has been completed for this project should do the following to the CUSTMAST file.

1. Add a record (from Project Fifteen).

2. Indicate DUP RECORD when trying to add an existing customer to the file (from Project Fifteen).

3. Update the customer record, changing any one or more than one of the fields: Customer Name, City, State, Zip, and Telephone Number.

4. Print a line when a field is updated, giving the field content before and after the change. Print BLANK if the field is to be blanked.

5. Indicate RECORD NOT FOUND on an update when trying to change a Customer Record that does not exist.

6. Blank any of the update fields.

7. Delete a Customer Record by placing a delete code in column 128 of the record.

The layout of the card input record is the same as that used to load the file except for the cases listed below.

1. Column 80 = A for an ADD transaction.

2. Column 80 = C for a CHANGE or UPDATE transaction.

3. Column 80 = D for a DELETE transaction

4. When column 80 = C, only those fields to be changed should be punched. When a field is to be blanked, punch an ampersand (&) in the first position of that field.

5. When column 80 = D, only the Customer Number should be punched.

6. In all cases, Customer Number is required.

Select five customers from the data deck to be changed. From these five data cards, select one, two, three, or more fields to be changed or blanked. The point is to test the program so that each field is tested at least once to see if the program is doing what it is supposed to do.

Delete the customer who was added in Project Fifteen. Now add a new customer with the new program to ensure that the function still works.

To test RECORD NOT FOUND, try to change a record that is NOT in the file.

Use Program 14B to test for all the results. Modify 14B so that column 128 will be printed in order to check the delete code.

COMPILATION INSTRUCTIONS

1. Develop a Print Chart for the Output Report. Use the Print Chart on page 464–465.

2. Code, keypunch, and compile this project to the satisfaction of your instructor. See the sample output on page 338.

3. Use coding sheets from Project 15. Additional Coding Specifications sheets are on pages 339 through 342.

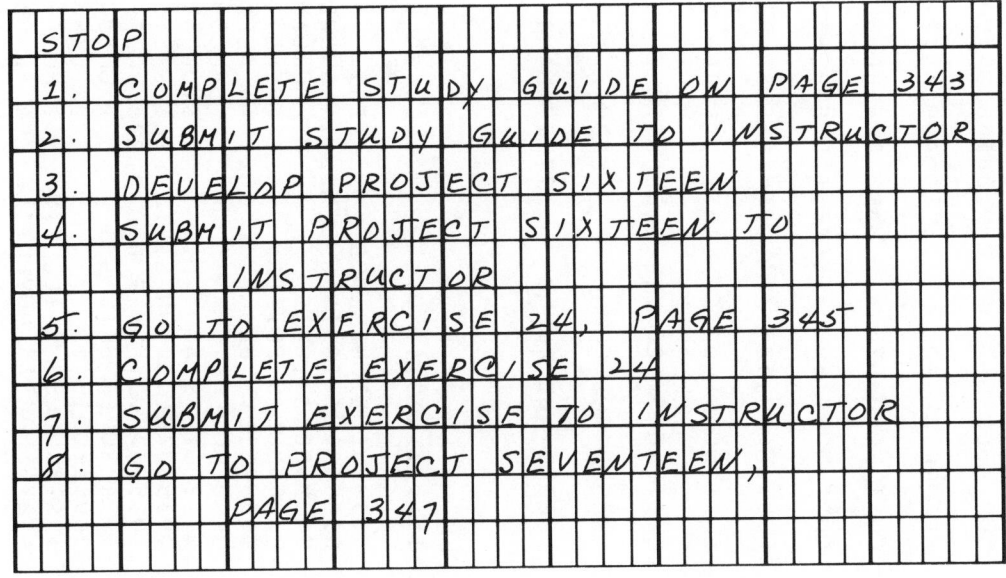

```
STOP
1.  COMPLETE STUDY GUIDE ON PAGE 343
2.  SUBMIT STUDY GUIDE TO INSTRUCTOR
3.  DEVELOP PROJECT SIXTEEN
4.  SUBMIT PROJECT SIXTEEN TO
        INSTRUCTOR
5.  GO TO EXERCISE 24, PAGE 345
6.  COMPLETE EXERCISE 24
7.  SUBMIT EXERCISE TO INSTRUCTOR
8.  GO TO PROJECT SEVENTEEN,
        PAGE 347
```

CUSTOMER FILE MAINTENANCE

DUP RECORD	88888CUSTOMER ADD	TEST	CARD	SS11112222222
RECORD ADDED	99999CUSTOMER ADD	TEST	CARD	SS11112222222
CUST NO-03824	NAME BEFORE-MCCARTHY GLASS		AFTER-MCCARTHY'S	
CUST NO-03893	STREET BEFORE-555 WEST STATE ST		AFTER-111 EAST STATE ST	
CUST NO-04597	CITY BEFORE-PRINTOWN		AFTER-PINNCETOWN	
CUST NO-04902	STATE BEFORE- MA		AFTER- VT	
CUST NO-07120 ZIP CODE BEFORE-03301			AFTER-04412	
REORD NOT FOUND	08839			
REORD NOT FOUND	77777CHANGE TEST CARD			7523780

CUSTOMER FILE LIST

```
1....+....10....+....20....+....30....+....40....+....50....+....60....+....70....+....80....+....90....+....100
99999CUSTOMER ADD          TEST              CARD              SS11112222222    CS
01854SCOT TRAIN'S & HBS414 SNOWDOWN ST       SAWER JUNCTION    NJ08001664466    CS
03824MCCARTHY'S            88 MORGAN ST.      FRYBURG          PA09523456987?   CS
03893MOM'S POTTERY         111 EAST STATE ST  MAKERVILLE       GA224102001040   CS
04597STEVE BABKEY & CO.1044 ALEXANDER DR PINNCETOWN    CA97120576889?   CS
04902RON FRIEMAN SHOP      27 BALCOURT WAY    NEW PICKERTON    VT680425220011   CS
07120GIFTS AND THINGS      5 STUBENVILLE RD   COUNTY LINE      RI044125011050   CS
09353JANE BROWN GIFTS      761 STETSON BLVD   GRACIOUS         IL152762143524   CS
10357GARVEY CHIP & DIP     228 PROSPECT ST.   MAJOR            KY120575521122   CS
32943SUPER ERIC'S          681 GUYOUT ST      AARNTOWNSVILLE   NY010107523265   CS
34982EDDIE'S               2222 GREAT TREE DRMERSER            ND784512561289   CS
39673RUBLEV SKILL CTR      311 HUNT ST.       BUNINGTON        WV152753510052   CS
45276SHART'S NOVELTIES     744 TERHAUT PL     FINGERTON        NH035247521358   CS
50389MAKING THINGS         EAST MAIN ST       DANDYTOWN        MN620059981133   CS
53898DUDLEY'S PLANT CTR668 DRIVEWAY RD        FLUGLETON        OH422533337721   CS
68935STRONG'S PARTS        351 WITHERSPOON DRROCKAWAY          VA145532121199   CS
69451GIFT SUPERMARKET      8 GROVER BLVD      GRANGEBURG       CT04445123700?   CS
83959STACY'S               MARKET ST          HUBBER           PA09552421557?   CS
88888CUSTOMER ADD          TEST               CARD             SS11112222222    CS
```

GX21-9093-2 UM/050* Printed in U.S.A.
*No. of forms per pad may vary slightly

IBM International Business Machine Corporation

RPG CALCULATION SPECIFICATIONS

Program

Programmer

Date

Punching Instruction

Graphic

Punch

Card Electro Number

Page ___ of ___

Program Identification 75 76 77 78 79 80

C	Line	Form Type	Control Level (L0-L9, LR, SR, AN/OR)	Indicators						Factor 1	Operation	Factor 2	Result Field				Resulting Indicators			Comments

Indicators: And N0, And, And N0, And, N0

Result Field: Name, Length, Decimal Positions, Half Adjust (H)

Resulting Indicators: Arithmetic — Plus, Minus, Zero; Compare 1>2 1<2 1=2; Lookup (Factor 2) is — High, Low, Equal

Column numbers: 3 4 5 6 7 8 9 10 11 12 13 14 15 16 17 18 19 20 21 22 23 24 25 26 27 28 29 30 31 32 33 34 35 36 37 38 39 40 41 42 43 44 45 46 47 48 49 50 51 52 53 54 55 56 57 58 59 60 61 62 63 64 65 66 67 68 69 70 71 72 73 74

Line numbers: 01 02 03 04 05 06 07 08 09 10 11 12 13 14 15 16 17 18 19 20

339

IBM International Business Machine Corporation

RPG   OUTPUT   SPECIFICATIONS

GX21-9090-2 U/M 050*
Printed in U.S.A.

Program					
Programmer		Date			

Punching Instruction
Graphic / Punch
Card Electro Number

Page [ ] of [ ]   1 2

Program Identification   75 76 77 78 79 80

Edit Codes table:

Commas	Zero Balances to Print	No Sign	CR	−
Yes	Yes	1	A	J
Yes	No	2	B	K
No	Yes	3	C	L
No	No	4	D	M

X = Remove Plus Sign
Y = Date Field Edit
Z = Zero Suppress

Constant or Edit Word

Column headers:
Form Type (6) · Filename (7–14) · Type (H/D/T/E) (15) · Stacker#/Fetch(F) (16) · Space Before/After (17–18) · Skip Before/After (19–22) · Output Indicators And Not / And Not / And Not (23–31) · Field Name (32–37) · *Auto (35–37) · Edit Codes B/A/C/1-9/R (38) · End Position in Output Record (40–43) · P/B/L/R (44) · Constant or Edit Word (45–70)

Line: 01 02 03 04 05 06 07 08 09 10 11 12 13 14 15 16 17 18 19 20

IBM International Business Machine Corporation

RPG OUTPUT SPECIFICATIONS

GX21-9090-2 U/M 050*
Printed in U.S.A.

Program				Card Electro Number	
Programmer		Date			

Punching Instruction — Graphic — Punch

Page 1 2 of ___

Program Identification 75 76 77 78 79 80

Commas	Zero Balances to Print	No Sign	CR	-
Yes	Yes	1	A	J
Yes	No	2	B	K
No	Yes	3	C	L
No	No	4	D	M

X = Remove Plus Sign
Y = Date Field Edit
Z = Zero Suppress

Constant or Edit Word

Output Indicators

Field Name

*Auto

Edit Codes

B/A/C/1-9/R

End Position in Output Record

P/B/L/R

And / Not

Skip — After / Before

Space — After / Before

Stacker #/Fetch(F)

Type (H/D/T/E)

Filename

Form Type

Line

O

IBM International Business Machine Corporation

RPG OUTPUT SPECIFICATIONS

GX21-9090-2 U/M 050*
Printed in U.S.A.

Program		Punching Instruction	Graphic		Card Electro Number
Programmer	Date		Punch		

Page 1 2 of ____

Program Identification 75 76 77 78 79 80

Output Indicators

Field Name

Commas	Zero Balances to Print	No Sign	CR	-
Yes	Yes	1	A	J
Yes	No	2	B	K
No	Yes	3	C	L
No	No	4	D	M

X = Remove Plus Sign
Y = Date Field Edit
Z = Zero Suppress

Constant or Edit Word

Line — Form Type — Filename — Type (H/D/T/E) — Stacker #/Fetch(F) — Space — Skip — Output Indicators — Field Name — *Auto — Edit Codes — B/A/C/1-9/R — End Position in Output Record — P/B/L/R — Commas — Zero Balances to Print — No Sign — CR

Date _____   Name_____

DIRECTIONS: *Answer the following questions in the spaces provided. Your answers should indicate the depth of understanding that you have toward the concepts and definitions presented. If there is insufficient space provided for your answer, complete your answer on the reverse side of the Study Guide.*

1. Explain how a delete code works.

2. Explain how more than one record type can be used in a file.

3. Explain the working between the Field Indicator and Record Identifying Indicator fields of the Input Specifications.

4. Explain the method by which a single character can be signaled out of a field for checking purposes.

5. Explain why it is necessary to have printed proof of the data before and after update has been effected.

6. Explain the GOTO and TAG operation codes.

Date _____   Name _____

TRUE-FALSE: *Each of the following statements is either true or false. Indicate your choice in the Answers column by encircling "T" for a true answer or "F" for a false answer.*

Answers

1. If a record is to be updated, the complete record must be changed rather than just a single field   T   F

2. It is not necessary to identify input records properly in an Add-Update program   T   F

3. The GOTO operation allows the program statements to be skipped over   T   F

4. If a record code is required for changing or updating a record, any code that the programmer decides to use will be acceptable to the computer   T   F

5. When a record is to be deleted from an indexed file, the space that it occupies cannot be used again   T   F

6. The updating process is such that the record is read, the field(s) of the record is/are updated, and then the record is written back in the same location on the disk from which it was read   T   F

7. There can be more than one Record Identifying Indicator associated with one file   T   F

8. A field that is not common to all records read from a file must have an appropriate Field Record Relation Indicator assigned to it   T   F

9. There is a direct relationship between the Record Identifying Indicator and Field Record Relation Indicator of the Input Specifications sheet   T   F

10. Defining the same field positions of an input record two or more differing ways is not allowed with RPG II   T   F

11. Input fields that are blank and defined as numeric are converted to zeros when read into an RPG II program   T   F

12. Single positions within a field cannot be checked for a specific character contained within   T   F

13. Part of the printed audit trail information is to show how part(s) of a record was/were before and after an update process   T   F

14. Records cannot be updated at detail output time   T   F

15. For every GOTO Statement there must be a TAG Statement   T   F

16. It is not necessary to punch the complete input card record if only one field is to be updated   T   F

17. The key used in the record must always be punched in the input card in an updating process   T   F

18. Whenever a new function is added to an already existing program, it should be tested to determine if it works correctly as intended   T   F

19. The character U of the File Type Field of the File Specifications sheet signifies that the data in the file is to be unchanged   T   F

20. Whenever a new function is added to an existing program, the old function should be tested again   T   F

COMPLETION: *Fill in the blank with the appropriate word or words.*

1. When a file is composed of several record types, each record type must have _____ _____ _____ _____ _____ to distinguish it from the others.

2. If numeric fields are blank when read into an RPG II program, they are converted to _____ .

3, 4. To check a single position of a field to see if it contains a specific character for comparison purposes, a programmer can use a series of _____ and _____ Operation Codes.

5. When an _____ _____ _____ record is to be punched, only those fields to be changed need be punched.

PROJECT SEVENTEEN

A Master Record is a record that contains all the information accumulated for a given entity. The entity could be a customer, an inventory item, a customer order, or a production order. Master Records can hold various types of indicative information, such as name and address of a customer. Indicative information does not change or need not be changed or updated unless the customer moves or changes his telephone number or the name of his company. The information contained within the Master Record is fairly static but always indicates or is indicative of the particular customer. Master Records hold not only indicative information but also variable information. Variable information, such as accumulated sales over a period of time, does change, depending on the given situation.

It is important to realize the relationship between a Master Record and a Detail Record. A Detail Record would be assigned as one invoice or line item of the invoice. A Detail Record would give only one transaction's information of a Master Record.

In this project you will be dealing with accumulative sales. The sales will be obtained from the Invoice Summary Records generated in Project Seven. The field to be concerned about from the Invoice Summary Record is the Invoice Total. It will be accumulated to a field called SALES in the Customer Master Record.

The programmer must decide how large the field in the Customer Master Record for accumulating information must be. It is assumed that no customer will have sales for any given period greater than $9,999,999.99. Therefore the field length will be nine positions long with two decimal places. If any customer were to have more than $9,999,999.99 in sales, then the field should be made large enough to accommodate the sales figure. The field could be enlarged to 11 or 13 positions in length. However, disk storage is at a premium in most computer installations or centers.

If 1000 customers each had two additional characters added to a field of the disk record, then 2000 more positions of disk storage would be needed for these 1000 customers. However, typically, there may be 10, 20, even 30 numeric fields holding dollar amounts or quantities of some kind. If these fields were unwisely made too large, it is clear that disk space would soon run out. For example, if there were 10 fields, each having two characters more than needed, the result would be 20 additional characters per record.

347

When this amount is multiplied by 1000 records, 20,000 additional characters of disk storage would be allocated. It is important to make the field large enough so that no one field in no one customer record is too small. On the other hand, the field should be conservative enough to avoid too much room being taken up on the disk file on the disk device. If the disk device has a 2-million-character capacity, 20,000 of them represent a significant amount of disk storage that is actually being wasted.

The disk device must also have work space for temporary files for sorting detail records. Whenever a sorting routine is applied to detail records, on disk, there must be sufficient room for the work file as well as the output file on the disk. The problem for a programmer is conservation, on the one hand, and being sufficiently informed, on the other, to ensure that the records will be sufficient in size to hold all the necessary pertinent information.

FILE DESCRIPTION SPECIFICATIONS SHEET

The Invoice Summary File (Input) is the primary file. The Customer Master File is the disk (Update-Chain) file. Finally, the Print File is the Output File.

INPUT SPECIFICATIONS

The Invoice Summary Cards created in Project Seven should be used for this project. The Invoice Total Field will be accumulated into the proper Customer Master Record. The Customer Record will be updated once for each control group.

The fields that are needed to run this program should be coded on the Input Specifications sheet. It is not necessary to code every field from the entire record being used as an Input record.

The CUSTMAST record has coded in it the field name SALES. However, the Customer Master Record does not have any data encoded into positions 83 through 91 at this time and yet it is being defined. The reason for this definition is so that the SALES field can be updated instead of merely being outputted. On an Update field it is necessary to code the field both on the Input Specifications sheet and on the Output Specifications sheet. Figure 106 shows how this field is coded on the Output Specifications sheet.

As can be seen in Fig. 104, the SALES field is to be read in from the Customer Master Record. It is going to be added to (updated) and then written out again with the additional information at output time.

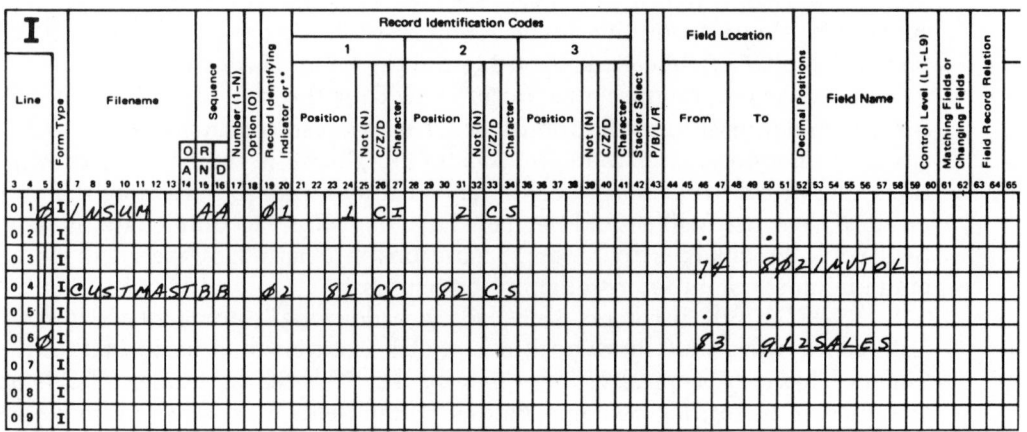

Figure 104

CALCULATION SPECIFICATIONS

In Fig. 105 the first statement is a comment statement. Statement 020 is coded with an L1 Control Level Indicator, which will cause the CHAIN operation to take place at detail time. The CHAIN operation will only occur on the first record within a Control Group. There must not be a CHAIN operation each time an Invoice Summary Record is read if it is for the same Customer Master Record. Once the Customer Master Record is placed in the machine (computer) memory, the field that is to be updated (Sales Field) will remain until another Customer Master Record is read into memory. This type of coding is shown in Fig. 105.

Indicator 03 is to check that the Customer Master Record is not found. In this case, Indicator 03 branches the program to the end of the Calculation Specifications because no addition should occur if the Customer Master Record is not found.

Line	Form Type	Control Level (L0-L9, LR, SR, AN/OR)	Not	Indicators And	Not	And	Not	Factor 1	Operation	Factor 2	Result Field Name	Length	Decimal Positions	Half Adjust (H)	Resulting Indicators
0 1	C	*		C CHAIN TO CUSTMAST ON FIRST RECORD OF CONTROL GROUP											
0 2	C			L L				CUSMR	CHAIN	CUSTMAST					03
0 3	C			03					GOTO	END					
0 4	C							.		.					
0 5	C							END	TAG						
0 6	C														
0 7	C														
0 8	C														

Figure 105

TIP TO PROGRAMMER

Whenever numerical information is read into a computer, a total should be given. In this program the total will be Total Sales for all the Invoice Summary Records being read in. In some cases, the total could be a Hash Total. For example, the Customer Number Field of each record could be added to a single field. At printout time this total would indicate that the data was read correctly or key-punched correctly from the data on the source documents. The totals should agree to a control tape which is a desk calculator tape taken on figures from the source documents.

OUTPUT SPECIFICATIONS

In Fig. 106 statements 010 and 020 indicate that printing is to be at detail time. However, the spacing of the printing will depend on whether it is the first record of the group or other than the first record of the group. Statement 010 is coded to cause one space to be effective before and one space after the line is printed. In other words, if this is the first record of a control group, meaning the first record for this customer, space before as well as space after printing the line. The effect of this type of coding would be to give two spaces between each customer group.

Statement 020 will cause one space after printing for each input record when it

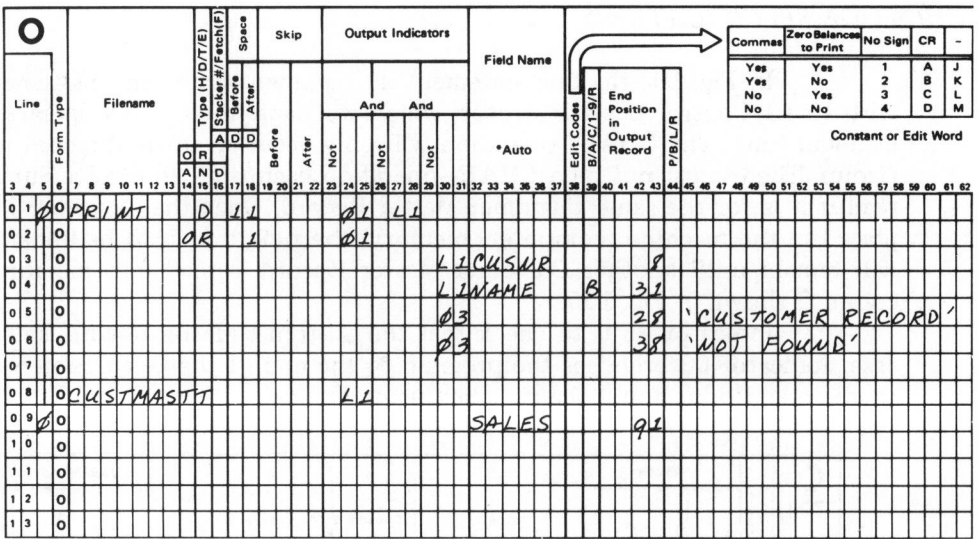

Figure 106

is other than the first record. The indicative information from the customer file will print on that line — that is, the first four fields: Customer Number, Name, City, and State. This data should not be repeated for every input detail record. It should be printed only once at the beginning of the Control Group. The method used for this type of printing is controlled by Indicator L1. The example shown in Fig. 106 is for Customer Name.

When a Customer Record is not found, a message should be printed indicating this fact. The message CUSTOMER RECORD NOT FOUND is printed when Indicator 03 is ON, as illustrated in Fig. 106. When Indicator 03 is ON, it indicates that the Customer Record that is being chained to is not found. The information that will be printed is the Customer Number and the message CUSTOMER RECORD NOT FOUND. The information from the Invoice Summary Record, Invoice Number, Invoice Date, Total, and Sales will also print with the message.

It is suggested that a fictitious customer number be punched into one of the Invoice Summary Records so that the appropriate message CUSTOMER RECORD NOT FOUND can be tested. An adding machine tape should be taken of the Summary cards to determine the total. This total must agree with the total accumulated by the computer.

Statement 080 defines the Customer Master Output Record. It will be outputted once per Control Group. It will be done on Indicator L1 at Total Time. This means that it will be written before the next record of the next Control Group is processed. In other words, as soon as the last record from the last Control Group is processed, the sales figure that has been accumulated is written to the disk. See Fig. 106 for the coding.

COMPILATION INSTRUCTIONS

1. Develop a Print Chart for the Output Report. Use the Print Chart on pages 464–465.

2. Code, keypunch, and compile this project to the satisfaction of your instructor.

3. Coding Specifications Sheets are on pages 353 through 357.

350

```
STOP
1.  COMPLETE STUDY GUIDE ON PAGE 359
2.  SUBMIT STUDY GUIDE TO INSTRUCTOR
3.  DEVELOP PROJECT SEVENTEEN
4.  SUBMIT PROJECT SEVENTEEN TO
        INSTRUCTOR
5.  GO TO EXERCISE 25, PAGE 361
6.  COMPLETE EXERCISE 25
7.  SUBMIT EXERCISE TO INSTRUCTOR
8.  GO TO TABLES AND ARRAYS,
        PAGE 363
```

CUSTOMER SALES UPDATE

CUST-NUM	NAME	CITY	STATE	INVOICE NUMBER	INVOICE DATE	INVOICE AMOUNT	SALES BALANCE
07120	GIFTS AND THINGS	COUNTY LINE	RI	532454	11/14/76	598.19	598.19
34982	EDDIE'S	MERSER	ND	532470	11/18/76	59.39	59.39
50389	MAKING THINGS	DANDYTOWN	MN	532465	11/16/76	72.95	72.95
68935	STRONG'S PARTS	ROCKAWAY	VA	532456 / 532472	11/14/76 / 11/18/76	3,215.07 / 320.82	3,215.07 / 3,535.89
09353	JANE BROWN GIFTS	GRACIOUS	IL	532451	11/13/76	2,705.54	2,705.54
45276	SHART'S NOVELTIES	FINGERTON	NH	532459	11/15/76	58.15	58.15
03824	MCCARTHY'S	FRYBURG	PA	532468	11/17/76	417.01	417.01
07120	GIFTS AND THINGS	COUNTY LINE	RI	532453	11/14/76	1,059.84	1,658.03
09353	JANE BROWN GIFTS	GRACIOUS	IL	532471	11/18/76	4,255.04	6,960.58
10357	GARVEY CHIP & DIP	MAJOR	KY	532452	11/13/76	393.98	393.98
50389	MAKING THINGS	DANDYTOWN	MN	532463	11/16/76	4,066.95	4,139.90
53898	DUDLEY'S PLANT CTR	FLUGLETON	OH	532474	11/18/76	3,096.83	3,096.83
68935	STRONG'S PARTS	ROCKAWAY	VA	532466	11/16/76	940.99	4,476.88
03824	MCCARTHY'S	FRYBURG	PA	532455	11/14/76	367.35	784.36
04902	RON FRIEMAN SHOP	NEW PICKERTON	VT	532457	11/14/76	2,926.68	2,926.68
32943	SUPER ERIC'S	AARNTOWNSVILLE	NY	532458	11/14/76	482.43	482.43
50389	MAKING THINGS	DANDYTOWN	MN	532462	11/15/76	51.98	4,191.88
01854	SCOT TRAIN'S & HBS	SAWER JUNCTION	NJ	532460	11/15/76	14.72	14.72
04597	STEVE BABKEY & CO.	PINNCETOWN	CA	532450	11/13/76	5,535.79	5,535.79
08839	CUSTOMER RECORD NOT FOUND			532473	11/18/76	979.35	5,535.79
10357	GARVEY CHIP & DIP	MAJOR	KY	532469	11/17/76	613.73	1,007.71
39673	RUBLEV SKILL CTR	BUNINGTON	WV	532461	11/15/76	106.00	106.00
69451	GIFT SUPERMARKET	GRANGEBURG	CT	532467	11/17/76	2,063.12	2,063.12
83959	STACY'S	HUBBER	PA	532464	11/16/76	624.32	624.32

TOTAL SALES   34,046.87

IBM
International Business Machine Corporation

RPG CONTROL CARD AND FILE DESCRIPTION SPECIFICATIONS

GX21-9092-3 UM/050*
Printed in U.S.A.

*No. of forms per pad may very slightly

Program	Punching Instruction	Graphic		Card Electro Number
Programmer	Date	Punch		

Page [ ] of ____

Program Identification
75 76 77 78 79 80

Control Card Specifications

Refer to the specific System Reference Library manual for actual entries.

H

Line — Form Type — Core Size to Compile — Object Output — Listing Options — Core Size to Execute — Debug — MFCM Stacking Sequence — Inverted Print — 360/20 2501 Buffer — Number Of Print Positions — Alternate Collating Sequence — Address to Start — Work Tapes — Overlay Open — Overlap Printer — Binary Search — Tape Error — 2152 Checking — Inquiry — Read/Write/Compute — Keyboard Output — Sign Handling — 1P Forms Position — Indicator Setting — File Translation — Punch MFCU Zeros — Nonprint Characters — Table Load Halt — Shared I/O — Field Print — Formatted Core Dump — RPG to RPG II Conversion

Model 20

Model 20

File Description Specification

F

Line — Form Type — Filename — File Type — File Designation — End of File — Sequence — File Format — Block Length — Record Length — Mode of Processing — Length of Key Field or of Record Address Field — Record Address Type — Type of File Organization or Additional Area — Overflow Indicator — Key Field Starting Location — Extension Code E/L — Device — Symbolic Device — Name of Label Exit — Extent Exit for DAM — Core Index — Continuation Lines — Option — Entry — File Addition/Unordered — Number of Tracks for Cylinder Overflow — Number of Extents — Tape Rewind — File Condition U1-U8

I/O/U/C/D — P/S/C/R/T/D — E — A/D — F/V/S/M/D — L/R — A/P/I/K — I/D/T or 2 — Labels S/N/E/M — K — A/U — R/U/N

IBM International Business Machine Corporation

RPG INPUT SPECIFICATIONS

GX21-9094-2 U/M 050*
Printed in U.S.A.

Program		Punching Instruction	Graphic	Card Electro Number
Programmer	Date		Punch	

Page (1 2) ___ of ___ Program Identification (75 76 77 78 79 80)

Line (3–5)	Form Type (6)	Filename (7–13)	Sequence (14–16) OR / AND	Number (1–N) (17)	Option (O) (18)	Record Identifying Indicator or** (19–20)	Record Identification Codes 1: Position (21–24)	Not (N) (25)	C/Z/D (26)	Character (27)	2: Position (28–31)	Not (N) (32)	C/Z/D (33)	Character (34)	3: Position (35–38)	Not (N) (39)	C/Z/D (40)	Character (41)	Stacker Select (42)	P/B/L/R (43)	Field Location From (44–47)	To (48–51)	Decimal Positions (52)	Field Name (53–58)	Control Level (L1–L9) (59–60)	Matching Fields or Changing Fields (61–62)	Field Record Relation (63–64)	Field Indicators Plus (65–66)	Minus (67–68)	Zero or Blank (69–70)	(71–74)
01	I																														
02	I																														
03	I																														
04	I																														
05	I																														
06	I																														
07	I																														
08	I																														
09	I																														
10	I																														
11	I																														
12	I																														
13	I																														
14	I																														
15	I																														
16	I																														
17	I																														
18	I																														
19	I																														
20	I																														
	I																														
	I																														
	I																														
	I																														
	I																														

GX21-9093-2 UM/050* Printed in U.S.A.
*No. of forms per pad may vary slightly

IBM International Business Machine Corporation

RPG CALCULATION SPECIFICATIONS

Program		
Programmer		Date

Punching Instruction — Graphic — Punch

Card Electro Number

Page □ of ___
1 2

C Calculation

Line	Form Type	Control Level (L0-L9, LR, SR, AN/OR)	Indicators							Factor 1	Operation	Factor 2	Result Field				Resulting Indicators			Comments
			And	10N	And	10N	And	10N				Name	Length	Decimal Positions	Half Adjust (H)	Arithmetic Plus Minus Zero / Compare 1>2 1<2 1=2 / Lookup (Factor 2) is High Low Equal			
3 4 5	6	7 8	9	10 11	12	13 14	15	16 17	18 19 20 21 22 23 24 25 26	27	28 29 30 31 32 33	34 35 36 37 38 39 40 41 42	43 44 45 46 47 48	49 50 51	52	53	54 55	56 57	58 59	60 61 ... 74
0 1	C																		
0 2	C																		
0 3	C																		
0 4	C																		
0 5	C																		
0 6	C																		
0 7	C																		
0 8	C																		
0 9	C																		
1 0	C																		
1 1	C																		
1 2	C																		
1 3	C																		
1 4	C																		
1 5	C																		
1 6	C																		
1 7	C																		
1 8	C																		
1 9	C																		
2 0	C																		

75 76 77 78 79 80 Program Identification

RPG   OUTPUT   SPECIFICATIONS

Program		Punching Instruction	Graphic		Card Electro Number	
Programmer			Punch			

Page [1] [2] of __

GX21-9090-2 U/M 050*
Printed in U.S.A.

75 76 77 78 79 80

Program Identification

Form Type

Line

Filename

Type (H/D/T/E)

Stacker #/Fetch(F)

Space — Before / After

Skip — Before / After

Output Indicators — And / And

Field Name *Auto

Edit Codes

B/A/C/1-9/R

End Position in Output Record

P/B/L/R

Constant or Edit Word

Commas	Zero Balances to Print	No Sign	CR	-
Yes	Yes	1	A	J
Yes	No	2	B	K
No	Yes	3	C	L
No	No	4	D	M

X = Remove Plus Sign
Y = Date Field Edit
Z = Zero Suppress

356

IBM International Business Machine Corporation

GX21-9090-2 U/M 050*
Printed in U.S.A.

Program _____

Programmer _____   Date _____

Punching   Graphic _____
Instruction   Punch _____

Card Electro Number _____

Page [1][2] of ___

Program Identification [75 76 77 78 79 80]

Commas	Zero Balances to Print	No Sign	CR	-	
Yes	Yes	1	A	J	X = Remove Plus Sign
Yes	No	2	B	K	Y = Date Field Edit
No	Yes	3	C	L	Z = Zero Suppress
No	No	4	D	M	

Constant or Edit Word

Date_____   Name _____

DIRECTION: *Answer the following questions in the spaces provided. Your answers should indicate the depth of understanding that you have toward the concepts and definitions presented. If there is insufficient space provided for your answer, complete your answer on the reverse side of the Study Guide.*

1. Explain the meaning of Indicative information on a Master Record.

2. Explain the relationship between a Master Record and a Detail Record.

3. Explain what techniques a programmer must use to conserve disk space.

4. Explain the use and significance of comment statements within a program.

5. Explain how the programmer codes the Output Specifications sheet to provide the proper spacing between the output print lines as required by the user.

Date _____   Name_____

TRUE–FALSE: *Each of the following statements is either true or false. Indicate your choice in the Answers column by encircling "T" for a true answer or "F" for a false answer.*

Answers

1. A master record is a record that contains all the information accumulated against a given entity   T   F

2. Indicative information does not usually change   T   F

3. Information that does not change is known as variable information   T   F

4. A master record and a detail record are one and the same   T   F

5. The programmer need not be concerned about the size of any given field   T   F

6. Disk storage is usually at a premium in most installations   T   F

7. Disk devices do not have sufficient space for temporary files   T   F

8. Disks can have work files as well as output files encoded on them   T   F

9. Checking computer totals to control tape totals is necessary because some computers can add incorrectly   T   F

10. Master records only hold indicative information   T   F

11. Any data that is encoded on a disk must come from card files   T   F

12. An updated field must be coded on the Input Specifications sheet as well as the Output Specifications sheet   T   F

13. The CHAIN operation can occur only at detail time   T   F

14. A different master record is read into memory each time that the CHAIN operation code is used in a program   T   F

15. When updating records, it is not necessary to test to see if master records exist in the file   T   F

16. Hash totals are mandatory in all programs   T   F

17. The data of an adding machine tape is taken from the keypunched data to prove its accuracy   T   F

18. The space before and space after concepts cannot be used on the same print line   T   F

19. There is the capability of having selected data of a control group printed while at the same time having all the detail data of the control group printed   T   F

20. Any accumulated data of a control group is written to disk at total time as soon as the first record of the next control group is read   T   F

COMPLETION: *Fill in the blank with the appropriate word or words.*

1. Data that has a tendency to change with a certain regularity is known as _____ _____ data.

2, 3. A field that is going to be updated must be coded on the _____ Specifications as well as on the _____ Specifications.

4. If the CHAIN operation will take place on the first record within the Control Group, the CHAIN must take place during _____ _____ Calculations.

5. A total not having any significance other than a checking for accuracy device is known as a _____ _____ .

TABLES AND ARRAYS

SPECIFICATIONS

Tables and arrays are groups or lists of related items or elements. The telephone directory is an excellent example of a table or array. It is actually two tables. One is a list of names in alphabetical order for easier reference, and the other is a list of telephone numbers. Looking up someone's name in the name list will tell you his telephone number. An example of a single table is an employee badge number list used by guards at a factory gate to check the employees as they enter their place of work.

In RPG II programming, the elements in a table or array must all have the same field length and number of decimal positions and must all be either alphameric or numeric. The program reserves certain areas of computer storage for tables and arrays. These reserved areas are loaded with data before or during program execution and are used during program calculations and output. The choice between a table or an array depends on how the elements of the table or array will be referenced in the program.

LOADING TABLES AND ARRAYS

Loading tables and arrays may be performed at: Compile Time, Pre-execution Time, or Execution Time of the RPG Cycle.

Compile Time

Loading of tables and arrays is performed with the compilation of the Source Program. The table or array is part of the source deck. A change to the table or array means that the program must be recompiled. The Compile Time method is used when the data in the table or array will not change with each program execution.

Pre-execution Time

Loading of tables and arrays is performed with the loading of the Object Program and just before the execution of the input, calculations, and output portions of the program. If the data in the table or array will change with each execution of the program, the Pre-execution Time method is used.

363

Execution Time

Loading of tables and arrays is performed during execution of the program. The table or array data may come from an input file or may be the result of program calculations. Execution Time tables and arrays are very dynamic within the program execution, and the data may change with every input record.

If every element of a table or array is not full of data, it is known as a short table or array. Figure 107 is an example of a short table.

Figure 107 shows a six-element alphameric and numeric table with only five elements loaded. For elements not loaded, numeric elements should be zeros and alphameric elements should be blank.

Element	Table 1		Table 2
1	J A N U A R Y þ þ	⎫	þþ123
2	F E B R U A R Y þ	⎪ Data	þ5678
3	M A R C H þ þ þ þ	⎬ Loaded	9þ12þ
4	A P R I L þ þ þ þ	⎪ into	51232
5	M A Y þ þ þ þ þ þ	⎭ Table	þþþ2þ
6	þ þ þ þ þ þ þ þ þ	No Data Loaded	þþþþþ

Alphameric — Numeric

Figure 107

Tables and arrays may be loaded from cards, disk, tape, or system console devices. For the purpose of this project, you will use only cards and the discussion will be limited to card input. Below is a list of rules for formatting the table or array input card for the Compile Time or Pre-execution Time method of loading tables and arrays. Figure 108 is an example of the card layout for a single table. An example of the card layout for an alternating table is shown in Fig. 109.

1. The first element must start in position 1 of the card.

2. The card may contain one or several table and array elements, but an element may not span cards. That is, one element must be contained (complete within itself) within a single card.

3. Each card, except the last card, must contain the same number of elements.

4. Tables and arrays may be loaded in alternating format. Alternating format. Alternating format is described as two related tables (like the telephone directory) being

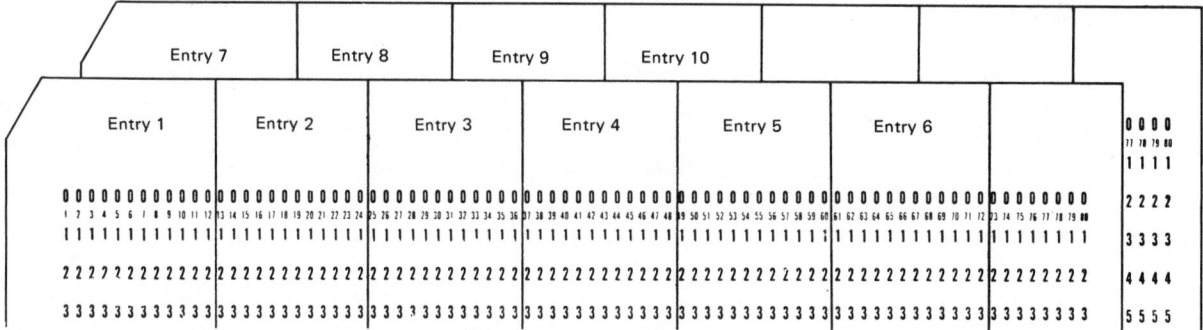

Figure 108 Example of card layout for loading a ten-element table having 12 positions in each entry.

part of one table or array with two elements per entry. The card would have the elements fielded as Name 1, Telephone Number 1, Name 2, Telephone Number 2, Name 3, Telephone Number 3, etc. The entry may not be split between two cards — that is, Name 3 and Telephone Number 3 must be on the same card.

EXTENSION SPECIFICATIONS

This Specifications sheet has the same common fields as described previously for the others. However, those fields necessary for the compilation of this project must now be described. See Fig. 110.

Statement 030 illustrates those fields that may be used by the programmer if the Loading of Tables and Arrays is to be performed at Compile Time.

Statement 050 illustrates those fields that may be used by the programmer if the Loading of Tables and Arrays is to be performed at Pre-execution Time.

Statement 070 illustrates those fields that may be used by the programmer if the Loading of Tables and Arrays is to be performed at Execution Time.

From Filename (Columns 11 through 18)

1. This is the name of the file described on the File Description Specifications sheet from which the Pre-execution Time table or array will be read to load the table or array.

2. When there is an entry in this field, the table or array is a Pre-execution Time table or array.

3. More than one table or array may be loaded from the same file.

4. The sequence of the Extension Specifications determines the order in which the table or array input cards are loaded or stacked in the input device of the computer being used.

5. The field is left-justified.

6. No Input Specifications are required.

To Filename (Columns 19 through 26)

1. This is the name of the file described on the File Description Specifications sheet that may be used to output the table or array at LR time.

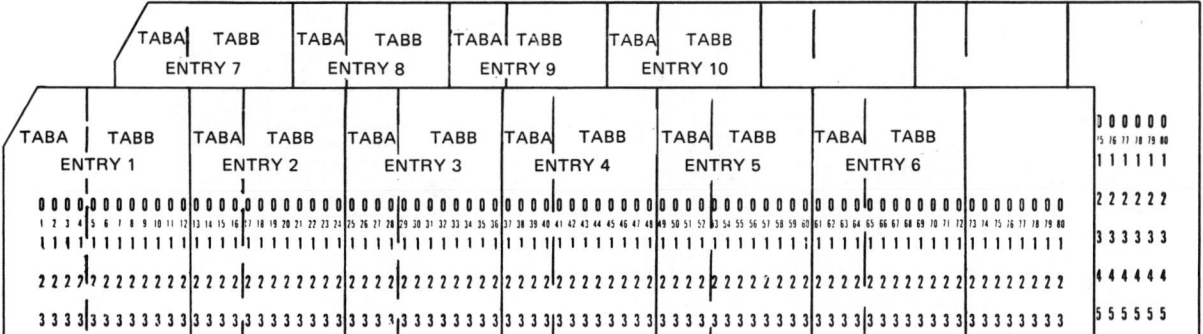

Figure 109   Example of card layout for loading a ten-element alternating table. TABA has four positions and TABB has eight positions in each entry.

File Description Specification

Form Type	Filename	File Type	File Designation	End of File	Sequence	File Format	Block Length	Record Length	Mode of Processing	Device		Extension Code E/L
0 2	TABLEIN	I	T			F	80	80		READER		
0 3	TABLEOUT	O	T			F	80	80		PUNCH		

Extension Specifications

Form Type	Line	From Filename	To Filename	Table or Array Name	Number of Entries Per Record	Number of Entries Per Table or Array	Length of Entry	Comments
E	0 1	TABLEIN	TABLEOUT	TABA	6	10	12	VALID FIELDS FOR
E	0 2							COMPILE TIME
E	0 3							
E	0 4							PRE-EXECUTION
E	0 5							TIME
E	0 6							EXECUTION TIME
E	0 7							
E	0 8							

Figure 110 TABLEIN is the Filename of the Input File where the Pre-execution Time Table TABA will load from. TABLEOUT is the Filename of the Output File where the Table TABA will go at LR Time in the program.

366

2. Only Compile Time or Pre-execution Time tables or arrays may be written at LR time.

3. The field is left-justified.

4. No Output Specifications are required.

Table or Array Name (Columns 27 through 32)

1. The field describes the name of the table or array. The name defined here is used in the Calculations and Output Specifications to reference the table or array.

2. Table names must begin with the characters TAB. The last three positions may be any valid characters.

3. Array names may be any valid name other than TAB.

4. The sequence of the Extension Specifications for tables and arrays is the order in which the table and array will be loaded.

5. Tables must be defined first.

6. The field is left-justified.

Number of Entries per Record
(Columns 33 through 35)

This is the number of entries on each input record used to load the table or array. The last input record may contain less than the required entries. For alternating tables or arrays, this is the number of each alternating set of entries. The field is right-justified.

Number of Entries per Table or Array
(Columns 36 through 39)

This field describes the number of elements of the table or array named in columns 27 through 32. The number also applies to the alternating table or array described in columns 46 through 51. This field is right-justified.

Length of Entry (Columns 40 through 42)

This field describes the length of each element of the table or array named in column 27 through 32. The maximum length for a numeric table or array is 15 characters. The maximum length for an alphameric table or array is 256 characters. All elements must be the same length. If the input entries are not the same length as described here, the input element must be padded with zeros or blanks if it is a numeric table or array and with blanks if it is an alphameric table or array. Notice, in Fig. 107, how the padding is accomplished.

Packed or Binary (Columns 43 through 43)

This field will not be considered here.

Decimal Positions (Columns 44 through 44)

This field (column) will be blank for alphameric tables or arrays. The number of decimal positions (0–9) for numeric tables or arrays must be coded in this column. This field describes the decimal positions for the table or array defined in columns 27 through 32.

Sequence (A/D) (Columns 45 through 45)

If the table or array is to be searched, looking for a high or low entry, an A for ascending sequence or a D for descending sequence must be entered here. Also, if an A or D is coded, the sequence of the Pre-execution Time table or array will be checked while the table or array is loading. If the table or array is loaded short, then consideration should be given to padding the beginning of the table or array with zeros or blanks, otherwise the end of the table or array must be padded with nines. See Fig. 107 for this type of padding.

Table or Array Name (Alternating Format)
(Columns 46 through 57)

These columns are used to describe the alternating table or array. This means that the table is loaded with alternating elements on the Input Record. The elements alternate with the elements from the table or array described in columns 27 through 45. The rules for coding columns 46 through 57 are the same as those described for coding columns 27 through 45. Figure 109 shows an alternating example.

Comments (Columns 58 through 74)

This field may be used for any comments that the programmer wishes to code. These comments have NO effect on the execution of the program.

FILE DESCRIPTION

Filename (Columns 7 through 14)

This is the same name that would appear on the Extension Specifications sheet under the following conditions.

      1. For Pre-execution Time table or array, it is the name of the Input table or array file. This file name is also coded in columns 11 through 18 of the Extension Specifications. No Input Specifications are required.

      2. If it is desired to output a Pre-execution Time or Compile Time table or array at LR Time, the Output File Name is coded in this field. This filename also is in columns 19 through 26 of the Extension Specifications sheet. No Output Specifications are required.

The rules for coding the Filename Field are the same as those previously described on page 49.

File Type (Columns 15 through 15)

Either an I for an Input File or an O for an Output File is valid for table or array files.

File Description (Columns 16 through 16)

For table or array files, a T is coded in this field.

Extension Codes (Columns 39 through 39)

For table or array files, code an E in this field.

Four other File Description fields to consider for table and array files are File Format, always coded with an F, Record Length, Device, and Symbolic Device. See Fig. 110 for the tie-in of the two Specifications sheets.

SEARCHING TABLES AND ARRAYS

LOKUP Operation (Columns 28 through 32)

The search of a table or array is accomplished with the LOKUP operation on the Calculation Specifications sheet. For tables, Factor 1 is the search argument. It is a field, table, array name, or constant that contains the data for the search. Factor 2 is the table name that is to be searched. A high, equal, or low indicator must be coded as a Resulting Indicator. The search will start at the beginning of the table and find the first element in the table that satisfies the high, equal, or low condition. If the search argument is equal to the table element, the equal Resulting Indicator is coded, which indicates that the search be stopped on the equal condition. Similarly, the high or low indicators coded will cause the search to stop on the first element that is higher than or lower than the search argument. The Resulting Indicator can then be used to condition other calculations or output. If the Resulting Indicator(s) does not come on, then the search was not successful. Observe this type of coding in Fig. 111.

If a second table name is coded in the Result Field, the special storage area will contain the contents of the corresponding element of that table. To reference that special storage area, the table name may be used in calculations that follow the LOKUP or coded as an element on the Output Specifications. See Fig. 112 for this type of coding.

Array elements can be referenced by an index. The total length of the array name, plus comma, plus index must not be greater than six characters in length except when used as Factor 1 or Factor 2 on the Calculation Specifications sheet.

Figure 111

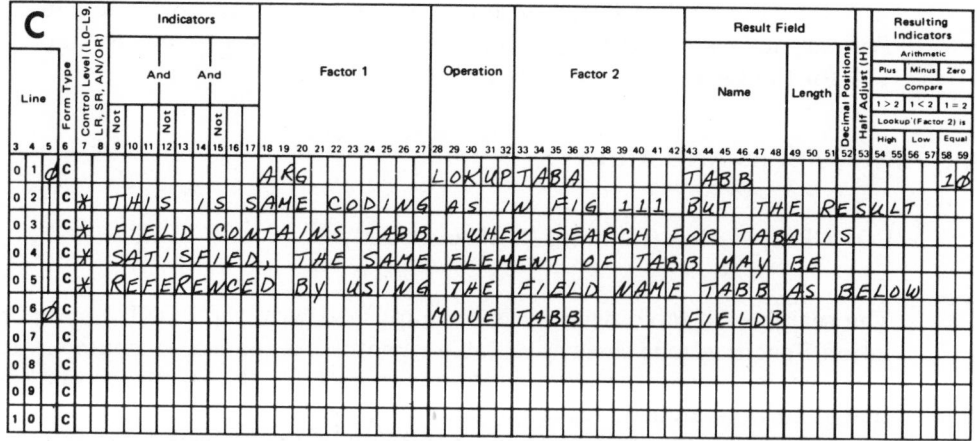

Figure 112   LOKUP with special storage area

On a LOKUP operation with an array, using an array name without an index is the same as a table; however, the element is not available in a special storage area. The Result Field may not be used. An index may be used with an array on a LOKUP operation; in this case, the LOKUP will start the search at the element indicated by the index number. If the index is a field name, then the index will contain the element number on a successful completion of the search. If the search is not successful, then the index field will be reset to 1.

An element of a table or array never changes as a result of a LOKUP operation.

USING TABLES

A special storage area, which contains the element contents of a table, is created as a result of a successful LOKUP operation. The special storage area is referenced by using the table name in Factor 1, Factor 2, or the Result Field of the Calculation Specifications or the field name on the Output Specifications. In this way, the contents of a table may be used in calculations or output. See Fig. 113, lines 010 and 020 for the coding.

Here, statement 010 will search TABA for 512. At the successful completion of the search, indicator 10 will be ON. If the fifth element of TABA contains 512, then statement 020 will multiply TABA (special storage area contains 512) by 2 and place the result in the fifth-element of TABB. The special storage area for TABB is changed, as well as the contents of TABB. If TABB were coded as a field name on the Output Specifications, then 1024 would be the output.

370

Line	Form Type	Control Level	And (Not)	And (Not)	Factor 1	Operation	Factor 2	Result Field Name	Length	Dec	HA	Resulting Indicators
01	C				512	LOKUP	TABA	TABB				10
02	C	10			TABA	MULT	2	TABB				
03	C				ARY	MULT	2	ARY				
04	C				ARY	ADD	ARX	ARZ				
05	C				ARY,2	SUB	10	TOTAL				
06	C				START	TAG						
07	C				IX	ADD	1	IX				
08	C				CNT	ADD	2	CNT				
09	C					ZADD	CNT	ARY,IX				
10	C				IX	COMP	10					99
11	C		N99			GOTO	START					
12	C				END	TAG						
13	C					XFOOT	ARY	TOTAL				
14	C											
15	C											
16	C											
17	C											
18	C											

Figure 113

USING ARRAYS

Arrays may be referenced on Calculations or Output Specifications in two ways: (a) the entire array may be referenced and (b) an element may be referenced by using an index. In Fig. 113, line 030 each and every element in ARY array is multiplied by 2.

The coding in Fig. 113, line 040 shows that each corresponding element of ARY array is added to each corresponding element of ARX array and that the result is placed in the corresponding element of ARZ array. In this example, the arrays should have the same number of elements. If they do not, the operation will stop when the element number of the shortest array is reached.

The coding illustrated in Fig. 113, line 050 is such that the second element of array ARY has 2 subtracted from it and the result is placed in the field named TOTAL.

In Fig. 113, lines 060 to 110 the coding is an example of a routine that will loop until CNT = 10. The results in ARY, when the loop is complete, will be 2, 4, 6, 8, 10, 12, 14, 16, 18, 20. Each entry represents each of the ten elements in array ARY.

The coding shown in Fig. 113, line 130 is a special operation for arrays. XFOOT will add together each element of the ARY array and place the results in the Result Field TOTAL.

TIP TO PROGRAMMER

If an index of an array is either zero or greater than the number of elements of the array, the program will terminate abnormally or stop with an error message. The computer operator will usually have to stop the program, and the programmer will have to debug the program. It is up to the programmer to ensure that the array index will be valid under all operating conditions.

Table elements may be output to a file by specifying the table name on the Output Specifications sheet in the field name (columns 32 through 37). The output data will be the table element that was the result of the last LOKUP operation. The element is written as part of the output record and may be edited just like any other output field.

Array elements can be written to an output file by specifying the array name and index number on the Output Specifications sheet. Normal field editing also applies. Arrays may also be written out in their entirety but only if the entire array will fit into the output record length. The array may not span records. If the array does not fit the output record length, then each array element must be referenced individually.

When writing arrays to disk or tape files, no editing is required. The whole array will be placed in the file just as it appears in memory — one element after another. It will be available as input to another program as an Execution Time array when its positions are referenced on the Input Specifications Sheet as part of the input record. If the array was written to a tape, disk, or card file, with no other fields but the array, then the file could be referenced as a Pre-execution Time array file. If the array was written to a card file, the cards could be inserted into the source deck of a program as input to a Compile Time array.

When printing arrays, the array must all fit on one print line. The length of the entire array plus editing symbols must be equal to or less than the printer line length. All normal editing symbols may be used when printing the whole array. Each element of the array will be edited the same. If an edit code in column 38 of the Output Specifications is used, two blank spaces will be put at the beginning of each element automatically. The ending position specified in columns 40 through 43 is the ending position of the last element of the printed array, including edit symbols.

The edit word in columns 45 through 70 of the Output Specifications may be used if an edit code does not give the desired results. You must specify your own blank spaces between elements by using the edit symbol &. In each of the following three examples, the input data is the same data. Note the following examples and how they appear as output.

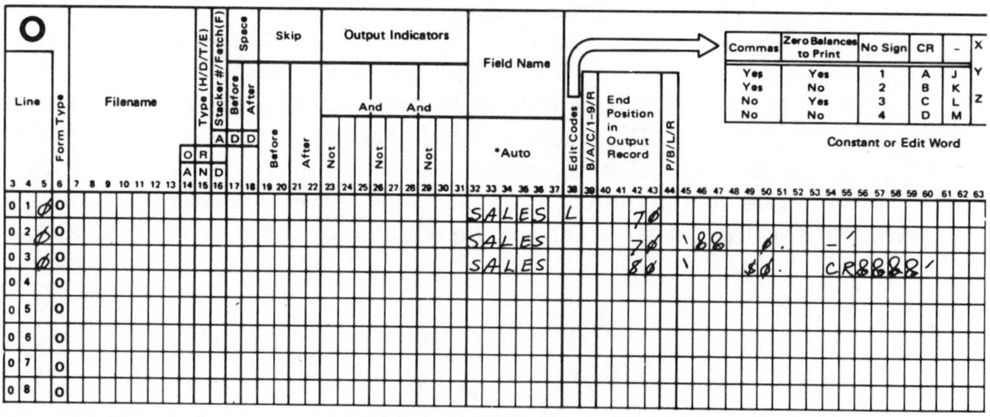

Figure 114

Contents of an array in memory called SALES

00765 12479 98700 00056 20101

The output of Example 1 (Fig. 114, line 010) is as follows:

ββββ7.65ββββ124.79–ββ987.00ββββββ.56βββ201.01β

    ↑ space for minus sign   ↑ ending position 70

The output of the example shown in Fig. 114, line 020 is identical to that of Example 1. It shows the actual edit word for the results of using Edit Code L. The output of Example 3 (Fig. 113, line 030) is as follows:

ββ$7.65ββββββ$124.79CRββββ$987.00βββββββββ$.56βββββ$201.01ββββββ

      └ Space for CR Symbol   Ending position 80 ──┘

INPUTTING TABLES AND ARRAYS DURING EXECUTION OF A PROGRAM

As indicated earlier, tables and arrays may be in a file as part of a record. Table data may be in the input file but must be handled as a normal field. Array data, however, may be handled as an array in its entirety or may be referenced by each element as a field or array name, plus index. By specifying the array name on the Input Specifications, giving its starting and ending positions for the complete array, the array defined on the Extension Specifications will be loaded with new data with each read of the input record.

Each element of the array can be specified with an index number, and the array element will replace the contents of the array defined on the Extension Specifications with each read of the input record. If the array positions are defined on the Input Specifications as a field name other than the array name, then the array defined on the Extension Specifications will not be affected and the field can be handled as a normal input field.

SUBROUTINES

Writing programs with many logical steps can be confusing and tedious. If the programmer were able to write program routines by individual functions, test and debug them, and then integrate them into the total program, program writing would be much easier. This is the purpose of writing programs with subroutines. Any subroutine can be used in any other program simply by inserting the subroutine code into the new program.

The Calculation Specifications Operations for Subroutines are:

EXSR   Execute subroutine

BEGSR   Begin subroutine

ENDSR   End subroutine

Note how the preceding codes are coded on the Calculation Specifications sheet of Fig. 115.

Statement 010 of Fig. 115 states that if Indicator 01 is ON, execute SUBR1. The program will branch to statement 100, which is the beginning of subroutine SUBR1, execute the statement through ENDSR, and branch back to statement 020.

Statement 040 will branch to SUBR2. If Indicator 02 is ON, execute the subroutine and return to the next statement — 050.

Statement 070 is executed at Total Time in the RPG cycle when L1 is ON during an input control break. Subroutine SUBR3 will execute if Indicators 01 and 02 are ON.

Subroutines must be inserted into the RPG Source Program after Total Calculations. All subroutines must begin with BEGSR and end with ENDSR. Branching by using a GOTO, from subroutine to subroutine or out of the subroutine to Detail or Total Calculations, is not permitted. Executing other subroutines from within a subroutine is permitted, however.

Line	Form Type	Control Level (L0-L9, LR, SR, AN/OR)	Not		Not	And		Not	And			Factor 1	Operation	Factor 2
0 1	C			Ø1									EXSR	SUBR1
0 2	C												•	
0 3	C													
0 4	C			Ø2									EXSR	SUBR2
0 5	C												•	
0 6	C												•	
0 7	C	L1		Ø1		Ø2							EXSR	SUBR3
0 8	C	L1											•	
0 9	C	L1												
1 0	C	SR										SUBR1	BEGSR	
1 1	C	SR											•	
1 2	C	SR											•	
1 3	C	SR											ENDSR	
1 4	C	SR										SUBR2	BEGSR	
1 5	C	SR											•	
1 6	C	SR											•	
1 7	C	SR											ENDSR	
1 8	C	SR										SUBR3	BEGSR	
1 9	C	SR											•	
2 Ø	C	SR											ENDSR	
	C													
	C													

Figure 115

STOP
1. COMPLETE STUDY GUIDE ON PAGE 389
2. SUBMIT STUDY GUIDE TO INSTRUCTOR
3. DEVELOP PROJECT EIGHTEEN
4. SUBMIT PROJECT EIGHTEEN TO
   INSTRUCTOR
5. GO TO EXERCISE 26, PAGE 391
6. COMPLETE EXERCISE 26
7. SUBMIT EXERCISE TO INSTRUCTOR
8. GO TO PROJECT NINETEEN, PAGE 399

PROJECT EIGHTEEN

Using tables, arrays, and subroutines, program a perpetual calendar. The only input is the year; the output is a calendar like the one shown in page 376. There is no rigid solution to this project. As many solutions exist as there are programmers. By using the following rules, create a calendar.

1. The input must be an Execution Time array.

2. All printed output must be from an array or table.

3. All three types of tables or arrays must be used—that is, Compile Time array, Pre-execution Time array, and Execution Time array.

4. Any year from the year 1899 must be able to be produced. Allowance for leap years must be included.

5. The program must be reentrant—that is, any number of years may be printed with one program load or execution.

Depending on your program design, a number of routines will be necessary—determining if the year is a leap year, determining the day of the week that the year begins, and so on. These routines should be subroutines and executed with the EXSR operation code.

TIP TO PROGRAMMER

Such a program must be in written in steps. Subroutines give the programmer the means to do so. Write the first subroutine and all the supporting code to produce an executable program. Compile it; debug it; test it. Proceed to do the same for the next subroutine. The idea is to build the complete program in this fashion. By building the program in this way, you will find it easier and less complicated. This approach will enable you to isolate any new bugs to new code.

It will be necessary to design and write several algorithms in this project. The important point to remember is that you cannot test too much at one time.

One hint: the days-of-the-month print line is an array with 58 elements, two positions each.

1 9 8 1

JANUARY

SUN	MON	TUE	WED	THU	FRI	SAT
				1	2	3
4	5	6	7	8	9	10
11	12	13	14	15	16	17
18	19	20	21	22	23	24
25	26	27	28	29	30	31

FEBRUARY

SUN	MON	TUE	WED	THU	FRI	SAT
1	2	3	4	5	6	7
8	9	10	11	12	13	14
15	16	17	18	19	20	21
22	23	24	25	26	27	28

MARCH

SUN	MON	TUE	WED	THU	FRI	SAT
1	2	3	4	5	6	7
8	9	10	11	12	13	14
15	16	17	18	19	20	21
22	23	24	25	26	27	28
29	30	31				

APRIL

SUN	MON	TUE	WED	THU	FRI	SAT
			1	2	3	4
5	6	7	8	9	10	11
12	13	14	15	16	17	18
19	20	21	22	23	24	25
26	27	28	29	30		

MAY

SUN	MON	TUE	WED	THU	FRI	SAT
					1	2
3	4	5	6	7	8	9
10	11	12	13	14	15	16
17	18	19	20	21	22	23
24	25	26	27	28	29	30
31						

JUNE

SUN	MON	TUE	WED	THU	FRI	SAT
	1	2	3	4	5	6
7	8	9	10	11	12	13
14	15	16	17	18	19	20
21	22	23	24	25	26	27
28	29	30				

JULY

SUN	MON	TUE	WED	THU	FRI	SAT
			1	2	3	4
5	6	7	8	9	10	11
12	13	14	15	16	17	18
19	20	21	22	23	24	25
26	27	28	29	30	31	

AUGUST

SUN	MON	TUE	WED	THU	FRI	SAT
						1
2	3	4	5	6	7	8
9	10	11	12	13	14	15
16	17	18	19	20	21	22
23	24	25	26	27	28	29
30	31					

SEPTEMBER

SUN	MON	TUE	WED	THU	FRI	SAT
		1	2	3	4	5
6	7	8	9	10	11	12
13	14	15	16	17	18	19
20	21	22	23	24	25	26
27	28	29	30			

OCTOBER

SUN	MON	TUE	WED	THU	FRI	SAT
				1	2	3
4	5	6	7	8	9	10
11	12	13	14	15	16	17
18	19	20	21	22	23	24
25	26	27	28	29	30	31

NOVEMBER

SUN	MON	TUE	WED	THU	FRI	SAT
1	2	3	4	5	6	7
8	9	10	11	12	13	14
15	16	17	18	19	20	21
22	23	24	25	26	27	28
29	30					

DECEMBER

SUN	MON	TUE	WED	THU	FRI	SAT
		1	2	3	4	5
6	7	8	9	10	11	12
13	14	15	16	17	18	19
20	21	22	23	24	25	26
27	28	29	30	31		

RPG CONTROL CARD AND FILE DESCRIPTION SPECIFICATIONS

IBM International Business Machine Corporation

GX21-9092-3 UM/050*
Printed in U.S.A.

*No. of forms per pad may very slightly

Program

Programmer

Date

Punching Instruction

Graphic

Punch

Card Electro Number

Page [1] [2] of ____

Control Card Specifications

Line / Form Type

Field	Columns
Form Type	6
Core Size to Compile	7 8 9
Object Output	10
Listing Options	11
Core Size to Execute	12 13 14
Debug	15
MFCM Stacking Sequence	16 17
Inverted Print	21
360/20 2501 Buffer	22
Number Of Print Positions	23 24 25
Alternate Collating Sequence	26 27
Address to Start (Model 20)	28 29 30
Work Tapes	31
Overlay Open	32
Overlap Printer	33
Binary Search	34
Tape Error	35
2152 Checking	36
Inquiry	37
Read/Write/Compute (Model 20)	38
Keyboard Output (Model 20)	39
Sign Handling	40
1P Forms Position	41
Indicator Setting	42
File Translation	43
Punch MFCU Zeros	44
Nonprint Characters	45
Table Load Halt	47
Shared I/O	48
Field Print	49
Formatted Core Dump	50
RPG to RPG II Conversion	51

Refer to the specific System Reference Library manual for actual entries.

Program Identification — 75 76 77 78 79 80

File Description Specification

Line / Form Type

Field	Columns
Form Type	6
Filename	7 8 9 10 11 12 13 14
File Type — I/O/U/C/D	15
File Designation — P/S/C/R/T/D	16
End of File — E	17
Sequence — A/D	18
File Format — F/V/S/M/D	19
Block Length	20 21 22 23
Record Length	24 25 26 27
Mode of Processing — L/R	28
Length of Key Field or of Record Address Field	29 30 31
Record Address Type — A/P/I/K	32
Type of File Organization or Additional Area — I/D/T or 2	33
Overflow Indicator	34 35
Key Field Starting Location	36 37 38
Extension Code E/L	39
Device	40 41 42 43 44 45 46
Symbolic Device	47 48 49 50 51 52
Labels S/N/E/M	53
K	53
Name of Label Exit	54 55 56 57 58 59
Continuation Lines	
Option	54 55 56 57 58 59
Entry	60 61 62 63 64 65
Extent Exit for DAM	60 61 62 63 64 65
Core Index	64 65
A/U	66
File Addition/Unordered	66
Number of Tracks for Cylinder Overflow	67 68
Number of Extents	69 70
Tape Rewind	70
R/U/N	70
File Condition U1-U8	71 72
73 74	

377

RPG EXTENSION AND LINE COUNTER SPECIFICATIONS

GX21-9091-2 UM/050*
Printed in U.S.A.

Programmer

Date

Punching Instruction

Graphic

Punch

Card Electro Number

Page [ ] [ ] of [ ]

1 2

Program Identification

75 76 77 78 79 80

Extension Specifications

Line	Form Type	Record Sequence of the Chaining File	Number of the Chaining Field	From Filename	To Filename	Table or Array Name	Number of Entries Per Record	Number of Entries Per Table or Array	Length of Entry	P/B/L/R	Decimal Positions	Sequence (A/D)	Table or Array Name (Alternating Format)	Length of Entry	P/B/L/R	Decimal Positions	Sequence (A/D)	Comments
3 4 5	6	7 8	9 10	11 12 13 14 15 16 17 18	19 20 21 22 23 24 25 26	27 28 29 30 31 32	33 34 35	36 37 38 39	40 41 42	43	44	45	46 47 48 49 50 51	52 53 54	55	56	57	58 59 60 61 62 63 64 65 66 67 68 69 70 71 72 73 74
0 1	E																	
0 2	E																	
0 3	E																	
0 4	E																	
0 5	E																	
0 6	E																	
0 7	E																	
0 8	E																	

RPG INPUT SPECIFICATIONS

Line	Form Type	Filename	Sequence	Number (1-N)	Option (O)	Record Identifying Indicator or **	Record Identification Codes 1 Position	C/Z/D	Not (N)	Character	2 Position	C/Z/D	Not (N)	Character	3 Position	C/Z/D	Not (N)	Character	Stacker Select	P/B/L/R	Field Location From	To	Decimal Positions	Field Name	Control Level (L1-L9)	Matching Fields or Changing Fields	Field Record Relation	Field Indicators Plus	Minus	Zero or Blank
3 4 5	6	7 8 9 10 11 12 13	14 15 16	17	18	19 20	21 22 23 24	25	26	27	28 29 30 31	32	33	34	35 36 37 38	39	40	41 42	43	44 45 46 47	48 49 50 51	52	53 54 55 56 57 58	59 60	61 62	63 64	65 66	67 68	69 70
0 1	I																												
0 2	I																												

IBM

International Business Machine Corporation

RPG CALCULATION SPECIFICATIONS

GX21-9093-2 UM/050* Printed in U.S.A.
*No. of forms per pad may vary slightly

Program

Programmer

Date

Punching Instruction — Graphic / Punch

Card Electro Number

Page _1_ _2_ of ___

Program Identification: 75 76 77 78 79 80

Line	Form Type	Control Level (L0-L9, LR, SR, AN/OR)	Indicators (Not / And / Not / And / Not)	Factor 1	Operation	Factor 2	Result Field Name	Length	Decimal Positions	Half Adjust (H)	Resulting Indicators (Arithmetic: Plus / Minus / Zero; Compare: 1>2 / 1<2 / 1=2; Lookup (Factor 2) is: High / Low / Equal)	Comments

Column positions: 3 4 5 6 | 7 8 | 9 10 11 12 13 14 15 16 17 | 18 19 20 21 22 23 24 25 26 27 | 28 29 30 31 32 | 33 34 35 36 37 38 39 40 41 42 | 43 44 45 46 47 48 49 50 51 52 | 53 | 54 55 56 57 58 59 | 60 61 62 63 64 65 66 67 68 69 70 71 72 73 74

C

Lines: 0 1, 0 2, 0 3, 0 4, 0 5, 0 6, 0 7, 0 8, 0 9, 1 0, 1 1, 1 2, 1 3, 1 4, 1 5, 1 6, 1 7, 1 8, 1 9, 2 0

379

IBM International Business Machine Corporation

GX21-9093-2 UM/050* Printed in U.S.A.
*No. of forms per pad may vary slightly

Program

Programmer

Date

Punching Instruction

Graphic

Punch

Card Electro Number

Page 1 2 of ___

75 76 77 78 79 80

Program Identification

Line	Form Type	Control Level (L0-L9, LR, SR, AN/OR)	Indicators						Factor 1	Operation	Factor 2	Result Field					Resulting Indicators			Comments
			And		And		And					Name	Length	Decimal Positions	Half Adjust (H)	Arithmetic / Compare / Lookup			

Arithmetic: Plus, Minus, Zero
Compare: 1 > 2, 1 < 2, 1 = 2
Lookup (Factor 2) is: High, Low, Equal

GX21-9093-2 UM/050* Printed in U.S.A.
*No. of forms per pad may vary slightly

RPG CALCULATION SPECIFICATIONS

IBM International Business Machine Corporation

Program		Punching Instruction	Graphic			Card Electro Number		Page	1 2	of
Programmer	Date		Punch							

C	Line	Form Type	Control Level (L0-L9, LR, SR, AN/OR)	Indicators							Factor 1	Operation	Factor 2	Result Field					Resulting Indicators				Comments

Program Identification: 75 76 77 78 79 80

RPG CALCULATION SPECIFICATIONS

IBM International Business Machine Corporation

Program	
Programmer	Date

Punching Instruction	Graphic		Card Electro Number
	Punch		

Page [1] [2] of ___

Program Identification [75 76 77 78 79 80]

GX21-9093-2 UM/050 • Printed in U.S.A.
*No. of forms per pad may vary slightly

Line	Form Type	Control Level (L0-L9, LR, SR, AN/OR)	Indicators									Factor 1	Operation	Factor 2	Result Field				Resulting Indicators			Comments
			Not	And	Not	And	Not							Name	Length	Decimal Positions	Half Adjust (H)	Arithmetic / Compare / Lookup			

Column numbers: 3 4 5 6 7 8 | 9 10 | 11 12 | 13 14 | 15 16 17 | 18 19 20 21 22 23 24 25 26 | 27 28 29 30 31 32 | 33 34 35 36 37 38 39 40 41 42 | 43 44 45 46 47 48 | 49 50 51 | 52 | 53 | 54 55 | 56 57 | 58 59 | 60 61 62 63 64 65 66 67 68 69 70 71 72 73 74

Resulting Indicators sub-headers:
- Arithmetic: Plus, Minus, Zero
- Compare: 1 > 2 (High), 1 < 2 (Low), 1 = 2 (Equal)
- Lookup (Factor 2) is: High, Low, Equal

Line
0 1
0 2
0 3
0 4
0 5
0 6
0 7
0 8
0 9
1 0
1 1
1 2
1 3
1 4
1 5
1 6
1 7
1 8
1 9
2 0

Form Type column: C

382

GX21-9093-2 UM/050* Printed in U.S.A.
*No. of forms per pad may vary slightly

IBM

International Business Machine Corporation

RPG CALCULATION SPECIFICATIONS

Program			Punching Instruction	Graphic		Card Electro Number		Page	1 2	of
Programmer		Date		Punch						

Program Identification: 75 76 77 78 79 80

C	Line	Form Type	Control Level (L0-L9, LR, SR, AN/OR)	Indicators						Factor 1	Operation	Factor 2	Result Field				Resulting Indicators	Comments
				And		And							Name	Length	Decimal Positions	Half Adjust (H)	Arithmetic / Compare / Lookup (Factor 2) is	
					Not		Not		Not								Plus Minus Zero / 1>2 1<2 1=2 / High Low Equal	

Columns: 3 4 5 6 7 8 9 10 11 12 13 14 15 16 17 18 19 20 21 22 23 24 25 26 27 28 29 30 31 32 33 34 35 36 37 38 39 40 41 42 43 44 45 46 47 48 49 50 51 52 53 54 55 56 57 58 59 60 61 62 63 64 65 66 67 68 69 70 71 72 73 74

Line numbers: 01 02 03 04 05 06 07 08 09 10 11 12 13 14 15 16 17 18 19 20

Right column numbers: 1 2 3 4 5 6 7 8 9 10 11 12 13 14 15 16 17 18 19 20 21 22 23 24 25 26 27 28 29 30 31 32 33 34 35 36 37 38 39 40 41 42 43 44 45 46 47 48 49 50 51 52 53 54 55 56 57 58 59 60 61 62 63 64 65 66 67 68 69 70 71 72

383

GX21-9093-2 UM/050* Printed in U.S.A.
*No. of forms per pad may vary slightly

IBM International Business Machine Corporation

RPG CALCULATION SPECIFICATIONS

Program

Programmer

Date

Punching Instruction

Graphic

Punch

Card Electro Number

Program Identification 75 76 77 78 79 80

Page 1 2 of ___

C	Line	Form Type	Control Level (L0-L9, LR, SR, AN/OR)	Indicators							Factor 1	Operation	Factor 2	Result Field				Resulting Indicators	Comments

Result Field: Name, Length, Decimal Positions, Half Adjust (H)

Resulting Indicators: Arithmetic — Plus, Minus, Zero; Compare — 1 > 2, 1 < 2, 1 = 2; Lookup (Factor 2) is — High, Low, Equal

384

GX21-9093-2 UM/050* Printed in U.S.A.
*No. of forms per pad may vary slightly

IBM International Business Machine Corporation

RPG CALCULATION SPECIFICATIONS

Program				Punching Instruction	Graphic			Card Electro Number		Page	1 2	of
Programmer		Date			Punch							

C	Line	Form Type	Control Level (L0-L9, LR, SR, AN/OR)	Indicators										Factor 1	Operation	Factor 2	Result Field								
				Not	And	Not	And	Not									Name	Length	Decimal Positions	Half Adjust (H)	Resulting Indicators				
																					Arithmetic		Compare		Lookup (Factor 2) is
																					Plus	Minus	Zero		
																							1>2	1<2	1=2
																							High	Low	Equal
Line 3 4	5 6	7 8	9	10 11	12 13	14 15	16 17	18 19 20 21 22 23 24 25 26 27	28 29 30 31 32	33 34 35 36 37 38 39 40 41 42	43 44 45 46 47 48	49 50 51	52	53	54 55	56 57	58 59	60	Comments 61 62 63 64 65 66 67 68 69 70 71 72 73 74

0 1	C
0 2	C
0 3	C
0 4	C
0 5	C
0 6	C
0 7	C
0 8	C
0 9	C
1 0	C
1 1	C
1 2	C
1 3	C
1 4	C
1 5	C
1 6	C
1 7	C
1 8	C
1 9	C
2 0	C

75 76 77 78 79 80
Program Identification

385

1 2 3 4 5 6 7 8 9 10 11 12 13 14 15 16 17 18 19 20 21 22 23 24 25 26 27 28 29 30 31 32 33 34 35 36 37 38 39 40 41 42 43 44 45 46 47 48 49 50 51 52 53 54 55 56 57 58 59 60 61 62 63 64 65 66 67 68 69 70 71 72

RPG   OUTPUT   SPECIFICATIONS

GX21-9090-2 U/M 050*
Printed in U.S.A.

Program						Card Electro Number	
Programmer		Date		Graphic			
				Punch			

Punching Instruction

Page [1] [2] of ___

Program Identification

75 76 77 78 79 80

Output Indicators

Field Name   *Auto

Filename

Form Type

Line

Type (H/D/T/E)
Stacker #/Fetch(F)
Space — Before / After
Skip — Before / After
And — Not / And — Not / And — Not

End Position in Output Record

Edit Codes   B/A/C/1-9/R   P/B/L/R

Constant or Edit Word

Commas	Zero Balances to Print	No Sign	CR	−
Yes	Yes	1	A	J
Yes	No	2	B	K
No	Yes	3	C	L
No	No	4	D	M

X = Remove Plus Sign
Y = Date Field Edit
Z = Zero Suppress

386

RPG OUTPUT SPECIFICATIONS

IBM International Business Machine Corporation

GX21-9090-2 U/M 050*
Printed in U.S.A.

Program
Programmer
Date

Punching Instruction
Graphic
Punch

Card Electro Number

Page 1 2 of ___

Program Identification
75 76 77 78 79 80

Commas	Zero Balances to Print	No Sign	CR	-
Yes	Yes	1	A	J
Yes	No	2	B	K
No	Yes	3	C	L
No	No	4	D	M

X = Remove Plus Sign
Y = Date Field Edit
Z = Zero Suppress

Constant or Edit Word

Field Name
*Auto

Edit Codes
B/A/C/1-9/R

End Position in Output Record
P/B/L/R

Output Indicators
And Not And Not And Not

Skip
After Before

Space
After Before

Stacker #/Fetch(F)
Type (H/D/T/E)

Filename

Form Type

Line

IBM   International Business Machine Corporation

GX21-9090-2 U/M 050*
Printed in U.S.A.
75 76 77 78 79 80

Program
Programmer   Date

Punching
Instruction   Graphic   Punch

Card Electro Number

Program
Identification

Page 1 2 of ___

Commas	Zero Balances to Print	No Sign	CR	-
Yes	Yes	1	A	J
Yes	No	2	B	K
No	Yes	3	C	L
No	No	4	D	M

X = Remove Plus Sign
Y = Date Field Edit
Z = Zero Suppress

Constant or Edit Word

Field Name
*Auto

Edit Codes   B/A/C/1-9/R
End Position in Output Record
P/B/L/R

Output Indicators   And   And
Not   Not   Not

Skip   Before   After
Space   Before   After
Stacker #/Fetch(F)
Type (H/D/T/E)

Filename

Form Type
Line

O

388

Date_____   Name_____

DIRECTIONS: *Answer the following questions in the spaces provided. Your answers should indicate the depth of understanding that you have toward the concepts and definitions presented. If there is insufficient space provided for your answer, complete your answer on the reverse side of the Study Guide.*

1. Explain the three methods used to load tables and arrays.

2. List the rules for formatting the table or array input card for the Compile Time or Pre-execution Time method of loading tables and arrays.

3. Explain how the "From Filename" and "To Filename" fields indicate the method of loading tables and arrays to be used.

4. Explain the length in a table or array as it pertains to padding.

5. Explain Alternating Format.

6. Explain the tie-in between the File Specifications and the Extension Specifications as far as tables and arrays are concerned.

7. Explain the LOKUP Operation Code and how it is used.

8. Explain the special storage area that contains the element contents of a table.

9. Explain the different ways to reference arrays on Calculations or Output Specifications sheets.

10. Explain how and why programmers use the special operation code XFOOT.

11. Explain how table elements and array elements are written to various output devices.

12. Explain the necessity of using editing symbols with output data and how the programmer must take them into account on the print line.

13. Explain how tables and arrays are inputted during the execution of a program.

14. Explain how a subroutine is used and the three subroutine operation codes.

Date _____   Name _____

TRUE–FALSE: *Each of the following statements is either true or false. Indicate your choice in the Answers column by encircling "T" for a true answer or "F" for a false answer.*

Answers

1. The telephone directory is an excellent example of a table or array	T	F
2. An example of a single table is an employee badge number list	T	F
3. Certain areas of computer storage are reserved for tables and arrays by the RPG II Program	T	F
4. There is no choice of using either a table or an array by a programmer in solving the problem of the user	T	F
5. The table or array is a part of the Source Program if it is loaded during Compile Time	T	F
6. If the data in the table or array will not change with each execution of the program, the Pre-execution Time method is used	T	F
7. Table or array data may come from an input file or may be the result of a calculation	T	F
8. If Execution Time is used to load the table or array, it is done during the execution of the program	T	F
9. Every element of a table or array must be of the same length	T	F
10. A short table or array is when every element of the table or array is not full of data	T	F
11. An element of a table or array input file can span or be split between two cards	T	F
12. The last card of a table or array input file must contain the same number of elements as every other card	T	F
13. More than one table or array may be loaded from the same input file	T	F
14. Table names must begin with the characters TAB	T	F
15. Array names may be any valid name, including TAB	T	F
16. If tables are an integral part of the source program, they must be defined first on the Extension Specifications	T	F
17. There is no need to have the same number of entries on each input record used to load the table or array	T	F
18. The number of elements of the table or array are assigned automatically during program execution	T	F
19. The maximum length of an element of a numeric table is 15 characters	T	F
20. If the table or array is going to be searched, then there must be a sequence check	T	F

21. The search of a table or array is accomplished with the LOKUP operation   T   F

22. Resulting Indicators as a result of a LOKUP operation cannot be used to condition other calculations or output   T   F

23. Array elements can be referenced by an index   T   F

24. XFOOT is an operation code used with arrays   T   F

25. If an index of an array is either zero or greater than the number of elements of the array, the program will terminate abnormally or stop with an error message   T   F

26. Table elements may be output to a file by specifying the table name on the Output Specifications sheet   T   F

27. Array elements can be written to an output file by specifying the array name and index number on the Output Specifications sheet   T   F

28. Output of an array cannot span records if each array element is indexed separately   T   F

29. When printing arrays, the entire array, plus any editing symbols, must fit on one print line of the printer being used   T   F

30. If table data is a part of the input file during program execution, it must be handled as a normal field   T   F

31. Subroutines are only applicable to the program for which they were originally written   T   F

32. Subroutines must be inserted into the RPG II Source Program after Total Calculations   T   F

33. Branching from one subroutine to another or out of the subroutine to detail or total calculations is not permitted in RPG II   T   F

COMPLETION: *Fill in the blank with the appropriate word or words.*

1, 2. Groups or lists of related items are known as _____ or _____ _____ .

3, 5. The loading of tables and arrays may be performed at _____ _____ , _____ _____ , and _____ _____ .

6, 9. Tables and arrays may be loaded from _____ , _____ , _____ , or _____ _____ devices.

10. Two related tables (like the telephone directory) are an example of _____ _____ tables.

11. If there is an entry on the "From Filename" field of the Extension Specifications sheet, the table or array is a/an _____ _____ table or array.

12, 13. If there is an entry in the "To Filename" field of the Extension and Line Counter Specifications sheets, the table or array is a/an _____ _____ or _____ _____ table or array.

14. If there is an entry in the "Table or Array Name" field of the Extension and Line Counter Specifications sheet, the table or array is a/an _____ _____ table or array.

15, 16. If the number of input entries of a table or array is not the same as the length, the table or array is padded with _____ if it is a numeric table or array; it is padded with _____ if it is an alphameric table or array.

17, 18. The coding in Factor 1 of the LOKUP operation is the _____ _____ , whereas the coding in Factor 2 is the _____ _____ .

19, 20. Arrays may be referenced _____ or they may be referenced _____ .

21, 22. If an editing code will not give the desired result on the printout, then the programmer uses the _____ to specify the blank spaces between elements. This coding must be in the _____ _____ _____ _____ field.

23, 25. The three subroutine operation codes are _____ , _____ , and _____ .

MATCHING RECORDS

SPECIFICATIONS:
MATCHING RECORDS

Matching Records is a method of controlling the reading sequence of records from a primary and one or more secondary input files in an RPG II Program.

Earlier it was learned that input files were processed in order — the primary file first and then the secondary files in the sequence that the files were coded on the File Description Specifications Sheets. All records were processed to the end of the file before the next file was processed.

There are two major requirements in using Matching Records.

1. Each file must have one or more fields that match. These, then, are called matching fields.

2. The files must have the matching fields in sequential order — ascending or descending.

NEW CONCEPTS

Sequence (A/D) — File Description Specifications

Match Record Field Indicators (M1–M9)

Matching Fields — Input Specifications

Matching Record Indicator (MR)

SEQUENCE A/D (COLUMN 18 THROUGH 18)

This column on the File Description Specifications sheet is left blank unless the Matching Records method is used. Matching Records requires the checking of the input files Matching Fields sequence. If sequence checking is necessary, the programmer codes an A for ascending order or D for descending order.

MATCH RECORD FIELD INDICATORS
(M1-M9) (COLUMNS 61 THROUGH 62)

In its simplest form, Matching Record Field Indicators can be used to check the sequence of a single input file. Coding an A for ascending or a D for descending sequence in column 18 of the File Description Specification sheet and the coding of a Matching Field Indicator (M1–M9) in columns 61 and 62 of the Input Specifications sheet next to the field that is to be checked for sequence will stop the computer. The computer operator must then check the input files to the program and make corrections to their sequence. Figure 116 illustrates the type of coding necessary for sequence checking of matching records.

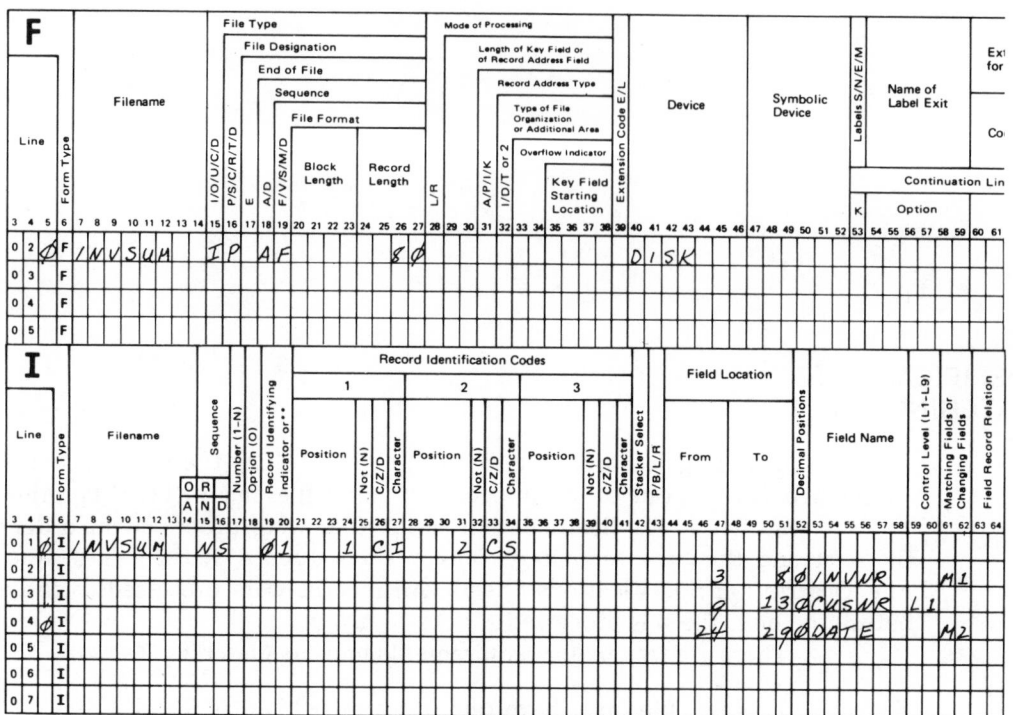

Figure 116

MATCHING FIELDS (COLUMNS 61 THROUGH 62)

Matching Field Indicators (M1–M9) have a hierarchy of M1 up to M9. M9 is most important. In Fig. 116 the Invoice Summary records are sorted by invoice number (INVNR) within date (DATE) sequence. DATE is most important in sequence and is assigned the highest Matching Field Indicator.

It is recommended that a change be made in Project Nine to include the coding as shown in Fig. 116 and rerun the program with the Invoice Summary cards in proper sequence. After the program has been run, change the order of one or two cards and see what happens when the program is rerun. The program will stop as soon as the record that is not in sequence is detected.

MATCHING RECORD INDICATOR (MR)

The primary purpose of the Matching Field Indicators is to control the Matching Record Indicator (MR). One to nine fields of a primary file may be matched with an equal number of fields of one or more secondary files.

An application example of matching records would be in matching a cash receipt with an invoice. The invoice file has the customer number and invoice number fields. The cash receipt file would also have a customer number and invoice number. A match of customer number and invoice number indicates that the cash receipt record goes with the invoice record.

The Matching Record Indicator will turn ON whenever there is a match between the primary and one or more secondary files with matching fields. MR is used in calculations and output to control the processing of the program. MR cannot be a Resulting Indicator as part of calculations. MR will remain ON as long as there is a primary and one or more secondary files that have matching fields. As soon as there is a record from one of the Matching Record files that has no match with another file, the MR Indicator will turn OFF and remain OFF until there is another match. Figure 118 is a flow chart that shows how matching records are controlled. All files that have no matching fields are processed first. Then a record is read from each Matching Record file, and processing continues as in the chart.

By using the MR Indicator and the Record Identifying Indicators, a programmer can control what processing will be accomplished with each input record. The following four conditions can occur.

1. Primary record read — matches secondary (MR ON)

2. Secondary record read — matches primary (MR ON)

3. Primary record read — no match (MR OFF)

4. Secondary record read — no match (MR OFF)

Fig. 117 shows the coding necessary to control the MR Indicator with a primary and one secondary file and one matching field in each file.

The four indicator possibilities of Fig. 117 are

1. If a primary record is read and Field A matches Field B, then 01 and MR are ON.

2. If a secondary record is read and Field A matches Field B, then 02 and MR are ON.

3. If a primary record is read and Field A does not match Field B, then only 01 is ON.

4. If a secondary record is read and Field A does not match Field B, then only 02 is ON.

Figure 117

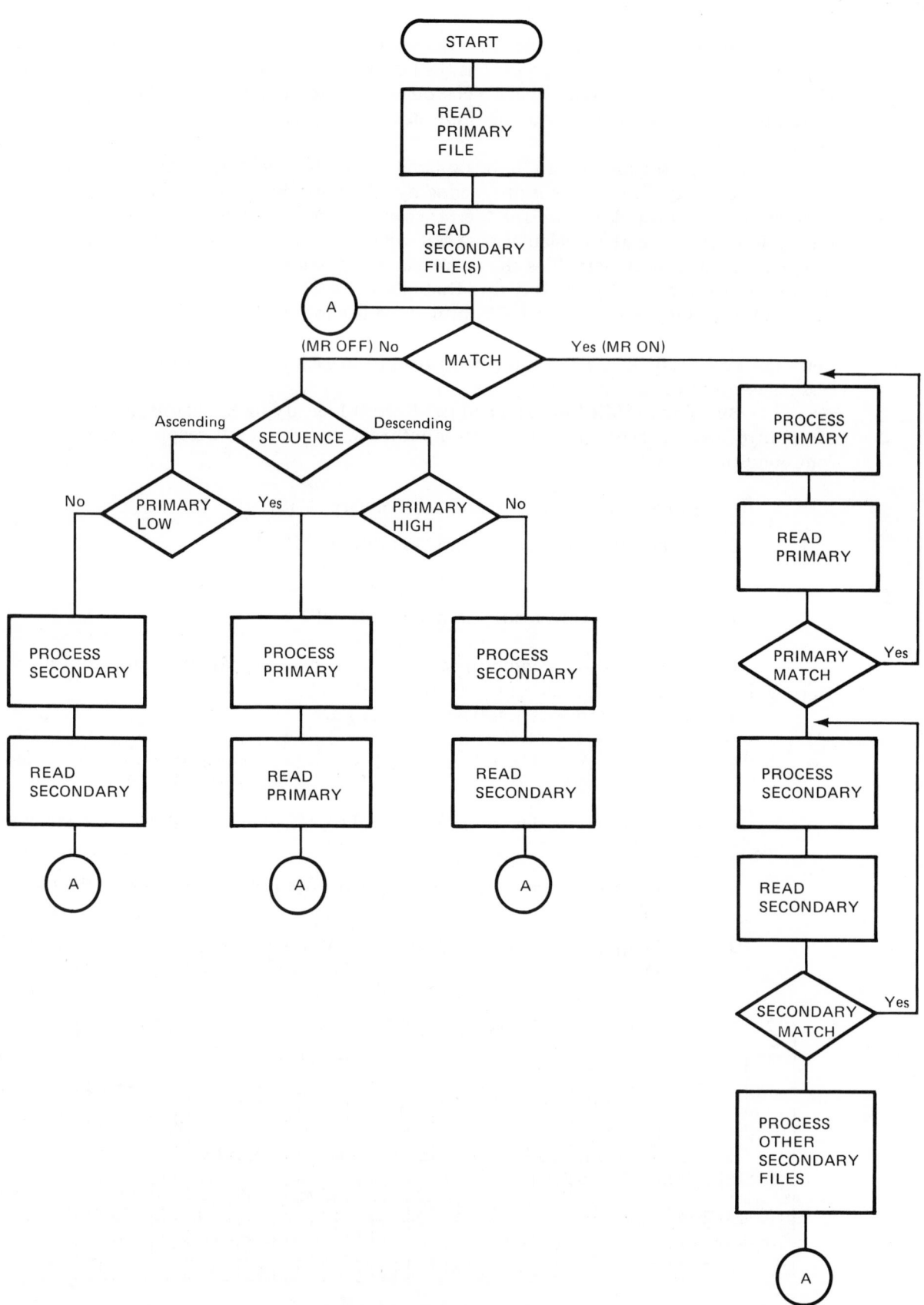

Figure 118   Matching record flowchart

PROJECT NINETEEN

In this project no major programming is required. You will get the chance to use matching records in an application program in Project Twenty.

1. Punch the primary and secondary cards on page 400.

2. Write a matching record program that will give the following lines of output.

PRIMARY RECORD MATCH	Contents of Input Card
PRIMARY RECORD NO MATCH	Contents of Input Card
SECONDARY RECORD MATCH	Contents of Input Card
SECONDARY RECORD NO MATCH	Contents of Input Card

3. Write four matching record programs that will

Program 1 Print both primary and secondary matching records. Add the contents of columns 5-6 from both primary and secondary matching records to a single total field.

Program 2 Print both primary and secondary NO matching records and add the contents of columns 5-6 from both primary and secondary NO matching records to a single total field.

Program 3 Print primary matching records only and print the total of columns 5-6 on primary NO matches.

Program 4 Print secondary NO matching records and print the total of columns 5-6 of the secondary NO matching records.

4. The output should appear like that on pages 400 and 401.

5. The primary purpose of these programs is to show you how to control input processing with matching records. Study your results carefully and you will understand how matching records works.

6. Extra practice with matching records can be gained if you introduce a third input file like the one provided on page 400.

Primary Card		Secondary Card		Third File	
Col. 1	Col. 5–6	Col. 1	Col. 5–6	Col. 1	Col. 5–6
A	01	A	12	A	30
B	02	C	13	D	31
C	03	D	14	F	32
E	04	E	15	H	33
G	05	F	16	I	34
H	06	F	17	J	35
J	07	G	18	J	36
M	08	H	19	J	37
N	09	H	20	K	38
O	10	I	21	O	39
P	11	J	22	P	40
		K	23	R	41
		L	24		
		M	25		
		N	26		
		P	27		
		P	28		
		Q	29		

Input data for Project 19

STEP 3 PROGRAM 1

Primary	Secondary
A 01	
	A 12
C 03	
	C 13
E 04	
	E 15
G 05	
	G 18
H 06	
	H 19
	H 20
J 07	
	J 22
M 08	
	M 25
N 09	
	N 26
P 11	
	P 27
	P 28
	Total 279

400

STEP 3 PROGRAM 2

Primary	Secondary	
B 02		
	D 14	
	F 16	
	F 17	
	I 21	
	K 23	
	L 24	
O 10		
	Q 29	
		Total 156

STEP 3 PROGRAM 3

Primary	Secondary	
A 01		
C 03		
E 04		
G 05		
H 06		
J 07		
M 08		
N 09		
P 11		
		Total 12

STEP 3 PROGRAM 4

Primary	Secondary	
	D 14	
	F 16	
	F 17	
	I 21	
	K 23	
	L 24	
	Q 29	
		Total 144

```
STOP
1.  COMPLETE STUDY GUIDE ON PAGE 407
2.  SUBMIT STUDY GUIDE TO INSTRUCTOR
3.  DEVELOP PROJECT NINETEEN
4.  SUBMIT PROJECT NINETEEN TO
        INSTRUCTOR
5.  GO TO EXERCISE 27, PAGE 409
6.  COMPLETE EXERCISE 27
7.  SUBMIT EXERCISE TO INSTRUCTOR
8.  GO TO PROJECT TWENTY, PAGE 411
```

RPG CONTROL CARD AND FILE DESCRIPTION SPECIFICATIONS

IBM International Business Machine Corporation

GX21-9092-3 UM/050*
Printed in U.S.A.

* No. of forms per pad may very slightly

| Program | | Punching | | Graphic | | | Card Electro Number | | |
| Programmer | | Date | Instruction | Punch | | | | | |

Page ☐ 1 ☐ 2 of ____

Program Identification: 75 76 77 78 79 80

Control Card Specifications

Refer to the specific System Reference Library manual for actual entries.

H

Line (3 4 5 6 — 0 1)

Form Type (6) = H

Columns/fields:
- Core Size to Compile (7 8 9)
- Object Output (10)
- Listing Options (11)
- Core Size to Execute (12 13 14)
- Debug (15)
- MFCM Stacking Sequence (16 17)
- Inverted Print (20 21)
- 360/20 2501 Buffer (22 23)
- Number Of Print Positions (24 25)
- Alternate Collating Sequence (26 27)
- Address to Start (28 29 30)
- Work Tapes (31)
- Overlay Open (32)
- Overlap Printer (33)
- Binary Search (34)
- Tape Error (35)
- 2152 Checking (36)
- Inquiry (37)
- Read/Write/Compute (38)
- Keyboard Output (39)
- Model 20 / Model 20
- Sign Handling (40)
- 1P Forms Position (41)
- Indicator Setting (42)
- File Translation (43)
- Punch MFCU Zeros (44)
- Nonprint Characters (45)
- Table Load Halt (47)
- Shared I/O (48)
- Field Print (49)
- Formatted Core Dump (50)
- RPG to RPG II Conversion (51)

File Description Specification

F

Line (3 4 5 6 — 0 2, 0 3, 0 4, 0 5, 0 6, 0 7, 0 8, 0 9, 1 0)

Form Type (6) = F

- Filename (7–14)
- File Type (15) I/O/U/C/D
- File Designation (16) P/S/C/R/T/D
- End of File (17) E
- Sequence (18) A/D
- File Format (19) F/V/S/M/D
- Block Length (20–23)
- Record Length (24–27)
- Mode of Processing (28) L/R
- Length of Key Field or of Record Address Field (29–30)
- Record Address Type (31) A/P/I/K
- Type of File Organization or Additional Area (32) I/D/T or 2
- Overflow Indicator (33–34)
- Key Field Starting Location (35–38)
- Extension Code E/L (39)
- Device (40–46)
- Symbolic Device (47–52)
- Labels S/N/E/M (53) K
- Name of Label Exit (54–59)
- Continuation Lines
- Option (55–57)
- Entry (58–64)
- Extent Exit for DAM (60–65)
- Core Index (64)
- A/U (66)
- File Addition/Unordered (66)
- Number of Tracks for Cylinder Overflow (67–68)
- Number of Extents (69)
- Tape Rewind (70) R/U/N
- File Condition U1-U8 (71–72)
- (73 74)

RPG INPUT SPECIFICATIONS

IBM International Business Machine Corporation

GX21-9094-2 U/M 050*
Printed in U.S.A.

Program

Programmer

Date

Punching Instruction

Graphic

Punch

Card Electro Number

Page 1 2 of ___

Program Identification 75 76 77 78 79 80

Line	Form Type	Filename	Sequence		Number (1-N)	Option (O)	Record Identifying Indicator or **	Record Identification Codes																								Field Location			Decimal Positions	Field Name	Control Level (L1-L9)	Matching Fields or Changing Fields	Field Record Relation	Field Indicators		
			OR	AND				1 Position		Not (N)	C/Z/D	Character	2 Position		Not (N)	C/Z/D	Character	3 Position		Not (N)	C/Z/D	Character	Stacker Select	P/B/L/R	From	To						Plus	Minus	Zero or Blank

I

GX21-9093-2 UM/050* Printed in U.S.A.
*No. of forms per pad may vary slightly

IBM International Business Machine Corporation

RPG CALCULATION SPECIFICATIONS

Program

Programmer

Date

Punching Instruction

Graphic

Punch

Card Electro Number

Page [ ] [ ] of ___

Program Identification

1 2

C

Line	Form Type	Control Level (L0-L9), LR, SR, AN/OR	Indicators									Factor 1	Operation	Factor 2	Result Field						Resulting Indicators						Comments
			Not	And	Not	And	Not								Name	Length	Decimal Positions	Half Adjust (H)	Arithmetic			Compare			Lookup (Factor 2) is	
																			Plus	Minus	Zero	1>2	1<2	1=2	High	Low	Equal

Indicators — And — And

Plus / Minus / Zero
Compare
1 > 2 / 1 < 2 / 1 = 2
Lookup (Factor 2) is
High / Low / Equal

405

IBM International Business Machine Corporation

Program				Card Electro Number
Programmer		Date		

Punching Instruction | Graphic | | Punch |

GX21-9090-2 U/M 050*
Printed in U.S.A.

75 76 77 78 79 80

Program Identification

Page ___ of ___

Constant or Edit Word

Commas	Zero Balances to Print	No Sign	CR	-
Yes	Yes	1	A	J
Yes	No	2	B	K
No	Yes	3	C	L
No	No	4	D	M

X = Remove Plus Sign
Y = Date Field Edit
Z = Zero Suppress

Edit Codes

B/A/C/1-9/R

End Position in Output Record

P/B/L/R

Field Name

*Auto

Output Indicators
And — Not
And — Not
Not

Skip — Before / After
Space — Before / After
Stacker #/Fetch (F)
Type (H/D/T/E)

O / R / A / N / D

Filename

Form Type

Line

O

1 2 3 4 5 6 7 8 9 10 11 12 13 14 15 16 17 18 19 20 21 22 23 24 25 26 27 28 29 30 31 32 33 34 35 36 37 38 39 40 41 42 43 44 45 46 47 48 49 50 51 52 53 54 55 56 57 58 59 60 61 62 63 64 65 66 67 68 69 70 71 72 73 74

01 02 03 04 05 06 07 08 09 10 11 12 13 14 15 16 17 18 19 20

STUDY GUIDE

Date _____   Name _____

DIRECTIONS: *Answer the following questions in the spaces provided. Your answer should indicate the depth of understanding that you have toward the concepts and definitions presented. If insufficient space is provided, complete your answer on the reverse side of the Study Guide.*

1. Explain why matching records are used.

2. List the two major requirements for using matching records.

3. Explain sequence A/D, column 18 of File Specifications.

4. Explain matching fields and how they are associated on the File and Input Specifications.

5. Explain the Matching Record (MR) Indicator and how it works.

EXERCISE 27

COMPLETION: *Fill in the blank with the appropriate word or words.*

1. If matching records are not being used in the program, the _____ field on the File Specifications is not used and therefore is blank.

2. The coding of an A in column 18 of the File Specifications indicates that the sequence is in _____ order.

3. The coding of a D in column 18 of the File Specifications indicates that the sequence is in _____ order.

4, 5. Matching Field Indicators have a hierarchy of _____ up to _____ .

6. The primary purpose of Matching Field Indicators is to control the _____ _____ _____ .

7, 8. The matching Record Indicator will turn ON whenever there is a match between the _____ and one or more _____ files with matching field.

9, 12. List the four conditions that can occur when using the MR Indicator to process an input record: _____ , _____ , _____ , and _____ .

13. The columns below represent the contents of a matching field of three input files. Place the number of order (1, 2, 3, etc.) that the records will be processed by a matching record program in the space provided next to each record.

Primary	Secondary 1	Secondary 2
1 ___	1 ___	1 ___
1 ___	1 ___	1 ___
2 ___	2 ___	1 ___
2 ___	2 ___	3 ___
3 ___	3 ___	3 ___
3 ___	4 ___	3 ___
4 ___	5 ___	5 ___
6 ___	7 ___	5 ___
7 ___	7 ___	8 ___
7 ___		9 ___

PROJECT TWENTY

This project will provide the opportunity of using most of the skills that have been learned so far with PRG II, Applied Fundamentals. Although the programs in this project are meant to tie in with the other programs that have been completed in this book, as a programmer you will be given the freedom to use your own designs and techniques. The three major sections of this project are:

1. Load and Maintenance of a Product Master File

2. Product Inventory Control

3. Customer Billing (Invoicing)

For each program, you are to design the input and output file layouts, print chart, and program logic specifications. Then code, debug, and test the program with your own test data. Successful compilation of this project depends on your demonstrating to your instructor the proper execution of each program with file listings or printed reports.

Section One (Load and Maintenance of a
Product Master File)

The Product Master File should include the following fields and be an indexed file.

Record Identification Code	Unit Cost
Product Code (item number) Key to file	Unit Price
Product Description	Quantity on Hand (in stock)
Unit of Measure (i.e., EA, FT, LB, etc.)	Quantity Sold (shipped)
Product Group Code	Quantity on Order (on order with your vendor)

411

The following programs are required for this section.

1. Load program to create Product Master File with Product Code, Description, Product Group, and Unit of Measure.

2. Maintenance program or programs to add, change, or delete a record. All fields should be able to be changed or blanked except Product Code.

3. Product file list program. Individual fields should be listed under separate field headings.

Section Two (Product Inventory Control)

There should be two programs: the first an Edit Program and the second an Update Program. The two programs should accept as input the transaction types listed below.

1. Purchase Order. A transaction to show the quantity of a product that you have placed on order with your vendor. This transaction will increase the Quantity on Order Field in the Product Master File. The transaction should have the Product Code, Purchase Order Number (yours), and Quantity of the order.

2. Inventory Receipt. A transaction to show the quantity of the product that you received from the vendor. This transaction will decrease the Quantity on Order and increase the Quantity on Hand in the Product Master File. The transaction should have the Product Code, Purchase Order Number, and the Quantity received.

3. Inventory Adjustment Up. This transaction has the Product Code and the Quantity that you wish to add to Quantity on Hand.

4. Inventory Adjustment Down. This transaction has the Product Code and the Quantity that you wish to subtract from the Quantity on Hand.

5. Customer Product Return. A transaction to decrease the Quantity sold and to increase the Quantity on Hand if a customer should return an item to you.

The Edit Program should check for proper Product Code and check to see that the transaction quantities will not cause the quantity in the Product File to go minus. All errors should be printed, and a total should be given on the number of each transaction type.

The Update Program should list each transaction and the effect that it has on the Product Master File quantities. The listing should provide a good audit trail of the transactions.

Extra Credit: Write a program to match the inventory receipts with the purchase order cards to show the Purchase Order Number, Product Code, Quantity on Order, Quantity Received, and the Outstanding Quantity on Order for each product still on order with your vendors.

Section Three (Customer Billing (Invoicing))

Billing programs and the programs to handle Customer Orders are generally very complex in the business world. In this project you will write the three basic programs for a sound billing system.

1. The Edit Program

2. The Invoicing Program

3. The Update Program

TIP TO PROGRAMMER

Although the Invoicing Program and the Update Program could be written as one program, there are very good reasons for not doing so. Two of them are

1. The invoice program is complex without adding update functions.

2. The invoice program prints on special forms. It is important to have the option of running the invoice program again in case of difficulties in printing on special forms. As a general rule, never update files while printing on special forms.

The input transaction should contain the following fields for each product on your customer's purchase order.

Customer Number

Customer Purchase Order Number (reference)

Product Code

Quantity Shipped

Salesman Number

Special Charges in dollars

Freight Charges in dollars

Program 1. Edit Program: Each transaction should be edited for

1. Proper Customer Number and Product Code.

2. Customer Purchase Order Number, Quantity Shipped, and Salesman Number not zero.

Program 2. Invoice Program:

1. The Invoice Program should produce an invoice like the one shown in Fig. 119. Since you won't have special forms, you must print the proper headings, provide the proper line spacing, and allow for eight line items between headings and total line.

2. State tax is calculated at 5% of the product extended totals only.

3. The program should punch the Invoice Summary card like that in Project Seven and the Product Summary card like that in Project Eleven.

4. The Invoice Number should be supplied to the program by a header card, and the number should increment with each invoice. At the end of the program a new invoice header card should be automatically punched with the invoice number for the next invoice run.

5. The customer name and address should come from the Customer Master File and should be accessed by using Matching Records.

6. The product information should be retrieved from the Product File by using chaining.

Program 3. Update Program: Write a program to update the Product Master File with the Product Summary card as input. The Product Quantity on Hand field should be decreased by the quantity shipped. A report should be produced showing a summary by product of

    Product Code

    Product Line

    Quantity Shipped

    Cost Extended

    Price Extended

    New on Hand Quantity

Totals at end of report for Total Cost, Total Price, Total Profit, and Profit Percentage should be shown.

Remit to:	YOUR COMPANY NAME Your company address City-State, Zip	

Customer Name
Customer Street Address
Customer City, State, Zip

Invoice Number — _____
Customer Number — _____
Salesman Number — _____

Customer Reference Number —

Date of Invoice — _____

Product Code	Product Description	Unit of Measure	Order Quantity	Price	Extension Price

State Tax _____

Special Charges _____

Freight Charges _____

Invoice Total _____

Figure 119

RPG CONTROL CARD AND FILE DESCRIPTION SPECIFICATIONS

IBM International Business Machine Corporation

GX21-9092-3 UM/050*
Printed in U.S.A.

Program

Programmer   Date

Punching Instruction

Graphic   Punch

Card Electro Number

*No. of forms per pad may very slightly

Page [1] [2] of ___

Program Identification

Refer to the specific System Reference Library manual for actual entries.

Control Card Specifications

Form Type																																															

H Line — Control Card with columns:
Form Type, Core Size to Compile, Object Output, Listing Options, Core Size to Execute, Debug, MFCM Stacking Sequence, Inverted Print, 360/20 2501 Buffer, Number Of Print Positions, Alternate Collating Sequence, Model 20, Address to Start, Work Tapes, Overlay Open, Overlay Printer, Binary Search, Tape Error, 2152 Checking, Inquiry, Read/Write/Compute, Keyboard Output, Model 20, Sign Handling, 1P Forms Position, Indicator Setting, File Translation, Punch MFCU Zeros, Nonprint Characters, Table Load Halt, Shared I/O, Field Print, Formatted Core Dump, RPG to RPG II Conversion

File Description Specification

F Line — File Description with columns:
Form Type, Filename, File Type, I/O/U/C/D, P/S/C/R/T/D, E, A/D, File Designation, End of File, Sequence, F/V/S/M/D, File Format, Block Length, Record Length, Mode of Processing, L/R, Length of Key Field or of Record Address Field, A/P/I/K, Record Address Type, I/D/T or 2, Type of File Organization or Additional Area, Overflow Indicator, Key Field Starting Location, Extension Code E/L, Device, Symbolic Device, Labels S/N/E/M, K, Name of Label Exit, Extent Exit for DAM, Core Index, Continuation Lines, Option, Entry, File Addition/Unordered, Number of Tracks for Cylinder Overflow, Number of Extents, Tape Rewind, File Condition U1-U8, A/U, R/U/N

415

RPG CONTROL CARD AND FILE DESCRIPTION SPECIFICATIONS

IBM International Business Machine Corporation

GX21-9092-3 UM/050*
Printed in U.S.A.

*No. of forms per pad may very very slightly

Program		Punching Instruction	Graphic
Programmer	Date		Punch

Card Electro Number

75 76 77 78 79 80
Program Identification

Page ☐ of ☐   1 2

Control Card Specifications

Refer to the specific System Reference Library manual for actual entries.

H — Form Type

Labels (left side, columns top to bottom):
- Core Size to Compile (8 9)
- Object Output (10)
- Listing Options (11)
- Core Size to Execute (12 13 14)
- Debug (15)
- MFCM Stacking Sequence (16 17)
- Inverted Print (20 21)
- 360/20 2501 Buffer (22)
- Number Of Print Positions (23 24 25)
- Alternate Collating Sequence (26)
- Address to Start (27 28 29 30)
- Work Tapes (31)
- Overlay Open (32)
- Overlap Printer (33)
- Binary Search (34)
- Tape Error (35)
- 2152 Checking (36)
- Inquiry (37)
- Read/Write/Compute (38)
- Keyboard Output (39) — Model 20
- Sign Handling (40)
- 1P Forms Position (41)
- Indicator Setting (42)
- File Translation (43)
- Punch MFCU Zeros (44)
- Nonprint Characters (45)
- Table Load Halt (47)
- Shared I/O (48)
- Field Print (49)
- Formatted Core Dump (50)
- RPG to RPG II Conversion (51)
- Model 20

File Description Specification

F — Form Type

Column labels:
- Filename
- File Type
- File Designation
- End of File
- Sequence
- File Format
- Block Length
- Record Length
- Mode of Processing
- Length of Key Field or of Record Address Field
- Record Address Type
- Type of File Organization or Additional Area
- Overflow Indicator
- Key Field Starting Location
- Extension Code E/L
- Device
- Symbolic Device
- Name of Label Exit
- Extent Exit for DAM
- Core Index
- Continuation Lines
- Option
- Entry
- File Addition/Unordered
- Number of Tracks for Cylinder Overflow
- Number of Extents
- Tape Rewind
- File Condition U1-U8

Column markers: I/O/U/C/D (15), E (17), P/S/C/R/T/D (16), A/D (18), F/V/S/M/D (19), L/R (28), A/P/I/K (31), I/D/T or 2 (32), A/U (66), R/U/N (70)

Labels S/N/E/M (53), K (53)

Line numbers 02–10

416

RPG CONTROL CARD AND FILE DESCRIPTION SPECIFICATIONS

IBM International Business Machine Corporation

GX21-9092-3 UM/050*
Printed in U.S.A.

*No. of forms per pad may very slightly

Program		Punching Instruction	Graphic		Card Electro Number
Programmer	Date		Punch		

Page (1 2) of ___ Program Identification (75 76 77 78 79 80)

Control Card Specifications

H

Columns	Field
3–5	Line
6	Form Type
7–9	Core Size to Compile
10	Object Output
11	Listing Options
12–14	Core Size to Execute
15	Debug
16	MFCM Stacking Sequence
17–20	
21	Inverted Print
22	360/20 2501 Buffer
23–25	Number Of Print Positions
26	Alternate Collating Sequence
27–30	Model 20: Address to Start
31	Model 20: Work Tapes
32	Model 20: Overlay Open
33	Model 20: Overlap Printer
34	Model 20: Binary Search
35	Model 20: Tape Error
36	Model 20: 2152 Checking
37	Inquiry
38	Model 20: Read/Write/Compute
39	Model 20: Keyboard Output
40	Sign Handling
41	1P Forms Position
42	Indicator Setting
43	File Translation
44	Punch MFCU Zeros
45	Nonprint Characters
46	
47	Table Load Halt
48	Shared I/O
49	Field Print
50	Formatted Core Dump
51	RPG to RPG II Conversion
52–74	Refer to the specific System Reference Library manual for actual entries.

Line: 0 1 H

File Description Specification

F

Columns	Field
3–5	Line
6	Form Type
7–14	Filename
15	File Type: I/O/U/C/D
16	File Designation: P/S/C/R/T/D
17	End of File: E
18	Sequence: A/D
19	File Format: F/V/S/M/D
20–23	Block Length
24–27	Record Length
28	Mode of Processing: L/R
29–30	Length of Key Field or of Record Address Field
31	Record Address Type: A/P/I/K
32	Type of File Organization or Additional Area: I/D/T or 2
33–34	Overflow Indicator
35–38	Key Field Starting Location
39	Extension Code E/L
40–46	Device
47–52	Symbolic Device
53	Labels S/N/E/M; Continuation Lines: K
54–59	Name of Label Exit; Continuation Lines: Option
60–65	Extent Exit for DAM; Core Index; Continuation Lines: Entry
66	File Addition/Unordered: A/U
67–69	Number of Tracks for Cylinder Overflow
68–69	Number of Extents
70	Tape Rewind: R/U/N
71–72	File Condition U1–U8
73–74	

Lines: 0 2 F; 0 3 F; 0 4 F; 0 5 F; 0 6 F; 0 7 F; 0 8 F; 0 9 F; 1 0 F; F; F

RPG INPUT SPECIFICATIONS

IBM International Business Machine Corporation

GX21-9094-2 U/M 050*
Printed in U.S.A.

Program		Punching Instruction	Graphic							Card Electro Number
Programmer	Date		Punch							

Page (1 2) ___ of ___ Program Identification (75 76 77 78 79 80)

Line (3-5)	Form Type (6)	Filename (7-13)	AND / OR (14-16) Sequence (15-16)	Number (1-N) (17)	Option (O) (18)	Record Identifying Indicator or** (19-20)	Record Identification Codes 1: Position (21-24)	Not (N) (25)	C/Z/D (26)	Character (27)	2: Position (28-31)	Not (N) (32)	C/Z/D (33)	Character (34)	3: Position (35-38)	Not (N) (39)	C/Z/D (40)	Character (41)	Stacker Select (42)	P/B/L/R (43)	Field Location From (44-47)	Field Location To (48-51)	Decimal Positions (52)	Field Name (53-58)	Control Level (L1-L9) (59-60)	Matching Fields or Changing Fields (61-62)	Field Record Relation (63-64)	Field Indicators Plus (65-66)	Minus (67-68)	Zero or Blank (69-70)	(71-74)
01	I																														
02	I																														
03	I																														
04	I																														
05	I																														
06	I																														
07	I																														
08	I																														
09	I																														
10	I																														
11	I																														
12	I																														
13	I																														
14	I																														
15	I																														
16	I																														
17	I																														
18	I																														
19	I																														
20	I																														
	I																														
	I																														
	I																														
	I																														
	I																														

RPG INPUT SPECIFICATIONS

IBM International Business Machine Corporation

GX21-9094-2 U/M 050*
Printed in U.S.A.

Program		Punching Instruction	Graphic		Card Electro Number	Page [1] [2] of [ ]
Programmer	Date		Punch			Program Identification [75][76][77][78][79][80]

Line	Form Type	Filename	Sequence			Number (1-N)	Option (O)	Record Identifying Indicator or **	Record Identification Codes																				Field Location			Decimal Positions	Field Name	Control Level (L1-L9)	Matching Fields or Changing Fields	Field Record Relation	Field Indicators			
			OR / AND						**1**					**2**					**3**					P/B/L/R	Stacker Select			From	To							Plus	Minus	Zero or Blank
									Position	Not (N)	C/Z/D	Character	Position	Not (N)	C/Z/D	Character	Position	Not (N)	C/Z/D	Character																
3 4 5	6	7 8 9 10 11 12 13	14	15	16	17	18	19 20	21 22 23 24	25	26	27	28 29 30 31	32	33	34	35 36 37 38	39	40	41	42	43	44 45 46 47	48 49 50 51	52	53 54 55 56 57 58	59 60	61 62	63 64	65 66	67 68	69 70	71 72 73 74
0 1	I																																
0 2	I																																
0 3	I																																
0 4	I																																
0 5	I																																
0 6	I																																
0 7	I																																
0 8	I																																
0 9	I																																
1 0	I																																
1 1	I																																
1 2	I																																
1 3	I																																
1 4	I																																
1 5	I																																
1 6	I																																
1 7	I																																
1 8	I																																
1 9	I																																
2 0	I																																

419

RPG INPUT SPECIFICATIONS

GX21-9094-2 U/M 050*
Printed in U.S.A.

| Program | | Punching Instruction | Graphic | | Card Electro Number |
| Programmer | Date | | Punch | | |

Page [ ] [ ] of [ ]   Program Identification [75 76 77 78 79 80]

I

Line	Form Type	Filename	Sequence	Number (1-N)	Option (O)	Record Identifying Indicator or **	Record Identification Codes																				Field Location			Decimal Positions	Field Name	Control Level (L1-L9)	Matching Fields or Changing Fields	Field Record Relation	Field Indicators			
			OR AND				1					2					3				Stacker Select	P/B/L/R	From	To						Plus	Minus	Zero or Blank	
							Position	Not (N)	C/Z/D	Character	Position	Not (N)	C/Z/D	Character	Position	Not (N)	C/Z/D	Character														

(blank form grid)

RPG INPUT SPECIFICATIONS

IBM International Business Machine Corporation

GX21-9094.2 U/M 050*
Printed in U.S.A.

Program

Programmer

Date

Punching Instruction

Graphic

Punch

Card Electro Number

Page ___ of ___

Program Identification

75 76 77 78 79 80

Line	Form Type	Filename	Sequence			Number (1-N)	Option (O)	Record Identifying Indicator or **	Record Identification Codes																			Field Location			Decimal Positions	Field Name	Control Level (L1-L9)	Matching Fields or Changing Fields	Field Record Relation	Field Indicators			
			AND	OR					1 Position	Not (N)	C/Z/D	Character	2 Position	Not (N)	C/Z/D	Character	3 Position	Not (N)	C/Z/D	Character	Stacker Select	P/B/L/R	From	To						Plus	Minus	Zero or Blank	

Record Identification Codes: 1, 2, 3

Field Indicators: Plus, Minus, Zero or Blank

421

IBM International Business Machine Corporation

GX21-9094-2 U/M 050*
Printed in U.S.A.

RPG INPUT SPECIFICATIONS

Program

Programmer

Date

Punching Instruction

Graphic

Punch

Card Electro Number

Program Identification

75 76 77 78 79 80

Page | 1 | 2 | of ___

I (Form Type)

Line	Filename	Sequence	Number (1-N)	Option (O)	Record Identifying Indicator or **	Record Identification Codes			Field Location		Decimal Positions	Field Name	Control Level (L1-L9)	Matching Fields or Changing Fields	Field Record Relation	Field Indicators		

Record Identification Codes: 1, 2, 3 — Position, Not (N), C/Z/D, Character

Field Location: From, To

Field Indicators: Plus, Minus, Zero or Blank

RPG INPUT SPECIFICATIONS

IBM International Business Machine Corporation

Program			Punching	Graphic		Card Electro Number	
Programmer		Date	Instruction	Punch			

Page $\frac{1 \quad 2}{\square \square}$ of ___

Program Identification $\square\square\square\square\square\square$

75 76 77 78 79 80

GX21-9094-2 U/M 050*
Printed in U.S.A.

423

RPG INPUT SPECIFICATIONS

IBM International Business Machine Corporation

GX21-9094-2 U/M 050*
Printed in U.S.A.

Program			Punching Instruction	Graphic		Card Electro Number	
Programmer		Date		Punch			

Page __1 2__ of ___

Program Identification: 75 76 77 78 79 80

Form Type: I

Column headers (left to right):

- Line (3 4 5)
- Form Type (6)
- Filename (7 8 9 10 11 12 13)
- Sequence — OR (14 AND 15)
- Number (1-N) (16 17)
- Option (O) (18)
- Record Identifying Indicator or ** (19 20)
- Record Identification Codes
  - 1: Position (21 22 23 24), Not (N) (25), C/Z/D (26), Character (27)
  - 2: Position (28 29 30 31), Not (N) (32), C/Z/D (33), Character (34)
  - 3: Position (35 36 37 38), Not (N) (39), C/Z/D (40), Character (41)
- Stacker Select (42)
- P/B/L/R (43)
- Field Location — From (44 45 46 47), To (48 49 50 51)
- Decimal Positions (52)
- Field Name (53 54 55 56 57 58)
- Control Level (L1-L9) (59 60)
- Matching Fields or Changing Fields (61 62)
- Field Record Relation (63 64)
- Field Indicators — Plus (65 66), Minus (67 68), Zero or Blank (69 70)
- (71 72 73 74)

Line numbers: 01 02 03 04 05 06 07 08 09 10 11 12 13 14 15 16 17 18 19 20

424

RPG INPUT SPECIFICATIONS

GX21-9094-2 U/M 050*
Printed in U.S.A.

IBM International Business Machine Corporation

Program		Punching Instruction	Graphic								Card Electro Number
Programmer	Date		Punch								

Page (1 2) of ___ Program Identification (75 76 77 78 79 80)

I

Line	Form Type	Filename	Sequence (OR / AND)	Number (1-N)	Option (O)	Record Identifying Indicator or**	Record Identification Codes 1: Position	1: Not (N)	1: C/Z/D	1: Character	2: Position	2: Not (N)	2: C/Z/D	2: Character	3: Position	3: Not (N)	3: C/Z/D	3: Character	Stacker Select	P/B/L/R	Field Location: From	Field Location: To	Decimal Positions	Field Name	Control Level (L1-L9)	Matching Fields or Changing Fields	Field Record Relation	Field Indicators: Plus	Field Indicators: Minus	Field Indicators: Zero or Blank	
3 4 5	6	7 8 9 10 11 12 13	14 15 16	17	18	19 20	21 22 23 24	25	26	27	28 29 30 31	32	33	34	35 36 37 38	39	40	41	42	43	44 45 46 47	48 49 50 51	52	53 54 55 56 57 58	59 60	61 62	63 64	65 66	67 68	69 70	71 72 73 74
01	I																														
02	I																														
03	I																														
04	I																														
05	I																														
06	I																														
07	I																														
08	I																														
09	I																														
10	I																														
11	I																														
12	I																														
13	I																														
14	I																														
15	I																														
16	I																														
17	I																														
18	I																														
19	I																														
20	I																														
	I																														
	I																														
	I																														
	I																														
	I																														

GX21-9093-2 UM/050* Printed in U.S.A.
*No. of forms per pad may vary slightly

IBM International Business Machine Corporation

RPG CALCULATION SPECIFICATIONS

Program		Punching Instruction	Graphic			Card Electro Number		Page	1 2 of
Programmer	Date		Punch						

Line	Form Type	Control Level (L0-L9, LR, SR, AN/OR)	|Indicators| Not	And	Not	And	Not	Factor 1	Operation	Factor 2	|Result Field| Name	Length	Decimal Positions	Half Adjust (H)	|Resulting Indicators|			Comments
3 4 5	6	7 8	9 10	11 12	13 14	15 16	17 18	19-27	28-32	33-42	43-48	49 50 51	52	53	54 55	56 57	58 59	60-74
0 1	C																	
0 2	C																	
0 3	C																	
0 4	C																	
0 5	C																	
0 6	C																	
0 7	C																	
0 8	C																	
0 9	C																	
1 0	C																	
1 1	C																	
1 2	C																	
1 3	C																	
1 4	C																	
1 5	C																	
1 6	C																	
1 7	C																	
1 8	C																	
1 9	C																	
2 0	C																	

Resulting Indicators:
Arithmetic — Plus, Minus, Zero (54 55, 56 57, 58 59)
Compare — 1 > 2, 1 < 2, 1 = 2 (High, Low, Equal)
Lookup (Factor 2) is High, Low, Equal

426

GX21-9093-2 UM/050* Printed in U.S.A.
*No. of forms per pad may vary slightly

IBM International Business Machine Corporation

RPG CALCULATION SPECIFICATIONS

Program

Programmer

Date

Punching Instruction

Graphic

Punch

Card Electro Number

Page [1] [2] of ___

Program Identification 75 76 77 78 79 80

C						
Line	Form Type	Control Level (L0-L9, LR, SR, AN/OR)	Indicators	Factor 1	Operation	Factor 2

Indicators: And Not, And Not, Not

Result Field: Name, Length, Decimal Positions, Half Adjust (H)

Resulting Indicators: Arithmetic — Plus, Minus, Zero; Compare — 1>2, 1<2, 1=2; Lookup (Factor 2) is — High, Low, Equal

Comments

427

RPG CALCULATION SPECIFICATIONS

IBM International Business Machine Corporation

GX21-9093-2 UM/050* Printed in U.S.A.
*No. of forms per pad may vary slightly

Program

Programmer

Date

Punching Instruction

Graphic

Punch

Card Electro Number

Page __ of __

Program Identification 75 76 77 78 79 80

C	Line	Form Type	Control Level (L0-L9, LR, SR, AN/OR)	Indicators										Factor 1	Operation	Factor 2	Result Field					Resulting Indicators		Comments
				And	Not	And	Not	And	Not								Name	Length	Decimal Positions	Half Adjust (H)	Arithmetic / Compare / Lookup		

Line numbers: 01, 02, 03, 04, 05, 06, 07, 08, 09, 10, 11, 12, 13, 14, 15, 16, 17, 18, 19, 20 — all Form Type C

RPG CALCULATION SPECIFICATIONS

Program

Programmer

Punching Instruction

Graphic

Punch

Card Electro Number

Date

Page ___ of ___

GX21-9093-2 UM/050* Printed in U.S.A.
*No. of forms per pad may vary slightly

Program Identification

75 76 77 78 79 80

| C | | | | | Indicators | | | | | | | | | | | Factor 1 | Operation | Factor 2 | | Result Field | | | | Resulting Indicators | | | | Comments |

Line | Form Type | Control Level (L0-L9, LR, SR, AN/OR) | Not | And | Not | And | Not | | | | | | | | | Name | Length | Decimal Positions | Half Adjust (H) | | | | | |

Result Field: Name, Length, Decimal Positions, Half Adjust (H)

Resulting Indicators — Arithmetic: Plus, Minus, Zero; Compare: 1>2, 1<2, 1=2; Lookup (Factor 2) is: High, Low, Equal

3 4 | 6 | 7 8 | 9 | 10 11 | 12 | 13 14 | 15 | 16 17 | 18 19 20 21 22 23 24 25 26 27 | 28 29 30 31 32 | 33 34 35 36 37 38 39 40 41 42 | 43 44 45 46 47 48 | 49 50 51 | 52 | 53 | 54 55 | 56 57 | 58 59 | 60 61 62 63 64 65 66 67 68 69 70 71 72 73 74

0 1 C
0 2 C
0 3 C
0 4 C
0 5 C
0 6 C
0 7 C
0 8 C
0 9 C
1 0 C
1 1 C
1 2 C
1 3 C
1 4 C
1 5 C
1 6 C
1 7 C
1 8 C
1 9 C
2 0 C

429

GX21-9093-2 UM/050* Printed in U.S.A.
*No. of forms per pad may vary slightly

IBM

International Business Machine Corporation

RPG CALCULATION SPECIFICATIONS

Program			Punching	Graphic			Card Electro Number		Page	1 2	of __	Program Identification	75 76 77 78 79 80
Programmer		Date	Instruction	Punch									

C

Line	Form Type	Control Level (L0-L9, LR, SR, AN/OR)	Indicators						Factor 1	Operation	Factor 2	Result Field				Resulting Indicators	Comments
			And		And		Not					Name	Length	Decimal Positions	Half Adjust (H)	Arithmetic / Compare / Lookup	

430

IBM International Business Machine Corporation

GX21-9093-2 UM/050* Printed in U.S.A.
*No. of forms per pad may vary slightly

RPG CALCULATION SPECIFICATIONS

Program

Programmer

Date

Punching Instruction — Graphic / Punch

Card Electro Number

Page 1 2 of ___

Program Identification 75 76 77 78 79 80

Line	Form Type	Control Level (LO-L9, LR, SR, AN/OR)	Indicators (Not / And / Not / And / Not / And)	Factor 1	Operation	Factor 2	Result Field (Name / Length / Decimal Positions / Half Adjust (H))	Resulting Indicators (Arithmetic: Plus / Minus / Zero; Compare 1>2 / 1<2 / 1=2; Lookup (Factor 2) is High / Low / Equal)	Comments
0 1	C								
0 2	C								
0 3	C								
0 4	C								
0 5	C								
0 6	C								
0 7	C								
0 8	C								
0 9	C								
1 0	C								
1 1	C								
1 2	C								
1 3	C								
1 4	C								
1 5	C								
1 6	C								
1 7	C								
1 8	C								
1 9	C								
2 0	C								

431

RPG   OUTPUT   SPECIFICATIONS

IBM International Business Machine Corporation

GX21-9090-2 U/M 050*
Printed in U.S.A.

Program

Programmer

Date

Punching Instruction

Graphic   Punch

Card Electro Number

Program Identification   75 76 77 78 79 80

Page 1 2 of ___

Constant or Edit Word

Commas	Zero Balances to Print	No Sign	CR	-
Yes	Yes	1	A	J
Yes	No	2	B	K
No	Yes	3	C	L
No	No	4	D	M

X = Remove Plus Sign
Y = Date Field Edit
Z = Zero Suppress

432

RPG OUTPUT SPECIFICATIONS

IBM International Business Machine Corporation

GX21-9090-2 U/M 050*
Printed in U.S.A.

Program

Programmer

Punching Instruction

Graphic

Punch

Date

Card Electro Number

Page [ ] [ ] of ___

Program Identification

Commas	Zero Balances to Print	No Sign	CR	-
Yes	Yes	1	A	J
Yes	No	2	B	K
No	Yes	3	C	L
No	No	4	D	M

X = Remove Plus Sign
Y = Date Field Edit
Z = Zero Suppress

Constant or Edit Word

433

IBM International Business Machine Corporation

GX21-9090-2 U/M 050*
Printed in U.S.A.

Program
Programmer
Date

Punching Instruction

Graphic
Punch

Card Electro Number

Page [1] [2] of ___

Program Identification

75 76 77 78 79 80

Commas	Zero Balances to Print	No Sign	CR	−
Yes	Yes	1	A	J
Yes	No	2	B	K
No	Yes	3	C	L
No	No	4	D	M

X = Remove Plus Sign
Y = Date Field Edit
Z = Zero Suppress

Constant or Edit Word

Field Name

*Auto

Edit Codes

B/A/C/1-9/R

End Position in Output Record

P/B/L/R

Output Indicators
And — Not
And — Not
Not

Skip
After
Before

Space
After
Before

Stacker #/Fetch(F)

Type (H/D/T/E)

Filename

Form Type

Line

O

1 2 3 4 5 6 7 8 9 10 11 12 13 14 15 16 17 18 19 20 21 22 23 24 25 26 27 28 29 30 31 32 33 34 35 36 37 38 39 40 41 42 43 44 45 46 47 48 49 50 51 52 53 54 55 56 57 58 59 60 61 62 63 64 65 66 67 68 69 70 71 72 73 74 75 76 77 78 79 80

IBM

International Business Machine Corporation

RPG   OUTPUT   SPECIFICATIONS

Program			Punching	Graphic			Card Electro Number	Page $\boxed{1}$ $\boxed{2}$ of ___	Program Identification	75 76 77 78 79 80
Programmer		Date	Instruction	Punch						GX21-9090-2 U/M 050* Printed in U.S.A.

O

Line	Form Type	Filename				O R	A N D	A N D	Stacker #/Fetch(F)	Space		Skip		Output Indicators						Field Name		*Auto	Edit Codes	B/A/C/1-9/R	End Position in Output Record	P/B/L/R								Constant or Edit Word												

Type (H/D/T/E)

Before / After (Space)

Before / After (Skip)

And / Not / And / Not / And / Not (Output Indicators)

Commas	Zero Balances to Print	No Sign	CR	–
Yes	Yes	1	A	J
Yes	No	2	B	K
No	Yes	3	C	L
No	No	4	D	M

X = Remove Plus Sign
Y = Date Field Edit
Z = Zero Suppress

GX21-9090-2 U/M 050*
Printed in U.S.A.

IBM International Business Machine Corporation

RPG OUTPUT SPECIFICATIONS

Program			
Programmer		Date	

Punching Instruction

Graphic

Punch

Card Electro Number

Program Identification: 75 76 77 78 79 80

Page 1 2 of ___

Commas	Zero Balances to Print	No Sign	CR	-
Yes	Yes	1	A	J
Yes	No	2	B	K
No	Yes	3	C	L
No	No	4	D	M

X = Remove Plus Sign
Y = Date Field Edit
Z = Zero Suppress

Constant or Edit Word

Output Indicators

Field Name

*Auto

Edit Codes

B/A/C/1-9/R

End Position in Output Record

P/B/L/R

Form Type

Line

Filename

Type (H/D/T/E)

Stacker #/Fetch(F)

Space — Before / After

Skip — Before / After

And / Not

O

436

IBM International Business Machine Corporation

RPG OUTPUT SPECIFICATIONS

| Program | | | | |
| Programmer | | Date | | |

| Punching Instruction | Graphic | | | |
| | Punch | | | |

Card Electro Number

Page ___ 1 2 of ___

GX21-9090-2 U/M 050*
Printed in U.S.A.

Program Identification: 75 76 77 78 79 80

Line — Form Type

Filename

Output Indicators — And / And

Type (H/D/T/E) — Stacker #/Fetch(F) — Space Before/After — Skip Before/After

Field Name — *Auto

Edit Codes

End Position in Output Record — B/A/C/1-9/R — P/B/L/R

Constant or Edit Word

Commas	Zero Balances to Print	No Sign	CR	–
Yes	Yes	1	A	J
Yes	No	2	B	K
No	Yes	3	C	L
No	No	4	D	M

X = Remove Plus Sign
Y = Date Field Edit
Z = Zero Suppress

439

IBM International Business Machine Corporation

RPG OUTPUT SPECIFICATIONS

GX21-9090-2 U/M 050*
Printed in U.S.A.

75 76 77 78 79 80

Program
Programmer
Date
Punching Instruction
Graphic
Punch
Card Electro Number
Page 1 2 of
Program Identification

Commas	Zero Balances to Print	No Sign	CR	–
Yes	Yes	1	A	J
Yes	No	2	B	K
No	Yes	3	C	L
No	No	4	D	M

X = Remove Plus Sign
Y = Date Field Edit
Z = Zero Suppress

Constant or Edit Word

O

Line
Form Type
Filename
Type (H/D/T/E)
Stacker #/Fetch(F)
Space — Before / After
Skip — Before / After
Output Indicators — And / Not
Field Name
*Auto
Edit Codes
B/A/C/1-9/R
End Position in Output Record
P/B/L/R

440

RPG   OUTPUT   SPECIFICATIONS

Program
Programmer
Date

Punching Instruction
Graphic
Punch

Card Electro Number

GX21-9090-2 U/M 050*
Printed in U.S.A.

Page [1] [2] of ___

Program Identification
75 76 77 78 79 80

Commas	Zero Balances to Print	No Sign	CR	−
Yes	Yes	1	A	J
Yes	No	2	B	K
No	Yes	3	C	L
No	No	4	D	M

X = Remove Plus Sign
Y = Date Field Edit
Z = Zero Suppress

Constant or Edit Word

Field Name

*Auto

Output Indicators
And   And
Not   Not   Not

Skip
Before   After

Space
Before   After

Stacker #/Fetch (F)
Type (H/D/T/E)

Filename

Edit Codes
B/A/C/1-9/R
End Position in Output Record
P/B/L/R

Form Type

Line

O

441

RPG OUTPUT SPECIFICATIONS

Program		
Programmer		Date

Punching Instruction

Graphic	
Punch	

Card Electro Number

GX21-9090-2 U/M 050*
Printed in U.S.A.

Page 1 2 of ___

75 76 77 78 79 80
Program Identification

Form layout (column headers)

Line | Form Type | Filename | Type (H/D/T/E) | O/R/AND | Stacker #/Fetch(F) | Space Before/After | Skip Before/After | Output Indicators (And/Not) | Field Name *Auto | Edit Codes | End Position in Output Record | P/B/L/R | Constant or Edit Word

Columns: 3 4 5 6 7 8 9 10 11 12 13 14 15 16 17 18 19 20 21 22 23 24 25 26 27 28 29 30 31 32 33 34 35 36 37 38 39 40 41 42 43 44 45 46 47 48 49 50 51 52 53 54 55 56 57 58 59 60 61 62 63 64 65 66 67 68 69 70 71 72 73 74

Lines: 01 02 03 04 05 06 07 08 09 10 11 12 13 14 15 16 17 18 19 20

Edit Codes table

	Commas	Zero Balances to Print	No Sign	CR	−
	Yes	Yes	1	A	J
	Yes	No	2	B	K
	No	Yes	3	C	L
	No	No	4	D	M

X = Remove Plus Sign
Y = Date Field Edit
Z = Zero Suppress

Edit Codes: B/A/C/1-9/R

IBM International Business Machine Corporation

RPG OUTPUT SPECIFICATIONS

GX21-9090-2 U/M 050*
Printed in U.S.A.

75 76 77 78 79 80

Program

Programmer

Date

Punching Instruction

Graphic

Punch

Card Electro Number

Page 1 2 of ___

Program Identification

Commas	Zero Balances to Print	No Sign	CR	—
Yes	Yes	1	A	J
Yes	No	2	B	K
No	Yes	3	C	L
No	No	4	D	M

X = Remove Plus Sign
Y = Date Field Edit
Z = Zero Suppress

Constant or Edit Word

Field Name

*Auto

Edit Codes

B/A/C/1-9/R

End Position in Output Record

P/B/L/R

Output Indicators

And

Not

And

Not

Not

Skip

After

Before

Space

After

Before

Stacker #/Fetch(F)

Type (H/D/T/E)

AND

OR

D

A

D

Filename

Form Type

Line

443

RPG OUTPUT SPECIFICATIONS

Program
Programmer
Date

Punching Instruction
Graphic
Punch

Card Electro Number

GX21-9090-2 U/M 050*
Printed in U.S.A.
75 76 77 78 79 80

Program Identification

Field Name
*Auto

Output Indicators
And And
Not Not Not

Skip
After Before

Space
After Before

Stacker #/Fetch(F)
Type (H/D/T/E)

Filename

Line
Form Type

Edit Codes
B/A/C/1-9/R
End Position in Output Record
P/B/L/R

Commas	Zero Balances to Print	No Sign	CR	−
Yes	Yes	1	A	J
Yes	No	2	B	K
No	Yes	3	C	L
No	No	4	D	M

X = Remove Plus Sign
Y = Date Field Edit
Z = Zero Suppress

Constant or Edit Word

IBM International Business Machine Corporation

RPG   OUTPUT   SPECIFICATIONS

GX21-9090-2 U/M 050*
Printed in U.S.A.

Program				Punching Instruction	Graphic		Card Electro Number		Page $\boxed{1}$ $\boxed{2}$ of ___	Program Identification	75 76 77 78 79 80
Programmer		Date			Punch						

Output Indicators

Field Name

*Auto

Edit Codes

Commas	Zero Balances to Print	No Sign	CR	–
Yes	Yes	1	A	J
Yes	No	2	B	K
No	Yes	3	C	L
No	No	4	D	M

X = Remove Plus Sign
Y = Date Field Edit
Z = Zero Suppress

Constant or Edit Word

B/A/C/1-9/R
End Position in Output Record
P/B/L/R

Type (H/D/T/E)
Stacker #/Fetch (F)
Space — Before / After
Skip — Before / After
And — Not / And — Not / And — Not

Filename

Form Type

Line

IBM International Business Machine Corporation
GX21-9090-2 U/M 050*
Printed in U.S.A.

RPG   OUTPUT   SPECIFICATIONS

Program
Programmer
Date

Punching
Instruction
Graphic
Punch

Card Electro Number

Program Identification
75 76 77 78 79 80

Page 1 2 of ___

Commas	Zero Balances to Print	No Sign	CR	–
Yes	Yes	1	A	J
Yes	No	2	B	K
No	Yes	3	C	L
No	No	4	D	M

X = Remove Plus Sign
Y = Date Field Edit
Z = Zero Suppress

Constant or Edit Word

Output Indicators

Field Name

End Position in Output Record

Edit Codes

B/A/C/1-9/R

P/B/L/R

*Auto

O Line Form Type Filename Type (H/D/T/E) Stacker#/Fetch(F) Space Skip And And

Before After Before After Not Not Not

0 1
0 2
0 3
0 4
0 5
0 6
0 7
0 8
0 9
1 0
1 1
1 2
1 3
1 4
1 5
1 6
1 7
1 8
1 9
2 0

446

IBM International Business Machine Corporation

RPG   OUTPUT   SPECIFICATIONS

GX21-9090-2 U/M 050*
Printed in U.S.A.

75 76 77 78 79 80

Program
Programmer

Date

Graphic
Punch

Punching
Instruction

Card Electro Number

Page | 1 | 2 | of ___

Program
Identification

Commas	Zero Balances to Print	No Sign	CR	-
Yes	Yes	1	A	J
Yes	No	2	B	K
No	Yes	3	C	L
No	No	4	D	M

X = Remove Plus Sign
Y = Date Field Edit
Z = Zero Suppress

Constant or Edit Word

Line

Form Type

Filename

Type (H/D/T/E)
Stacker #/Fetch(F)

Space
Before / After

Skip
Before / After

Output Indicators
And / And

Field Name

*Auto

Edit Codes
B/A/C/1-9/R

End Position in Output Record
P/B/L/R

RPG   OUTPUT   SPECIFICATIONS

IBM International Business Machine Corporation

Program						
Programmer				Date		

Punching Instruction — Graphic / Punch

Card Electro Number

Page 1 of 2

GX21-9090-2 U/M 050*
Printed in U.S.A.

Program Identification: 75 76 77 78 79 80

Commas	Zero Balances to Print	No Sign	CR	-
Yes	Yes	1	A	J
Yes	No	2	B	K
No	Yes	3	C	L
No	No	4	D	M

X = Remove Plus Sign
Y = Date Field Edit
Z = Zero Suppress

448

APPENDIX

THE RPG CYCLE

For a better understanding of how to program in RPG II and take advantage of its features, you should know just what the cycle is and does.

With most programming languages the programmer controls *when* an input or output record will be read or written with the use of an input/output control statement. The RPG programmer controls IF an input or output record is read or written through the use of indicators. Indicators are discussed in the main portion of the book. The RPG II cycle is flowcharted in Fig. 120 and is the illustration that will be used in the following discussion.

1. As the program begins execution,

    a. The 1P or first page indicator is turned on by RPG II.

    b. Heading lines conditioned by 1P on the Output Specifications sheet will be written.

    c. This occurs only once during the RPG cycle.

2. Heading and detail output

    a. Nothing will happen the first time through the cycle because no indicator(s) is ON.

    b. On subsequent passes through the cycle, all heading and detail lines that are conditioned to be written will be written.

    NOTE: It should be carefully understood by the RPG programmer that each phase of the cycle is executed (exceptions are the total calculation and total output phases) on every RPG II cycle.

3. Read a record

    a. Read the record into the input buffer. Buffers are areas set aside in the computer memory as intermediate or holding areas for information. The programmer need not be concerned with them when programming. But this step is important as will be shown later in the cycle.

449

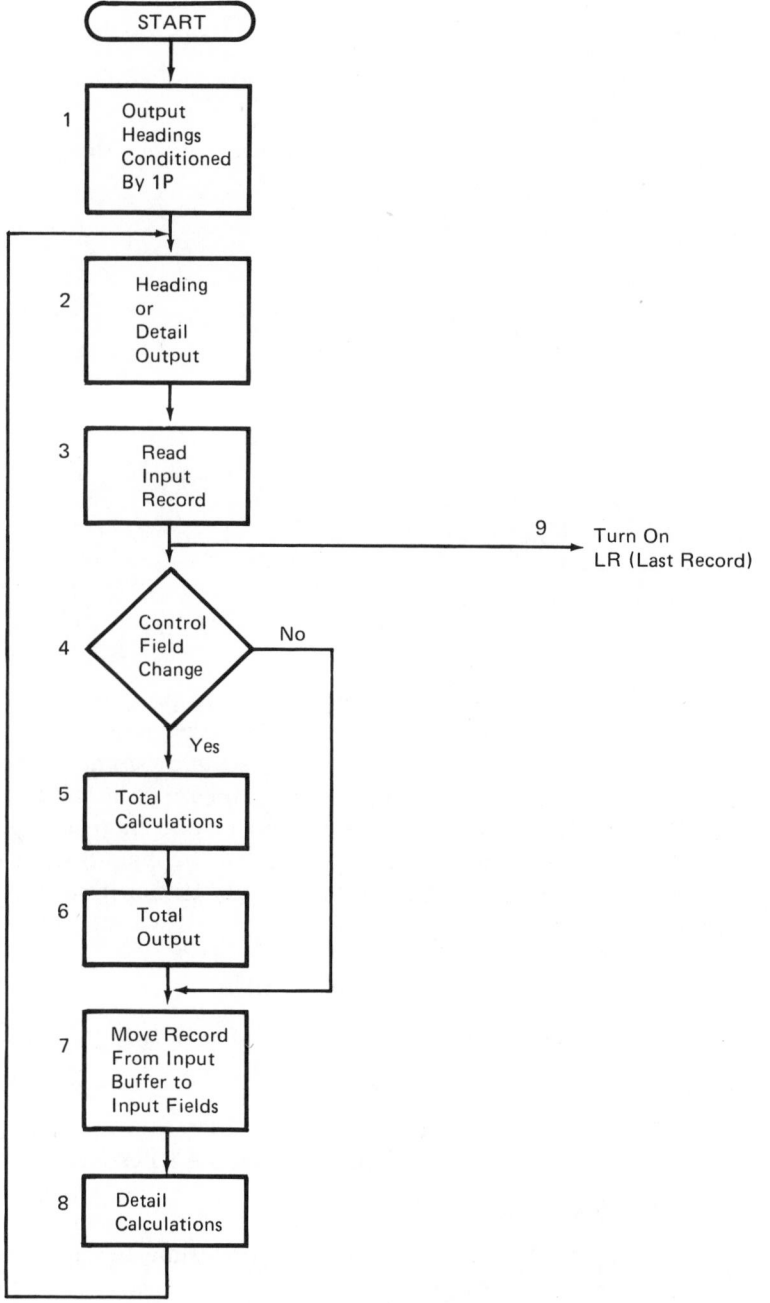

Figure 120

b. Turn on Record Identifying Indicators.

c. If more than one input file, read from the primary file first.

d. When all primary records are read, read from the next secondary file coded. This means that if there is more than one secondary file, they are processed in the sequence that they are specified on the File Description Specifications sheets.

e. For interweaving the reading of primary and secondary records, the Matching Record Feature is used. This option is discussed in the chapter on Matching Records.

4. Set Control Level Indicators

$$\overline{1000}$$
$$\quad\overline{1000}$$
$$\qquad\overline{1000}\quad\text{Change}$$
$$\qquad\quad\overline{1010}$$
$$\qquad\qquad\overline{1010}\quad\text{Change}$$
$$\qquad\qquad\quad\overline{1020}$$
$$\qquad\qquad\qquad\overline{1020}$$
$$\qquad\qquad\qquad\quad\overline{1020}\quad\text{Change}$$
$$\qquad\qquad\qquad\quad\overline{1040}$$

A group of records having the same control number may have to be totaled as a group. These records may be of the same customer or salesman and customer sales totals, or salesman commission totals could be of interest to the company.

If a Control Level Indicator (L1 to L9) was coded on the Input Specifications sheet in columns 59-60, next to the control field (customer number or salesman number), then RPG will set a level indicator ON when the control number changed. This indicator can now be used to condition calculations and/or output. A full discussion of Control Level Indicators is discussed in Projects 9 and 10.

5. Total Calculations

a. This part of the cycle will be processed if a control break (Control Level Indicator ON) occurs.

b. The fields from the last record read during the read part of the cycle are not yet available for processing because the record is still in the input buffer.

c. The fields from the last record of the last control group are available and can be used in calculations at this time.

6. Total Output

a. Write the output total lines.

b. The fields of the last record from the last control group are still available for output at this time.

7. Move Input Field

a. Move fields from input buffer to input fields. When the programmer describes the fields on the Input Specifications Sheets, RPG II reserves the desired spaces in computer memory for them. This space is reversed for the entire run of the RPG program. The fields then can be used in all other parts of the RPG cycle.

b. As discussed above in total calculations, the fields of the last record of the last control group are available to total calculations and total output parts of the cycle.

c. After this phase is completed, the fields from the last record read are now available through the rest of the RPG cycle.

8. Detail Calculations

a. This part of the cycle will process the last record read.

b. Fields within the last record read can be calculated or moved.

c. After this part of the cycle, the processing continues with Heading and Detail output and continues processing input records until the LR (Last Record) indicator comes ON.

9. LR Indicator

a. LR comes on with the processing of the last record on the input file.

b. If only one input file is used in the program, when End of File is reached, LR comes ON.

c. If more than one input file is used, then all files must be processed to End of File to turn ON the LR Indicator.

d. If an E is coded on the File Description Specifications sheet, in column 17, then when that file reaches End of File, the LR Indicator will come ON.

e. End of File condition causes the LR Indicator to come ON.

f. All records read will be processed to completion.

g. The total calculations and total output parts of the cycle will be processed.

h. The program stops.

PRINT CHARTS

SUGGESTIONS FOR USE OF THE PRINT
CHARTS (pages 454-467)

Sufficient space on the Print Chart has been allotted for diagramming. As a student programmer, learn to diagram only a portion of each concept of the program output.

1. When assembling each set of Print Charts (2 pages), be sure that the alignment is correct. Make sure column 71 is adjacent to column 70.

2. Place a small piece of tape at the top and bottom margins of the set in the area of columns 70 and 71.

3. The right portion of one set of Print Charts (Columns 71-150) becomes the left portion (Columns 1-70) of the next set of Print Charts.

150/10/6 PRINT CHART

PROG. ID _____

PAGE _____

(SPACING: 150 POSITION SPAN, AT 10 CHARACTERS PER INCH, 6 LINES PER VERTICAL INCH)

DATE _____

PROGRAM TITLE _____

PROGRAMMER OR DOCUMENTALIST: _____

CHART TITLE _____

CARRIAGE CONTROL

TAPE   CHAN.

Part III
of Output
Specifications
Test

Project 3

Project 4

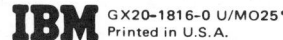

Fold in at dotted line.

GX20-1816-0 U/M025*
Printed in U.S.A.

NOTE: Dimensions on this sheet vary with humidity. Exact measurements should be calculated or scaled with a ruler rather than with the lines on this chart.

71 72 73 74 75 76 77 78 79 80 81 82 83 84 85 86 87 88 89 90 91 92 93 94 95 96 97 98 99 100 101 102 103 104 105 106 107 108 109 110 111 112 113 114 115 116 117 118 119 120 121 122 123 124 125 126 127 128 129 130 131 132 133 134 135 136 137 138 139 140 141 142 143 144 145 146 147 148 149 150

71 72 73 74 75 76 77 78 79 80 81 82 83 84 85 86 87 88 89 90 91 92 93 94 95 96 97 98 99 100 101 102 103 104 105 106 107 108 109 110 111 112 113 114 115 116 117 118 119 120 121 122 123 124 125 126 127 128 129 130 131 132 133 134 135 136 137 138 139 140 141 142 143 144 145 146 147 148 149 150

*No. of sheets per pad may vary slightly.

Fold in at dotted line.

PROGRAM TITLE _____

PROGRAMMER OR DOCUMENTALIST: _____

CHART TITLE _____

CARRIAGE CONTROL
TAPE   CHAN.

Project 5

Project 6

Calculation
Specifications
Sheet Test
Part II

IBM GX20-1816-0 U/MO25*
Printed in U.S.A.

NOTE: Dimensions on this sheet vary with humidity.
Exact measurements should be calculated or scaled
with a ruler rather than with the lines on this chart.

7777777778888888888999999999900000000000111111111122222222223333333333444444444 5
1234567890123456789012345678901234567890123456789012345678901234567890123456789 0

7777777778888888888999999999900000000000111111111122222222223333333333444444444 5
1234567890123456789012345678901234567890123456789012345678901234567890123456789 0

*No. of sheets per pad may vary slightly.

← Fold in at dotted line.

150/10/6 PRINT CHART

PROG. ID _____ PAGE _____

(SPACING: 150 POSITION SPAN, AT 10 CHARACTERS PER INCH, 6 LINES PER VERTICAL INCH) DATE _____

PROGRAM TITLE _____

PROGRAMMER OR DOCUMENTALIST: _____

CHART TITLE _____

CARRIAGE CONTROL

TAPE   CHAN.

Project 7

Project 8

← Fold in at dotted line.

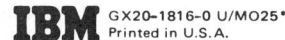

IBM GX20-1816-0 U/MO25*
Printed in U.S.A.

NOTE: Dimensions on this sheet vary with humidity. Exact measurements should be calculated or scaled with a ruler rather than with the lines on this chart.

71 72 73 74 75 76 77 78 79 80 81 82 83 84 85 86 87 88 89 90 91 92 93 94 95 96 97 98 99 100 101 102 103 104 105 106 107 108 109 110 111 112 113 114 115 116 117 118 119 120 121 122 123 124 125 126 127 128 129 130 131 132 133 134 135 136 137 138 139 140 141 142 143 144 145 146 147 148 149 150

71 72 73 74 75 76 77 78 79 80 81 82 83 84 85 86 87 88 89 90 91 92 93 94 95 96 97 98 99 100 101 102 103 104 105 106 107 108 109 110 111 112 113 114 115 116 117 118 119 120 121 122 123 124 125 126 127 128 129 130 131 132 133 134 135 136 137 138 139 140 141 142 143 144 145 146 147 148 149 150

*No. of sheets per pad may vary slightly.

← Fold in at dotted line.

150/10/6 PRINT CHART   PROG. ID _____   PAGE _____

(SPACING: 150 POSITION SPAN, AT 10 CHARACTERS PER INCH, 6 LINES PER VERTICAL INCH)   DATE _____

PROGRAM TITLE _____

PROGRAMMER OR DOCUMENTALIST: _____

CHART TITLE _____

CARRIAGE CONTROL
TAPE   CHAN.

Project 9

Project 10

Project 11

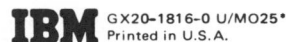

Fold in at dotted line.

IBM GX20-1816-0 U/M025*
Printed in U.S.A.

NOTE: Dimensions on this sheet vary with humidity. Exact measurements should be calculated or scaled with a ruler rather than with the lines on this chart.

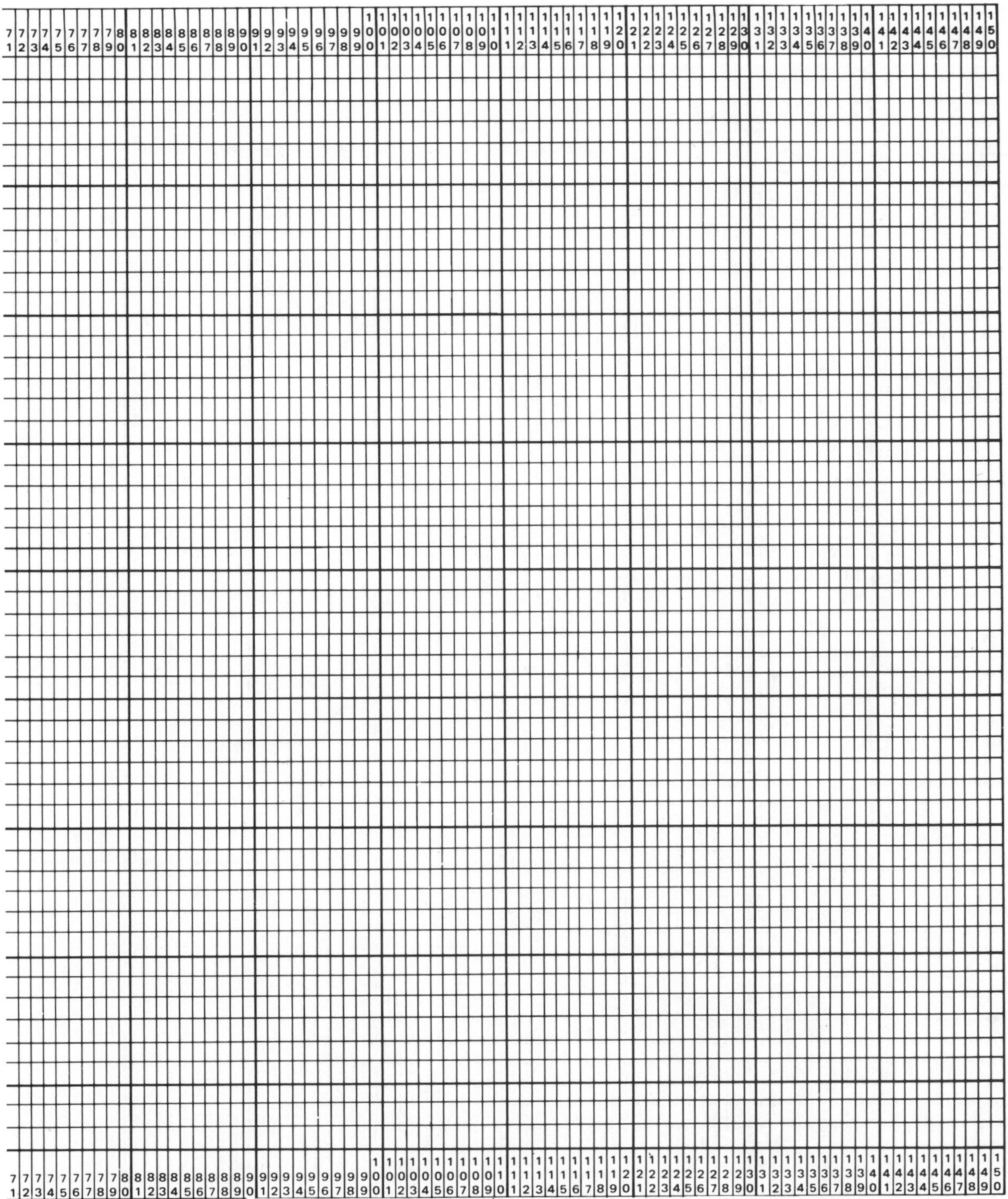

*No. of sheets per pad may vary slightly.

Fold in at dotted line.

150/10/6 PRINT CHART   PROG. ID ———————————————— PAGE ————

(SPACING: 150 POSITION SPAN, AT 10 CHARACTERS PER INCH, 6 LINES PER VERTICAL INCH)   DATE ————————

PROGRAM TITLE ————————————————————————————————————

PROGRAMMER OR DOCUMENTALIST: ————————————————————————

CHART TITLE ————————————————————————————————————

CARRIAGE CONTROL
TAPE   CHAN.

Project 13

Project 14
A & B

Project 15

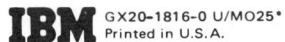

IBM GX20-1816-0 U/MO25*
Printed in U.S.A.

NOTE: Dimensions on this sheet vary with humidity.
Exact measurements should be calculated or scaled
with a ruler rather than with the lines on this chart.

7 7 7 7 7 7 7 7 7 8 8 8 8 8 8 8 8 8 8 9 9 9 9 9 9 9 9 9 9 0 0 0 0 0 0 0 0 0 0 1 1 1 1 1 1 1 1 1 1 1 1 1 1 1 1 1 1 1 1 1 1 1 1 1 1 1 1 1 1 1 1 1 1 1 1 1 1 1 1 1 1 1 1 1 1 1 1 1 1 1 1 1 1 1 1 1 1 1 1
1 2 3 4 5 6 7 8 9 0 1 2 3 4 5 6 7 8 9 0 1 2 3 4 5 6 7 8 9 0 1 2 3 4 5 6 7 8 9 0 1 2 3 4 5 6 7 8 9 0 1 2 3 4 5 6 7 8 9 0 1 2 3 4 5 6 7 8 9 0 1 2 3 4 5 6 7 8 9 0 1 2 3 4 5 6 7 8 9 0

7 7 7 7 7 7 7 7 7 8 8 8 8 8 8 8 8 8 8 9 9 9 9 9 9 9 9 9 9 0 0 0 0 0 0 0 0 0 0 1 1 1 1 1 1 1 1 1 1 1 1 1 1 1 1 1 1 1 1 1 1 1 1 1 1 1 1 1 1 1 1 1 1 1 1 1 1 1 1 1 1 1 1 1 1 1 1 1 1 1 1 1 1 1 1 1 1 1 1
1 2 3 4 5 6 7 8 9 0 1 2 3 4 5 6 7 8 9 0 1 2 3 4 5 6 7 8 9 0 1 2 3 4 5 6 7 8 9 0 1 2 3 4 5 6 7 8 9 0 1 2 3 4 5 6 7 8 9 0 1 2 3 4 5 6 7 8 9 0 1 2 3 4 5 6 7 8 9 0 1 2 3 4 5 6 7 8 9 0

*No. of sheets per pad may vary slightly.

150/10/6 PRINT CHART

PROG. ID _____ PAGE _____

(SPACING: 150 POSITION SPAN, AT 10 CHARACTERS PER INCH, 6 LINES PER VERTICAL INCH)   DATE _____

PROGRAM TITLE _____

PROGRAMMER OR DOCUMENTALIST: _____

CHART TITLE _____

CARRIAGE CONTROL

Project 16

Project 17

Project 18

464

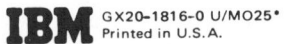

GX20-1816-0 U/MO25*
Printed in U.S.A.

NOTE: Dimensions on this sheet vary with humidity.
Exact measurements should be calculated or scaled
with a ruler rather than with the lines on this chart.

*No. of sheets per pad may vary slightly.

150/10/6 PRINT CHART

PROG. ID _____ PAGE _____

(SPACING: 150 POSITION SPAN, AT 10 CHARACTERS PER INCH, 6 LINES PER VERTICAL INCH)

DATE _____

PROGRAM TITLE _____

PROGRAMMER OR DOCUMENTALIST: _____

CHART TITLE _____

Project 20

466

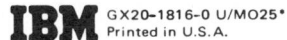

IBM GX20-1816-0 U/MO25*
Printed in U.S.A.

NOTE: Dimensions on this sheet vary with humidity.
Exact measurements should be calculated or scaled
with a ruler rather than with the lines on this chart.

*No. of sheets per pad may vary slightly.

Fold in at dotted line.

INDEX